Protecting Your Children on the Internet

D1516876

Protecting Your Children on the Internet

A Road Map for Parents and Teachers

Gregory S. Smith

ROWMAN & LITTLEFIELD PUBLISHERS, INC.
Lanham • New York • Toronto • Plymouth, UK

How to Protect Your Children on the Internet: A Road Map for Parents and Teachers, by Gregory S. Smith, was originally published in hard cover by Praeger Publishers http://www .greenwood.com/praeger, an imprint of Greenwood Publishing Group, Inc., Westport, CT. Copyright © 2007 by Gregory S. Smith. Paperback edition by arrangement with Greenwood Publishing Group, Inc. All rights reserved.

Published in the United States of America
by Rowman & Littlefield Education
A Division of Rowman & Littlefield Publishers, Inc.
A wholly owned subsidary of The Rowman & Littlefield Publishing Group, Inc.
4501 Forbes Boulevard, Suite 200, Lanham, Maryland 20706
www.rowmaneducation.com

Estover Road
Plymouth PL6 7PY
United Kingdom

British Library Cataloguing in Publication Information Available

Library of Congress Cataloging-in-Publication Data

Smith, Gregory S., 1963–
    How to protect your children on the Internet : a roadmap for parents and teachers / Gregory S. Smith.
        p. cm.
    Includes bibliographical references and index.
    1. Internet and children.   2. Technology and children.   3. Internet—Safety measures.
4. Safety education.   I. Title.
    HQ784.I58S65   2007
    305.235—dc22   2007016348

ISBN-13: 978-0-275-99472-3 (cloth : alk. paper)
ISBN-13: 978-1-57886-800-1 (pbk. : alk. paper)

∞™ The paper used in this publication meets the minimum requirements of American National Standard for Information Sciences—Permanence of Paper for Printed Library Materials, ANSI/NISO Z39.48-1992.
Manufactured in the United States of America.

To all parents and children who have been harmed, duped, or deceived via the Internet. Also, for all of the hard-working law enforcement, child therapists, parents, teachers, and Internet security professionals dedicating their time and effort to protecting children.

This book is intended for parents with children between the age of 8 and 17 who have access to the Internet and the educators that teach them. The Internet and technologies that enable online interaction and access to a variety of content can be a perilous place for minors. The dangers are real, and parents today are confronted with many threats that they simply don't understand. Simply stated, the purpose of this book is to share the risks of the Internet via exposing some recent real-world tragedies, while providing a pragmatic approach and road map to help parents protect their children against the threats of going online.

Contents

PREFACE   xi

ACKNOWLEDGMENTS   xv

Part One: Introduction to Technology and Risks on the Internet

CHAPTER 1   3
Welcome to the Internet
     Growing Up   *3*
     The Internet: What Is It?   *6*
     Recommendations   *12*

CHAPTER 2   15
Back to School
     Internet Technologies Defined: Education 101   *15*
     Recommendations   *42*

CHAPTER 3   45
Risks Overview: Are Parents Making the Grade?
     An Overview of Online Risks   *45*
     Some Statistics for Kids Going Online   *62*
     How Are Parents Doing Protecting Their Kids?   *64*
     Protection at School and in Libraries   *69*
     Recommendations   *71*

CHAPTER 4   74

The Risks of Going Online

A Sampling of Unfortunate Events   *74*

Recommendations   *80*

Part Two: A Road Map to Protect Children While Online

CHAPTER 5   85

How to Monitor Your Kids Online

To Monitor or Not to Monitor   *85*

Tricks Kids Use to Hide What They're Doing   *85*

Nontechnical Parental Monitoring   *88*

Software for Better Monitoring   *89*

Recommendations   *97*

CHAPTER 6   101

Internet Surfing, Blogs, and Social Networking

Surfing/Browsing the Internet   *101*

Search Engines: The Good, the Bad, and the Ugly   *101*

Social Networking and Blogging   *105*

Video Cameras Gone Wild   *109*

Firewalls and Wireless   *112*

Recommendations   *114*

CHAPTER 7   118

Email

Email Options and Programs   *118*

Email Risks   *120*

Kid-Friendly Email Programs   *121*

Tricks Kids Use to Hide Email Activities   *122*

Blocking Free Email Services   *122*

File Attachment Risk   *123*

Don't Forget about Spam   *123*

Recommendations   *124*

CHAPTER 8   129

Instant Messaging and Voice-over-IP

IM Basics and Tools   *129*

IM Lingo Parents Must Know   *132*

Blocking IM: It's Not Easy   *132*

Chat Rooms: A Hangout for Predators   *136*

Making Phone Calls over the Internet   *137*

How Predators Find Their Victims 137

Recommendations 139

CHAPTER 9 142

Cell Phones and PDAs

An Overview of Portable Communication Devices 142

Text Messaging: How Teens Communicate 149

Monitoring Call Logs and Bills 149

Browsing and IM Challenges with PDAs 150

Recommendations 151

CHAPTER 10 155

A Glimpse into the Future

Converging Devices 155

Free Stuff Everywhere (Advertisers' Heaven) 156

Global Positioning Takes Off 156

Built-in Security for Future Operating Systems 156

Futuristic Ways to Stay Connected 157

Recommendations 161

CHAPTER 11 162

Talking to Your Kids about Online Risks

An Internet Usage Contract 162

When and How to Be Firm 164

What Not to Say to Your Teen 164

Advice from the Pros (Child Psychologists) 165

Recommendations 167

NOTES 171

BIBLIOGRAPHY 181

INDEX 187

Preface

I am an international expert in the field of information technology and the parent of two children. Like many other parents, I walk a fine line of analyzing and determining just how much technology freedom to give my kids. The Internet is an abundant resource of interconnected networks, servers, and, yes, content that with the advent of World Wide Web and browser technology has transformed the way that people research, shop, conduct business, and communicate. That said, the Internet and online interaction technologies can be a perilous place for kids. The dangers are real, and parents are confronted with many threats that they may not fully grasp. The purpose of this book is to share the risks by describing some recent real tragedies and hidden secrets of online activities, while providing a pragmatic approach and plan to help parents protect their children against the threats of going online.

THE NEED

Parents today with children ranging from the age of 8 to 17 are often somewhat clueless about the real risks when their children access the Internet via a variety of devices and applications such as (1) email, (2) instant messaging (IM), (3) browsing, (4) blogs, (5) cell phones with text messaging, (6) personal digital assistant (PDA) devices, (7) online chat, and (8) social networking sites (such as MySpace). More and more youths today around the world are going online and engaging in activities that are quite risky, such as viewing mature and adult content and being exposed to predators that use the Internet to target minors for sex and other harmful intent. Many parents have read some of the horror stories printed in local and national newspapers or exposed by TV media such as NBC's *Dateline* about potential harm that can come to children online.

Most teenagers simply don't understand the risks of accessing the Internet and can be harmed greatly as a result of their naiveté. This book exposes the risks and provides a road map for parents to become more engaged in their children's online activities as well as techniques and tips to help protect their children. Kids today are using technology in ways that parents don't even know are going on, such as conducting private phone conversations over the Internet with friends and sometimes strangers. Voice technologies integrated with free instant messaging tools provide children with an opportunity to fly under the parental radar undetected, as there is no log of calls made or received.

As I write this, there are over 6 billion people in the world, and more than a billion have access to the Internet. The United States accounts for over 300 million people as of October 2006. According to the 2000 U. S. census, there are approximately 34.5 million households (32.8 percent) with children under the age of 18. Children at risk today between the ages of 5 and 19 years old comprise over 60 million of the total population estimated by the Census Bureau. The numbers speak for themselves and highlight the fact that millions of parents are challenged with the dilemma of how to protect their kids from online risks.

THE SOLUTION

How to Protect Your Children on the Internet brings to light some chilling examples of how minors and adults conduct themselves online and follows up with recommendations to mitigate the risks by a variety of online tools and countermeasures. Part One provides an introduction to the Internet with a highlight of the benefits and risks of going online. The bulk of this part of the book explains some key technologies and why they're important for parents and educators to understand, along with the risks associated with going online and what parents are doing to protect their children.

Part Two is designed to give parents and educators a map and clear set of recommendations on how to protect children if they use a variety of the Internet-enabled tools and technologies that introduce risk in the first place. These include email, IM, Internet browsing, blogs, cell phones with text messaging, PDAs, online chat, social networking sites, and even Internet-connected video cameras. The final chapter concludes with some helpful hints for parents to talk to their children about the risks associated with using the Internet.

TARGET AUDIENCE

This book is targeted primarily toward parents, most of whom are not aware of the real and potentially dangerous risks when their children connect to the Internet. The book provides parents with a computer technology primer to educate them about the tools that enable online activity and their associated risks and provides with a set of software solutions and recommendations to mitigate harmful risk to children. Parents in North America are the most connected to the Internet, with well over 50 percent of households going online in some form or another. Teenagers today are usually more sophisticated than their parents with regard to accessing and using online technologies. They are also getting smarter at hiding their methods for doing the wrong things online. Many other industrialized nations around the globe (in Asia, Europe, and South America) are going online more, and as a result, their children are being exposed to the good and bad portions of the Internet. Parents around the world with computers and other connected devices are exposing their children to risks in ways that they simply don't understand.

A secondary audience includes private and public school educators (K–12) as they attempt to guide and teach students the benefits and risks of the Internet. Technology permeates the K–12 educational environment, so risk is introduced. Many schools attempt to limit those risks with Internet filters and blocks, but many dangers persist. More technologies are using encryption to bypass sophisticated Internet filters and security software. By doing so, they can go virtually undetected. Examples include voice calls over the Internet (such as Skype), encrypted pornography sites, and IM tools that use common protocols and ports that change to allow users to browse the Internet. Unfortunately, there is no standard boilerplate at schools today and as a result, some have better technology to protect children than others.

APPROACH

The information presented in this book, along with recommendations, come from a variety of sources including research reports, case studies, child advocacy organizations and Web sites, interviews with experts, interviews and surveys involving parents with children that have access to the Internet, and my own experiences as both a parent and a technology professional with over 20 years of information technology experience as well as a decade in the classroom educating the next generation of IT leaders.

Acknowledgments

Over the past 20 years, I've had wonderful opportunities to learn, grow, and apply information technology (IT) best practices to businesses, deliver results for customers, and mentor and teach technical staff and graduate students craving more knowledge and best practices. I believe that it's the responsibility of today's leaders to give back to their community in one way or another. This book is one way for me to do just that—by sharing my knowledge and expertise in technology and education with an eye for helping millions of parents and teachers better protect their children from the risks associated with accessing the Internet. One specific person along the way taught me some of these leadership traits. I'd like to recognize Deborah Hechinger as a mentor and a role model. By her own actions, Debbie teaches others to do their best and to make a difference in life. My first interaction with her was in a professional nature, but that has clearly grown into a more trusted and true friendship. Thanks for being a great role model, Debbie!

Proofreading is an art form, often missed by an author who may be too close to his or her own work. I'd like to personally thank Catherine Golden and Anne Topp for their eyes on this project. Also, a special thanks goes out to Stan Wakefield, the literary agent who introduced me to the publishing team at the Greenwood Publishing Group. Thanks again!

Honest sounding boards are very important to me, especially in the development of a book as controversial and technically complex as this one. I'd like to thank two particular friends of mine, both initially via professional association, who supported my decision to write this manuscript with solid encouragement and subtle tones of friendship and were instrumental in getting the word out in the press. They are Martha Heller of the Z Resource Group and Eric Lundquist of *eWeek* magazine.

In closing, I pay special thanks to the wonderful folks at Praeger and the Greenwood Publishing Group, especially Suzanne Staszak-Silva for her efforts in making this book a world-class publication. Last and most important, I thank my family for their continued and generous support during the writing of this manuscript, and my parents, Josephine and Carl, for their never-ending encouragement to take risks and succeed. They've instilled a key motto for how I live my life—*never give up*!

PART ONE

Introduction to Technology and Risks on the Internet

Welcome to the Internet

Everything that you can imagine is real.

—Pablo Picasso

GROWING UP

Most parents today don't have a clue how to protect their children from the risks of using the Internet. In fact, most would probably admit that their teenagers know more about technology than they do—putting themselves at a disadvantage from the start. *Everything that you can imagine is real.* If Picasso were alive today, the reality of his words when applied to the Internet would blow him away. It's true—if you can think it, it can be built, packaged, and sold.

When I was a kid growing up in Flemington, New Jersey, we listened to rock and roll bands like KISS and Bruce Springsteen, rode our bikes, played sports, went to school, and checked out the opposite sex at school-sponsored dances and the mall. We didn't have online predators. We didn't have hard-core pornography accessible at the click of a mouse. We didn't have email accounts, text messaging, and caller ID. We didn't have instant messaging and definitely could not make private phone calls over the Internet without our parents' knowledge. Hell—we didn't even have phones in our bedrooms! Our parents were in complete control of our upbringing, and they liked it that way.

For the most part, parents today are clueless about computer technology and the Internet along with the risks. Simply put, adults are at a technological disadvantage when compared to teens and are confused on how to gain control again.

I know—I've spoken to many parents, and the topic of Internet risks comes up frequently. Within minutes into those types of conversations, I'm often asked for advice. My first tip: read this book cover to cover and pay clear attention to the recommendations section at the end of each chapter. Tip number 2: get up to speed on technology and regain control over your children. Tip number 3: don't be afraid to be a parent. Some parents I've spoken with are more interested in being their kid's best friend. It's important at times to play both roles, but parents should never lose sight of the fact that it is their obligation and responsibility to parent and protect their children. Those who bow to pressure from their kids, especially teenagers, and relax their responsibilities are potentially putting their children at risk. More important, if their children are harmed physically or emotionally as a result of going online and the parent has failed to provide protection, they are partly to blame for the tragedy. It's easy to knuckle under to pressure, especially from teens, but parents must be strong and take responsibility for properly raising their children. That includes learning when to say no to certain things in an effort to guarantee their safety.

When I was a teen, to access semi-nude and somewhat respectable photos of naked women, we had to get older kids to buy magazines such as *Penthouse* or *Playboy* for us. The biggest problem I ever had growing up was hiding a *Playboy* from my mother that a friend had given me for my fourteenth birthday, and even that didn't work out well. She found it under my mattress, gave me holy hell, and sent me to my room for the afternoon, where I waited for my father to address the issue when he came home from work. "Wait until your father gets home," she said to me with her index finger pointed at my face. I waited for hours in my room for my father to come home from work. I can still remember the sound of his footsteps coming up the stairs and walking down the hallway toward my room. He knocked on my bedroom door and then came in. After a brief pause, he said with a slight smile on his face, "Don't let your mother catch you with this again," and promptly walked out. Whew—all that worrying for nothing. If I could go back and do that decision over again, I'd probably hide the magazine under my parent's mattress—on my father's side.

I am an internationally recognized expert in the field of information technology. I'm also the parent of two children. Like many other parents, I walk a fine line of analyzing and determining just how much technology freedom to give my kids. The Internet is a wonderful and abundant resource of interconnected networks, servers, and, yes, content that with the advent of Web and browser technology has transformed the way that people research, shop, conduct business, and communicate. That said, the Internet and online communication technologies can be a perilous place for minors. The dangers are real, and parents are confronted with many threats they simply don't fully comprehend. At the end of each chapter, I provide clear and concise recommendations to parents and teachers. To begin Part Two of the book, the recommendations are broken down into three different age groups that mimic the typical school system environment and the social challenges that go along with each increasing age level. These three categories are:

- Category 1: Elementary School (ages 8–11).
- Category 2: Middle School (ages 12–14).
- Category 3: High School (ages 15–18).

Chances are good that most parents know a bit more about technology than their children while their kids are in the first category, elementary school. That lead usually erodes quickly as kids enter the socially awkward and more competitive environment of middle school, where technology is more often used in support of school projects and to keep up with the latest tween and teen fad. By the time most youths reach high school, they usually surpass their parents with knowledge of technology, especially if the parents are not involved in the technology or education profession. Teens in category 3 are at an age that effective monitoring, sometimes via stealth software, best comes into play as they may try to conceal their online activities.

Parents today with children, minors ranging from the age of 8 to 17, are at least moderately in the dark about the risks when their children access the Internet via a variety of devices and applications, such as email, instant messaging (IM), surfing or browsing, blogs, cell phones with text messaging, personal digital assistant (PDA) devices, chat rooms, and social networking sites. Youth around the world are going online more often and engaging in activities that are quite risky, such as viewing mature and adult content and being exposed to predators that use the Internet to target minors for sex and other harmful intent. Some have read some of the horror stories printed in local and national newspapers or exposed via TV media such as NBC *Dateline* about harm that can come to children that go online.

According to the 2000 U.S. census, there are slightly more than 281 million people living in the United States, with approximately 34.5 million households (32.8 percent) that have children under the age of 18.[1] Unofficially, the population total in the United States crossed the 300 million mark sometime in October 2006. Children at risk between the ages of 5 and 19 years old comprise over 60 million of the total U.S. population estimated by the Census Bureau.[2] Of those, over half are estimated to be online in some form and connected to the

Internet. The numbers speak for themselves and highlight that many millions of parents are challenged with the dilemma of how to protect their kids. According to a survey commissioned by Cox Communications and NCMEC, 71 percent of teens age 13 to 17 have reported receiving messages online from strangers; 45 percent have been asked for personal data by someone they don't know; 30 percent have contemplated a one-on-one meeting with an online acquaintance; and 14 percent have actually had a face-to-face meeting with someone that they've conversed with over the Internet.[3] Another alarming statistic is that 40 percent of teens say that they'll respond to a blind or unknown chat request.[4] Research also suggests that 61 percent of teens age 13 through 17 have a personal profile or Web page on a social networking site such as Friendster, MySpace, or Xanga.[5] Of those, approximately 50 percent have also posted pictures of themselves online for view by the full public or their online friends.[6]

Teachers, school administrators, lawmakers, and law enforcement professionals are *not* entirely responsible for protecting today's children. They can help and clearly play an integral part. That said, it's the *parents'* responsibility to educate children about the risks of going online, make the right call as to when they should be granted access to these technologies, and take responsibility for properly raising their children. Parents and teachers today have to get smart on technology and use it to their advantage. No more excuses.

THE INTERNET: WHAT IS IT?

The Internet, simply put, is a collection of millions of computers around the world that are interconnected via wires, wireless, and sometimes satellite connections using computer protocols, networking devices, security appliances, and Internet providers enabling businesses and individuals to access and share information. Although many have contributed to the success and sometimes scary elements about the Internet today, it is appropriate to highlight some of the key milestones and individuals that contributed to this communications medium that may be relative when explaining strategies for protecting children (see Figure 1.1).

On February 7, 1958, the U.S. Department of Defense (DOD) established the Advanced Research Projects Agency (ARPA), which was intended to provide "for the direction or performance of such advanced projects in the field of research and development as the Secretary of Defense shall, from time to time, designate by individual project or by category."[7] It was essentially a response to the Soviet Union's launch of the first artificial satellite, *Sputnik*. Over the years, ARPA's name flip-flopped between ARPA to DARPA (Defense Advanced Re-

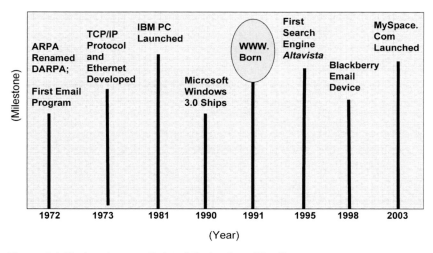

Figure 1.1 Modern Internet-Related Technology Timeline

search Projects Agency) until settling with the final name of DARPA in 1996 as a result of Public Law 104–106, under Title IX of the Fiscal Year 1996 Defense Authorization Act.[8]

In 1962, J. C. R. Licklider of the Massachusetts Institute of Technology (MIT) penned a series of memos outlining his galactic network concept, where he described a series of interconnect computers.[9] In 1962, another MIT researcher, Lawrence G. Roberts, went to DARPA to develop the ARPANET computer network.[10] In 1969 and with the assistance from the group Bolt Beranek and Newman (BBN), the first node of the network came into play at the University of California at Los Angeles (UCLA).[11] By the end of 1969, four host computers were connected into the initial ARPANET—UCLA, SRI at Stanford University, the University of California at Santa Barbara, and the University of Utah.[12] In short, ARPANET became the Internet and as a result, DARPA is essentially the inventor of the Internet as we know it today. Folks from DARPA back in 1958 and even through the late 1960s could not have imagined the types of technologies that we see today that would stand on the incredible achievement of building an information superhighway.

Another great invention was electronic mail, or email. In 1972, Ray Tomlinson at BBN wrote the "first initial hot application"—electronic mail, or email as it is commonly referred to today.[13] While working with other researchers at DARPA, Tomlinson made history when he created the email name format, including the @ sign.[14] According to the Internet Society, "he sent himself a message, the contents of which have been lost in time."[15] Over 25 years later, the first email program, written by Steve Dorner at the University of Illinois, was made available to the public.[16] It was called Eudora, and it changed the way human beings communicate around the globe.

Vinton Cerf, hailed by many as the father of the Internet, invented the TCP/IP protocol, which allows computers of different operating systems (Windows, Apple, Unix, etc.) to communicate.[17] Though not a sexy invention, the TCP/IP protocol is the core of how the Internet works and is installed on almost every computer worldwide, and thus is a major milestone for technology. The IP address is essentially a unique address for a device that is connected to the Internet. Today, most organizations and computers are running version 4 of the IP protocol, commonly referred to as IPv4. IPv4 is essentially a 35-year-old technology that has a limit of approximately 4.2 million individual IP addresses.[18]

IPv6, developed in the 1990s and starting to be implemented, will allow for literally trillions of IP addresses for the future.[19] Why is this important? Because IPv6 is foreshadowing a future that will include a broad array of consumer and professional devices, including watches, cameras, PDAs, cars, MP3 players, and telephones, that will always be online and connected to the Internet. IPv6 will enable the proliferation of these devices; within years, people will be carrying multiple devices that can access the Internet in real time.

Ray Tomlinson, with BBN, is credited with writing the first email program in 1972. Email is one of the major milestones in technology that has persisted for well over three decades. It is the most used Internet application today, for businesses as well as for consumers. I get over 100 emails on a normal day for business and about 10 or so personal messages. Those who are connected to the net use email more often than they do any other technology, including a telephone. Email is the de facto method of online communication today, followed closely by instant messaging. Hail to Tomlinson for getting us started!

In 1974, the first microprocessor was invented, followed shortly by the first commercially available personal computer from Apple Computer, called the Apple II. in 1977.[20] This was a major milestone in the history of computing and Steve Jobs, Apple's brilliant CEO, was leading the way. This brilliance, however was interrupted in 1981 when IBM introduced the personal computer or PC.[21] IBM's PC and Compaq's clone quickly caught on in the corporate workplace and has become the gold standard for business computing.

In November 1985, the world changed when Microsoft released the Windows 1.0 operating system.[22] Between 1985 and 1992, Microsoft made several upgrades to Windows and hit the big time, convincing businesses with it's 3.1

version.[23] The rest is pretty much history. Microsoft went on to dominate the PC operating system market as well as capture a significant portion of the server-based market that runs today's Web and commerce sites, corporate databases, and even popular email programs. Although Apple Computers is still around today and produces desktop and laptop-based operating systems, its share of the operating system market is well below 10 percent. As a result, Apple has successfully transformed itself into a non-PC consumer product company, focusing on music players like the iPod and download services like iTunes. Without them, Apple would have gone away a long time ago.

In 1991, the World Wide Web (WWW) was launched by CERN, the European organization for Nuclear Research and the world's largest particle physics center that resides on the French–Swiss border near Geneva, Switzerland.[24] Tim Berners-Lee of CERN is credited with the birth of the World Wide Web by creating the hypertext markup language, or HTML, which is used to display content from Web sites in a browser running on a computer.[25] In 2004, Berners-Lee was formally recognized for his accomplishment when he won $1.23 million along with the world's largest technology award—the Millennium Technology Prize—by the Finnish Technology Award Foundation.[26] According to CERN, the first Web server in the United States went into production in December 1991 at the Stanford Linear Accelerator Center in California.[27]

In 1993, the University of Illinois National Center for Supercomputing Applications (NCSA) released the Mosaic browser software in a Windows-based graphical user environment.[28] This technology was one of the most important developments in the history of the Internet because it was responsible for displaying Web pages by translating the HTML coding in documents to an easy-to-read page. The rest of the browser software story can be summed up with two companies—Netscape and Microsoft. According to CERN, in 1993 the NCSA released version one of the Mosaic browser application that allowed users to surf the Internet in a user-friendly and Windows-like environment on computers running the Unix operating system.[29] Versions for other computer systems followed shortly thereafter, and by late 1993, there were approximately 500 known Web servers on the Internet.[30]

Marc Andreessen, the leader of the Illinois team, and Jim Clark, a founder of Silicon Graphics, founded Mosaic Communications in 1994, and it was later renamed Netscape Communications. Their product, the Netscape Navigator Web browser, quickly became a success and was hailed by many as one of the most important software applications written in the modern computing era. By the end of 1994, the Internet had approximately 10,000 servers online, 2,000 of which were for commercial use with approximately 10 million users going online after the information posted.[31] By 1995, Microsoft had entered the browser war competition when it released its Windows 95 operating system with a built-in browser application, Internet Explorer. What ensued over the next five to eight years was a hard-fought browser war that Microsoft went on to dominate mainly by catching up to Netscape on technology capability and the fact that they essentially gave the product away, causing Netscape to do the same, but a little too late.

Another key milestone in the history of the Internet came in 1995 when Digital Equipment Corporation (DEC) introduced the powerful search engine Altavista.[32] DEC was an early adopter of the Internet and one of the first commercial companies to launch a public Web site. Altavista quickly became the de facto Internet search engine for two primary reasons. First, it became popular for the vast information that it seemed to offer as a result of an aggressive spider and search of public Web sites. Second, it was a hit with users because of the amazing speed at which it provided results.

Today, search engines are an interesting challenge for parents and educators when trying to protect children from harm while online. They allow minors to quickly hone in on content that may not be appropriate with just a few words typed into a query box. Google is by far the most popular search engine available today, with quick access to billions of pieces of content, images, and information on the Web in a variety of languages. Its name has become a pop culture icon and is often used as both a noun and a verb. It's quite common to Google (or search) for somebody on the Internet to find out more about them. The founders at Google came up with the name from the term *googol*, which is the mathematical term for the number 1 followed by 100 zeros.[33] Though not the number one search engine today, Altavista still exists, and its technology has been licensed and embedded into many other commercial software products that search extensively within them.

In 1998, Research in Motion (RIM) introduced the Blackberry instant email device about a decade after the company was founded in Waterloo, Ontario, in 1984.[34] This unique device, sometimes referred to as a Crackberry because of its addicting nature, is more commonly called a personal digital assistant (PDA) and is one of the most popular tools used in business and government, with millions of paying subscribers. The Blackberry revolutionized receiving email by packaging nearly instant send and receive capabilities that didn't require users to manually check for new mail. That differs greatly from Webmail packages and sites where users have to periodically check to see if they have new messages. In addition, the folks from RIM (as well as other PDA competitors) have packaged a number of additional capabilities into their products, most important, instant messaging, voice, and Internet browsing. I use a Blackberry as my phone, calendar, instant email, and Web browser and find it to be nearly impossible to do without it as I manage my work and home life. The PDA has thus become a modern success and will also complicate the task of protecting children by moving the access point from the home or school into the palm of the user's hands.

One final invention that deserves recognition is the notion and technical capabilities within today's social networking Web sites. Social networking sites are simply places for people to interact, share information, and communicate online. The most popular sites are MySpace, Xanga, and Facebook. Founded in 2003, MySpace is probably the most popular site with millions of members. These sites typically are good draws for people that want to interact and socialize online with many different types of other people that they may never meet in person. Users can post content, pictures, videos, and favorites lists and build friendships and even romances with others. Many sites also offer online chat forums with hundreds of thousands of forum topics to choose from. Although popular with teens and adults alike, it's amazing to see how much information members of these sites disclose about themselves to potentially millions of other strangers. Therein lies the risk to minors—they are often exposed to controversial topics while logged into these sites, or they expose too much about themselves, putting them at risk, potentially to sexual predators. Social networking is here to stay and seems to be a popular method for socializing in cyberspace.

Today, the Internet is used by so many people it's hard to even gather accurate statistics because thousands of new users get online daily. According to a *Wall Street Journal* article, as of May 2006, 143 million Americans accessed the Internet from home, with 72 percent of them connecting via a high-speed data connection.[35] Statistics compiled from the Computer Industry Almanac, a firm that publishes market research reports for the technology sector, show an unbelievable growth that is simply staggering:

- In 1995, the number of Internet users was 45 million.
- By 2000, that number reached 420 million.
- In 2005, the number of users going online surpassed 1 billion.
- By 2011, the number of Internet users is expected to surpass 2 billion.[36]

Of the current 1 billion plus users of the Internet, the top six countries that make up approximately 50 percentage of the total user base includes the United States (18.3 percent), China (11.1 percent), Japan (8 percent), India (4.7 percent), Germany (4.3 percent), and the United Kingdom (3.3 percent).[37] As one of the leaders in Internet usage, the number of U.S. online users is nearing 200 million, which would account for more than half the total population.[38]

More and more children are using computers, either at home or in school. According to a 2003 study released by the National Center for Educational Statistics (NCES) in the United States, 91 percent of children ages 3 and over in nursery school through grade 12 use computers, and 59 percent of them have access to the Internet.[39] Despite the sheer number and growth of youth using the Internet today, there still appears to be a digital divide between races for access at home versus in school. The NCES study goes on to report that 54 percent of white students use the Internet at home, compared with 26 percent of Hispanics and 27 percent of blacks.[40] Internet use by poverty level flip-flops for children who use the Internet at only one location, with 30 percent of use at home and 60 percent of use at school for those under the poverty line versus 63 percent use at home and 33 percent of use at school above the poverty line.[41]

Regardless of access privileges, the challenges associated with protecting minors is daunting enough given these statistics, but what is really scary is that anticipated growth for online access is based on an accelerating increase in mobile devices, such as smart phones and PDAs, especially as price points drop to bring mobile devices to more socioeconomic groups. That's where things will get tricky in trying to lock those devices down.

So why is all of this important to parents? Because everything that kids will learn as they move through middle and high school and into college is based on past computer history, protocols, and operating systems. Simply put, without understanding the technological building blocks, parents don't have a chance at protecting their kids from the risks of going online.

RECOMMENDATIONS

The Internet is a wonderful resource that offers a plethora of information, knowledge, truths, fallacies, and yes, risks, too. It is the world's electronic stage, where companies conduct business, market and advertise their products and services, and billions of messages get sent to and from one person to another. It's a haven for academics, a place of worship for the religious, the conduit for today's pornographers, and the stealth superhighway for predators and criminals. Most parents are both scared by computer technology and marvel at the advances made in the past couple of decades. Many adults take control of their lives and teach their children to lead a moral and good life, but most don't know how to guide their children to the safe content and away from the harmful information on the Internet. Parents that think they understand the risks and computer technology usually really don't. Most are sold mediocre standalone software packages designed to be only part of the solution to safety on the Internet.

Children between the ages of 8 and 17 are not growing up in an environment similar to their parents' childhoods. Children of past generations couldn't even fathom the kinds of hard-core pornography available today at the click of a mouse, nor predict the actions of today's teens while they are online. Start this journey by taking an inventory of all devices and programs available to you that can connect to the Internet. The following recommendations are designed to help parents gear up for the online world and start parenting with confidence by using technology.

- Spend time getting up to speed on the operating systems that are in use in your home. Read up on user accounts, password management, and privileges so that you'll be ready to create effective user accounts for your children with limited rights that prevent the ability to install software. Read up on the administrator account and privileges. This account or accounts with administrator privileges has the ability to manage the computer's operating system, all accounts, and passwords.
- Take inventory of all computers in your home and write down the user IDs and passwords for each person that have access to the Internet.
- Take an inventory of the computer programs and version numbers used in your home, including email, Web browsers, instant messaging tools, voice-over-Internet systems, anti-virus, anti-spam, and Internet filtering/ monitoring software. The more applications and devices with online access, the more complex it is to create a safe computing environment. A simple way to take inventory of the programs running on your Windows-based computers is to click the Start button, then Control Panel, then Add or Remove Programs. Windows will build a list of application programs that are installed on that computer.
- Talk to your kids and ask them questions about what they're doing online. Sit down with them when they go online. If you get resistance, your children might have something to hide.
- Review the Web sites your children are visiting for each computer with online access. This will provide an insight into their online activities, including visits to adult Web sites and social networking sites such as MySpace or Facebook. For Internet Explorer browsers, from the browser's menu, click View, Explorer Bar, then History to see a list of previously viewed Web sites. Pressing Ctrl+H is a shortcut. For other browsers, consult the owner's manual or Help menu.
- Search your home computers for pictures and videos. Look for all *.JPG,

.JPEG,.GIF, *.MPG, *.MPEG (common photo and video file formats). This provides a good glimpse into what's been stored, copied, and possibly left over from an Internet browsing session. Surfing the Internet often leaves behind temporary files, including pictures. The easiest way to do this is to double-click and open the My Computer icon, click on Search, select the pictures, music, or video link, select Pictures and Photos and Videos, then click the Search button.

- Take an inventory of all devices—PDAs, phones, computers, laptops, TVs, and so on—that have access to the Internet.
- Ask your kids how many email accounts they have, if they use instant messaging programs, if they have a profile on a social networking site, and where they use computers outside of your home. Honest answers include school, the library, and other kids homes, which can sometimes be the greatest risks. Be prepared for some lies.

Back to School

Training is everything. The peach was once a bitter almond.

—Mark Twain

INTERNET TECHNOLOGIES DEFINED: EDUCATION 101

I feel for today's parents. Most feel technically challenged, frustrated that their teenagers know more than they do about computers, and don't have any idea where to start to fix things so that they can be aware of what their kids do online and proactively protect them from the risks. A key part of this book is to get parents up to speed with technologies that their kids are using or will be using in the very near future. I'm an educator of over 10 years, and I tend to discuss the building blocks associated with a topic before delving into details, strategies, and recommendations. This chapter defines some key technology terms and describes why parents need to know about them as they build an effective strategy for keeping their children safe. As stated previously, the Internet is composed of millions of interconnected computers (PCs and servers), through myriad wiring and technology devices through Internet providers (see Figure 2.1). All computers have an operating system, computer protocols to connect to the network, and a series of applications (browsers, email, instant messaging, etc.) that facilitate online activity.

Because few people read a glossary and to help you get up to speed with technology terminology, this chapter gives parents and educators the basics of some key topics along with an explanation as to why the technology is important

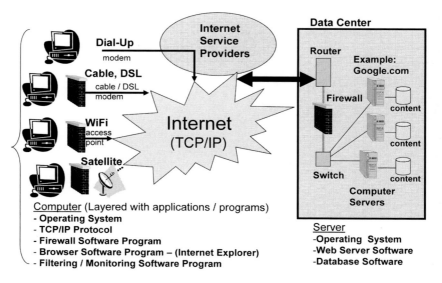

Figure 2.1 The Internet and Components

and relevant in helping to protect children. They are listed in alphabetical order for convenience.

Administrative accounts/privileges: Administrative accounts control what other accounts on that computer can do, such as what directories they have access to or even what programs others can run. Most operating systems have an administrative account. Windows XP does, and it can be used to set up other user accounts and security for a particular computer.

Why it's important: Parents can set up accounts for their children in such a way as to block them from using certain programs that may be harmful or conflict with your work. It's common for parents to set up separate user accounts for each of their children and add the programs that they can see and run. Thus, it's possible to block the Internet for one child and allow it for another by using the administrator account associated with a computer's operating system. Also, most monitoring and filtering software requires administrative rights or has to be installed by the administrator user account. *It is therefore essential that parents know and retain the password for all administrative accounts for computers in their home.* If your kids change their account password on the computer, you'll be able to reset it.

　　　How to Protect Your Children on the Internet

Blocking software: Programs that are installed on computers to block or prevent access to a particular Web site or group of Web sites by information categories (such as adult content). These programs can bet set up to block sites and other Internet-related technologies like instant messaging or voice-related services.

Why it's important: As children get older, it becomes necessary to block access to harmful sites. Parents need to know how to install these types of programs, how to configure their options for blocking sites and categories, and how to interpret usage reports that show what's being attempted but blocked. Teachers in many states will come in contact with such programs as a result of legislation requiring their use in public schools.

Blog/blogging: A kind of diary or online journal on the Internet (a contraction of *Web log*). Many social networking sites like MySpace have features that allow their members to post messages, content, images, and videos online for either semi-private or public viewing. Interestingly enough, more and more teens are using alternatives to MySpace because parents are aware of it and actively blocking it. There are many alternative sites that pose the same risk, and parents need to keep up with them and treat blogging sites as a category and not just by name. Stealth monitoring can come in handy to see exactly what your child is doing online.

Why it's important: Blogging can be fun, yet dangerous. Children have a tendency to post and expose too much information online and put themselves at risk of dangerous solicited and unsolicited content and requests. Sexual predators often look for addresses and other personal data that they can use to approach their victims. Parents need to know if their children use blogs, what they post, and whether they're at risk. Internet monitoring software is an effective way to do this.

Browser: The program that one uses to surf or browse the Internet and Web sites. Browsers are software programs that are installed on top of a computer's operating system that uses underlying computer protocols to communicate to the Internet. Browsers are available for multiple different computer operating systems, including Macintosh, Microsoft, and a variety of Unix versions. Popular browsers include Microsoft's Internet Explorer (IE), Mozilla's Firefox, and Apple's Safari.

Why it's important: Parents need to know how to configure and use features available in today's browsers. These include the use of cookies, seeing the history of sites viewed, blocking sites, and setting security and content levels to protect children. Simply put, a downloaded version from the vendor without any configuration settings may be a security risk to your computer as well as the user and your child.

Cable/Cable Modem, DSL/DSL Modem: A device that connects a single computer or multiple computers to the Internet. It's essentially your direct connection to an Internet Service Provider (ISP), whose job is to connect your computers to a corridor on the Internet.

Why it's important: Parents don't need to know the ins and outs of cable or DSL modems, just that they are the device that connects a computer to the Internet. As technology has evolved, wireless devices are becoming more common. Thus, computers today can potentially gain access to the Internet via another person's cable or DSL device if they have a wireless device connected to it. So why is this important? If the speed on your Internet connection is slowing down and you have a wireless device or access point connected to your DSL or cable modem, someone may be hijacking your Internet connection. If the information that is being sent and received on that connection is not secured via encryption technology, your personal information may be compromised.

Cache: Space on a hard drive where files are stored during normal use. Caches, which can be permanent or temporary, are used to speed up data transfers and certain types of activities, such as browsing the Web. Examples of caches include temporary directories and files when using word processing or spreadsheet programs. Software makers typically design an auto-backup feature that keeps a copy of the file you working on to protect it from being inadvertently deleted.

Why it's important: Most browsers have settings by default that store Web pages previously viewed on the hard drive in a cache. Kids that want to hide their online activities will typically delete the cache with the click of a mouse in the configuration settings of their Web browser. For those that don't delete cache manually, the browser manages the cache as it sees fit and deletes old content as the files grow too large. If not deleted, you can check a fair portion of the files or Web pages your children have previously viewed simply by browsing to the cache directory and opening the files in a browser. It's just one way to get a glimpse of what your child is doing online. If the cache on your home computer is always empty or deleted, your child may be trying to hid something.

Chat/chat room: A place where a computer user can go to converse online with other users. Chatting is a common online and real-time Internet activity.

Not all chat rooms are harmful, but beware—there are a lot of adult and sexual chat sites out there ranging from ones that talk about graphic sex (heterosexual and homosexual), sadomasochism, bondage, and even bestiality. Users must typically enter or log in to a chat room to begin conversing with others online. There are hundreds of thousands of chat rooms hosted and sometimes monitored by a variety of Internet service companies.

Why it's important: Parents must understand the risks of letting a child have access to chat rooms or entering one. Most children use an alias name when entering a chat room to hide their true identity. Online predators do the same, often posing as other teens in attempt to start up a conversation that may lead to a youth exposing personal information that can potentially lead to an in-person meeting.

Cookie: A cookie is a small file that is placed onto a computer by a Web site after visiting the site. A cookie can store information about the visitor, such as name, account number, last visit, user preferences, online purchasing information, or even a password to the site. Many banks and professional Web sites use them to recognize their customers with a friendly "welcome back, Greg" message when they reenter the site. Browsers can also be configured to notify a user when a cookie is about to be downloaded and placed on the hard disk. Those that use this feature can simply accept or reject the pending cookie.

Why it's important: Cookies can be used to track where a user goes online. Many children accept cookies for their email systems so that they don't have to keep entering a password when they go online to check email. That said, cookies are essentially a useful tactic for Web site developers but a mild invasion of privacy. Kids who want to keep their Web sites hidden from parents will often delete cookies stored on their computer after they're done browsing. They do this by simply clicking a button in the browser's configuration menu. Parents who want to see where their kids are going online can view the cookies directory for their particular browser. Consult the documentation for the browser of choice or simply search for "help cookies" and more information will be displayed.

Cybersex: Sexual discussions or online conversations pertaining to the topic of sex or sexual acts. Some adult sites allow for these types of online chats and integrate real-time video feeds that can show graphic sexual situations and acts.

Why it's important: Parents need to be aware that there are some very adult and graphic sites on the Internet that go beyond just viewing nude photos or sexual situations. A good Internet content filtering program will likely block access to most of these sites, but the software companies simply can't keep up with the number of them and how some of them are disguised via innocent names. Cybersex can also occur via the use of other common technology programs, such as email or instant messaging. To get up to speed on what's out there, simply type in one of the following search keywords and be prepared to view some hard-core material: xxx, porn, cybersex, *or sex. Parents must employ a combination of Web content filtering technology, parental policies and rules, and if necessary stealth software to reveal exactly what your child is doing online.*

Data key: A small, portable device capable of storing large amounts of files and content; also called a flash drive or a thumb drive. Most data keys connect to computers via a USB port, usually located on the front or rear of a computer. Newer and larger devices, some as large as several gigabytes, can store thousands of files. These devices are essentially mini-hard drives that are capable of storing files permanently after a computer is turned off.

Why it's important: Data keys or flash drives are small and portable, making them ideal choices for teens who want to store and potentially hide content from his or her parents. If a file retrieved from email or downloaded from the Internet is only stored on a data key and not the local hard drive on the actual computer, it becomes almost invisible to the parent monitoring their computer. Thus, pay attention to what devices are connected to your home computers when your children are online and if necessary, employ monitoring applications that can show all of their activities, including storing or copying content to small portable devices. If your child has such a portable drive, ask to see it from time to time. Review the content on it, and don't take no for an answer. If a child is unlikely to turn over a thumb drive, they might have something to hide. If you think that kids today aren't creative and will always turn over controversial or objectionable content to their parents—you are dead wrong. Even good kids have things to hide and are curious. Flashback—the thought *never* crossed my mind to give the *Playboy* magazine that my friend gave me for my birthday to my parents. I was curious and made an active attempt to hide it. Your kids are likely the same—good kids, curious, and protective of their stuff as they get older.

Domain name: A domain name identifies the name of the computer (PC or server) where a particular Web page or document is stored. Behind every domain name is a unique address called an IP address that identifies the exact computer. In the example of www.yahoo.com, yahoo.com is the domain name. The domain suffix, .com in this case, identifies the country, organization, or enterprise; .com is for business, .edu is for education, .org is for nonprofit, .mil is for U.S. military, .gov is for U.S. government, and so on.

Why it's important: The domain name tells you where your child has been on the Internet. Most computer logs and monitoring software will list the locations and sites by domain name that your child has visited. Beware—not all domain names are as friendly as they appear. A simple name could easily be hosting and displaying inappropriate content to your child so you may need to go beyond just the name to find out what's behind the web front door of their site. For example, *www.whitehouse.com* which has adult content, versus *www.whitehouse.gov* which is the actual White House.

Email: Email is the most common form of online communication today. Almost anyone that goes online has one or more email accounts. Some are free, and others are paid, such as ones with your name in the domain (Example: person1@gregoryssmith.com). There are a variety of email programs on the market; some are preinstalled on a computer, and others are Web-based and thus only require a browser to access.

Why it's important: Web-based email accounts are more common for teens than ones that are installed on an actual computer. Why? Because a child with access to the Internet can sign up for one, potentially without their parents knowing about it. Risks of email for minors include unsolicited messages from businesses and other strangers, some with legitimate content, others with sexually explicit messages, pictures, or links to pornographic sites. Chapter 7 goes into much more detail on this topic, including when to allow your child to have an email account and how to monitor it to minimize risk.

Encryption: Encryption is typically a software program or algorithm that scrambles messages, content, Web sites, and so on from one computer to another. Essentially, it makes the online communication nearly impossible to intercept, read, or monitor. The U.S. government maintains encryption keys to unlock and view secure sessions, but parents do not have access to this to find out what their kids are doing.

Why it's important: More sites, including adult hard-core pornography, and IM tools are using encryption to prevent programs and firewalls from blocking their traffic to your home computer. Most home and business computers allow encrypted sessions to flow to the Internet, usually through port 443 on a firewall. All online banking, stock trading, and financial sites use them to secure transactions. By encrypting a pornographic Web site or IM session, the Web site owners are trying to make it more difficult to block access to their sites. Chapters 5 and 6 goes into strategies to detect and block pornographic content, regardless of whether the site is encrypted. Stealth monitoring is often very effective to reveal exactly what your teens are doing online— regardless of whether the session is encrypted.

File sharing programs: A file sharing program is a software application that facilitates the distribution of content, usually photos, videos, and music, from one computer to another. These programs usually require software to be installed before one can share or download from another computer. The most common examples of file sharing sites include Napster, Kazaa, and Limewire.

Why it's important: Many of these programs facilitate sharing of illegal files or content. A recent example includes the evolution of Napster from a free service that facilitated the illegal transfer of music files to a fee-based service that is now legitimate. Other risks of these types of programs include the capability for other users on the Internet to be able to browse limited directories on your computer, potentially exposing personal data. Thus, proceed with caution with regard to file sharing programs. They can open up your computer to outside eyes.

File transfer protocol (FTP): A protocol for downloading and uploading files. FTP sites are simple servers that facilitate downloading and sharing of content. Most companies have FTP sites so that their customers can download updated programs or bug fixes for software they make and sell. FTP sites are essentially a poor man's file sharing site. Some are secure, and others are completely wide open to the public. An example of an FTP site is designated by ftp://username@ftp.company.com , where the username may or may not require a password.

Why it's important: Some teens that share files on FTP sites can create an FTP server on your home computer if they have administrative rights to do so. Thus, they can download content from others or turn your home computer into an Internet showroom without your knowledge, potentially exposing personal content about themselves or your family. In addition, there are a variety of FTP sites that offer hard-core pornography with somewhat cryptic names, making them difficult for parents to detect. Not all FTP sites are blocked by filtering software and can therefore introduce content risk to teens. FTP sites are alternatives to getting content from standard Web sites. Blocking FTP as a service is an option at the firewall, but then no FTP sites can be accessed. These sites need to be managed and monitored just like standard Web sites. Chapters 5 and 6 talk about how to monitor and block FTP sites if necessary.

Filtering software: Filtering software is used to prevent access to a particular Web site or type of content. Many filtering programs are configurable and allow parents to permit and deny content by categories, such as adult, sports, shopping, and so on. Filtering programs come in two flavors—ones that are installed on your computer or ones offered as a service via your Internet service provider. If configured properly, they can be somewhat effective, but not foolproof.

Why it's important: This software is popular with many parents today, and there are a variety of providers on the market. Filtering software, however, will not fully protect your child. More Web vendors are devising schemes to bypass filtering software algorithms. Most popular search engines offer a backdoor glimpse into adult porn sites by providing thumbnail image results to simple Web searches—even with some of the most sophisticated content filtering products. The links to the sites returned may be blocked, but the images can reveal hard-core sex even with safe searching options turned on. Also, most products can't protect against backdoor threats like friends sharing picture or video files through email or sharing files via data keys. Chapters 5 and 6 go into more detail on this topic and provides parents with more tools to detect and reduce threats. These include recommendations for restricted access for teens to standard search engines like Google and Ask.

Firewall: A firewall can be a physical device or a software program. Its main purpose is pretty simple—to prevent harmful viruses and unwanted content from going into or out of your computer. That said, most firewalls are complex to set up and maintain and require a bit more computer knowledge than what it takes to just browse the Web. Many businesses maintain sophisticated, powerful firewall devices to protect their business information. Home computers are usually protected by one or more software firewalls. Some are built into the operating system, like the firewall by Microsoft, whereas others are downloaded and installed. I believe in the common saying in life, "you get what you pay for." The free Microsoft product built into the Windows operating system is adequate at best. A version worth a look is BlackICE (www.blackice.iss.net). I use a combination of products from Microsoft and F-Secure and configure them to block everything (inbound and outbound) except what I want to flow to the Internet. In conclusion, a firewall when combined with anti-virus software is the gatekeeper of information flowing in and out of your computer to the Internet— and thus pretty important.

Why it's important: By the time most kids reach the teen years, they already know about firewall technology, what it blocks and allows, and how to reconfigure them to pass the type of traffic that they want to see. Thus—parents need to get up to speed on firewalls and lock them down to prevent their children from changing the settings. Firewalls if configured properly can block traffic to file sharing sites, block individual web sites, and block access to FTP sites if needed. Firewalls, used in conjunction with monitoring software, filtering software, and sound parental policies can make for a safe Internet experience in your home. Firewalls also protect your home computer from other potential threats including viruses and spyware by only allowing the ports or services that you want to go in and out of your computer connected to the Internet.

Gamer: This is a person who plays games on the Internet. Many young children play online or computer games as a mechanism to learn techniques, spelling, mathematics, and grammar. Some teenagers become obsessed with Internet games, many of which have online real-time chat capabilities and chat rooms where they share secrets about their favorite games

Why it's important: Gaming can become an addiction and affect children in a negative way, including becoming reclusive and less social. In addition, Internet predators use gaming sites to meet their prey, first building relationships with them and then gathering personal information. Internet games today are not entirely innocent.

Hacker: This is a person that intends to infect your computer with a virus or program that can compromise or steal information and files from you.

Why it's important: Without firewall technology, anti-virus, anti-spyware, and filtering software, your computer may be at risk. Kids today have an uncanny way of exposing risk to your computer just from the Web sites that they visit. Many gaming sites install software on home computers and create back doors for information, such as online banking passwords, to be collected by an external hacker. Parents need to reign in their kids to protect them from harm on the Internet as well as protect the assets stored on your computers.

Home Page: The top-level page of a Web site. All subordinate pages flow from or are linked to from the home page for a particular site.

Why it's important: Most kids today have one or more personal Web sites or home pages on a social networking site, such as MySpace. Children often expose too much information about themselves that can potentially introduce risk from online predators. In some cases, online Web page postings by minors provide a view into what's on their mind or what they may do in the future. Parents today must be knowledgeable of both the number of Web sites their kids have and the content within them. Monitoring tools (discussed in Chapter 5) provide a road map and set of recommendations.

Hyperlink: A Web page link to another page, site, or document posted on a computer.

Why it's important: Most teens have one or more personal Web sites, and the text alone doesn't always reveal what is on their site. A link to another page or document may be named something straight forward like *homework*, but may actually be a link to other types of content, such as pictures or videos. Most kids don't fully understand the risk of going online or posting too much content about themselves. It's not out of the ordinary for them to disguise content via parent-approved types of content links. Click on them to find out what they expose.

Hypertext Markup Language (HTML): HTML is the language that was invented by Tim Berners-Lee that renders content into displayable pages on the Web.

Why it's important: By the time kids reach age 12 or so, they are well versed at creating Web pages either via a tool or by coding them manually. Some of the tags, usually metatags, in their sites can advertise the site to a number of search engines. Parents may need to learn how to view the source code for their kids' Web pages to see whom they're trying to attract online. This is typically done in a browser by selecting Show source code from the appropriate browser menu on the page that you want to see. Look for words after the tag <meta name="KEYWORDS"> section, which are what search engines use to build their databases.

Hypertext Transfer Protocol (HTTP) and (HTTPS): These are the basic protocols that allow for a Web browser on a computer to communicate with a Web server on the Internet. The *S* at the end of HTTP indicates a secure site.

Why it's important: Sites that use HTTP are not secure. Sites that use HTTPS are encrypted and are typically secured. Examples include online banking sites. However, more porn sites are using HTTPS to bypass firewall rules attempting to block their traffic. Parents should regularly review the list of sites that their kids visit, especially ones that are encrypted.

Instant Messaging (IM): Instant messaging is the newest craze in online communication. Teens to adults are IMing each other to communicate. Most IM tools and services are free. Popular ones include Yahoo! Messenger, MSN, and AOL Instant Messenger. Unlike email, IM tools show when another user is online.

Why it's important: Instant messaging is a common tool used by sexual predators on the Internet. Much of the traffic sent is only logged by the Internet provider, and it also may allow for files to be sent from one computer to another without a proper parental audit trail or log. Many IM programs also encrypt data during transmission to bypass tools designed to block the service and pass through most firewall technology. Last but not least, many IM tools allow users to send and receive voice calls over the Internet. Although this is a great and cool technology, parents have no log of the calls, originators, or content; simply put, your kids might be talking to a stranger or sexual predator. IM use is soaring, and traffic is projected to surpass email traffic by 2010 or 2012, making this technology a real challenge for parents to monitor. Chapter 8 goes into more details about IM and provides parents with solid recommendations on how to monitor and control the risk.

IP Address: An IP address is the unique address of a computer, usually tied to the network interface card (NIC) that is commonly installed or shipped with most computers or devices today. Without getting too technical, the IP address is like the Social Security number of a computer or Internet-enabled device running the TCP/IP protocol that is designed to connect to either an internal data network or the Internet via a cable or wirelessly. An IP address is made up of four sets of numbers separated by periods, and the address can either be private (one that is not registered and exposed to the public) or public. An example of an IP address is 24.120.220.165. Internet service providers give home users access to the Internet by providing them with a fixed IP, sometimes referred to as a static IP address, or a dynamically allocated one at the time that a computer connects. Most dial-up connections to the Internet use dynamic IP addresses because they can be reused by the ISP when the user is no longer online. However, most home users (especially in developed countries) are connecting to the Internet more often with digital (non-dial-up) connections that can be allocated for longer periods of time. Thus, the IP address for a home computer in the United States may very well be always on and static.

Why it's important: Parents don't need to know whether their computers contain public or private IP addresses, but they do need to understand the concept that each device or computer that connects to the Internet will likely have a separate IP address and go through some conduit or channel to get connected to the Net. Teens with wireless network cards enabled on their laptops pose an interesting challenge for parents because they may be able to access the Internet through another connection outside of the home. In addition, the adoption of always-on PDA devices will also complicate putting in parental controls. My BlackBerry is able to bypass strong content filters enabled at work or home, and usage reports by user are not reviewed due to labor shortages. (More on this risk in later chapters with some tips to help mitigate the risks.) To quickly obtain the TCP/IP configuration from a Windows-based computer, open a command prompt (via Start, Run, Command), and type "ipconfig" and press Enter. The results will include the IP address of the network interface (wired or wireless—some computers can have both) along with other technical information suitable for IT pros. The ping command is also helpful to identify the IP address of another computer or Web site. Simply type "ping" followed by the full IP address or Web site (example: ping www.microsoft.com) and press Enter. The results will show the time, usually in milliseconds, that it takes to talk to the other computer (or yours if you ping yourself). As parents get more comfortable with networking concepts, the ping command comes in handy to identify and test connections to wireless access points, firewalls, and other computers in the home that are networked. By the time your kids are in their mid-teens they will have these concepts nailed down, and it will be even more important to keep up with them without calling the Geek Squad.

Internet: As stated previously, the Internet is a collection of millions of computers that are interconnected via wires, wireless, and sometimes satellite connections using computer protocols, networking devices, security appliances, and Internet providers enabling businesses and individuals to access and share information. Information on the Internet consists of useful research, educational materials, corporate sales and marketing collateral, information on products and services, software, and, yes, objectionable content and hard-core adult and child pornography.

Why it's important: Parents have an obligation and right to help protect their children and other minors from dangers that lurk on the Net. In addition, parents and educators alike need to better understand the components and devices that connect to the Internet; the risks; and tools to monitor, block, and filter inappropriate content to properly execute on a strategy to ensure safe computing for minors. More teens are becoming Internet savvy, and parents need to catch up and take a proactive role in granting permission and access to the Internet via the variety of devices and connections on the market today.

Internet Service Provider (ISP): An ISP is the link or conduit to the Internet for a particular computer or device. Examples include (but are not limited to) (1) T-Mobile for BlackBerry PDA wireless email and Internet access, (2) AOL for computer-based access to the Internet and email, (3) Vonage and Skype for phone service over the Internet, (4) Earthlink for home and small business computer access, (5) AT&T for voice, text messaging, and PDA Internet access, and (6) Qwest for business-grade access and high-speed connections to the Internet for larger organizations and businesses. Each ISP maintains the hardware (and sometimes software) needed for their users to connect to the Internet, and most charge a fee to connect, usually monthly. Lower speed connections like dial-up are usually more cost-effective but result in longer times to download or view content. Higher speed digital connections provide a more enjoyable surfing environment that usually results in fast download speeds and quick access to content. ISPs can also supply other services beyond just connecting to the Internet, such as email or Web hosting.

Why it's important: Parents will likely be paying the bill for all of the methods and channels that their home computers and children can access the Internet. It's easy to see how costs can quickly get out of control and increase as most households in the United States have broadband (high-speed) Internet connections for their home computers, as well as multiple cell phone and PDA-enabled accounts that provide access to the Internet. The good news is that you'll know how you're household is connected by the bill you pay, unless of course your child is hijacking a neighbor's unsecured wireless Internet connection without your knowledge or approval.

Java: Java is a software development language invented by Sun Microsystems designed to run on a variety of computer, devices, and operating systems. In contrast, applications typically written for the typical PC running Microsoft Windows requires a specific version of the Windows operating system or Internet browser to run properly.

Why it's important: Java applications are here to stay, and more software developers are writing in Java to allow their applications to run on any computing platform, including the Macintosh, Windows PC, Unix, PDA, cell phone operating system platforms, and more. The BlackBerry device includes a Java runtime client application that enables running Java applications on the PDA itself. Java applications can run on a computer, as a plug-in download file to an Internet browser, or simply as preinstalled software on any device. Most browsers allow administrators to set security protection and either allow or prevent the use of Java applications. Why? Because Java applications can have access to the files and information on a computer and potentially communicate sensitive information to hackers if the application is written to do so. What can parents do about this? Not much, because they generally don't know which applications may be harmful or not. What is important, however, is to only install or run Java applications from reputable firms. Avoid downloading (via blocking the capability to install an application at the account level of your child), any application, Java or otherwise, from online gaming sites, which are frequently used to deposit spyware or programs designed to compromise personal information stored on computers.

JavaScript: JavaScript is a software scripting language used by software programmers to build logic and features into Web-based application pages. Unlike Java, it doesn't pose the same threat of access to information stored on a local computer. Common uses of JavaScript in Web pages include validating data entered into a form—such as an email address, ZIP code, state, or country. JavaScript runs on local computers after the files are downloaded from the Web site being accessed. Most browsers have the capability to turn off JavaScript, but most users allow it.

Why it's important: This technology is really about Web site and application performance than security. The slower the Internet connection, the slower the response to displaying pages with JavaScript embedded in them and the longer it takes to process or submit online forms. A high-speed Internet connection allows JavaScript run much faster. No real harm here.

Monitoring Software: Monitoring software is an application program that is either installed on your computers or used as a service via your ISP to help you potentially block sites, content, and services. Monitoring software can log online activities that include downloading files, accessing Web sites or FTP servers for restricted content, using IM programs, making voice calls over the Internet, and standard email usage.

Why it's important: These programs are not only helpful in protecting children but essential for parents and educators today. Monitoring programs can also be installed in what's called stealth mode so that kids don't even know they are there. Savvy teens will look for monitoring programs running on their computers and may attempt to uninstall them (if they have the privilege on their account) or remove them from memory. A common tactic on computers running the Windows operating system is to press the Ctrl-Alt-Delete key combination to reveal a screen (the task manager) that allows them to see what programs and processes are running. Programs are clearly displayed in the window, and users can easily shut them down if desired. Examples of common programs include a browser, Microsoft Word, and Excel. Many other software applications and monitoring tools are displayed as more cryptic processes. A program is usually made up of one or more processes running in the memory of your computer. Examples of processes that are not displayed as programs include anti-virus and anti-spyware applications. Some processes are easily discernible by their name and can be killed to terminate the application. Other processes are not so obvious and can be difficult for teens to crack and disable. Well-designed stealth monitoring programs fall into this category.

Multimedia (audio, video, etc.): Multimedia files typically display more than just text. Examples include pictures, audio files, and videos. Many of these files are readily available for download and viewing, and some of them come with significant risks. You wouldn't want your teen downloading or viewing a portion of the Paris Hilton sex video clip online. Without proper filters or blocks, files like these are just a click away, usually through an industrial-strength search engine like Google, MSN, Yahoo!, or Ask. Multimedia files come in a variety of types that include common file extensions like .wav, .au, and .mp3 for audio files; .jpeg, .jpg, .bmp, or .gif for photos and images; and .mpg, .mpeg, .avi, .mov, and .qt for videos.

Why it's important: There are many options for formatting content, and several free options including browser plug-ins for viewing or playing multimedia files. Parents need to be cognizant of the types of files and applications that their children use to ensure that they're not at risk. Most pornography is distributed or viewed by images or links to photos from Web sites and email messages. If done properly, images can be embedded directly into the content of an email so that they display on opening without any other action from the user. Users on social networking sites like MySpace frequently post audio, video, and photos that many parents might object to. Although many of these sites have terms of use and methods for reporting questionable content, they don't get all of the bad stuff. And for a lot of them, you don't even have to be logged on or registered to search and find objectionable content.

Access to multimedia content, including adult and hard-core pornography images and videos, is just a click away with the help of a search engine. Parents need to be aware of the file types and content that they provide as well as the most common methods for accessing it. Once you are fully educated, lock down those computers and monitor your kids to see what they're up to. Don't forget those data keys . . .

Operating System (OS): At a high level, an operating system is the key program that controls the basic functions of a computer, which include how software programs get loaded into memory and run, how files get saved onto disk drives, and how data is displayed on a monitor. They come in a variety of version and flavors. Microsoft currently dominates the PC operating system market for home and business computers and laptops. Older versions of their operating system that are still in use today include Windows 98, Windows NT,

Windows 2000, Windows XP, and Windows 2003. Newer versions have become much more proficient and intelligent at performing tasks quickly, adding to the enjoyment of user computing. Other operating systems that are less common in homes and the office include Apple's Macintosh OS and various versions of Linux and Unix. Most popular Web browsers have been adapted to run on all of these operating systems. Because the market share is so large for Windows-based PCs in homes today, this text focuses predominantly on computers equipped and running Windows.

Why it's important: The most important aspect of an operating system for parents to know is how to create user accounts and manage their security. I'm a strong advocate that children should not have user accounts on home computers that let them administer the PC, create new user accounts, change their profiles to allow for more functions like installing software applications and changing passwords. Parents must get up to speed on how to create user accounts for their children that grant them appropriate privileges on their computers. Part of this important role includes password management for all administrative user accounts, Web content and filtering software, and email accounts. Take charge of the computing environment in your family and manage it proactively. One of my colleagues asked me why I thought it was ok to run such a tight ship in my house with regards to computer access to the Internet and whether I thought that it was an invasion of my children's privacy. My answer was swift—*It is my role, right, and obligation to do what is necessary to keep my kids safe and I don't need anyone's permission to take the appropriate actions. They're my kids!* Get up to speed on the operating systems used in your home and kids' schools and, if possible, consolidate to one or two in the home to ease management and administration.

Phishing: This is a common tactic by hackers and scammers to trick users into giving up personal or confidential information like addresses, bank accounts, and Social Security numbers. The most common form of phishing occurs through email and in most instances contains some official-looking text and a link to a Web page where users are encouraged to confirm or change personal content and information about themselves. Banking scams are most common—unsuspecting users are redirected to a bogus Web site that looks like their bank's Web site but isn't. Most phishing sites have IP addresses in the Web link compared to a properly qualified domain name in the link, like www.-Wachovia.com. Some phishing email links also redirect users to sites that can install spyware or other harmful programs designed to collect personal information from home computers.

Why it's important: Parents should be aware of this for their own protection as well as that of their children and need to pay attention to Web URLs when being asked to confirm or edit any personal or financial information online. Most top-level banks have other methods to thwart phishers that include the use of special passwords or image file uploads to their site so that their customers know they are on a secure and authentic Web site. Parents need to talk with their children about not giving out information while on-line—including address and phone numbers, as teens can be more easily duped than adults. Anti-spyware and anti-spam programs are also helpful in an attempt to reduce phishing. Every email account should have these protections. If they don't, close them down and look for a viable alternative that better protects your kids and your personal information as well.

Plug-in: A plug-in is a special kind of program that installs on your computer and works with your browser to enhance going online and accessing content from Web sites. The most common types of plug-in programs facilitate viewing PDF content and documents, viewing pictures, listening to audio or music files, and viewing video within the browser's window. Plug-ins are a great way to enhance the interactive experience.

Why it's important: Some plug-in files can damage your computer or create back door programs that can compromise personal information to hackers and scammers. Accept only plug-ins from reputable sites that have fully named Web pages (Example: www.adobe.com) and not Web sites using IP addresses as part of their domain name. In addition, you might restrict what teens can install, limiting their ability to install a potentially harmful plug-in without your knowledge and consent. This can be easily done by using user account privileges applied to their accounts. Remember, the operating system rules the computer's activities. A simple request by a teen to install software or a plug-in can be overridden by the security settings at the operating system applied to their account. When applied correctly, this is a good safe surfing tactic.

Podcasts: Podcasts are audio files that are accessible for listening online and downloadable to audio players, usually in MP3 format. Most podcasts are played with the assistance of either a browser plug-in or a separate audio player like Windows Media Player or iTunes.

Why it's important: The majority of podcasts are usually recorded and published for business, educational, or product/promotional purposes. Keep in mind that anyone with the right equipment can create and record a podcast, publish it to a Web page, and promote it relatively easily. Podcasts can contain a variety of inappropriate content and discussion. To complicate matters, audio files are extremely difficult to filter and restrict by content filtering software, mainly because the audio is not transcribed to text that can be filtered. Thus, the wrong type of podcast can easily fly under the radar and into the hands of young teens without parents' knowledge. I recommend that parents search their computers from time to time for a variety of file types that include .mp3 and .wav (audio) and play the content to ensure that it's appropriate for children. Look for these files in all hard drive directories and any mobile data keys.

Pornography: Adult-oriented and sometimes graphic sexual content (images, text, and videos) that can include sex with minors, adults (homosexual and heterosexual), and sex acts with animals.

Why it's important: Pornography sites are some of the most profitable on the Internet today. Many require a credit card or paid subscription to access the majority of their content, but a lot have free sections that are teasers for would-be paying customers. These teaser sections can contain graphic content including (but not limited) to all kinds of sex acts. Some adult sites are more extreme than others and provide discreet access to images, photos, and videos. One that comes to mind is Playboy. While appropriate for adults, it is certainly not appropriate for children. Thus, parents today must employ some kind of Internet filtering or blocking software to prevent their children from seeing mature adult content and hard-core pornography. The most common form of access to this type of material is through a standard search engine. Lock them down for children.

Search Engine: Search engines are one of the greatest software inventions as well as the one of the biggest risks for minors for accessing inappropriate content. There are a variety of great search tools on the Internet today including popular search engines like Google, Ask, Altavista, Yahoo!, and MSN. They regularly patrol the Internet, looking for new content to catalog in their search databases. Some search engines offer more content than others. A recent test search using the same keyword, *sex*, revealed 699 million results (or links to Web pages), and another search engine revealed a mere 90 million for the same search word.

Why it's important: Search engines are the most common and easiest way for teens to look for and find inappropriate content. Teens looking for adult content can simply type a variety of keywords into a search engine, which will quickly return millions of Web page links or images. It's just that easy. Several search engines offer safe or family search settings for their users, and these settings do filter search results and block potentially harmful content. The real problem with these sites is that the setting can easily be changed by minors and requires no additional passwords or parental approvals to do so. Thus, most teens can simply set them to not filter search results when they're online, find what they want, save the good stuff to data keys to hide it, set the safe search settings back on, then clear the browser's cache and history to cover their tracks. There are however, alternatives to protecting children from harmful results served up by search engines that include safe search sites and engines. Chapter 6 goes into depth about which search sites are safe for teens along with recommendations on which sites to grant access to your children and how to prevent some really harmful content with search filters that don't work that well.

Secure Socket Layers (SSL): Secure socket layers or SSL is a fancy technical term for a kind of encryption technology. Essentially, SSL is the software that provides a secure session over the Internet to most public Web sites. Financial institutions like banks and online brokerage companies use SSL to encrypt Web sessions from logging on to their site, moving money, and trading stocks and bonds. Browsers typically indicate that a Web session is secure by the placement of a small lock and key icon somewhere in the browser's window. Placing the mouse pointer over the lock will usually reveal the level of encryption is being used. These layers range from weak encryption (40-bit) to strong encryption (128–256-bit). The stronger the encryption, the more secure the sites are and less likely that the site or session (content exchanged between the requesting PC and Web site) will be compromised. In short, this is fantastic technology that has enabled a tremendous growth of self-service Web sites for financial management.

Why it's important: Some controversial sites use SSL to encrypt entire Web sessions and access to their content. Why? Simply put, their operators are getting smarter and are attempting to prevent Web filtering software applications from blocking them. Most firewalls by default allow encrypted SSL sessions through port 443. Blocking SSL essentially prohibits one's ability to do online banking and trading, accessing secure corporate email systems, buying and selling on eBay, purchasing a good or service online with a credit card, or logging into a legitimate but secure Web site to do research that may be available via a subscription. In addition, more instant messaging applications are going secure via SSL to bypass applications attempting to block them. Parents can't get around this one, but note when kids are accessing secure sites and investigate further if warranted. Secure Web sites are typically denoted with an additional "s" in the http protocol section of the Web address, such as https://securelogin.bankname.com. Monitoring software can also come in handy when trying to find out exactly what content your child is accessing from a secure Web site. More in Chapters 5 and 6.

Services: Services are usually programs that run on sophisticated and high-powered servers. Examples of applications that run as services include a Web site or FTP service. As PCs have become more powerful and desktop operating systems more sophisticated, these capabilities are now available on most home computers. Services usually don't show up as applications when a user opens a Windows task manager to view applications and processes running performance and network activity. Services are more complicated and usually show up as one or more cryptic processes running on a computer, making them harder to detect.

Why it's important: A smart teen can turn your home computer into a publicly accessible Web site in a short period of time. If your child has access to the administrator password on your home computer, he or she can set up a Web server and operate a site without your knowledge over your high-speed Internet connection. The site itself and any content displayed may be accessed from anywhere in the world, drawing traffic to your home computer and potentially exposing your new site to hackers and viruses. Parents are encouraged to consult their operating system's user manuals and look for the types of application services that can be enabled. Look for services that are automatically started on bootup. When in doubt, ask your child or set up stealth monitoring to really find out what's running on your home computer.

Social Networking: Social networking sites are Web sites that offer users a forum to share information about themselves with other private and public friends.

Why it's important: Social networking sites are prime target areas for sexual predators. They gather information such as schools, pictures, email addresses, and friends to piece together the necessary types of personal data to launch an assault. Many children don't understand the risks of social networking sites and put themselves in danger by publishing too much private data about themselves. Parents should beware of this technology.

Spam: Spam is simply unwanted email or messages. It comes in a variety of flavors, but the main categories of annoying spam include (1) unsolicited special offers/sales, (2) racially insensitive material, (3) get-rich-quick schemes, and, my all-time favorite (4) adult content. Most companies have sufficient anti-spam solutions in place to reduce (but not totally eliminate) unwanted email, and those algorithms are usually worth the money that organizations spend on them. Junk email can range from 40 percent of incoming email to as much as 75 percent for large multinational and high-worth companies. Free anti-spam solutions are moderate at best in reducing unwanted and sometimes downright profane email. Good anti-spam solutions not only block most unwanted email but also allow users to create and manage their own "accept" and "blocked" lists of email addresses.

Why it's important: Parents will undoubtedly run into email messages that are not intended for children. Inappropriate messages that I've seen from a variety of consumer email products and services include advertisements to grow hair, increase genital or breast size, last longer in bed, or view the latest hot chick's naked pictures. Simply put, parents today *must* pay attention to spam and take precautions to minimize inappropriate content for their children. More on this in Chapter 7, along with clear recommendations on how to see how effective your anti-spam solutions are.

Spyware: Spyware is an interesting phenomenon and fairly recent technology challenge that has significant risks for today's corporate and home computers. In a nutshell, spyware is a program or a script that if downloaded to your computer is capable of causing harm to your system and potentially compromising personal information stored on your system. Many spyware (or adware) programs can turn systems into zombies by taking control of them and using their computing power with hundreds or thousands of other computers to collectively launch an attack against a public Web site, say, Google. Spyware can also store and run simple hard-to-detect programs that can capture user IDs and passwords for what most think are secure financial Web sites. Many companies invest in programs to combat spyware, but few consumers do so. Most consumers I've talked to think that free anti-spyware downloads will get the job done. Let me be frank—in this case, nothing free is really that good. In short, spyware is a dangerous threat that can be protected against if appropriate steps are taken. Chapter 6 goes into strategies for protecting against spyware.

Why it's important: Anti-spyware solutions usually come as separate software products. Spyware can be delivered to computers in a variety of ways. The most common way a computer gets infected is by visiting a public Web site that has been embedded with programs intended to do harm that are downloaded on visiting the site. Common sites that have spyware programs include gaming sites, gambling sites, and pornography sites. Parents can limit the spyware problem via two simple ways: (1) block harmful sites via Internet filtering software, or (2) install and regularly update anti-spyware. The computer industry is evolving, and most anti-virus vendors will employ anti-spyware solutions as part of their offerings in the near future. Thus, parents need to do their research and pick the right products for the job today as well as tomorrow.

Surfing: Another name for browsing the Internet using a standard Web browser. The most common way for adults and children to navigate the Web is to use a search engine to begin finding content. Content found from surfing the Web can come in a variety of forms, mostly from standard Web sites and pages. However, surfing is usually expanded in its definition to include browsing content from social networking sites like MySpace, viewing videos on YouTube, and entering a chat room for a conversation with others. Thus, surfing the Web is no longer classified as just looking at Web sites and pages.

Why it's important: The Internet is a vast resource of information—some truthful, some false. With so much content and the help of sophisticated and powerful search engines, searching the Internet can be a risky proposition in the hands of children. It's quite common for a child to come across inappropriate content as a result of searching for something else. Case in point: Searching for a female friend's name could easily yield pornographic content, including graphic pictures. Parents need to be proactive and set rules for what sites and search engines children have access to and use capable technology to enforce it. In my professional work, I never set a policy that can't be enforced with technology. I apply this to protecting my children as well and it works.

TCP/IP: TCP/IP stands for Transmission Control Protocol/Internet Protocol. In a nutshell, these are the software and networking protocols that allow computers to talk to one another via local area networks or over the Internet. Most computers come already loaded with a TCP/IP software stack so that they can plug into computer networks and the Internet. There's usually nothing to configure at home unless you're setting up a network (wired or wireless) or using a firewall for your home computers. Either way, each device, computer, cable modem, and firewall device has an IP address so that TCP/IP can talk properly.

Why it's important: The only thing that parents need to know about TCP/IP is that it works and requires a unique IP address for each device, whether it be a Windows-based PC, Macintosh, or a computer loaded with the Linux operating system. They all require IP addresses and run TCP/IP. Parents should maintain an inventory of all computers in their house, know the IP addresses for each one, and use appropriate monitoring software for each computer.

Temporary Internet Files: These are files that are stored on a local computer's hard drive that contain actual content (HTML Web pages, pictures, audio, video, etc.) from sites that have been visited. When a user calls up a Web page, the resulting page and content is actually downloaded to the requesting computer's hard disk, retrieved by the requesting Web browser, and then displayed. Once the browser is closed and the computer is shut off, these files usually stay on the local hard drive for some time unless they are manually deleted by the user. Temporary Internet files usually sit in their own subdirectory and can be opened and viewed like they were from a Web page without being connected to the Internet. Most browsers have settings for how these files are managed. Options include setting up a large temporary disk space for improved speed when accessing sites to deleting them once the browser is shut down. The default is usually to let the browser manage an appropriate amount of space, usually a small percentage of the hard disk size, and delete older temporary files as newer pages and sites are viewed.

Why it's important: Parents can get a feel for what their child is doing online by simply using the My Computer icon to search for the appropriate directory and view files stored there. Double-clicking on an HTML file should open the file and display it in the default browser. The default location for temporary Internet files for a Microsoft XP Windows computer is usually stored in a subdirectory for each user. For my computer, it's stored in the following directory: C:\Documents and Settings\Greg\Local Settings\Temporary Internet Files. My browser is automatically set to store up to 596 megabytes of temporary Internet files. Most browsers also allow users to easily view these files. In Internet Explorer, it's as easy as clicking on the Tools menu, Internet Options, General tab, Settings, then View Files. Parents are encouraged to view these files to see what their child is up to. If the temporary Internet directory is always empty, your child may be proactively deleting content from it in an effort to conceal their tracks online.

Text Messaging: Text messaging, or texting, is very popular with the young crowd and even highly used among adults. Essentially, it involves sending a simple message without graphics or attachments, from one device to another. The most popular form of test messaging with teens is through cell phones that are configured to permit outgoing and incoming text messages. Many carriers charge for these messages, some as much as $0.10 per message, so beware of increased costs on your child's phone bill. There are also text messaging capabilities built into to several Web sites that also allow simple messages to be sent from one person to another.

Why it's important: Parents need to understand the risks of texting, especially for younger children. More advertisements and unsolicited messages are being sent to text-enabled cell phones and are exposing children to information that might not be pertinent for them. In addition, texting doesn't leave a good audit trail for parents to review content. In contrast, parents can often review messages sent from and received by their children's email account and even set up forwarding capabilities to allow them to see all inbound messages. Text messages essentially go undetected by parents, leaving children with and an unmonitored communication capability. Grant this technology carefully and when your kids are ready for the responsibility.

Uniform Resource Locator (URL): A URL is a fancy name for a Web address. Figure 2.2 depicts the components in a standard URL and explains each segment.

Why it's important: URLs are the footprints of sites that your children are visiting. Parents should know the kinds of Web sites and pages their children are accessing, including search engines and social networking sites. Most browsers offer a history feature that lists the most recently visited sites. Parents are encouraged to consult their browser's help section and learn exactly how to view this information. If the history list is empty, your child may be deleting it and trying to hide where they've been online.

http://www.domain/directory/sub-directory/file-name.htm
Example: http://www.gregoryssmith.com/profile.html

http	The **HyperText Transfer Protocol** (http), or standard for communication that governs the transfer of several types of web objects.
www	World wide web portion (web pages / sites) of the Internet. Note: Using FTP in this spot would denote a file transfer protocol associated with the web.
gregoryssmith .com	The **domain name** identifies the computer where the document is stored. The domain suffix identifies the country (as in ca for Canada), organization (org), school (edu), commercial enterprise (com) and so on.
profile.html	The document name (or web page) that is stored as a hypertext markup language (htm or html) document.

Figure 2.2 The Uniform Resource Locator (URL)

Webcam/Videocam: Webcams are usually simple and inexpensive camera add-ons (or built-ins) to a computer that allows for taking either still pictures or real-time video of anything in the camera's view. This technology can be used for business purposes to integrate video links into online presentations into a single session, for personal phone calls with video between two parties over the Internet via VOIP, or for sexual situations that often require fees to view the more interesting stuff on the net.

Why it's important: Parents need to know just how easy it is for teens to either proactively or accidentally find this type of live adult content. A recent search for the phrases *+adult +video +cam*, which instructs the search engine to return results where all three words are matched (implied Boolean AND), returned 6.3 million links to sites. Most adult and sex sites allow users to either text chat or video chat with people on the other side of the online video camera, and it can be very easy to get access. Don't believe me? Try the search phrases above to learn just how easy it is to get very adult content and live interactions that are not appropriate for children. Also, if your home computers have Webcams installed on them, pay attention to how your children are using them. It's easy to set one up and expose oneself to the world via live feeds. This technology needs to be monitored by parents. They also need to ensure that content filters are preventing access to adult video and live sex camera sites.

Web Site: A collection of Web pages that usually contains content in a variety of formats and links to other pages within the same site or a different site. The top-level page of a Web site is typically called the home page.

Why it's important: Not only do parents need to monitor what their kids are looking at online, they also should know if their children are hosting their own Web sites. If so, content should be reviewed to ensure that only appropriate material is posted that does not include too much information about themselves—such as personal phone numbers, home/email addresses, or IM names.

Wireless Access Point: A wireless access point is essentially a small computer networking appliance that performs a couple of functions. First, it directly links to a digital broadband or high-speed Internet connection. Second, it can act as a networking switch and allow for computers to be directly connected to it via a data cable. Third, it works with compatible wireless networking cards installed in desktop and laptop PCs to facilitate a wireless transfer of content from the access point to the requesting computer with a wireless card installed in it. Wireless devices are still evolving and come in many flavors with phrases like 802.11b and 802.11g. Wireless access points can be set up to talk to specific computers in the home and do so using encryption technology in an attempt to protect content and Web sessions. Most laptop computers come already equipped with a wireless network card that is ready to integrate with a number of access points. Wireless access points can be configured to be secure or unsecure, open to anyone within range. Using an unsecured wireless access point from a computer without asking permission is known as hijacking an Internet connection. The most common term for a wireless access point is Wi-Fi, which stands for wireless fidelity. The typical range for a wireless access point to a computer is a few hundred feet. WiMax technology, which is coming soon commercially, will broadcast a signal to a range of miles instead of feet, making it even more attractive to teens wanting to go online.

Why it's important: It's not important for parents to understand the intricacies of the various wireless networking options, devices, and versions. It is important however, for them to understand the risks of kids going online via a wireless connection that might not be controlled in their own house. This dilemma will only get worse as more powerful and free wireless access points cover a larger geographical range. By the time most children reach the age of 15 or so, they are quite adept at (1) finding unsecured access points, (2) configuring a laptop computer to access a wireless access point, and (3) setting up a wireless access point, including enabling encryption. Parents need to join in and catch up on this knowledge fast. This technology is wonderful, but it can provide several avenues for teens to access the Internet under the parental radar. It's not uncommon for a teenager to use someone else's wireless access point to find inappropriate adult content. Today's teenagers are Web-savvy, smart, and sometimes deceitful. It will become increasingly difficult to lock down a computer and protect minors when the avenues through which they can get onto the Internet fall outside of protections that may be set up within their own homes. Parents need to get up to speed with this technology, install it in their own homes with the assistance of an IT professional, and learn how to lock it down securely. My home network is comprised of a wireless access point connected to a cable modem, employs encryption, and only allows certain computers in the home to use it. Thus—I've blocked my neighbors from hijacking my Internet connection or viewing content as it travels wirelessly from my computers to my access point. Parents—wake up to this technology. Understanding this technology is a key component to protecting kids online.

World Wide Web (www, the Web): The World Wide Web is a broad term for the collection of publicly accessible Web sites. There are millions of Web sites on the Internet, with thousands being added each week. Content is exploding on the Internet as more people join the digital and online revolution. The

Web portion of the Internet is one of the most widely used and known, but it is not the only avenue for people to exchange information and content online. Other avenues include email, FTP, bulletin boards, IM, and voice-over-Internet calls.

Why it's important: Parents need to be up on all of the avenues through which their children can get on the Internet. The Web portion of the Internet deals content displayed via browser software and browser plug-ins. Parents should always think of the Web as the "world wild web" due to the variety of interesting and often inappropriate content that children can find online.

Virus: A program or script that can potentially render a computer useless. Viruses come in a variety of shapes and forms. Some are more dangerous than others. Bad viruses can destroy content on the infected computer and also use that computer to spread to other computers. Viruses attack weaknesses in a computer's operating system. Computers running Linux or the Mac OS are not frequently targeted by coders that write viruses. The majority of viruses are designed to attack computers running one of the many versions of Microsoft's operating system—Windows NT, 98, 2000, XP, 2000 Server, 2003 Server, or any of their application programs designed to run on these operating systems.

Why it's important: First and foremost, parents need to get decent anti-virus software for their home computers. An anti-virus program is only as good as its last update, which can sometimes help protect against hundreds of new virus threats. Decent anti-virus programs for purchase include offerings from F-Secure, Norton, and Symantec. For systems connected to the Internet via digital or high-speed lines, the anti-virus programs should be set to update at least daily (if not hourly). So what does a conversation about viruses have to do with protecting kids online? Not much other than to say that many Web sites that offer inappropriate content for free or fee, such as sites promoting computer games, pornography, and gambling, have a higher probability of delivering a virus than more reputable sites. Some of these sites can also install spyware, which can inflict a stealthy kind of pain that may compromise key passwords to work accounts or even online banking and brokerage ac-counts. Thus, do your part and block access to these sites for children, and you'll benefit in the long run with fewer viruses and spyware.

RECOMMENDATIONS

It's important that parents and educators stay abreast of recent developments in computer technology and the Internet as a whole. Tools, devices, and technologies change frequently. By the time most children reach 14 or 15 years of age, they have completely surpassed their parent's knowledge of computers and the Internet. If left unchecked, these kids may get into some trouble, whether or not they mean to. Parents have an obligation and right to nurture, educate, and protect their children from the risks associated with going online. Those that feel they are violating their children's privacy by keeping ahead of them from a technology and monitoring perspective may actually be contributing to their risk. That said, I leave you with the following recommendations.

- Take control of all administrative computer accounts and passwords for your computers in the home. Without these controls, you're helpless.
- When your kids are younger and in middle school, place your Internet-enabled computers in a common space that is viewable. Don't allow them to have unfettered access to the Internet, especially from their rooms.
- Get up to speed on firewall programs and learn how they work. They can be very useful in protecting your kids from harmful content and programs as well as any personal or confidential data stored on your home computers. Every computer—home, work, or school—should be protected by either a firewall program or a device.
- Take an inventory of the items and services that have access to the Internet, including computers, cell phones, and PDAs. Reduce risky services where appropriate. Simply put, the fewer devices connected to the Internet, the easier it is to manage them. You may even save some money by restricting or consolidating services.
- Research the types of Internet filters and programs that can block harmful content and monitor online activities. Chapters 5 and 6 may be helpful in this research. No computer or device that is used by a child should be without some type of protection or monitoring. As a parent, you are responsible for what your child has access to or is doing online. Take some responsibility—install and configure software to monitor and filter out adult or objectionable content for minors, and review your children's online activities from time to time. Blocking applications don't prevent all of the risks, which is why I recommend monitoring applications as well. Teens blocked from certain Web sites may get creative and get the content that they're looking for from another, less protected or entirely unprotected computer. They also often share content and files via portable data keys (flash drives), which are easy to hide. Pay attention to what's connected to your home computers and ask to see what's on those data keys.
- Get up to speed on content and security filters that are readily available in

the browser software installed and running on your computers. There may be multiple versions, so take an inventory of the number and type of browsers. It's not uncommon for a teen to download Firefox or Netscape and hide it from their parents, who may only be concerned with security on the installed version of Internet Explorer. If possible, reduce the number of browser applications to one and hone your skills on the settings and capabilities for just that browser.

- Using the administrator account for your computers, set up individual accounts for each child. Where appropriate, restrict those accounts from installing new software or applications. This is commonly referred to as either an administrative or power-user privilege that is associated with a user account. If your child's account has either of these privileges, they can download and install software without your knowledge and configure them to their desires. Lock down your home computers and learn about the operating system's capabilities for assigning security settings by account. No child needs to install software without a parent's consent, unless of course there is stealth software installed.

- Ask questions at your child's school to find out how they are helping protect children using computers in class. Don't settle for generic answers. Get names of products used and discuss and learn about strategies at the school. Engage your child's teacher in a conversation on Internet safety. You may be surprised how little they know.

- Most kids need and use a search engine to do research for school projects. Search engines pose one of the greatest risks for exposing children to adult content. Get your kids using safe search engines instead of a standard version. These include (but are not limited to) Ask Jeeves for Kids (www.ajkids.com), Yahooligans (www.yahooligans.com), or family filtering options on commonly used search engines and sites. Where appropriate, help your child perform the search and approve each results page to ensure that they're not being exposed to inappropriate content. I hate to remind you, but it's your job as a parent to get involved and that includes spending time with your child on the computer and enforcing safe surfing. Chapter 6 provides some additional tips and recommendations on using search engines.

- Last, but not least, keep an open dialog with your children about the risks associated with accessing the Internet and be clear on what tools and sites that they can use.

Risks Overview: Are Parents Making the Grade?

The best way to teach morality is to make it a habit with children.

—Aristotle

AN OVERVIEW OF ONLINE RISKS

Let me be really clear at the start of this chapter—all of the privacy advocates that pontificate about how wrong it is for parents to spy on their kids' activities, some online, in an attempt to keep them safe—can just go pound sand. There, I said it. I don't need anyone's permission to look at my kids' email accounts, see where they've gone online, or even log into their social networking site to see what they've posted privately. I have every right as a parent to do what it takes to keep them safe. My house is not a democracy and is a far cry from a dictatorship, but my rules apply as long as I'm footing the bill. The Internet is definitely an interesting place, especially for parents trying to protect their children from adult content, harmful adult predators, and others intending to physically or emotionally harm children. I write this from Brussels, Belgium, where I'm reminded that technology is global and access to the Internet spans the entire world, even in remote places. As I strolled the streets of this city, I notice a number of Internet cafés that offer access to the Net at an hourly rate, some charging for as little as 15 minutes. I stopped inside one to see who was there and what they were doing. To my surprise, most of the patrons of this particular café were teenagers, with an occasional businessman looking frenzied. Anyway, I glanced at what many of the teenagers were doing as I walked through. Most were using email and updating social networking sites, entering what appeared to be additions to long-winded blogs. Two young boys, likely 15 or 16, were toward the back, and as I approached, they minimized the screen. I caught a glimpse before they cleared the screen entirely, and it looked like they were browsing porn sites. That's when it hit me: Creative kids will look for opportunities to gain unfettered access to the Internet. That said, most children in industrialized countries are exposed to the Internet via four primary uses and locations:

1. computers at home,
2. computers in school,
3. computers at other friends' houses, or
4. Internet cafés or shared Wi-Fi sites like coffeehouses.

According to a Pew Internet and American Life Project Teens and Parents Survey, 87 percent of children between the ages of 12 and 17 (approximately 21 million) use the Internet.[1] In addition, 74 percent of teens most often go on the Internet at home, followed by 17 percent at school.[2] The Pew study goes on to report that overall teens use computers to access the Internet 87 percent of the time at home, 78 percent at school, 74 percent at a friend's house, 54 percent at the library, and 9 percent at a community center, youth group, or community church.[3] The highest percentage of growth in use came at libraries, where reported use went from 36 percent in 2000 to 54 percent in 2004.[4] The Pew survey goes onto report that 60 percent of children as young as sixth grade go online, with the numbers steadily increasing as they get older (82 percent for seventh grade, 85 percent for eighth grade, and up to 94 percent for twelfth grade).[5]

There are a variety of risks and potential harms associated with going online for both adults and minors. The following is a list of some of the consequences that can happen to anyone (see Chapter 4 for specific cases).

- Exposure to sexual content, exploitation, and harassment—potentially from sexual predators
- Computer viruses and spyware
- Hacking attempts to steal personal information
- Gambling and addiction
- Illegal purchase or distribution of drugs
- Exposure to extreme violence and mutilation
- Exposure to racially insensitive/hate content

- Fraud and identity theft
- Personal injury and harm

To keep things simple and help parents and teachers develop a solid road map for protecting children, I've categorized the top five risks of going online into the following general categories targeted toward children between the ages of 8 and 17.

1. Viewing graphic pornography and other adult content
2. Computer viruses, worms, and spyware that can compromise personal content
3. Sexual predators looking for victims
4. Adults looking to inflict other harm on children, including kidnapping, rape, murder
5. Content promoting hate crimes, weapons, and harm to others

These risks can be delivered or accessed in a variety of ways, ranging from simply browsing the Internet, blogging, using email, instant messaging, swapping files between computers, using cell phones and PDAs, or conversing with others in online chat rooms (see Figure 3.1).

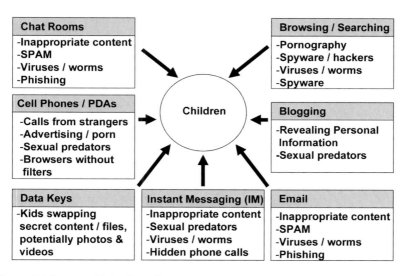

Figure 3.1 Internet Risks Overview

Browsing/Searching

Browsing the Web and using search engines is one of the most common activities for teens and adults online today. Risks of unfettered browsing includes exposure to graphic pornography, risk of spyware being placed on home computers, exposure to viruses, and hackers attempting to steal personal or financial information, such as banking passwords and accounts. I recently performed an experiment and searched for the phrase *sex* on five popular search engines, both with and without content filters. Content filters are essentially efforts by the search site to filter out adult and mature content from being displayed on the results page. Interestingly enough, search engines produce very different results in both the number of search results returned and the effectiveness and security of their family filters (see Table 3.1). Microsoft's new Live.com produced the greatest number of search results, totaling almost 700 million pages, whereas Ask.com produced the least, with just over 90 million page results returned. Three of the five search sites asked for confirmation to turn off family filters and return all results, regardless of content. All of the sites appeared to use cookies to store the search setting (family safe, moderate safe, or no filtering) on the local computer's hard drive. Although the intent by these search firms is good, most teens simply get around the settings by changing them, deleting the cookies, or just downloading another browser and setting their own search settings.

What I found most interesting about these family filters was that they were, for the most part, not effective at all. With the exception of Microsoft's Live .com, all of the other search engines still returned a significant number of results

Table 3.1. Search Results

Search Engine	Returned Links to Pages with Safe Search On (requires cookies to be enabled to work properly)	Returned Links to Pages with Safe Search Off
Google	146 million	599 million (returned 1.5 million graphic images)
Ask.com	90.7 million	90.7 million
Altavista	229 million	393 million (asked to confirm turning off safe surfing)
Live.com	0 (The only search site that worked with strict filters turned on)	695 million (asked to confirm turning off safe surfing)
Yahoo!	236 million	394 million

with family filters turned on. Ask.com didn't seem to work at all and returned the exact same number of links to pages for unfiltered and filters turned on. My point is simple: At 236 million links to pages returned for a site like Yahoo!, it can't possibly be effective at returning family-safe content for children. Even though Microsoft's new tool is a late entry to the search engine family, it impressed me the most and returned zero links to pages when family filters were turned on.

Another risk associated with using a search tools is that they expose children to graphic images. Using Internet Explorer (versions 6 and 7), I set up filters within the browser itself to block harmful content. These work somewhat well, but they are not fully effective. With these settings in place, I attempted to go to a known adult Web site. The content filter setting in the browser appropriately blocked the Web site from displaying content on the screen. I then set the browser to block all sites and only allow those that are approved by a parent (by entering an administrative password) to be viewed. I allowed Google to be one of those approved sites and began searching for adult terms to see what would be viewable. With safe settings on Google turned on and content filters in Internet Explorer set to the most aggressive level, the search tool still returned 146 million links to content pages. When I attempted to view those pages, the browser blocked them as expected. However, when I clicked on the Images tab on the Google results search page, I was able to view images easily, bypassing both filters. When I turned safe searching off, I was able to view graphic photographs with the click of a mouse, bypassing the content filters that had been set in the browser altogether. The nature of the photographs that were easily viewable included close up shots of vaginal, oral, and anal sex.

I recently also ran the image tab test on an expensive, industrial-strength filtering software. The product, Websense, is a software service used by many organizations and is considered to be one of the leading Internet filtering tools on the market. It also failed my test, revealing access to a many graphic adult images that should have been blocked in the first place. These examples demonstrate that software designed to detect and block harmful content may be playing catch-up when compared to sites that want to distribute their information to the masses, regardless of the content rating.

The risks to children don't just stop at being exposed to mature content but also include being a victim of child pornography. According to CNN.com, in October 2006 U.S. federal officials arrested more than 125 people accused of subscribing to a Web site that had content and photographs of children, including infants, engaging in sexual activities with adults.[6] The article states that the suspects included over a dozen convicted sex offenders that had accessed the site starting in late 2005.[7] Disturbingly, among the suspects was a former counselor at a Bible camp, a Boy Scout leader, and middle school sports coach.[8] U.S. Attorney Christopher J. Christie also indicated that such pornographic sites can make up to $2 million per month in subscription fees.[9] These facts clearly support the need for parents and schools to implement separate programs to filter and block harmful content in a way that search engines have not been able to do successfully to date. Security settings within browsers and search engines are not effective enough to protect children from harmful content. The technologies implemented in these tools simply aren't sophisticated enough to determine whether a particular photo, video, or audio is suitable for a child. Most rely on a Web site's ratings (safe, mature, adult) to trigger a content filter. Chapter 5 goes into more detail on how to implement safe browsing environments.

Email

Congressman Mark Foley wrote a series of emails to an underage page working at the U.S. House of Representatives. Foley's online activities, which included lewd and sexually suggestive emails and instant messages, ultimately led to his downfall from politics in 2005.[10] The emails "freaked me out," said a page who was asked by Foley to send a picture of himself.[11] After being warned by Congressman Shimkus, who was responsible for the Page Board, the emails continued and began showing up in newsrooms in Florida.[12] On September 24, 2005, the Stop Sexual Predators Web site published scanned images of Foley's emails sent to pages.[13] By 2006 the event was well publicized in the media and in the fall of 2006, Foley resigned and the FBI launched a probe. According to *Newsweek*, "It is unlikely he [Foley] will be prosecuted unless evidence emerges that he tried to lure minors into physical sex, not just e-mail sex."[14]

Kids give away their email address to too many people and can potentially expose themselves to a flood of unwanted email if they post their address online at social networking sites. The more exposed their email address is, the more potential risk from sexual predators, spam, phishing, and viruses. Many anti-spam filters are simply not effective at blocking inappropriate content from arriving in a teen's email inbox. In addition, some teens send adult and pornographic content as file attachments and disguise the file names as something innocent—easily bypassing content filters. Email and other online tools like instant messaging are common methods that sexual predators use to prey on victims, both adult and underage. Chapter 7 talks about safe email programs, how to protect children from Internet predators, and how to communicate safely online.

Instant Messaging

Instant messaging (IM) tools have become the online program of choice for most children and teens today, surpassing even email as the preferred method for communicating with friends and, yes, strangers. They are easy tools to learn, can be installed on computers and other personal communication devices like PDAs, and, more important, don't usually leave a footprint or audit trail for parents to snoop around and see what their children are doing. Teens like IM because it's a stealth tool of choice. They can go online, converse with friends, meet new ones, and have private conversations beyond their parents' control. In addition, these tools provide technical mechanisms to send file attachments, potentially bypassing anti-virus scans because they can be encrypted. They can even conduct phone conversations over the Internet by simply adding an inexpensive headset to a standard computer.

Unfortunately, IM is also the tool of choice with sexual predators that are looking for teens to chat with and potentially exploit them in hopes of engaging them in sexual activity. A U.S. Justice Department study found that "one in seven children on the Internet has been sexually solicited and one in three has been exposed to sexual material."[15] The article describing this study goes on to list a series of public service announcements supported by the U.S. Attorney General and how they are designed to "warn teen girls against posting images or information that would put them at risk."[16] I support these types of advertisements to raise awareness, but they simply do not do enough to curb risks of going online. Be aware that there are plenty of sexual predators looking to engage in sex acts with young boys (as well as girls). Hundreds have been arrested and prosecuted to date.

To highlight the sometimes open and rude approach that predators take, the following is an excerpt obtained by ABC News from instant messages sent by Congressman Mark Foley, using the screen name Maf54, to an underage male page.

> Maf54: What ya wearing?
> Teen: tshirt and shorts
> Maf54: Love to slip them off of you.
> Maf54: Do I make you a little horney?
> Teen: A little.
> Maf54: Cool.[17]

People like Mr. Foley that are caught or exposed deserve to lose their job at a minimum. These actions, usually calculated and intentional, are not acceptable, and perpetrators should be held accountable and, if appropriate, prosecuted to the fullest extent of the law, both federal and state.

Chat Rooms

Chat rooms are another form of communication favored by teenagers today. They offer a way for people to converse online with others and expose their identity or fly under the radar with a different name or alias. As indicated in a previous chapter, chat rooms are all over the Internet, are offered by a variety of providers, and are easy to use. Most looking for a site simply navigate the various chat room names after searching for one or navigating by chat room title. Once online, users can converse with one another in a real-time conversation—most of which is never logged by the user, but usually by the chat room hosting provider. For obvious reasons, chat rooms, along with IM and email (for one-on-one communication) are the preferred tools by criminals, pornography distributors, and sexual predators. Allowed use and monitoring of these sites are recommended to parents.

Online Predators

So what is an online predator anyway? The typical Internet predator is male, middle-aged, and married with children.[18] Though the majority of sexual predators are male, up to 25 percent are female.[19] According to a comprehensive study in Canada in 1996, "Mounting research evidence about sexual abuse perpetration at the hands of teen and adult females has begun to challenge our assumptions."[20] The study goes on to report that "the percentage of women and teenage girl perpetrators recorded in case studies is small and ranges from 3% to 10%," and that another study found that female adults were abusers of male victims 37 percent of the time compared to 19 percent for female victims.[21] According to a BBC News program, "Women commit 25% of all child sexual abuse," and 250,000 children in the United Kingdom have been sexually abused by women.[22]

The stereotype of sex-crazed pervert lurking in the shadows is a misconception that needs to be dispelled. According to Marie D. Marth, who works for the Northampton County Adult Probation and Parole, "They are very intelligent, they know how to navigate the Web and hide files on their computers."[23] Some predators want more timely interactions both online and offline and move quickly to meet their online pen pal, often requesting personal phone numbers and addresses or suggesting meeting places within hours or days of conversing online. Others will take a more calculated approach over a longer period of time to gain more trust from their online partner before taking steps that often include swapping photos and email addresses and coordinating a meeting place. Some common definitions that parents need to know include the following.

- **Child pornography:** the illegal use of children in pornographic films or pictures; more recently expanded to include the use of any technology medium and the portrayal of children depicted in an inappropriate sexual manner.
- **Child sexual abuse:** "exposing or subjecting the child to sexual contact, activity, or behavior. Sexual abuse includes oral, anal, genital, buttock, and breast contact. It also includes the use of objects for vaginal or anal penetration, fondling, or sexual stimulation."[24]
- **Child solicitation:** solicitation of a child to engage in sexual conduct. *Solicit* can mean that the conduct (commanding, entreating, or attempting to persuade a specific person) may be accomplished in any manner, including in person, by telephone, by letter, or by computerized or other electronic means.[25]
- **Child exploitation:** exploitation of a minor through video, filming, phone cameras, photographs, or other technical reproduction means depicting sexual acts involving a minor.
- **Pedophile:** According to a Netsmartz article, "A pedophile is a person who has a sexual preference for prepubescent children and fantasizes about having sex with them."[26]

How do sexual predators reach children today? The answer is via a variety of means and technology that usually starts after an online meeting, followed up by a personal one-on-one meeting. Some predators simply abuse their roles in their jobs or as a volunteers and make a personal connection with a minor before attempting to exploit or harm them. Examples of sexual abuse of children not involving technology include abuse of power and interaction with minors by teachers, coaches, priests, baby-sitters, family members, and friends. Avenues for approaching a child online include postings on social networking sites, email, IM, and chat rooms. What I find fascinating about today's wired teens is their willingness to disclose personal information and day-to-day drama to strangers via the Internet or those posing as friends online. I've had many conversations with friends, colleagues, and children over the course of researching this book, and I believe that teens are more trusting of others while online and they don't really understand the mind of an Internet predator, nor the risks of posting personal information for the world to see—especially things that they probably wouldn't tell some of their friends in person. In any case, it is the parents' and teachers' jobs to monitor the children they care about in an effort to protect them from risks they simply don't comprehend or choose to ignore.

In the course of my research on Internet predators, I came across a group that is working hard to help protect children: Perverted Justice (www.perverted-justice.com). They were featured on an *NBC Dateline* television story that exposed some shocking scenarios and discussions with alleged sexual predators, many resulting in convictions after engaging law enforcement officials. The following is an example of a conversation between an online predator and a potential victim. *Caution:* Some of the text below is graphic, but I feel it's necessary to highlight it to help educate parents and teachers of the dangers of children accessing the Internet. Comments in bold highlight sexually graphic approaches sometimes taken by predators or a cunning approach to win over their victim. Comments in brackets highlight any additional comments pertaining to statements in the conversation.

The initial introduction takes place in a chat room where a predator hones in on a child who has posted pictures and personal data on a social networking site. The following conversation is portrayed as a series of private IM conversations after the predator, a 38-year-old man, requests to move the conversation from a public forum to a more private medium with little or no audit trail. In this scenario, the predator is pretending to be a mature young boy trying to lure a younger girl into more adventurous situations.

Day 1, Conversation after School

Predator: nice screen name . . .

Cutegirl666: thanks! It kind of balances me out—the good and the bad.

Predator: we've had some nice conversations in the teen chat room. Good to get out of the crowded space.

Cutegirl666: i guess so.

Predator: did you just get out of school?

Cutegirl666: yep. kinda sucks . . . i'm sooooo bored.

Predator: where are you now?

Cutegirl666: at home.

Predator: do you ride the bus to school? [an attempt to find out if she is unsupervised during her day]

Cutegirl666: nah . . . I walk. It's pretty close.

Predator: are your parents home too?

Cutegirl666: no. still at work. always working . . .

Predator: gotta pay the bills . . . what are you doing tonight?

Cutegirl666: don't know. maybe watch a movie or chat online again . . .

Predator: oh? Well, how old are you?

Cutegirl666: i'm turning 13 in 3 months. can't wait—maybe my parents will take me seriously then . . .

Predator: I see. do they treat you like a kid now?

Cutegirl666: yeah. I'm the youngest and they don't seem to have time for me.

Predator: where do you live?

Cutegirl666: Boston. [he already knows that from a prior conversation in a chat room]

Predator: I live just outside . . . if your parents don't pay attention to you then you can pretty much do what you want then. right?

Cutegirl666: sometimes. they wouldn't know anyway. I could runaway and they probably wouldn't find out for days.

Predator: too bad you aren't older—like 17 . . .

Cutegirl666: why? do you like older women? LOL . . .

Predator: not really, just girls that are more mature or like to try new things . . .

Cutegirl666: like what? The 666 in my name isn't there for no reason.

Predator: I don't know. Ever play spin the bottle or 30 seconds in a closet?

Cutegirl666: yeah, but I had to kiss this really ugly geek guy.

Predator: I'm not a geek . . . and I kinda like girls that can be my best friend and spend time hugging and kissing . . .

Cutegirl666: I can do that . . . but only for the right guy, ya know?

Predator: yeah I know. I've had a few girlfriends, but am still looking for one that can go beyond my good looks . . .

Cutegirl666: so you're hot!!!

Predator: I don't know. I think i'm kinda normal, but all the girls tell me i'm cute.

Cutegirl666: send me a picture.

Predator: ok, but don't laugh . . . It was taken when I was 16. [outright lie]

Cutegirl666: ok . . . i'll send you one of mine and we'll compare. let's rate each other.

Predator: be nice . . . i'm sure you're really pretty. you seem very nice online and i love talking to you. let's talk again tomorrow . . .

Cutegirl666: ok, but send me your photo via IM. [predators prefer using tools like IM to send files because they don't usually leave an audit trail of the transfer like email would]

In this case, the predator would likely send a photo of an attractive 17-year-old boy in an attempt to lure her in for a meeting. At this point, he changes gears and starts a discussion about sexual experiences.

Day 3: After Several Days of Trivial Conversations and Getting to Know Each Other

Predator: ok. let's play truth or dare . . . [time to find out how playful she may be, hoping she selects dare]

Cutegirl666: ok. dare.

Predator: I dare you to take off your top and run to the mailbox and back . . .

Cutegirl666: serious????

Predator: chicken. afraid somebody else is going to see that cute body of yours? I put your picture above my computer so that I can see you while we chat . . .

Cutegirl666: oh . . . don't call me a chicken. you just wait until it's my turn. be right back . . .

Predator: wish I had a video camera for this . . . funny stuff.

Cutegirl666: i'm back!!!! i think the old guy down the street saw me . . . that was fun . . . my turn.

Predator: how long did it take you?

Cutegirl666: once i took my top off—30 seconds. i'm really fast.

Predator: fast in what way?

Cutegirl666: running stupid . . .

Cutegirl666: my turn: truth or dare?

Predator: truth.

Cutegirl666: how far have you gone?

Predator: you mean???

Cutegirl666: yes.

Predator: round the bases . . . it's a rush, but only with girls that I really like. have you done it yet? [trying to determine sexual experience]

Cutegirl666: kinda.

Predator: kinda. it's really a yes or no answer. it's alright if you're waiting for the right guy. I don't blame you, but it really feels great when you connect with someone you really like . . .

Cutegirl666: ok, so not all the way but close . . .

Predator: how close?

Cutegirl666: i'm afraid of going all the way . . . one of my friend tells me it hurts. i like giving BJs instead . . .

Predator: ok, nothing to be afraid of. maybe i can help . . .

Cutegirl666: what??? you serious? what kinda tips can you give me?

Predator: i'm serious . . . we seem to hit it off well. Let's meet and get to know each other. you never know . . . i could be gentle with you . . .

Cutegirl666: that's funny. i would like to meet you though.

Predator: glad to hear that. I can't get the image of you running down the driveway with your minis bouncing in the wind . . .

Cutegirl666: you crack me up. they're not that big—but they're growing . . . LOL.

Predator: I think your really nice and hot too . . .

Cutegirl666: I think you're cute . . .

At this point, he changes his tone to be more sexual, then backs off a bit and reintroduces the idea of meeting.

Predator: are your parents home?

Cutegirl666: no, why?

Predator: I'd like to hear what your voice sounds like . . . i have a feeling you have a sexy voice for your age . . .

Cutegirl666: hah! you wish. what do you sound like? young boy or old man?

Predator: nice boy silly . . . Do you know how to make a recording to an audio file?

Cutegirl666: no . . .

Predator: I could teach you or if it's easier just call you? Is there a phone number where I can reach you that only goes to you—like a cell phone? [predators usually look for ways to reach out that don't involve parents and can't be tracked easily]

Cutegirl666: yes. my dad let's me have a cell phone to keep touch with me since he's always working or traveling for his job . . . My cell is 617-xxx-xxxx. What's your phone number?

Predator: I'll just call you. hang on . . .

Cutegirl666: ok . . . getting jittery . . .

Predator: All around? tits perky too?

Cutegirl666: serious? Yeah—a bit of that too . . .

Predator: cool . . . Do you have small or big nipples? I'm calling you now.

He dials a prefix to prevent caller ID from displaying his number and pretends to be a older teenager. After the call, he resumes online.

Cutegirl666: you sound older than 17 . . .

Predator: Nope . . . just have a deep voice. girls at school tell me it's sexy . . .

Cutegirl666: do you have a girlfriend?

Predator: nope, but i'd like one. your voice is sexy . . . maybe we can spend some time together and get more mature???

Cutegirl666: ahh . . . the teacher in you again. wait your turn . . . in good time.

Predator: so, maybe you'll let me see a little more than that photo you sent me? how about a quick PC video-cam flash? do you have one?

Cutegirl666: no. dad thinks it's too risky for me . . . he's right!!!!!

Predator: ok. can I ask you a personal question since you're hot and all???

Cutegirl666: okay.

Predator: what color underwear do you have on now?

Cutegirl666: I'm not wearing any . . .

Predator: nice.

Cutegirl666: i'm kidding . . . i have on red and white ones . . .

Predator: what are they covering up? anything interesting???

Cutegirl666: like what? if i'm a guy or a girl . . . LOL

Predator: no, you know what I mean . . . do you have any hair? [some sexual predators that prey on young girls are fanatic about clean or shaven genitals]

Cutegirl666: that's funny . . . yes, why?

Predator: don't know. seems like the older girls are big into shaving. kinda looks sexy that way. would you ever try it? [an attempt to get her to try and act more mature and do things more mature women would do; a common approach by predators]

Cutegirl666: ooouuucchhh! i'd probably cut myself and bleed all over the floor . . . that's gross.

Predator: it's not that bad. check out the following site to see what i mean . . . [he gives her an address to a teen Web site that shows naked girls engaged in a variety of risqué poses]

Cutegirl666: this i gotta see . . . hold on while i bring up the site . . . that's pretty freaky!!!! some of those girls look like their my age! do you look at sites like this a lot???

Predator: nah . . . one of my friends told me about it. my last girlfriend was *clean* shaven though . . . it's pretty sexy. you should give it a try. try clipping first, then using some cream . . .

Cutegirl666: you serious??? pervert!!!

Predator: ok, so don't try it. I'm not a PV . . . the older girls are mature about this kinda stuff. maybe i thought you could handle it . . . [coercion attempt]

Cutegirl666: maybe I can. I think i'm mature for my age . . .

Predator: prove it. [capitalizing on his prior approach for a dare]

Cutegirl666: ok . . . ok, maybe i'll give it a try . . .

Predator: that's my girl . . . we should get together soon in person . . . how about thursday after school?

Cutegirl666: i can't. i'm studying with a friend of mine. how about next week?

Predator: what day? can't wait to meet you and start the process of making you into an older woman! like shaving . . . maybe we can start you on a six-step program and shake those fears of having sex quickly . . .

Cutegirl666: easy romeo . . . in due time . . .

Predator: so i have a chance? cool . . . would love to be your first . . . you seem special to me . . . i promise i'll be gentle when I fuck you!!! i don't like to wear condoms—hope you don't mind . . . [sexual predators often jump in and out of graphic conversations as a mechanism to test the waters and gauge a reaction]

Cutegirl666: what?

Predator: just kidding . . . can't you take a joke?

Cutegirl666: yeah, but that's just rude . . . i prefer to call it *making love.* that's what my mom tells me . . .

Predator: here we go again. I thought you told me you had a little 666 in you? seriously, all kidding aside, I'd love to meet you in person and get to know you. maybe catch a movie or something?

Cutegirl666: that sounds like fun.

Predator: can you meet me outside the library on 7th and Maple about a mile from your school on monday at 7 pm?

Cutegirl666: why so late and in the dark?

Predator: i have to do something with my brother before . . . maybe we can go to a movie at 8 and get to know each other . . . [darkness allows him a lot of options, which include kidnapping. Many sexual encounters have occurred after a brief kidnapping, resulting in a sexual assault, possibly in the car or at a nearby location. Some predators keep their victims for days and even weeks, sometimes sexually torturing them. Others drop off their victims at another location after the initial assault.]

Cutegirl666: sounds like fun. let me ask my mom later . . .

Predator: no parents!!! just figure out a way to get away . . . kinda like a romantic first meeting . . . I'm getting jittery now . . .

Cutegirl666: i'm kinda excited about meeting you too. ok. i'll tell my mom i'm going to a friend's house to study. don't know about a movie. it depends on how my mom reacts before i leave . . .

Predator: ok. can't wait to meet you in person. I'll be in a hot dark blue mustang! my older brother lets me borrow his car every once in a while . . .

Cutegirl666: wow—hot!!! hope you're as hot as that car stud . . .

Predator: you'll see . . . see you monday. I'll call you on your cell phone at 6 pm that day to make sure you can make it. make sure your parents don't see you take the call or they'll never let you go and your shot at meeting prince charming will be gone . . .

Cutegirl666: what a drama queen . . . I'll be there.

Predator: don't forget to wear something hot! everyone that sees us will want to be me with the hottie, who's also a nice person . . .

Cutegirl666: really?

Predator: sure. can't wait to see you for our first meeting. remember—don't tell anyone . . . can't wait to see you. chow!

Conversations like these and some even more graphic occur all the time. Children who enter chat rooms, use IM, or maintain a social network page or Web site are at risk. The first step for parents is to ask their children what tools and sites they use and visit. Don't always believe their answers, as children have a propensity to cover up activities that they believe they are mature enough to handle. The next step is to use stealth software, discussed in Chapter 5, to capture their online passwords. Once parents have these passwords, they can explore the sites for content and record online activities like chat conversations to find out what the kids are up to. The Internet can be a scary place, and the only defense for parents and teachers is a solid offense. Sometimes that requires adults to delve into their children's online world in a stealth manner. Parents need to do whatever it takes to keep predators like these and inappropriate content away from their kids. Check the Perverted Justice Web site to look for excerpts from convicted offenders.

Blogs and Social Networking

Blogging is essentially just an online diary posted onto a Web site. It's a catchphrase that's gotten a lot of traction in the last year or so and is popular with the younger generation. Sexual predators, including older ones, have adjusted quickly to be able to understand social networking sites like MySpace and Friendster to prey on others. MySpace and other sites have many benefits, but they come with some risks, including providing teens (and children posing as teens) with an online avenue for expressing themselves. Chapter 4 provides several examples of some real-world tragedies that have taken place as a result of children exposing too much about themselves or meeting the wrong person online.

Text Messaging via Cell Phones

Text messaging is another popular medium for online communication, one that has exploded across the globe as inexpensive cell phones have proliferated. In some countries that have stricter cultures that prohibit unmarried teens of the opposite sex to engage in personal meetings, text messaging is an alternative way to communicate even across very short distances, like café seats or in cars. Many phone vendors bundle text messaging services as part of the monthly bill at no additional cost, whereas others charge a small fee per message sent. These charges can add up quickly with actively texting teens, so check the bills to see just how often your child is on a cell phone and then determine if you need to monitor and review the activity. Call your cell phone provider and asking them for the best way to review text content being sent and received over their service.

Where teens often make mistakes regarding text messaging is by giving out their phone number or starting an online conversation with someone that they don't know and disclosing personal information such as full name, address, school, and so on. Online predators are quite effective at exposing information and using small pieces of personal data to gain more information. Chapter 4 exposes some tragedies involving text messaging and phones that are unfortunate but well worth the read.

PDAs

PDAs, personal digital assistants, are devices that evolved from cell phones and include additional features beyond making voice calls. Common features in PDAs include voice calls and voicemail, text messaging, IM clients, a built-in Internet browser, a calendar, contact list, notes section, and memo pad. PDAs come from a variety of vendors including BlackBerry, Microsoft, Hewlett Packard, Sony, and Palm. What's interesting about these devices are the features they have, the continually falling cost, and their adoption by teens. Teens use these devices as they gain adoption by their parents, teachers, and other professionals, which facilitates acceptance by adults who end up purchasing them for their children.

The risks of using PDAs is that they can complicate a parent's ability to protect a child and monitor online activity because they are decentralized and not connected to computers. That makes it harder to control their use, monitor what software has been installed on them, and review the people and sites that their children visit while using them. I carry a sophisticated BlackBerry and couldn't do without it for work and personal life. However, my wife has no knowledge of what I do with it or what Web sites I access with it—reaffirming just how difficult is to for an adult to manage these small devices. Most Web sites that people visit or messages sent are not recorded or reviewed by employers or parents. Parents who decide to let their teen have one of these multifeatured devices should consult with their provider (examples: T-Mobile, AT&T, etc.) for assistance in getting reports of online usage. Everything is usually logged at the provider, and provided to law enforcement if subpoenaed, but not kept forever due to the cost of storing information on servers and disk systems.

SOME STATISTICS FOR KIDS GOING ONLINE

There are a number of excellent published studies that examine teen use and risks on the Internet along with safety statistics. I highlight three reports here that offer up some humbling and scary realities associated with today's wired youth.

Netsmartz

The NetSmartz Workshop is a great resource from the National Center for Missing and Exploited Children (NCMEC) and Boys & Girls Clubs of America (BGCA).[27] Here are some of their data.

- 61 percent of 13- to 17-year-olds have a profile page on a social networking site.
- 71 percent have received messages online from someone that they did not know.
- 45 percent have been asked to give out personal information by people they did not know.
- 30 percent have considered meeting a person that they've met online.
- 14 percent have actually met people they've met online (9 percent of 13–15-year-olds, 22 percent of 16- and 17-year-olds).[28]

National Center for Missing and Exploited Children (NCMEC)

NCMEC, established in 1984, helps prevent child abduction and sexual exploitation, helps find missing children, and assists victims.[29] In addition to operating the CyberTipline, it serves as a clearinghouse for information about miss-ing and exploited kids.[30] According to a 2000 NCMEC study of 1,501 minors who regularly use the Internet,

- 1 in 33 teens surveyed received aggressive sexual solicitation from a person that asked to meet them somewhere.
- 1 in 17 was threatened or harassed.
- 25 percent of those who received a sexual solicitation actually told their parents.
- 33 percent of parents surveyed with home computers indicated that they had Internet filtering software installed to help protect their children.
- Girls were twice as likely as boys for sexual solicitations at 66 percent versus 34 percent.
- Younger teens (aged 10 to 13) were more likely to be distressed than older children, suggesting that the younger set has a harder time getting past unwanted solicitations.
- Just over 66 percent of solicitors were reported as males compared to 25 percent from females.
- 70 percent of youth surveyed reported that they were at home when sexu-ally solicited online compared to 22 percent at someone else's house.[31]

A sampling of some scary testimony from youth in the NCMEC report turns up the following.

- A 13-year-old girl was asked her bra size.
- A 12-year-old girl indicated that her online contacts described sexual activ-ity they were doing and asked her to masturbate.
- A 13-year-old boy indicated that a female asked him how big his private area was and wanted him to masturbate to completion.[32]

The Exposure of Youth to Unwanted Sexual Material on the Internet: A National Survey of Risk, Impact, and Prevention

The University of New Hampshire published a study in 2003 that surveyed over 1,000 youths (796 boys and 705 girls), 10- to 17-year-olds, and their caretakers. The following provides some interesting highlights that support risks outlined in this chapter.

- 25 percent of youth reported at least one unwanted exposure to sexual pictures while online in the previous year.
- 73 percent of such exposures happened while surfing or browsing the In-

ternet, and 27 percent occurred while reading email or clicking on links provided through IM conversations.

- 67 percent of the incidents happened at home, but 15 percent happened in school, 13 percent at someone else's home, and 3 percent in a library.
- 32 percent of images displayed showed people having sex, and 7 percent of those involved violence in addition to the nudity.
- 92 percent of email exposure came from unknown senders.
- Boys encountered more unwanted sexual material (57 percent) than girls (42 percent).
- Older youth (15 or older) were more exposed (60 percent) than younger youth.
- Troubled youths who reported physical, sexual abuse, or depression had more exposure.[33]

Needless to say, there is plenty of research to support the need for parents and educators to take a more proactive approach in helping protect today's minors and tomorrow's leaders from some of the tremendous risks online.

HOW ARE PARENTS DOING PROTECTING THEIR KIDS?

Before jumping into an overview of the tools that kids use to access the Internet, take a look at the results of two parental surveys gauging how well parents are doing to protect children.

Parents' Internet Monitoring Study

Cox Communications, NCMEC, and Netsmartz.org conducted a study of 503 parents and teens (between 13 and 17) in February 2005 who had Internet access from home. Below are the key findings.

- The highest placement of home computers that had access to the Internet was in the family room (34 percent), followed by the bedroom (30 percent).
- 51 percent of parents do not have software or do not know if software is installed on their home computers to monitor what their children do on the Internet.
- Of the 49 percent that do use software to monitor their children, 87 percent review their children's activities, with 23 percent reporting daily and 33 percent reporting monthly at best.

- 61 percent of parents report that their teenagers use chat rooms and IM tools.
- 42 percent of parents do not review what their teenagers read or write in chat rooms or via IM.
- 96 percent of parents were unable to identify the meaning of P911 as parent alert, and 92 percent were unable to identify what A/S/L (age, sex, location) meant in IM lingo.[34]

Smith Survey of Child Internet Usage and Parental Protection

I ran an anonymous survey of 100 parents in the United States that have children between the ages of 8 and 17. I intentionally expanded the age bracket for my survey to include children below the age of 10, because I've seen elementary school children using computers at school and home in the past few years. I also intentionally asked specific questions as to how and with what tools parents use to monitor or block inappropriate content. The results from this survey are staggering, especially for young children, and clearly demonstrate that parents are clueless with regard to the risks of going online and how to really monitor and protect their children. See for yourself in Table 3.2.

The overall results of my survey were mainly consistent with results from other large-scale surveys. What my survey revealed is that parents think that looking over their kid's shoulder periodically or placing the computer in a common area in the house is effective monitoring. In addition, although the use of Internet Explorer Content Advisor is well intentioned, it rarely stops a technology-savvy teenager, who can simply do one of the following to bypass its controls.

- Dodge the Content Advisor's limits. Many parents that I've spoken to who use IE Content Advisor check the adult content box as their only method of using technology to prevent inappropriate content. The IE Content Advisor allows for the following categories to be managed: language, nudity, sex, and violence. It doesn't allow a more sophisticated set of restrictions that other software packages have. Most teens will still be able to access social networking, chat, IM, and so on with the way most parents use IE Content Advisor.
- Guess the password and bypass it. Once this is done, one can regularly delete temporary Internet files (cache), cookies, and history to cover one's tracks. My own children have become quite adept at guessing passwords, which is why we change them frequently and suspend their online activities for a period of time if we catch them at it.

Table 3.2 Smith Poll Results

Q1. Do your children under the age of 18 have access to the Internet or other related Internet technologies? Examples include: (a) Web browsing, (b) phone text messaging, (c) email accounts, (d) instant messaging accounts, (e) personal digital assistants (PDAs) with text messaging.

Yes: 96 percent
No: 4 percent

Q2. What ages are your children with online access? Results listed averages in order from youngest to oldest for families with multiple children.

1. Child #1: 11.6 years old
2. Child #2: 10.6 years old
3. Child #3: 10.3 years old
4. Child #4: 12 years old

Interestingly enough, I also tracked the oldest and youngest child with Internet access. Surprisingly, the youngest child was at age 4 and the oldest was 17. Several parents indicated other younger children as well, which included 5–7-year-olds.

Q3. Do you think that the Internet poses any risks to children today?

Yes: 98 percent
No: 2 percent

Q4. Do you monitor your children's access to the Internet?

Yes: 95 percent
No: 5 percent

These responses included soft Internet monitoring, such as periodically looking on a computer screen to see what a child is doing. Soft monitoring is not very effective, especially as children get into the teenager years.

Q5. If so, how do you monitor them?

The following answers were most common (in descending order).

1. The computer is in a common room and we check what they are doing regularly. They do not have computers in their bedrooms.
2. I am in the same room with them, always.
3. I sit next to them if they need to respond to an email or if they want to look up something online. They use browsers such as askforkids.com, kidsclick.com, and yahooligans.com to filter out some of the questionable material online.
4. Walk in on them when they are using it. Question them about what they are going online for, and then "spot check" the usage.
5. All emails received are forwarded to my personal email as well.
6. Through the use of CyberSitter and by looking at logs created by IE and CyberSitter. I get a daily email on all IM activity.
7. Content filters in the IE browser.

The following answers were less common.

1. Keylogger software, computer placement (in the middle of the family room), time limits, and parental control software.
2. Parental blockers and email checks.

Table 3.2 *(continued)*

3. I have AOL, which has very good parental controls. They block sites that are inappropriate and as the parent you can block any additional things you find inappropriate. At the end of the day they will send you an email that lets you know the Web sites that they successfully visited, and the ones that were blocked. They also tell you how many people they IM with and how many email messages were sent and received. I can set the limit for how long they are allowed daily on the Internet, and I have blocked complete access to chat rooms.

To complete this section, an interesting and very personal response.

Rule # 1: An adult must be present while my daughter is on the computer. Moreover, I have tried very hard to instill good Christian values in my children and ask them to follow the 10 commandments in all aspects of their life. I am, however, not naive enough to believe these standards will not be tested by the most cunning and conniving of individuals who continue to infest our society through their lack of respect for life and God's divine will. It is a sick world we live in and only a parent's presence can keep a child safe!

Q6. What age did you allow your children to access the following technologies?

	Low Average Response (for those with access)	Average Age Response (for those with access)	High Age Response (for those with access)
Note: 0 was entered where children didn't have access.			
1. Internet/Web page browsing	4	8.8	15
2. Email accounts	4	9.6	15
3. Cell phones without text messaging	7	12.2	16
4. Cell phones with text messaging	10	13.6	16
5. Instant messaging accounts	8	11.4	16
6. Accounts on social networking sites/Web blogs (like MySpace)	10	14.2	17

Q7. What' s the most common reason you allow your children to access the Internet or other related online technologies?

1. Peer pressure—other kids have access	3 percent
2. School work and projects	68 percent
3. To stay in contact with me—I work	0 percent
4. They're good kids and I trust them	18 percent
5. Other	11 percent

Q8. Do you block or filter Internet sites or pages for your children?

Yes: 39 percent
No: 61 percent

Note: These numbers are in line with other studies done, where parents are asked if they use specific software to help block objectionable content, sites, or services such as IM and online chat.

(continued)

Table 3.2 *(continued)*

Q9. If so, what is the primary tool(s) that you use to block or filter Internet content for your children? The following answers were most common among responses listed of the parents that did employ software for safety in descending order.
  1. Internet Explorer Content Advisor (lead choice by 2:1 of any other option)
  2. AOL Parental Controls
  3. CyberSitter
  4. SurfPatrol
  5. Norton Internet Security
  6. Not sure of the name, my husband installed it
  7. Earthlink Parental Controls
  8. SafeEyes
  9. KidsWatch

One final interesting response: I tried to block Runescape, but they figured it out and unblocked it. Other than that, I don't worry and don't block because I trust them.

Q10. Do you know anyone whose children (17 or under) were harmed emotionally or physically by using or accessing the Internet?
  Yes: 22 percent
  No: 78 percent

- Install another browser and hide it from the Desktop. Favorites include Firefox and Netscape. IE controls simply don't work on these browsers, and they can gain access to any site or service they want.
- Use a proxy site that masks where minors go online. Once connected to a proxy site, future Web pages viewed through the site are hard to log and monitor, thus camouflaging the real destinations many teens use on the Internet. Sophisticated Internet filtering software can block access to these sites and remove the risk.
- Borrow a neighbor's wireless Internet service and bypass any firewall restrictions put in place at their own home. A wireless network card is needed to dodge controls in this manner.

I found it fascinating that parents allowed very young children to browse the Internet, have email accounts, and use IM tools. These parents may be too lenient with their children's access to the Web, and perhaps they don't fully understand the risks. Hopefully, after reading this chapter along with Chapter 4, parents will begin to rein in some of those privileges and establish some real monitoring that involves using more sophisticated software (discussed in Chapter 5).

I found that the average age for kids using social networking sites, just over

14, was a bit young, because most sites only allow those 14 and older to register. I also found it interesting that the parents were able to say with almost complete certainty that their children did or did not use email, IM, and social networking sites. With 61 percent of respondents indicating that they did not use software to filter or monitor their children's online activities, how would they know if the kids have a Web mail account, use IM, or have posted personal information to a social networking site? Without logging software, the only thing they have to go on is their own two eyes.

I was also surprised at the larger response than anticipated (22 percent indicated yes) to the question, "Do you know anyone whose children (17 or under) that were harmed emotionally or physically by using or accessing the Internet?" I was expecting the number to be smaller. This may indicate that there are a larger set of minors than I anticipated that have been harmed emotionally or physically by going online. I would like to see larger national polls explore this question to see the impact on a larger sample size before drawing any formal conclusions.

PROTECTION AT SCHOOL AND IN LIBRARIES

Although schools and libraries have made great progress to help protect minors on the Internet, they have a long way to go. Two specific laws in the United States have made some progress with regard to protecting minors. The Children's Online Privacy Protection Act (COPPA) of 1998 was drafted to prevent online services and Web sites from collecting personal information from a child as defined by the law as an individual under the age of 13.[35] The Children's Internet Protection Act (CIPA), signed into law in December 2000, requires schools that use certain federal funds and E-rate discounts to have an Internet safety policy and provide technology to protect and shield children and adults from unacceptable content, including visual deceptions that are obscene, harmful to minors, or contain child pornography.[36] Other countries have similar laws and have passed a number of statutes intended to protect minors and prosecute those who abuse them. CIPA requires certain schools to establish policies and software protection. However, there is no standard for what software protection is taken. Simply put, some schools use better Internet filtering and monitoring solutions than others, exposing some children to additional risks.

To prove my point, I ran a series of tests in November 2006 at a large public school system with the following profile: over 100,000 students, over 150 schools in the county, over 15,000 employees. The school system had Internet policies and software installed throughout the county. I conducted my test using a second-grade user account. The following reveals what I was and was not able to do while accessing the Internet during that test.

Successfully Accessed

- Accessed Google and changed the safe surfing settings from moderate filter to none. This setting saves preferences on the local computer and impacts search results greatly.
- Searched for *sex*, resulting in 415 million page links returned.
- Accessed many graphic sexual images via the Google Images tab after page results were returned.
- Viewed a homemade video posted on the Internet (one of the resulting links returned from the Google search) of two adults having sex in their kitchen.
- Downloaded another browser program (Netscape).
- Accessed personal/consumer email Web pages (e.g., MSN mail).

Unsuccessful Attempts

- Was not able to access several adult content sites by name (e.g., www.playboy.com).
- Could not access Web sites commonly used to mask online use.
- Could not remove programs that were installed on the computer.
- Was not able to alter programs listed on the Start menu within the operating system.
- Could not access a command line window to enter operating system or program commands manually.

Private school systems often have Internet protection in place, but again they vary in the quality of those tools and staff supporting them, mainly due to costs. The wealthiest schools can thus afford to have better protection, but only if the support staff or outsourced systems professionals are engaged to provide that protection. At one private school that I visited, monitoring software was in place to detect what sites and services (IM, VOIP, etc.) kids were using, but they didn't actually block access to those sites or services.

Public libraries in the United States offer another area for children and predators alike to view inappropriate content or simply communicate via online tools, many of them encrypted to hide the online conversation from library attendants. I visited a public library in Maryland and found the following rules and circumstances.

- The library maintains access to the Internet as a matter of policy grounded in the First Amendment and existing laws.
- Users must have a library card, must have a PIN, and sign up to use a computer that has Internet access.
- Customers are expected to be considerate of others when viewing material online and, if necessary, use a privacy screen to view certain content and materials that children shouldn't see.
- Library staff may call the police if they believe that a customer is printing, downloading, emailing, or distributing child pornography on their systems.
- Computers in the children's section of the library are equipped with filtering software to prevent viewing inappropriate content.
- The library contained computers with unfiltered access to the Internet and recommends using search engine filters to filter content.

Thus, as long as an individual is being discreet, is not engaged in viewing or distributing child pornography, and complies with state laws to prevent viewing of mature content by minors, they can access pretty much anything they want. This is perhaps not a great place to turn your teen loose.

RECOMMENDATIONS

The risks associated with going online are real, and most children can't (or refuse to) recognize the problems of what has become a very open and socially online population facilitated by content growth technological innovation, making it easy and fun to communicate online. Parents are encouraged to learn as much as they can about the risks associated with the Internet and how predators are using it to abuse and inflict physical and emotional harm on youth. This book advocates an eight-step plan (see Figure 3.2) designed to mitigate online risks for children. The plan includes the following.

1. Establish computer use policies at home.
2. Maintain administrative passwords for computers in their homes. This includes putting restrictions on what each child account can do, such as install new software.
3. Use safe email programs that include anti-spam protection.

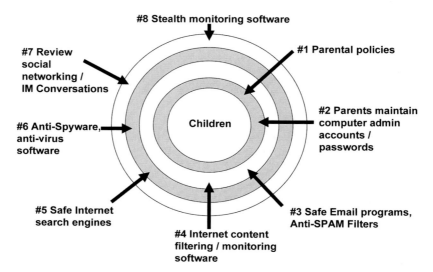

Figure 3.2 Insulating Against the Risks

4. Use Internet content filtering and monitoring software to limit content and programs for children.
6. Use safe Internet search engines or lock down consumer ones.
7. Use anti-spyware and anti-virus programs to protect personal data.
8. Review social networking and IM conversations.
9. Using stealth monitoring software to see exactly what your child is doing online

The following recommendations should help parents and educators understand the risks of going online and reporting an incident to the appropriate authority.

1. There are hundreds of good Web sites designed to reinforce the risks of going online and help parents and teachers protect children. The following Web sites are exemplary in both content and approach.

   - FBI: www.fbi.gov/hq/cid/cac/crimesmain.htm
   - The Pew Internet and American Life Project: www.pewinternet.org
   - NetSmartz Workshop: www.netsmartz.org
   - Wired Safety, one of the largest online safety sites: www.wiredsafety.org
   - The National Center for Missing and Exploited Children: www.missingkids.com

How to Protect Your Children on the Internet

2. The CyberTipline was created to provide a way for people to notify professionals of a specific risk on the Internet or a person that they know is being harassed, potentially exploited, or stalked by an Internet predator. Concerned individuals can either call (800)The-Lost (843–5678) or fill out an online form at www.cybertipline.org to report an incident.

3. Julie Clark and John Walsh have put together a great educational video to help protect children online. For parents with younger children below the age of 12, check out the www.thesafeside.com to purchase a video that creatively educates younger children and their parents of the risks associated with using chat rooms, email, and browsing.

4. For more information on female sexual predators, consult the 45-minute video *When Girls Do It: The Story of Female Sexual Predators*, produced by Vancouver filmmaker Glynis Whiting. The video provides a provocative and compassionate look at the motivations behind women who abuse children and the effects of their crimes on their victims. This film can be ordered from www.nfb.ca, NationalFilmBoardofCanadaInternational@nfb.ca, 1-800-542-2164 (US), or 1-800-267-7710 (Canada).

5. For more information about how some courageous volunteers are fighting the threats of online predators and working with law enforcement officials, visit the www.perverted-justice.com. Beware, some of this site contains graphic content, conversations, and transcripts of conversations with convicted sexual predators.

6. For information about what the FBI is doing to combat and investigate crimes against children, check out their Investigative Programs, Crimes Against Children Web page at www.fbi.gov/hq/cid/cac/crimesmain.htm. This is an excellent resource for parents and teachers and includes listings of federal statutes related to crimes against children as well as direct links to each state's sex offender registry Web site.

7. Get involved at your child's school. Ask school officials questions about the security and tools that they've put in place to protect children. Test their systems using the techniques described in this chapter, and report any weaknesses in their software solutions.

Four

The Risks of Going Online

You cannot go around and keep score. If you keep score on the good things and the bad things, you'll find out that you're a very miserable person. God gave man the ability to forget, which is one of the greatest attributes you have. Because if you remember everything that's happened to you, you generally remember that which is the most unfortunate.

—Hubert H. Humphrey

A SAMPLING OF UNFORTUNATE EVENTS

Although technology is a powerful tool, it can provide an anonymous conduit for children and teenagers to access content that may not be appropriate or, more important, communicate with individuals that may do them harm. I've pointed out several statistics in this text and will highlight more where appropriate. According to the Crimes Against Children Research Center's Youth Internet Safety Survey, "One in five children each year receives a direct e-mail solicitation from a child predator," usually after seeing a picture or a profile page online.[1] Predators looking for sex with minors aren't the only bad thing that can happen by going online. Pornography is a serious problem and has a correlation to child molesters, some of whom kill their victims to hide their actions. According to the New Jersey State Police High-Tech Crime Unit based in Trenton, "53 percent of convicted child molesters admit they used child pornography just prior to sexually abusing a child."[2]

When trying to communicate just what can go wrong if children are left to their own, I find it easiest (but unfortunate) to describe some of the bad events, horrors, crimes, and victims of these modern tragedies. Following is a sampling of things that have and can go wrong as a result of a child interacting with the wrong person online or via content seen on the Internet.

Kacie Woody

On December 3, 2002, 13-year old Kacie Woody, who lived in a small town in Arkansas, was abducted and later killed by an Internet predator while her father, a police officer for the city of Greenbrier, was at work.[3] Shortly after it was discovered that Kacie was missing, several law enforcement agencies in Arkansas along with the FBI were engaged and "in less than 20 hours they had a suspect, a suspect vehicle and had located the predator and Kacie."[4] According to documents, the predator was a 47-year-old man from California posing online as a 17-year-old.[5] "Investigators searched the home computer, found an alias that the predator had been using, and traced him to a motel in Conway."[6] Officers found the young girl, who was shot in the head, in a van inside a storage facility in another town in Arkansas.[7] When law enforcement officers closed in on the abductor, he shot himself.[8]

Christina Long

A 25-year old man from Greenwich, Connecticut, pleaded guilty and was sentenced to 30 years in prison for the death of 13-year-old Christina A. Long of Danbury, Connecticut. The predator, Saul Dos Reis, had met his victim online.[9] "Prosecutors contend Dos Reis strangled Long in his car after the pair had sex at the Danbury Fair Mall, and then he dumped her body in a shallow stream in a secluded Greenwich subdivision."[10] Reis's defense attorneys insisted that the death was an accident.[11] Long allegedly published a Web site that contained frequently used racy screen names and had sex with people she'd met in a variety of chat rooms.[12] According to a Netsmartz.org article, "She was the captain of her school cheerleading squad and an altar girl."[13] You never can tell what kids are up to, which is why I advocate a more aggressive approach to managing technology and using stealth tools to find out what kids really do online before it's too late.

A British Minor

A 12-year-old girl vanished for a while to meet a 31-year-old man she met on the Internet.[14] According to the Netsmartz.org recap of the story, the girl had been emailing the man up to five hours per day, and they were planning to meet in Paris.[14] As the investigation unwound, police allegedly found sexual digital photos of children on the alleged predator's computer as well as "sexual allegations involving two underage girls in the U.S."[16] Authorities also found records on his computer indicating that he clearly knew she was underage even though he claimed she lied about her age and said that she was 19.[17] Her parents may have been aware of the massive amount of time the young girl spent on the Internet and may have positioned their computer in a common area in their home and talked with her about not giving out personal information to strangers online.[18] The article concludes with the following statement and advice: "Allowing a child unmonitored access to the Internet is like putting him or her out on a street corner and not watching what happens."[19]

Assault Cases

A 13-year-old girl in Georgia was raped by a man she had met during an online conversation.[20] According to investigators, her alleged predator, a 40-year-old man, pretended to be 17 years old while chatting online.[21] After getting her address, the man attacked and raped her in her home after posing as a repairman to gain access.[22]

Another 13-year-old girl in Minnesota met her alleged sexual predator in a chat room, and the online chat moved to a telephone call, through which they agreed to meet in person.[23] The girl told police that she was taken to a hotel room, raped, and then driven home by her assailant.[24]

Triple Threat Abuse

In 2001, James Warren, age 41, Beth Loschin, age 46, and Michael Montez, age 35, were arrested on multiple charges related to an alleged kidnapping and sexual assault of a 15-year-old girl.[24] The girl, who had been exchanging messages online for several months with Warren, agreed to meet him at a mall where she worked, and she told him that she wanted to run away.[26] The girl told police that within a short period of time after meeting Warren and Loschin, she was "handcuffed much of the time and kept under constant surveillance," and that she'd been sexually assaulted by all three of the adults.[27] According to the *USA Today* article, Loschin and Warren were arrested. Loschin was charged with sodomy and sexual abuse, and Warren and Montez were charged with kidnapping, sodomy, rape, and sexual abuse.[28]

Webcam Minister

Simon Thomas, a 44-year-old minister with the United Reformed Church in Hythe, Hampshire, England, and a married man with several children, pleaded guilty to 35 charges, including two offenses of raping an 11-year-old boy.[29] An investigation revealed that Thomas had been contacting young boys over Internet chat rooms and telling them to perform sex acts over Webcams.[30] Police found a schedule of over 1,000 names of individuals he had met on the Internet on computers seized from his home, with just under 100 that were under the age of 16.[31] A court hearing revealed that Thomas also exposed himself to several boys over the Internet via Webcams and had arranged to meet four of the boys in town, where he took them to quiet locations and abused them.[32] Thomas was given a sex offender prevention order, banning him from communicating with children.[33]

Julie Doe

A 14-year-old teen, dubbed Julie Doe, and her mother filed a $30 million lawsuit against MySpace after she claimed to be sexually assaulted by a 19-year-old Texas college student.[34] In an interesting twist to this case, the defense attorney for the male student is considering suing MySpace because he says the alleged victim portrayed herself on the social networking site as older than her actual age.[35] According to a *Time* article, the girl set up a MySpace profile in 2005 when she was 13, even though the Web site's rules prohibit accounts for children under 14.[36] Once online, she met the male student, exchanged emails for over a month, exchanged phone numbers, and agreed to meet in person, where he allegedly sexually assaulted her.[37]

Ryan Adams

Ryan M. Adams, 20 years old, was accused of having sex with two boys he met on the Internet and was indicted on six counts of statutory rape of a 14- and 15-year-old boy that he met on MySpace.[38] MySpace and other popular social networking sites are common online venues for Internet predators, and they often represent themselves as another persona.

Supalover666

Police allegations revealed that a 21-year-old man from Kingston, Ontario, built an online environment in which children were groomed for sex.[39] Supalover666, the online screen name (or handle) of Mark Bedford, was allegedly used to enter online chat rooms and look for young girls.[40] Police claim that Bedford tried a variety of things to connect with teens, ranging from looking for interests in sports, music, and dancing or, as a last resort, hacking into their email accounts to gain access to their online buddy lists.[41] According to police, girls as young as nine were "threatened with rape, bodily harm, and even death if they failed to co-operate and perform sex acts on their webcams."[42] According to Ontario Police Detective Sergeant Frank Goldschmidt, who led the nine-month investigation, "I have never seen this many victims involved and it's safe to say that, in this early stage of this investigation, we're looking at well in excess of 100."[43] Bedford allegedly also threatened to post images of his online encounters on Web sites and show them to family members if they refused his requests.[44] Bedford was charged with two counts of luring a child by means of a computer, two counts of possessing child pornography, three counts of making child pornography, two counts of distributing child pornography, and three counts of extortion.[45]

In a related case, 21-year-old Lee Costi was jailed after contacting a 13-year-old girl via a chat room and convincing her to perform sex acts for him over a Web camera.[46] According to the girl, "He kept saying how beautiful I was."[47] Police found over 350 logs of online conversations with young girls on Costi's computer, including conversations with other pedophiles around the world.[48] Costi admitted to three counts of sex with children, three counts of Internet child grooming, and five counts of creating indecent images of children.[49]

A Swedish Case

A 36-year-old Stockholm man was taken into custody on suspicion of raping three young girls after allegedly contacting them via the Internet on a popular youth Web site.[5] The girls, aged 14 and 15, tipped off the police, alleging that the man had raped them, and two indicated they had been forced to have sex with him.[51] The attacks allegedly took place in the man's home, at his work in the city, and at the home of one of the girls.[52] Swedish law states that sex with a minor under the age of 15 is rape, regardless of consent.[53]

Jose Marino

Thirty-six-year old Jose A. Merino was charged with three counts of rape of a child, six counts of sodomy on a child, and four counts of sexual abuse of a child.[54] Police believe he posted a profile on MySpace and posed as a 16-year-old to lure young girls for sexual encounters.[55]

Jacobo Rivera

Thirty-two-year-old Jacobo Rivera of Orem, Utah, agreed to two federal counts of possession of child pornography and faced state other charges, including seven first-degree felony counts of sodomy on a child, rape of a child, and aggravated sex abuse of a child.[56] Rivera's girlfriend at the time discovered pictures on his cell phone of her niece and two daughters and notified police, who arrested him.[57] Because the photos were created on a cell phone, he was also charged with five federal felony counts of production of child pornography.[58]

Online Blackmailing

Two girls, then 13 and 15 years old, went to police to expose an Internet sicko who was preying on them.[59] Their ordeal started when they received an email from a man posing as their friend, which led to a prank flash exposure via a Webcam after conversing in a chat room.[60] They quickly received a message stating, "I'm not who you think I am," followed up by several requests and threats of exposing the pictures to friends, parents, and even posting them to Web sites.[61] An investigator for the case indicated that the alleged predator was suspected of blackmailing over 100 girls on two continents into performing sex acts.[62] The man was subsequently charged with several counts of making and distributing child pornography and extortion.[63]

Joseph Colasacco

Police arrested 30-year-old Joseph Colasacco and charged him with four counts of promoting pornography to a minor, three counts of electronic enticement of a minor, and one count of sexual assault after he was allegedly found in the bed of a 14-year-old boy.[64] According to the prosecutor's spokesperson, the two met on MySpace.[65] According to an affidavit, the boy's mother found pornographic magazines and a DVD in his bedroom "depicting nude men in sexual acts and poses" that according to the boy was brought by Colasacco to his house.[66]

Matthew Gargill

A 29-year-old Hawaiian man was accused of sexually assaulting a 15-year-old girl in his car near a college campus after initially meeting her online.[67] Police say that Matthew Gargill posed as a 16-year-old boy on MySpace and arranged to meet the girl.[68] According to Captain Frank Fuji of the Honolulu Police Department, "The young people using the Internet, you need to realize that if you're being less than truthful about the information you put on the screen, you can be pretty certain that the other people on that screen are probably putting less than truthful information."[69] Officers arrested Cargill for investigation of seven counts of sex assault and one count of electronic enticement of a child.[70]

Paul Bennett

Paul Bennett, 24 years old, was arrested in San Francisco in 2004 and subsequently convicted for transporting a 13-year-old girl across state lines with the intent on engaging in sexual activity.[71] Bennett and the victim met online after a series of email exchanges that led to an Internet romance.[72] The young girl testified that she had sex with Bennett on multiple occasions after leaving League City, Texas, and heading north to Oklahoma, where the pair hitchhiked to California after learning that the FBI was looking for him.[73]

Ronald Elmquist

Radio Shack Corporation reported in November 2006 that its board accepted the resignation of director Ronald Elmquist, who was charged with three counts of possessing child pornography and entered a not guilty plea.[74]

Molesting Son for "Master"

A 38-year-old Canadian woman pleaded guilty to one count of sexual interference with a person under the age of 14 and another count of transmitting child pornography after apparently sending sexual pictures of herself and her 8-year-old son to her master in a bondage-themed online chat room.[76]

Ottawa police also charged Thomas Brian Feehan, 56, with possession of child pornography after seizing his computer from his home.[76] The woman said her master started her submissive training that over time evolved to her using sex toys over a Webcam and eventually to sending him nude pictures of her son touching himself.[77]

RECOMMENDATIONS

This chapter highlights only some of the tragedies that have happened in recent years and will continue to happen in years to come. Part of protecting children and minors from the dangers of the Internet and other technologies is learning just what can go wrong. There are a lot of dangerous people in the world, many of whom inflict harm (sexually, emotionally, physically) on children. Blackmail and tricks to get children to reveal personal details and (sometimes body parts) are commonly used by intelligent predators. Kids need to hear sensitized versions of the events described in this chapter to help better prepare themselves and protect themselves while they are online. The following recommendations close this gruesome reality.

- Have *frequent* conversations with children about the risks of going online, and where appropriate, let them know some of the bad things that have happened to others and how they were duped. I don't advocate a grotesque or detailed account, but children need to know that there are bad people in the world with intent to harm them and how they attempt to do so. I used this approach with my children when I explained why I wouldn't allow them to have an IM account. They're smarter as a result of the conversation and have talked to their friends about some of the risks of going online and communicating with strangers.
- Develop a contract or agreement with your children about things not to do while on the Internet and have them sign it. Reinforce that they should never give out personal information (name, address, phone number, schools, etc.) to anyone they don't know in chat rooms, IM conversations, online games, social networking sites, or email. People aren't always who they say they are.
- Politely explain some of the consequences if they send a photo to a stranger or post one online. Although this seems enticing sometimes, communicate that they shouldn't open picture files sent by strangers. They may be graphic or fake. It's common for Internet predators to send photos of young teens, concealing their real identity and age in an effort to lure them to a personal meeting. Real-world examples of tragedies, if communicated properly, are an excellent way to get a message across to children, especially teenagers, of the potential dangers of going online.
- Set up communication guidelines for conversing with others online, regardless of the medium. These include never responding to rude or inappropriate messages or requests. They should cut off communication with these individuals and inform their parents or teacher immediately. Also, make sure they know that they should *never* agree to meet someone in person that they've met online and reinforce this message with some real-world tragedies that have unfortunately left others as victims, some sexually abused and dead.

PART TWO

A Road Map to Protect Children While Online

How to Monitor Your Kids Online

I've arrived at this outermost edge of my life by my own actions. Where I am is thoroughly unacceptable. Therefore, I must stop doing what I've been doing.
—Alice Koller

TO MONITOR OR NOT TO MONITOR

One thing is for sure when raising children—they will lie at some point. Some lies are minor, but others are more serious. I've watched my kids and others grow up and have noticed the era of "that's my stuff." As children grow into young teenagers, they become more protective of what is theirs and move into a phase of more independence, which includes trying to conceal things from their parents. This chapter discusses three main topics.

1. The types of tricks kids use to hide their online activities
2. Nontechnical parental monitoring
3. Effective technical software to filter and monitor (overt and covert)

TRICKS KIDS USE TO HIDE WHAT THEY'RE DOING

Children with access to the Internet are smarter than we parents give them credit for. My own kids get great grades, play team sports, and are mostly a parent's dream to manage. But they do lie from time to time and on a number of occasions have attempted to get past the software that I've put in place to limit their online activities. (I'm their worst nightmare from a technology standpoint because they'll never surpass my knowledge of computer technology as long as I'm still in the IT profession.) The following list shows some examples of how children use technology to camouflage and hide their online activities.

- *Kids often set up and use multiple email accounts.* When parents monitor their primary email accounts, looking at both sent and received messages, kids may use hidden accounts to send information to their online acquaintances and friends. Stealth software (discussed later in this chapter) will help parents identify those accounts so they can stamp them out and disable them.

- *Teens use a variety of IM tools and sometimes make voice calls over the Internet with these tools.* Parents often lay down the rule that their kids are not allowed to use IM. Rules don't work—technology does. Unless parents use software to block these types of tools at the appropriate age, children can easily misuse them and potentially get into trouble.

- *Technically adept teenagers cover their online browsing tracks by deleting temporary Internet files and recorded history.* It's actually quite easy to do this in most browsers. Microsoft's Internet Explorer now has just one button to click to delete the history, cached temporary Internet files and pages, and data entered into Web page forms. Once the data is gone, parents can't tell where their kids have been on the Web. If you find that this is happening on your home computers, your children may have something to hide.

- *Tech-savvy children often use proxy sites to hide where they're going on the Internet.* These Web pages allow users to enter the Web page that they'd like to go to directly on their site and thus make surfing anonymous and hidden from that point forward. These sites also make it harder for Web logging software to report what sites children have visited. Stealth software fixes that and gives parents a true report of Web usage.

- *Teenagers often create personal Web pages on a free service and update content as desired.* Yahoo!'s GeoCities is one such popular service. Teens often publish too much personal content on their personal Web pages, which are available to everyone and often picked up by search engines. Savvy teens can actually turn their home PCs into a Web server by starting a Web publishing service or program. This approach is usually less popular with teens because all of their content is on their home computers and searchable by their parents.

- *Teenagers frequently download and install different browser software, hide the icon from the Desktop, and surf the Internet bypassing content controls in the browser that their parents have set up.* A common example: a parent enables content filtering in Internet Explorer to block adult content. His or her teen downloads Firefox , hides the shortcut icon from the Desktop, and even deletes it from the list of programs on the Application menu, but stores a hidden shortcut in a directory where they can run the program and bypass all IE content filters.

- *Curious children wanting more from the Internet try to crack administrative passwords by watching their parents type on the keyboard.* My own kids have done this a number of times and I type at ninety words a minute! Once a child has an administrative password for a particular computer or Internet content filtering program, they can bypass the controls, setup new accounts, and delete their online tracks and log files. Stealth software and key loggers help mitigate this along with changing administrative passwords on a monthly basis.

- *Teenagers often delete sent and received email and IM messages that they don't want parents to see.* Stealth software reveals exactly what they're trying to hide by capturing screen shots at the desired intervals.

- *Sophisticated teens save private email attachments and downloaded files (pictures, videos, etc.) to data keys (flash drives) instead of the hard drive.* Data keys can store large amounts of information, including full-motion videos of pornography like the infamous Paris Hilton sex frolic. Stealth software reveals all activities on a particular computer, including copying files to data keys.

- *Some teenagers use hot keys to quickly switch between screens and programs when parents walk by the computer.* By pressing the right key combination, kids can bring up a word processing file that looks like a homework assignment in less than a second to conceal what's being accessed via another tool or window.

- *IM- and chat-savvy teenagers use shortcuts and jargon to warn others online when they can no longer converse freely.* These quick phrases and characters are often not known by parents. Some interesting examples include the following. (Chapter 8 provides a detailed list to get parents up to speed.)

- :-*) = kiss
- POS = parent over shoulder
- SA = sibling alert
- IPN = I'm posted naked
- NIFOC = naked in front of the computer
- WTGP? = want to go private?
- KPC = keeping parents clueless
- CTN = can't talk now

- *Teens that want to hide personal IM conversations simply turn off logging within the IM tool itself, leaving no record of the online exchanges.* Email programs by default leave an audit trail, and users must manually delete them to hide the content of the messages. In contrast, IM users only save messages of online conversations to disk on demand. Keep in mind, Internet providers keep a log of content for a period of time, but they usually don't keep them for longer than required by law.

• *Children often change social networking sites frequently and select nonmainstream sites to hide postings from their parents.* In addition, many have profile pages on multiple sites, so if their parents find one and shut it down, they still have another. Given the recent press about social networking sites, most parents already know about MySpace and check to see if their kids have a profile page with inappropriate or personal content posted. They don't usually know about the less advertised alternatives to trendy sites. Internet filtering software that logs Web activity and stealth software that records all activities can help parents find out exactly what sites their kids are posting to. Key loggers also allow adults to capture passwords so they can log in as their child to see their private profile pages. This is not an invasion of privacy. Parents shouldn't feel guilty snooping around and don't need to justify prying to help protect their children. As long as my kids are still minors and living under the roof that I provide for them, they don't have many rights. The privacy advocates can look somewhere else for a discussion on this topic.

• *Smart kids rename files to nondescript names and file types when sending email attachments to prevent parents who monitor their email accounts from viewing them when they try to open the file.* Changing a nude picture file from JPEG to, say, a nonexistent file type like JTT complicates the viewing of such files because the operating system doesn't know what program to launch to see what's inside. An example would be for a teen to rename a file called nakedgirl2.jpeg to hw2.doc or hw2.gss. Most parents wouldn't look into a file that looks like a homework document. To pull off the exchange, the intended recipient simply changes the file extension back, saves it for viewing at a later time (maybe on another computer to a data key), and deletes the email itself. Stealth software exposes these types of tricks and tips off monitoring adults that there may be an issue with online behavior.

Parents and teachers need to learn these types of tricks and start thinking like the opposition to protect children on the Internet today. A tech-savvy parent or teacher with the right tools and techniques can mitigate many of the risks and be at a competitive advantage with their children against the sexual predators that are stalking kids every day.

NONTECHNICAL PARENTAL MONITORING

Although not as effective, the following nontechie approaches to monitoring your kids' activities may help reduce risk, but the recommendation is to employ a technical software solution on every computer in your home and school.

1. Put the family computer in a common room with open access so that it's easy to see what's on the screen.
2. Set time limits for when children can go online, and prohibit them from accessing the Internet when parents or guardians are not home, especially if there isn't any monitoring and filtering software installed.
3. Regularly review what Web sites your child goes to by viewing the browser history.
4. Regularly review your child's sent, deleted, and received emails.
5. If your child has a data key or flash drive, ask to see it from time to time and review the files for inappropriate content.
6. Create sound family policies and agreements of what is acceptable and not acceptable Internet use.

These approaches attempt to reduce the risks associated with using the Internet, but they're not fully effective alone, which is why the remainder of this book is focused on using the right types of technology that do help protect minors that access the Internet. Why take a software approach instead of a more casual approach? Because software doesn't lie and is far more effective at disclosing the truth regarding what children do online. It's also very helpful and more effective at protecting children from inappropriate content and sexual predators. Parents who can see actual conversations between their children and strangers are in a better position to do something about it than those that are in the dark.

SOFTWARE FOR BETTER MONITORING

First I want to clarify the difference between filtering and blocking software. *Filtering* software is usually designed to block access to specific sites containing a series of keywords that are either preprogrammed or keyed in manually. The problem with filtering solutions alone is that Web site operators are pretty smart with regard to misspelling typical keywords. Filters can be used as a set of keywords or combinations of categories such as *adult, drugs, violence,* and so on and turned on or off in most programs. *Blocking* software typically maintains a database of sites by category that, when a filter is set, can block access to those sites. Many companies that offer these solutions employ people to troll the Internet in an attempt to add new sites to the database, keeping the product more current and increasing the effectiveness of the block. As with filtering solutions, the best blocking products also allow parents to add to the bad and good site list. Today's best products employ both strategies—blocking and filtering—and often add components of monitoring or logging as well to help you sift through the data collected when used to monitor online activities.

Filtering and blocking software will still allow the Internet experience to survive and move forward. Given the amount of content and the varying degrees of appropriateness for minors, laws and societies have evolved to institute provisions designed to protect minors while still preserving free speech. Some countries not only filter and block but do it openly, as China regularly does. Saudi Arabia has openly stated that all Internet traffic in and out of the country is routed through a set of central servers that review each Web page requested.[1] If the user's requesting page is on the government's black list or blocked pages, the page is blocked from being viewed by the user.[2]

Browser-based content filters, like Internet Explorer Content Advisor, and search engine parental filter settings are not effective tools for protecting children. Simply put, they don't cut it, especially if children's accounts have rights to install new software or use other nonsecured wireless Internet connections. In addition, Internet-based services that filter and block certain sites and services are not totally effective either. Many who use these services like the functionality and effectiveness, but they don't realize that they can be bypassed. These tools are effective only if their users access the Internet through their provider. Let me be quite honest when I say that the Internet will include many wireless options and providers in the future. It's as easy as tapping into an unsecured wireless connection and using a different browser to bypass many of the online services content filters. Teenagers who have laptop computers with wireless networking cards can simply take their computer to a friend's house, use it at a Starbuck's, or as stated before, tap into another unsecured Internet access point to go where they want on the Internet and download almost anything.

According to a recent U.S. government study, approximately 1.1 percent of Web sites that were searched and indexed by MSN and Google and 1.7 percent of sites indexed by AOL, MSN, and Yahoo! are sexually explicit.[3] In 1998, the U.S. government passed the Child Online Protection Act (COPA), which required commercial Web sites to collect credit card information or other proof of age before allowing users to view material deemed harmful to minors.[4] In 1997, the U.S. Supreme Court deemed portions of the law unconstitutional because they said it was too vague and impacted the free speech rights of adults.[5] In 2004, the Supreme Court blocked COPA and indicated that filtering software may be more effective at protecting children against pornography.[6] According to American Civil Liberties Union attorney Chris Hansen, "COPA—right out of the bat—doesn't block the 50 percent (posted) overseas" and thus "COPA is substantially less than 50 percent effective."[7]

It often takes a very public scandal involving sex or crimes against children to raise awareness of the risks of using the Internet. According to a *Wall Street Journal* article, in the two weeks after the Congressman Mark Foley scandal broke, some sales of monitoring and filtering tools for parents saw double-digit growth.[8] According to Philip B. Stark, a professor at the University of California at Berkley, "Filters are more than 90 percent effective."[9] Does that mean that most software filtering programs are by default 10 percent ineffective? If so, that's already putting them into the B grade, at best, right out of the shrink-wrapped box. I believe that only a few filtering/monitoring software programs are effective, and not many can claim 90 percent effectiveness. Many of the packages I tested failed my images and video tab test when searching for adult content. When they fail, they fail big, often returning very graphic content. We're not just talking about the percentage of successfully blocked pages, we're dealing with the varying degrees of inappropriateness of content returned.

As a result, my recommendation is clear: install the right monitoring/filtering software on all computers, desktops and especially laptops, where children access the Internet. I evaluated a variety of software solutions before coming up with the following recommendations for parents and teachers. As a result, I've selected two software products to help parents and teachers do a better job protecting children on the Internet, regardless of the browser or Internet-based communications tools children use. I used the following criteria. The product must be:

- effective and work as advertised (50 percent weighting)
- easy to set up and use and produce accurate reports (40 percent weighting)
- cost-effective (10 percent weighting)

Cost represented only a small portion of the total weighting when selecting products. As with many other things in life, you get what you pay for. To be effective, a product must not only work as advertised but pass a series of tests. Many products failed my search engine test and displayed graphic sexual photos and videos. At no time during my evaluation of software solutions was I coerced, bribed, given free software, or paid to select any product.

There are a lot of products on the market, and most parents are confused at the offerings and simply don't know which ones are effective or not. As a result, they rely on independent analysis, reviews, articles, and recommendations from friends. Many articles recommend a number of products for a particular category, like keystroke loggers. The following products are my recommended picks and what I consider to be best of breed in their respective categories.

- Content filtering/monitoring recommendation = CyberPatrol
- Stealth monitoring/keystroke logging recommendation = PC Tattletale

CyberPatrol

CyberPatrol is one of the easiest products to use and is very effective at blocking inappropriate content. It also blocks undesirable services and tools like IM and chat. The product is developed and distributed by Surf Control and is sold via a subscription model for approximately $40 for a one-year subscription and $60 for a two-year subscription. You can purchase the product online at www.cyberpatrol.com. Once purchased and downloaded, simply enter an appropriate license key. The product can be configured for automatic or manual updates. I recommend automatic daily updates that start 10 minutes after your Internet access for that day is initiated. This should be the default setting, so no need to worry about this setting unless you desire less frequent updates. In addition to being an effective tool, CyberPatrol has the following helpful features,

1. Parents can set up individual user profiles for different family members with different filtering permissions. The program has a default user profile that applies to any user on that computer. To simplify configuration, opt for this setting instead of creating multiple user profiles on each computer. You can override any blocks with an administrative password if need be.
2. The product comes with preconfigured filters that are already set up for different age categories. Simply select the filter setting that best applies for the members of your family and it does the rest, which includes automatically setting up permissions for minimum to maximum blocking by information category. Examples of preset filters include Allow All, Adult—Security, Mature Teen, Young Teen, Child, and Custom. I opted for a Custom setting and then went into each of the information categories and set them for the desired filter strength (see Figure 5.1).
3. The product comes with 13 different information categories to allow setting filters at a more detailed level. Categories include Adult/Sexually Explicit, Chat, Criminal Activity & Phishing, Drugs, Alcohol & Tobacco, Gambling, Glamour & Intimate Apparel, Hacking & Spyware, Hate Speech, Remote Proxies, Sex Education, Violence, and Weapons. Figures 5.2 and 5.3 provide screen shots of the various filter options, access levels (on/off, allow, block), and custom settings for each filter option.
4. The product also allows parents to set permissions on a variety of tools

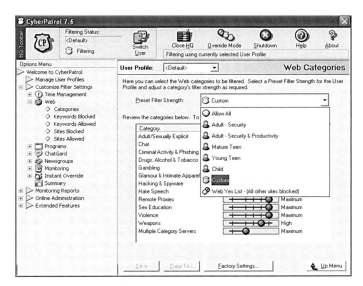

Figure 5.1 Setting Custom Filters
Used with permission from SurfControl PLC.

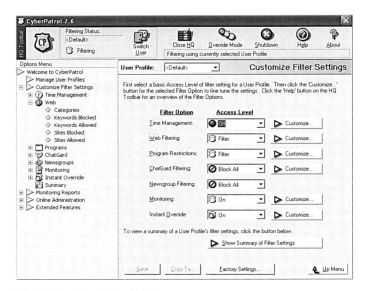

Figure 5.2 Customizing Filter Settings
Used with permission from SurfControl PLC.

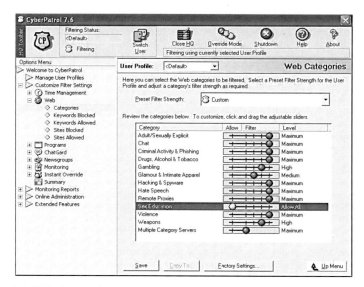

Figure 5.3 Web Categories
Used with permission from SurfControl PLC.

along with blocking them or allowing them individually. An example
would be to turn on Web Filtering and customize it while blocking all
ChatGard and Usegroups.

5. CyberPatrol allows you to set time restrictions by user account. Parents
can allow certain programs to be used only at specific times of the day for
each user, if necessary. This may be a helpful feature for working parents
whose children may return from school before their parents with a couple
of hours to kill on the Internet.

6. The program comes with an instant override feature that allows parents
to enter the administrative password for the application and bypass blocks
and restrictions that have been set up. I use this feature on all of my home
computers and use it to get past blocks that are intended for my children.

7. For Internet Web filtering, the program allows parents to set up blocked
and allowed keywords and Web sites that can automatically trigger blocking a Web page from being viewed.

8. Last but not least, the program has a great reporting feature that shows
pretty much what was attempted and blocked if monitoring is enabled. I
recommend that parents enable this feature at all times.

When a user attempts to access a Web page or Internet service that is blocked, CyberPatrol displays a blocked page/service message prominently for the user. Thus, this product is an overt package for effective Internet monitoring and filtering. For the price, functionality, and automatic updates, CyberPatrol is a must-have for parents with children between the ages of 8 to 17. Unlike individual browser-specific content filters, CyberPatrol works across all browsers with up-to-date licenses. It even protects and logs activities by teenagers trying to access the Internet using a different service provider with their laptop and CyberPatrol installed.

PC Tattletale

PC Tattletale is one of the most unique and effective software programs I've come across in a long time. As a former software developer, I appreciate a good product that doesn't take a whole lot of computing resources and can be set to be completely hidden from the user. Teenagers won't even know that it's installed because the program doesn't show up in the Task Manager as an application, hides all shortcut icons, doesn't show on the program listings, and isn't seen as an installed program from the Control Panel. In addition, the application was engineered to take about as much memory and computer processing power as a small IM program. Thus, it's got a small footprint and can't be seen once it's been installed. Parents can access the management screen by either typing a Ctrl-Alt-function key combination followed by an administrative password or by entering a four letter command in a command prompt window, followed by the correct administrative password. The PC Tattletale product has the following helpful features.

1. The product comes with an effective keystroke logger that traps all passwords for any program or Web-based form. This is extremely helpful for parents who want to login as their child and see personal profile pages posted on their children's favorite social networking sites or sift through emails sent and received on that special account that their children may have hidden from their parents.
2. PC Tattletale records all Web site activity and clearly displays what sites were visited by looking into the Web Sites Recorded section from the main menu (see Figure 5.7).
3. The program can be put into a stealth mode, making it invisible to most users. Access to the management console can only occur if the correct

command and password are entered from a DOS-like command window. Refer to the user's manual for this critical information.

4. The best function of this software is its ability to take a picture of the screen every few seconds, store it in a hidden location, and allow you to play it back like a movie when desired (see Figure 5.4). PC Tattletale's Screen Captures section shows all activity performed on the computer, including any attempts to delete online history, cache, messages, move pictures to and from data keys, and so on. It can be configured to take a snapshot every few seconds. The default is four seconds, but you can set it to, say, eight seconds to save space on the hard drive. This feature is well worth the price of this package. The package automatically deletes screen captures older than 30 days in an effort to prevent filling up the hard drive. Once a screen capture movie is viewed, parents can easily delete the logs by clicking on the appropriate icon on the left side of the management console page. This stealth package is a parent's dream and puts you back in control so that you can be more effective at protecting children while on they're on the Internet.

The following steps will help anyone who wants to know more about what their children are doing online get up and running quickly.

1. Download and install the program, then enter the master password that is required to manage the application and settings.
2. Select the Options button at the bottom of the main menu page (see Figure 5.5).
3. Check (a) Record all Website activity, (b) Record screen shots every 8 seconds, (c) Record all keystrokes, (d) Record all windows opened, and (e) Turn off Ctrl-Alt-F5 hot key (see Figure 5.6). Turning off the hot key will prevent teenagers from detecting that the software is even running. To access the management console with this control key sequence turned

Figure 5.4 PC Tattletale VCR Controls
Used with permission by Parental Controls Products, LLC.

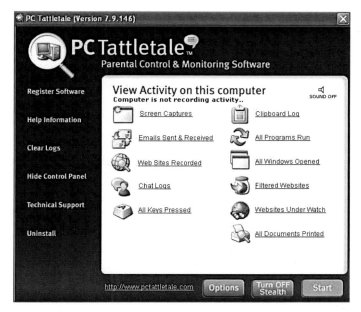

Figure 5.5 PC Tattletale main menu
Used with permission by Parental Controls Products, LLC.

off, please refer to the user's manual for the command to be entered at the command prompt.

4. From the PC Tattletale main menu, turn on stealth monitoring by selecting the Turn ON Stealth button on the bottom of the page.

5. Optional: from the PC Tattletale option menu, select the Scheduling icon on the left to configure the package to turn stealth monitoring on and off at certain times.

6. Optional: from the PC Tattletale option menu, select the ReflexMail icon to be notified via email if certain Web watch keywords are used (say, xxx, sex, etc.) during hours of monitoring.

7. Save your settings.

RECOMMENDATIONS

Parents and teachers who want to monitor children and their online activity need to augment nontechnical monitoring and get up to speed on best practice software solutions like the ones listed in this chapter. Content filtering and

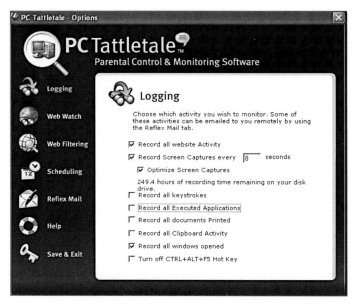

Figure 5.6 PC Tattletale Logging Options
Used with permission by Parental Controls Products, LLC.

monitoring software has come a long way in the past few years and is getting more powerful with every new release. That said, it's by no means perfect and should not be the only technical solution that adults rely on to ensure that their kids are doing the right things and are not putting themselves at risk by posting personal information or conversing with strangers in cyberspace. That's where stealth software like PC Tattletale comes into play. It removes any doubt about what your children are doing on the Internet by providing the clear facts of

Figure 5.7
Used with permission by Parental Controls Products, LLC.

How to Protect Your Children on the Internet

their online habits, tools, and even with whom they are conversing, regardless of the tool used. Stealth software also fills in the gaps that imperfect content filtering solutions have in the marketplace.

The following recommendations should help parents and teachers get started with great technical solutions that can help keep children safe online. I've also provided recommendations by age category, because from this point on, recommendations will vary by age.

- Avoid external service offerings that are tied to a single Internet service provider. They may be fine as long as your child is younger, but as soon as they get into high school and have access to more mobile types of technology like laptops, PDAs, and so on, these services become less effective as most teens break away from standalone solutions.
- Browser-based content filters like those in Internet Explorer are not effective and are tied to a single browser. Move away from these types of content filtering solutions and install tier-one content filtering software like CyberPatrol. Configure them to update daily and remember to install the software on each PC that is connected to the Internet.
- For the real skinny on what your kids are doing, install the PC Tattletale stealth software on your home computer before installing any content filtering and monitoring software that is overt. Overt software tips children off that they're being monitored. Covert or stealth software reveals what they're really doing. If you find that their activities are less than desired or they are at risk, then by all means install CyberPatrol to better protect them and leave the stealth software up and running to appropriately track their activities, including IM chats, file transfers, and other attempts to cover their online tracks.

Category 1: Elementary School (Ages 8–11)

- The only strong recommendation for this age group is to put Internet filtering software on all computers that children use to access the Internet. My recommendation is CyberPatrol.
- Internet filtering settings should be strong and tied to their age to prevent access to inappropriate content, which is usually by accident. I recommend blocking the following categories for this age group: social networking sites, file sharing/peer-to-peer services, email, FTP, adult content, IM tools, and chat rooms. CyberPatrol makes it easy to apply these settings by selecting the appropriate age profile.

Category 2: Middle School (Ages 12–14)

- Children aged 12–14 are usually going through a transition from child to teenager, which includes all of the wonderful and sometimes interesting mood swings that go along with puberty. All children at this group should have all Internet filtering software installed on all of the computers they use to access the Internet.
- I recommend blocking the following categories for this age group: social networking sites, file sharing/peer-to-peer services, IM tools, FTP, adult content, and chat rooms. CyberPatrol has easy-to-use settings that accomplish this by selecting the appropriate age profile.
- If you decide to allow certain more mature categories like social networking or IM, I highly recommend installing PC Tattletale to capture passwords and monitor their activities so that you can see what they're really doing online. Actions required by parents may include logging into their children's email and social networking accounts to see what they've sent, received, and posted to private audiences vs. the public Internet.
- Change administrative passwords for your Internet filtering and stealth software from time to time, perhaps monthly, as teens at this age may attempt to bypass these controls.

Category 3: High School (Ages 15–17)

- Children aged 15–17 are evolving into young adults, which will probably require allowing more online liberties and freedom. Children in this group should have Internet filtering software like CyberPatrol installed on all of the computers that they use to access the Internet, especially those with wireless network cards.
- Internet filtering settings should be more permissible and tied to their age to prevent access to inappropriate content. I recommend blocking the following categories for this age group: adult content, FTP, file sharing/peer-to-peer services, and chat rooms.
- For this age group, I highly recommend installing PC Tattletale to capture passwords and monitor activities so that you can see what they're really doing online. Teens often use laptop PCs and other Internet providers, some wireless. Stealth software will capture exactly what they're doing online, regardless of where they take their laptop. Parents should review logs weekly and delete as appropriate to free up space as needed for future stealth logs.
- Change administrative passwords for your Internet filtering and stealth software from time to time, perhaps monthly, as teens at this age may attempt to bypass these controls.

Internet Surfing, Blogs, and Social Networking

You're two clicks away from just about anything.

—Gregory S. Smith

SURFING/BROWSING THE INTERNET

It's official—we crossed the 100 million mark for the number of Web sites on the Internet.[1] According to Netcraft, an Internet monitoring company based in Bath, England, the milestone was reached sometime in October 2006.[2] "There are now 100 million web sites with domain names and content on them," according to Rich Miller.[3] That doesn't include all of the sub-domain and personal Web sites on the Net, which are typically not registered and take up only a few pages. The growth in the number of Web sites and content therein is simply staggering and has grown from approximately 18,000 thousand Web sites in 1995.[4] What's more interesting is the rate at which content and number of sites is increasing on the Internet. According to a Microsoft advertisement for their search engine, Live.com, "7 million new pages are added to the Internet every day."[5]

SEARCH ENGINES: THE GOOD, THE BAD, AND THE UGLY

Surfing the Internet today is a crapshoot with regard to what people can find and how easily. The quote at the beginning of this chapter is really true. A well-structured set of keywords with the appropriate Boolean logic (and, or, not, etc.) usually returns relevant links to desired content in a matter of seconds. That content could be anything—schoolwork related, history, computers, travel, pornography photos and movies, S&M, violence, mutilation, racism, guts and gore, gay and lesbian, suicide, eating disorders, drugs, and weapons—all of which can be found with just two clicks of a computer mouse, one to execute the desired search and the second to view the resulting link. From Chapter 3, we know that search engines are great at finding information on the Internet, fast, and yes, dangerous if children are left to use them without proper supervision or filtering software. A recent report conducted by the Harvard Law School's Berkman Center for Internet and Society criticized Google's adult content filter for blocking nonporn sites (such as the American Library Association) when Google's Safe Search is turned on, pointing out that its filters are not 100 percent effective.[6] What does that mean about how accurate their algorithms are for blocking inappropriate content? These algorithms are not that accurate.

The most popular search sites are usually marketed well by the owning company or via social networking. Adults and teens alike seem to gravitate to public search engines that have the lion's share of Internet traffic. The following list includes some popular search sites along with the percentage of searches handled as of July 2006 according to a review of 57 search sites by Hitwise.[7]

- Google (www.google.com): 60.2 percent
- Yahoo! (search.yahoo.com): 22.5 percent
- MSN (search.msn.com): 11.8 percent
- Ask (www.ask.com): 3.3 percent
- AOL (search.aol.com): 1.0 percent
- Others: 1.0 percent collectively

Most of the search tools on the market offer parental or safe search filters, but according to my own research and testing, they don't work as well as I would like, and I don't recommend them for protecting children from potentially harmful content. Not all search sites are the same. My testing reports that Google and Live contain the most content when comparing search phrases and results across the various search engines. Search engine size is usually determined by one statistic—the number of documents indexed or ready for search. Over the past few years, a number of search engines have claimed to be the biggest. In 1997, Altavista claimed the largest repository with nearly 150 million pages indexed.[8] By 2003, the biggest site battle was between AlltheWeb and Google.com with 3.3 billion and 3.2 billion, respectively.[9] Toward the end of 2004, Google had taken over the lead again with 8 billion pages compared to its next rival, MSN, with 4 billion.[10] Today, success of a search engine is determined by a number of factors, including size, speed, marketing, the coolness factor, and growth potential (usually driven by advertising revenue). Google is at the top of that list, but Microsoft is back in the hunt with Live.com.

Search engines can search not only Web pages or HTML documents but within more than 250 file types including some popular files like Word, Power Point, Excel, PDF, WordPerfect, CorelDraw, and even relational databases from vendors like Oracle and IBM. Search engines update their content by sending search robots to look for new and updated content by spidering through pages and links to follow other pages and then updating their directory of indexed content. Many search engines also license their technology for purchase so that companies and organizations can implement sub-search site capabilities on their own corporate, government, and organization-wide public Web sites. Google is one such company that sells hardware appliances loaded with their search tool for groups to use internally on intranets as well as for external public Web sites. As a result, we surf the Web in an environment of organizational search sites specific to each company's content or message, along with a vast repository of external public free search sites with billions of pages of indexed and searchable content. That's really cool, but it comes with a cost. Let me be really clear as I lead into the next section—public free search sites are dangerous for children and should be greatly restricted and limited. It's that simple. I block them for my children using CyberPatrol.

Fortunately, there are a variety of options for parents today. The following sites are good alternatives and can be added (if necessary) to your approved site list in CyberPatrol.

- www.ajkids.com (Ask Jeeves for kids)
- www.kidsclick.org (Web search for kids by librarians)
- www.yahooligans.com (Yahoo! for kids)

Ask Jeeves for kids is one of my favorites because it supposedly contains no content on CyberPatrol's master block list, which is updated frequently.[11] I also like Yahooligans, which is designed for children between the ages of 7 and 12 and contains no adult-oriented advertisements.[12] Other lesser known safe sites include the following.

- www.ala.org/greatsites (American Library Association safe sites for kids)
- www.awesomelibrary.org (32,000 carefully reviewed Web sites for kids)
- www.education-world.com

- www.factmonster.com (a kid-friendly online dictionary, encyclopedia, and almanac)
- www.family-source.com (a family-friendly search engine across 1 million pages)
- www.kids.gov (a U.S. government–sponsored site with content by category and links to other safe sites)

Because it's so easy to search for and find hard-core pornography on the Internet, I wanted to spend a bit of time talking about the risks of exposing children to this material. According to Dr. Mary Anne Layden, co-director of the Sexual Trauma and Psychopathology Program, Center for Cognitive Therapy at the University of Pennsylvania, exposing adults and children to pornography can damage an individual's beliefs and behaviors.[13] In her testimony to the U.S. Senate Committee on Commerce, Science and Transportation, she described some additional harms of pornography.

1. Viewing pornography increases the possibility of sexual addiction for the viewer.
2. Clinical research supports that sex addicts are 40 percent likely to lose their spouse; 58 percent are likely to have a negative impact on their finances; and 27–40 percent may lose their jobs.[14]

The impact on children is just as bad, but in a different way that includes the following.

1. They may develop ideas that the images and videos they see are normal and can apply to them.
2. It may increase the likelihood that children will engage in the sexual behaviors that they see.
3. It may increase the likelihood of sexual exposure at an earlier age, thus increasing the risk of pregnancy and sexually transmitted diseases.[15]

A report from Australia stated that children who eventually became sexual predators all had access and experienced pornography on the Internet.[16] In her testimony, Layden also indicated that "there are no studies and no data that indicate a benefit from pornography use."[17] The following teen testimonials regarding their experience with pornography helps substantiate some of the risks.

- Bill (started viewing at 12 years old): "It led me to having sexual intercourse at age 13, trying to do what I saw on the Internet. I got into drugs and wound up at House of Hope."[18]

- Troy says "cyber-porn skewed his view of women. A guy starts treating a girl like a ho. They're just a piece of meat."[19]

One study of 932 sex addicts revealed that 90 percent of men and 77 percent of women who took part in the study indicated that pornography significantly contributed to their addiction.[20]

As I close out this section, there are four main takeaways:

1. Don't rely on search engine safe search settings—they don't work well by themselves.
2. Block popular search engines for younger children through middle school.
3. If you allow mainstream search sites like Google and Live, use adult filter settings within CyberPatrol to block and limit potentially harmful content. CyberPatrol is very effective at blocking harmful text and visual content.
4. Exposure of pornography to children, especially teenagers, can damage their view of what is a normal sexual relationship and lead to inappropriate and demeaning behavior later in life.

SOCIAL NETWORKING AND BLOGGING

I wrote this portion of the book on Santa Cruz Island in the Galápagos, where I expected technology and access to the Internet to be more of a pipe dream than a reality. Not so. Wireless Internet access and Internet cafés are vibrant on the island, and Internet access is available at most hotels via broadband connections. One traveler described the house where she was staying on a recent boat trip to do some snorkeling on the island of Bartolome. She described her friend's house on Santa Cruz as clean with basic amenities, no air conditioning and no hot water, but fully equipped with high-speed wireless Internet access, two computers, and an iPod. I also spoke to a few teenagers who live on Santa Cruz and they seemed quite aware of the types of content available on the Internet. Several of them indicated that they had free email accounts. I don't know how many teens on the island are aware of or use social networking sites, but it's just a matter of time before this becomes common even in remote locations. Technology is permeating most cultures and locations around the globe, which means that the risks to children on the Internet are just as real on remote islands as they are anywhere else, if not more so.

Social networking and supporting Web sites present real challenges for parents, teachers, and children. Popular sites such as MySpace, Xanga, and Friendster are drawing millions of teens and adults in what appears to be a race for the largest online diary of members. Although hip for kids, who often post pictures of themselves and friends, describe their personal interests, and blog (the act of writing an online diary, a Web log) about daily life, these sites are a parent's worst online nightmare. Kids frequently post too much personal information about themselves, and some operators of these sites have security issues and don't have sufficient mechanisms to protect private profile content for their members. On September 7, 2006, Xanga agreed to pay a $1 million fine for violations of the Children's Online Privacy Protection Act (COPPA) for allegedly collecting and disclosing personal information from kids 12 years old and under.[21] COPPA requires that all commercial Web sites obtain consent from parents before collecting personal information from kids younger than age 13.

What's interesting is what drives average people to blog on the Internet and potentially disclose personal information to millions of strangers. The Internet and social networking sites have helped create a new class of personal reporters and commentators that are eager and willing to write just about anything. A national survey reveals that most bloggers focus on describing their daily life and personal experiences targeted to a small audience; and that only a small percentage of bloggers target their information for larger audiences that include subject areas on politics, media, and government.[22] Although blogging is wildly popular with teens, they're not the only ones writing about their experiences. According to the Pew Research Center, the number of adult bloggers in the United States is on the rise as well—to approximately 12 million adults or 8 percent of adult Internet users.[23] The Pew study goes on to report the following summary findings.

- 54 percent of bloggers say they've never published before anywhere else.
- 54 percent of bloggers are under the age of 30.
- Women and men are almost evenly split among the blogging population.
- 76 percent of bloggers share their personal experiences.[24]

So how big is the social networking market? The answer is simple—it's huge! Table 6.1 offers a slice of data about the larger sites, plus a few alternatives that most parents have not yet heard of by name, along with the number of visitors in 2006 and growth rates from 2005.

Other lesser known sites include XuQa and Hi5, which offer nontraditional add-on services like games and music players.[26] Some kids spend several hours a day on social networking sites, keeping in touch with friends, uploading pictures, and writing in their online journal. As kids have learned that parents are

Table 6.1 Social Networking Sites

Site	2006 Visitors	Percent Change from 2005
MySpace	79.6 million	+243%
Facebook	15.5 million	+86%
Friendster	15.4 million	−1%
LiveJournal	11.6 million	+4%
Piczo	10.2 million	+216%
Bebo	9 million	+185%

Source: comScore World Metrix.[25]

aware of sites like MySpace, they sometimes move to lesser known sites like Piczo to fly under the parental radar. Some sites are more focused on younger teens, whereas others (like Facebook) target older teens to college students. Facebook started out requiring college domain email addresses (like .edu) to register but later opened their site to include high school students.[27]

Although it may be fun for kids and college students to converse online and post personal journals, social networking sites are prime lurking spots for sexual predators. According to a *Washington Post* article, a MySpace member discovered that a stranger had copied her photos from the site, set up a fake page, posted copies of those photos on the new site, and used it to start a relationship with a boy on the west coast.[28] How easy is it for a predator to find potential prey that live close by to them? Unfortunately, it's really simple. On MySpace, predators can simply click on the Browse menu item, enter search information into the categories (including sex, age, country), and then enter the desired ZIP code to search for prospective prey. The ZIP code search can even be refined to include a radius surrounding the desired area to hone in to members within, say, 5 or 10 miles.

Predators often pose as minors on social networking sites, including posting fake photos of themselves, to target victims. Using search technology, they can easily find publicly available content, including email addresses, IM screen names, hobbies, favorite chat rooms, and school names before attempting to establish an online conversation with their next potential victim. "This is the kind of place that clearly attracts sexual predators," states FBI's Child Sexual Victims Agent Jim Clemente.[29] "It's a huge risk," he concludes. How revealing are some of the postings on social networking sites? More revealing than most parents would allow. According to recent RecordOnline.com article, a random search through a dozen or so member profiles in a particular ZIP code revealed a photo of a nearly topless woman who's an admitted dancer, along with a racy bio.[30] A recent search on MySpace resulted in numerous photos, postings, and videos with sexual undertones that are not suitable for children.

Predators also use other tools to hone in on their victims after gaining some ground with key personal facts. Chapter 8 discusses some scary approaches and tools used, including IM and chat rooms, that allow predators to actually locate the address and school within an hour or so of online research. One 14-year old girl is suing MySpace, on which she met a man she alleges sexually assaulted her.[31] The man claims he's not guilty and that the girl, then 13, portrayed herself as 15 years old to get listed on the site, which prohibits users under 14 years old.[32]

Some adults aren't taking the risks of social networking sites lying down. Seven students at a New Jersey high school were suspended for posting photos and profanity on a Web site about other students and teachers.[33] According to school officials, the students used cell phone cameras to secretly take pictures of others without their permission.[34] So, what can parents do about social networking sites? The following quick tips can help.

- Block social networking sites for elementary and middle school children.
- Frequently remind children to never post anything personal that can tip off a sexual predator.
- If access to social networking sites is allowed, stealth monitor via PC Tattletale and review the movie presentations frequently to ensure that your children are not talking to the wrong people online or posting personal content that can be used against them or put them at risk.
- Don't underestimate the appeal of social networking sites for teenagers. They sometimes feel more independent expressing themselves online than in person and don't have to deal with one-on-one embarrassment if they say something wrong.

Don't Forget about FTP Sites

FTP sites are very simple and nongraphical sites for storing and exchanging files among users. Businesses use them to securely send and receive files between vendors and partners. An FTP site uses a different software protocol, denoted by ftp in the Web browser's address line, that is different than the http protocol that is used to access standard Web sites and pages. FTP sites can be accessed with a typical browser in one of two ways:

- anonymous (no user ID/password required), such as ftp://ftp.sitename.com
- user ID/password required, such as ftp://username@ftp.sitename.com; this will likely prompt the user to enter a password

The bad news about FTP sites is:

- Porn (pictures/video) can easily be shared among others who know the FTP address of a particular site.
- FTP sites are popular for sharing illegal music videos, violating copyright, and are also used by hackers to disguise audio files with computer viruses and worms if downloaded, potentially compromising the user's computer and any confidential data on it.
- Many content-filtering packages don't accurately block access to these sites because they often use cryptic file names and no other content.
- Most parents are clueless about FTP sites and how to access them.

The good news is, the FTP protocol itself can be blocked, denying children access to these sites and content.

I recommend that parents block FTP via a firewall application, which is discussed later in this chapter. For parents who are not running a firewall application on their home computer, *you should*. PC Tattletale will easily expose kids using FTP sites to access inappropriate content and which ones they're accessing.

Most adult users have no need to access FTP sites because most content and file downloads are stored on Web servers and not FTP servers. If you do have a need for using FTP, you're probably in the information technology profession and know how to quickly grant and revoke access when needed so that kids are not exposed to the risks of FTP.

VIDEO CAMERAS GONE WILD

Over the past few years, computer-based video cameras have become increasingly popular among teens and adults as a way to humanize communication over the Internet. Two key drivers that have propelled an increase in the use of these devices are the low entry price of cameras and the increase of broadband Internet connections to homes, schools, and businesses. A fully functional video camera attached to a computer retails for about $50 and includes software that is easy to install and use. Lower grade video cameras are also proliferating in today's cell phones, making them viable devices for recording and distributing mini-movies.

The business world has been using computer video cameras for years to add to encrypted and private online meetings that can display slide presentations and real-time video images on the same screen. The technology has become so simple that many professionals use it without assistance from IT pros. I enjoy plugging in a USB camera to my computer and launching an online meeting with a distant colleague. The online meeting software senses the device and automatically opens a window to display live video.

Video cameras and sites that display videos come with significant risk for children today. Several years ago, a creative young woman named Jenny launched a Web site named Jennycam with nothing more than a computer, a camera, and an always-on Internet connection from her bedroom. The camera was left on at all times and displayed to anyone watching her every move and activity, which included sex. The site became wildly popular and famous, with many curious strangers around the world watching to see her next moves. Fast forward to today and we've got several large amateur video sites like YouTube that contain a variety of homemade video clips, many of which are not suitable for children. These sites make it easy for users to upload new content that can be viewed by thousands across the world within minutes. The explosion of online video-sharing Web sites like YouTube, MySpace (who recently added video capabilities), Yahoo!, Google, and even Microsoft has become the latest challenge for parents trying to protect their kids. YouTube is by far the largest and most successful site, with 20 million visitors per month and an average of 50,000 new video uploads per day.[35]

Most video sharing sites require those uploading clips to acknowledge an agreement, usually via checkbox or button, prohibiting content that is obscene, pornographic, or involves nudity. Like most users on the Web, those who upload rarely read the fine print and often upload objectionable content any-way—many knowing that their postings may be removed at a later date. Thus, these objectionable video clips are accessible for a period of time and are only pulled off the site after viewers alert the hosting company about inappropriate content. According to a YouTube spokesperson, "The really objectionable material gets flagged very quickly," and is pulled from the site within 15 minutes.[36] However, not all flagged content is removed from many of these sites, but instead only made available to registered users who are 18 years and older.[37] This approach doesn't help protect children from viewing racy videos. Kids may simply lie about their age when registering; the sites know that this is a common practice, but they have not gone far enough to protect minors. One good way would be to require a credit card to register as 18 and older, but many compa-nies know that they would lose members if they did so. I personally think that management at social networking and video sharing sites are part of the problem and trade child safety for more members and advertising revenue. Shameful!!!

So what are the risks for children using computer-based video cameras and sharing sites? The following summarizes the main risks to children.

- It's easy for children to access inappropriate and mature video content from video-sharing sites.
- These sites, including social networking components, may expose personal information, including what the child looks like or other facts revealed in homemade videos like street names or schools to predators and kidnappers.
- Content including still pictures and video clips can be used by sexual predators to blackmail children into performing other online activities, including sex acts, or even force a face-to-face meeting.

In addition to sometimes entertaining but risky video sharing sites like YouTube, there are thousands of adult sites that have free viewable teaser video clips of people engaging in a variety of sex acts—all accessible without a credit card or being a member of their service. These sites are easily found with a search engine by typing phrases like "sex video."

It is not uncommon for sexual predators to pose as a friend or classmate of a child they've met online. Over the course of days and sometimes weeks of online conversations, predators attempt to build trust and can falsely convince a child that they are really one of their friends at school. In this type of an environment, one thing leads to another and what starts out as, say, a casual topless flash by the child/teenager, turns into a blackmail request (perhaps to post still photos of the flash on the Internet or even mail them to the teen's parents, teachers, and friends). On the extreme side, a misused video camera by a teenager could lead to becoming an online or in-person sex slave to a sexual predator. There are many documented cases that attest to this type of approach and risk.

Parents are thus cautioned to carefully monitor their child's use of video equipment, including cell phones and Webcams. An extreme case of an attempt to block inappropriate video content from children is the recent announcement by a Brazilian telecommunications giant Brazil Telecom SA that they blocked YouTube in part of the country after a steamy sex video of a model and her boyfriend was posted on the site.[38] The widely viewed video became even more notorious after the telecom giant's news to block YouTube made headlines worldwide, but by then the video had been posted to a number of other Web sites, making it almost impossible to block from viewers in Brazil or around the world.[39]

Parents should limit the use of computer-attached video cameras in the home and block video-sharing sites. If computer-based video cameras are installed and used at home, pay attention to how your kids are using them and what sites they are viewing. If necessary, PC Tattletale will tell all on this one.

FIREWALLS AND WIRELESS

Firewalls

Chapter 2 defined a firewall and briefly discussed why parents and teachers need to know about them. Here I cover how to get started selecting and using them. In short, firewalls help parents by:

1. protecting their computer from hackers,
2. blocking certain types of applications from accessing the Internet (usually through a specific firewall port number),
3. blocking certain harmful file types (MP3, EXE, PIF) from being sent by your computer or received by another), and
4. blocking certain protocols (like FTP) from your computer.

This book is not designed to teach parents the ins and outs of firewall technology. Instead I cover just the portions that can help protect children on the Web (e.g., blocking FTP services), so I'll focus on the last benefit. Recommendation: Each computer in your house should have a firewall program installed and running if the computer is connected to the Internet. While most businesses run on expensive hardware/software combined firewalls to protect their computers, consumers typically run free software-only firewalls. Windows XP and Vista come with software firewalls pre-installed. Although these are not as effective as other firewall products, they can be a good first line of defense and are easy to activate with as little as a checkbox. I turn on the firewall for each computer in my home. To activate the Microsoft firewall, simply consult the built-in help program (F1 key) and follow the easy instructions.

Recommendation: Although there are several good software firewall products on the market, I specifically recommend one of the following two.

1. BlackICE PC Protection from Internet Security Systems (ISS), www. BlackICE.iss.net. This program retails for a one-time cost of about $40, but it can be purchased for multiple computers (up to three) for about $100.

2. F-Secure Internet Security 2007, www.f-secure.com. License for one to three computers is approximately $80)

After you've selected a program and downloaded and installed it, please consult the product's online help on how to specifically block FTP as a service. This may require you to block a specific port number, possibly port 21, which is commonly used by FTP. Once blocked, try to access a site like ftp://ftp.micro soft.com and see if the request is stopped by your new firewall rule. If so, congratulations! You've just created a security role in your firewall product.

Wireless

Wireless (Wi-Fi) computing is becoming more the norm these days than the exception. Companies and individuals alike are using wireless access points and networking cards from vendors like Linksys and D-Link to create fast, inexpensive wireless networks, where all connected computers are capable of accessing the Internet. It's certainly cheaper to set up a Wi-Fi network at home than pay to have each room wired with networking cables. Wireless is here to stay, and it presents additional challenges to adequately protect children on the Internet. Today's caregivers and teachers *must* get up to speed on how best to monitor and protect children in a wireless world. The following outlines some of the risks of wireless networking and children using a desktop, but mainly laptop computers equipped with wireless cards (often called wireless NICs).

- Mobile computers with wireless access can bypass Internet security service protections by simply connecting to another unsecured wireless access point to access the Internet.
- Laptops can be used in places where parents can't easily monitor them. PC Tattletale should be installed on them to accurately report what they're being used for, regardless of where they are connected.
- Laptops can bypass home hardware firewalls (sometimes called firewall appliances) by accessing the Internet through another Wi-Fi access point. I recommend installing software firewalls on the computer itself, and then blocking children from uninstalling them with a user account with full operating system administrator privileges.
- Instead of spending the next several pages talking about wireless networks and security, I offer the following simple advice.

1. Install CyberPatrol and set blocks for appropriate ages on any laptop used by a child.
2. If Wi-Fi is enabled, install PC Tattletale with stealth and review usage frequently.
3. If unacceptable violations occur, warn once, then revoke the laptop and give them use of a desktop PC with or without Internet depending on the severity of inappropriate use.
4. Laptops should be considered a luxury item for your children, and they need to know that if the privilege is misused, there will be repercussions, including revoking Internet access or the laptop itself.

RECOMMENDATIONS

I know that there's a lot of material to digest in this chapter, but the topics are important for parents and educators to understand. This chapter contains important information to have a solid grasp of, along with Chapter 5, which discusses specific software programs to help monitor and protect children. The following recommendations are provided to help parents get started in this area. Recommendations are broken down by age category.

All Ages

- Use the built-in personal firewall in Windows.
- Use a software firewall program (BlackICE or F-Secure) to better protect incoming and outgoing traffic.
- Lock down children's user accounts on computers in the home to prevent them from installing software. This should work well without any resistance from elementary and middle school children. For Windows XP, open the Control Panel, select User Accounts, select the appropriate user, select Change my account type to limited.
- Install PC Tattletale on all laptops in the home and enable stealth mode from time to time for middle and high school children. Review usage via the play-back feature as needed.
- Using your software firewall, block the FTP protocol for all users.

Category 1: Elementary School (Ages 8–11)

- Enable CyberPatrol Internet filtering software on all computers that children use to access the Internet and set the filter strength to Custom. For this age category, I recommend blocking newsgroups and chatgard.

- Within CyberPatrol, set *all* of the Web categories (adult/sexually explicit, chat, etc.) to the *maximum* strength filter. The easiest way to do this is to select the preset filter strength = Child, which is accessible in the Web categories section.
- Add the following search engines and social networking sites to Cyber Patrol's blocked list:

  - www.google.com
  - www.altavista.com
  - www.ask.com
  - http://search.aol.com
  - http://search.msn.com
  - www.live.com
  - http://search.yahoo.com
  - www.myspace.com
  - www.friendster.com
  - www.xanga.com
  - www.facebook.com
  - www.livejournal.com
  - www.piczo.com
  - www.bebo.com
  - www.xuqa.com
  - www.hi5.com

- If necessary, add the recommended safe search sites listed in this chapter to the CyberPatrol approved site list.

Category 2: Middle School (Ages 12–14)

- Children aged 12–14 are going through an interesting transition from children to teenager. All children in this group should have Internet filtering software installed on all of the computers that they use.
- Within CyberPatrol, set *all* of the Web categories (adult/sexually explicit, chat, etc.) to a *high* or *maximum* strength filter. The easiest way to do this is to select the preset filter strength = Young Teen, which is accessible in the Web categories section.
- Add the following search engines and social networking sites to Cyber Patrol's Web sites blocked list:

  - www.google.com
  - www.altavista.com

- www.ask.com
- http://search.aol.com
- http://search.msn.com
- www.live.com
- http://search.yahoo.com
- www.myspace.com
- www.friendster.com
- www.xanga.com
- www.facebook.com
- www.livejournal.com
- www.piczo.com
- www.bebo.com
- www.xuqa.com
- www.hi5.com

- Read *MySpace Unraveled* by Larry Magid and Anne Collier (available at bookstores and online at Amazon.com). This book is not terribly long, but it serves as a good reference for how the hottest social networking site works along with some helpful tips for parents.
- If you decide to allow certain more mature categories like social networking or IM, I highly recommend installing PC Tattletale and enabling stealth mode so that you can appropriately monitor what they're doing online. Actions required by parents may include logging into their children's social networking accounts to see what they've sent, received, and posted to private audiences versus the public Internet. If you find activities of sites accessed that you don't approve of, simply add those sites to the Cyber Patrol list of blocked sites.
- Change administrative passwords for CyberPatrol, PC Tattletale, and your home computer's operating system from time to time. I recommend monthly to quarterly as teenagers may attempt to bypass these controls by guessing your passwords.
- Using your software firewall, block the FTP protocol for all users.
- Add appropriate keywords to CyberPatrol's blocked keywords list to ensure that kids can't find inappropriate material. Add the following: porn, sex, xxx, gay, lesbian, nude, and naked. Use your imagination and add to this list as you see fit.

Category 3: High School (Ages 15–17)

- Children aged 15–17 are evolving into young adults, which requires allowing more online liberties and freedom. Teenagers should have Internet filtering software installed on all of the computers that they use to access the Internet, especially those with wireless network cards.

- Within CyberPatrol, set *all* of the Web categories (adult/sexually explicit, chat, etc.) to a *medium* through *maximum* strength filter. The easiest way to do this is to select the preset filter strength = Mature Teen, which is accessible in the Web categories section. Keep in mind, using this setting allows chat, so I recommend setting it to a much higher filter strength (say, high)—chat rooms are risky even for mature teens.
- Teenagers will most likely be using full-strength search engines in support of their schoolwork, so you'll need to add to CyberPatrol's approved Web site list:

  - www.google.com
  - www.altavista.com
  - www.ask.com
  - http://search.aol.com
  - http://search.msn.com
  - www.live.com
  - http://search.yahoo.com

- If you decide to allow more mature categories like social networking or IM, install PC Tattletale and enable stealth mode so that you can appropriately monitor what they're doing online. If you find activities on sites accessed that you don't approve of, simply add those sites to the CyberPatrol list of blocked sites. For this age group, PC Tattletale exposes more sophisticated approaches to sharing and concealing inappropriate content. Data keys seem to be the tool of choice for storing files away from the home computer where they can be easily searched by parents. PC Tattletale puts parents back in charge of computer and Internet security for their children. For this age category, it should be used frequently to ensure that kids are safe on the Internet. It will record all activities, including data key file transfers and thus help keep children safe by keeping parents in the loop.
- Change administrative passwords for CyberPatrol, PC Tattletale, and your home computer's operating system from time to time. I recommend monthly to quarterly as teenagers may attempt to bypass these controls by guessing your passwords.
- Maintain a list of blocked keywords in CyberPatrol that are appropriate for your mature teen.

Seven

Email

Email is the electronic leash of the modern day. Instant messaging will replace it in the near future.

—Gregory S. Smith

EMAIL OPTIONS AND PROGRAMS

This chapter will likely be one of the easiest for parents and teachers to understand because many adults in industrialized and developing nations have and actively use an email account. Quite a few working parents have two accounts, one for business and one for personal messages. Most children, starting with middle school and into high school, have multiple email accounts, sometimes as many as five or six. Why? Usually for the following three reasons: (1) It's easy to set up a free account. (2) They do so to assert their independence. (3) They do so to elude monitoring from their parents. If you think you're on top of monitoring your teenager's online mail, you're probably mistaken—they may have multiple free accounts at mail services like Yahoo!, Google, Microsoft, and Lycos. According to About.com, the following are some of the top free email Web sites and services available.

1. Gmail (Google)
2. Inbox.com
3. Yahoo! Mail
4. AIM Mail (AOL)

5. Goowy Mail
6. Hotmail
7. Lycos Mail[1]

Beyond these examples, there are literally hundreds of alternative sites that children can use to sign up for free and use Web-based email programs—many without their parents' knowledge. If this isn't a great reason to stealth monitor your child's email activities, I don't know what is. Parents can't possibly have the time to keep track of the various email accounts and passwords. A far better use of their time is to use PC Tattletale (see Chapter 5) and let the software program do what it does best—record children's online activities.

Types of Email Service

There are essentially three main types of email services.

- Web-based
- POP3
- IMAP[2]

Web-based mail is probably the most common among children, especially teens, because they can access their account from a Web browser and an Internet connection from pretty much anywhere on the planet. All messages, sent, received, and stored in personal folders are maintained online at the mail hosting provider for each user.

POP3 email services initially store email on the hosted server from the email provider. Users select from a variety of robust email packages, like Outlook or Eudora, and install the desired program to have more features. POP3 users usually access their email on the remote POP3 server, download new messages to their computer, and send messages authored and queued to be sent. Users can typically configure a POP3 account to delete messages already downloaded from the hosted server or keep a second copy. Most POP3 users use local email and POP3 services because it's easier and faster to write and read messages on their computer, especially with low-speed Internet connections, compared to waiting for Web pages to refresh in a browser's window. This approach also allows users to manage larger amounts of email and file attachments on their own computer and not have to worry about disk space limitations for most online Web email services, which tend to limit disk space per user to between 50 MB and 2 GB. Email messages with large file attachments can quickly fill up a Web-based email system quota. Like POP3, IMAP works with an email program to download email messages from a remote server. In addition, IMAP allows more control such as synchronizing mail folders between a local computer and a remote IMAP server.

The following are several popular free email programs that can be downloaded and installed on Windows-based computers.

- Mozilla Thunderbird
- Eudora
- Opera
- Outlook Express
- Pegasus Mail[3]

Thunderbird, Opera, and Outlook Express are probably the most popular programs; each has solid third-party reviews and robust features. Your child is probably using either a Web-based service or accessing email through one of these programs.

EMAIL RISKS

So what are the risks of children using email today? The following are what I consider to be the top five threats.

1. Predators look for email addresses on Web sites and social networking sites, then expand their search for more relevant and personal information.
2. Spam (unwanted email) can reach children with a variety of tricks (scams) or inappropriate content, such as graphic pornography or seemingly harmless links that actually go to adult content sites.
3. Computer viruses and worms can damage a computer, increase the risk of information loss, and require expensive consulting to repair. Kids typically open more file attachments or messages from strangers than adults. Some of these files contain harmful computer viruses. Special offer scams typically try to trick teens into giving up personal information to obtain a fake prize, like winning an iPod.
4. Many children using email software disclose their full name every time they send an email. This is often referred to as a "user name," "full name," or "real name" in email programs like Outlook Express. Send yourself an email from your child's installed email program and see if their full name appears in the From heading. If it does, it should be changed in the

program to only disclose, say, a first name or an irrelevant alias, which is even safer. Consult your specific email program's help section for instructions on how to change the sent user name.

5. Some free Web mail isn't secure, which is usually indicated by the lack of a locked key logo on the browser's window. User IDs and passwords can be compromised by hackers and predators, because the text for the account and password pass across the Internet unencrypted.

KID-FRIENDLY EMAIL PROGRAMS

Fortunately, there are a number of kid-friendly email programs available, most for a small monthly fee. Several are fairly good at greatly reducing spam and eliminating porn from arriving in your child's inbox. Of course, no one can guarantee a risk-free email experience, especially if your child posts his or her email address on a public Web page or social networking site or trades inappropriate files and photos. The following services are some great alternatives to risky free email services for children and teenagers.

- Kidmail.net (currently $6 per month after a free trial or $30 per year for up to 10 email addresses; www.kidmail.net)
- Zoobuh.com (30-day free trial, then $1 per month per child account; www.zoobuh.com)
- AOL email with AOL Parental Controls enabled (site.aol.com/info/parent control.adp)
- Earthlink with Parental Controls enabled (earthlink.net/software/free/ parentalcontrols)

The first two are typically geared toward parents with younger children (elementary to the beginning of middle school) and have lots of parental controls, such as determining who can email the child's account, parental review/approval of unknown incoming mail before it gets to a child's inbox, and redundant copies of sent and received emails sent to a parent or guardian's email address as kind of an audit trail. Other more mature offerings from Earthlink and AOL (with parental controls enabled) are more suitable for older middle school to high school teenagers and don't come with an adolescent email domain name. Many children use these services but don't enable parental controls. They're missing a valuable option in the arsenal to protect their children. These services without parental controls are too risky even for middle school kids. Offerings like AOL email with parental controls is even configurable for different age ranges, such as young teen (ages 13–15) and mature teen (ages 16–17), that are similar to what CyberPatrol has to offer to ease configuration for Internet content filtering.

TRICKS KIDS USE TO HIDE EMAIL ACTIVITIES

If parents want to be one step ahead of their kids, they need to be tech-savvy and think creatively, like cunning children often do. Kids (mainly teenagers) use the following activities to hide or conceal what they do on email.

- Maintain multiple accounts, often Web-based services, and rotate through them as needed.
- Delete messages from their sent folder and inbox that they don't want their parents to see.
- Send questionable file attachments with innocuous file names, such as homework1.doc or class-notes.xls.
- Save questionable file attachments to data keys or thumb drives to conceal their contents.
- Delete temporary Internet files and history from their browser and hard drive to conceal what they've seen via the Web.

I applaud creativity, but it's no match for PC Tattletale, which records all activity and allows parents to play back hidden recorded files like they're watching a movie (see Chapter 5). That's why I recommend using stealth software for troubled or vulnerable middle school children and all high school teens who are active on the Internet.

BLOCKING FREE EMAIL SERVICES

This part is simple. To block free email services that are risky, such as the ones listed earlier in the chapter, simply add the Web sites to the CyberPatrol blocked sites list and voilà! You're done! If you think your child is using another version of an email program, you can do the following.

- Install PC Tattletale and enable it in stealth mode.
- Capture Web site activities, including account names and passwords.
- Log into their new email accounts and take a look for suspicious or inappropriate email.
- If desired, add the new email site/service to the CyberPatrol blocked list.

Some Web sites/services make it harder for minors to open a new account than others. Security-conscious sites not only ask for age verification but also require a credit card to activate a free account in an attempt to protect minors. Unfortunately, it's still relatively easy for a child to find a free email service and sign up without any parental involvement or approval. Within about three minutes, I was able to successfully set up Web-based email accounts on both Yahoo! mail and Mail.com by simply lying about my age, selecting an email address name, and accepting the terms displayed on the site—all without any parental approval or requirement for a credit card. The recommendations section at the end of this chapter contains specific free email Web site addresses that parents can block to help protect their children. This list is not all-inclusive, but PC Tattletale will expose any others that children are using and can be shut down and blocked by CyberPatrol. Thus, part of the strategy of this book is to arm parents with the right technology and an effective road map to protect their children. PC Tattletale combined with CyberPatrol is the one-two punch that can do the job.

FILE ATTACHMENT RISK

Given that most parents use email and are aware of the risks associated with file attachments, this section will be short and sweet. Talk to your children about the risks (viruses, inappropriate content, predators, etc.) and repeatedly tell them *not* to open attachments or email from anyone they don't know. If you see your children using data keys frequently, they may be storing traded file attachments to avoid inspection by a parent. Ask to see their data keys from time to time and do a file inventory using your computer. Turning on thumbnails for images will allow parents to quickly view image pictures without having to open them one by one. To find out any other file attachment concealment strategies, it's PC Tattletale to the rescue!

DON'T FORGET ABOUT SPAM

Spam is unwanted email. It comes in a variety of forms that can be risky for children, including adult content, inappropriate advertisements, special offers and scams, racially insensitive content, and get-rich-quick schemes. Children who see an offer to receive a free iPod will be more likely click on the link because they truly believe, especially at younger ages, that they've just won a free prize. The reality is that they could be directed to a site that may attempt to capture personal data or, even worse, relay the user to an adult site that displays graphic content, including video clips or still pictures. According to Postini , a world leader in anti-SPAM and anti-virus products and services, spam represents a significant portion of email and is a threat to businesses and consumers.[4] The Postini Resource Center, which tracks spam for their customers, recently reported that every 10 out of 12 email messages, or just over 81.5 percent, were tagged as spam and quarantined for their customers in a normal day.[5] On the particular day that I was monitoring the Postini Web site, the number of messages tagged as spam reached 371,541,404 in a 24-hour period, out of 562,866,069 messages scanned.[6] In addition, during that same 24-hour period, 1 in 335 messages was determined to contain a virus.[7] The numbers reported by Postini clearly demonstrate that spam is a problem for email customers worldwide.

To mitigate the risks of spam, parents can choose one of two options. The first is to install an anti-spam program on their computer, configure it, and set up the program to receive updates as necessary. The second option is to select an email provider that incorporates anti-spam and anti-virus capabilities directly into their email service and attempts to block them before the email is delivered to the account. I strongly advocate the latter approach. It's easier for parents and doesn't require any complicated installations and update procedures. The email services listed earlier in this chapter provide decent anti-spam features as part of their offerings. It's a no-brainer that requires less time and energy. Parents already expend enough energy working, raising children, and trying to protect them online. When something comes along that can help them reduce spam and viruses, even for a fee, it is well worth the cost.

RECOMMENDATIONS

The following recommendations are provided to help parents protect their children against the risks of email and related technologies.

Recommendations for All Ages

- Lock down children's user accounts on computers in the home to prevent them from installing new email software on your computer.
- Install PC Tattletale on all laptops in the home and enable stealth mode from time to time for middle and high school children. Review usage via the movie playback feature as needed and remember to delete log files to prevent filling up disk drives.

- Set a family policy that email account passwords are to be known by parents and not changed by children. If they are changed, revoke their account for a month and add the email service/site to the blocked site list in Cyber Patrol. I'm a fan of warning once before fully revoking a privilege. If your child repeatedly changes an email account password, he or she may be trying to conceal what they're doing online. In this scenario, parents have two options: use PC Tattletale to see exactly what the child is using email for and, if necessary, revoke the privilege, or just revoke email as a privilege until they are older and can better respect the rules. Remember—parenting is not a democracy. It's the parent's job to make the best decisions necessary to protect their children and that means establishing some rules with clear repercussions.

Category 1: Elementary School (Ages 8–11)

- Children in this age category should *not* have an email account. When my children were in this age bracket, I held firm on this position, even though they asked repeatedly and threw tantrums when I said no. Don't budge on this. Cell phones are safer alternatives to email accounts at this age in the event that a child needs to stay in touch with a parent or caregiver.
- My recommendation above is strong, and I recognize that there may be exceptions, such as the use of school email accounts to support homework assignments. If you do allow your younger child to have an email account, use one of the kid-friendly email programs or one that is provided by the school itself. If school provided, check to see if spam is being blocked and, if not, raise the issue with the school principal.
- Kid-friendly email accounts alone won't help keep your child safe, so parents will need to monitor what their kids are doing online. Inspect their email accounts by logging in as them once a week and reviewing files sent and received by navigating through folders and their inbox. If possible, set their deleted folder to not purge data for at least seven days. This will allow parents to view what their child has deleted in the course of using the service over the last week.

Category 2: Middle School (Ages 12–14)

- Set a family policy of one email account per child and enforce it. Allowing children to maintain multiple accounts adds risk and can be time-consuming for parents to monitor. A classic trick that kids at this age use is to use an approved email account while their parents are observing and then use another free email *unapproved* account to elude their parents. If you suspect your child is using multiple accounts, turn on PC Tattletale in stealth mode and analyze their usage. As appropriate, add unapproved sites to the CyberPatrol blocked list to clamp down on violators.

- Kid-friendly email accounts alone won't keep your child entirely safe, so parents will need to monitor what they're kids are doing online. Inspect their email accounts by logging in as them once a week and reviewing files sent and received. If possible, set their deleted folder to not purge data for at least seven days. This will allow parents to view what their child has deleted in the course of using the service.
- Have frequent conversations with your children about the risks of opening and responding to emails from senders they don't know. They should *never* respond to an email from someone that they don't know and *never* open a file attachment from unknown senders as well. If they don't respond to email, they can't potentially give out personal data to a stranger.
- Teach your child to *never* knowingly publish or allow his or her email account names to any public Web site, including a school Web site, which can expose risks of sexual predators. If this occurs unknowingly, contact your school's administrator immediately.
- Ensure that the email provider that you select doesn't flood your child's email account with potentially inappropriate spam. If it does, contact your provider and see if they can correct it. If they cannot, switch to another provider that offers a better anti-spam solution that is built into their email offering. Select one of the four safe email sites/services described earlier in this chapter.
- Add the following free email sites to CyberPatrol's blocked list.

  - http://gmail.google.com, www.google.com/accounts/SmsMailSignup1, www.google.com/accounts/ServiceLoginAuth
  - www.inbox.com, www.inbox.com/register/email.aspx
  - www.goowy.com
  - https://login.yahoo.com/config/mail?.intl=us, www.yahoo.com/r/m1, www.yahoo.com/r/m2
  - http://webmail.aol.com, https://new.aol.com
  - http://hotmail.msn.com, http://login.live.com/login.srf?id=2, http://join.msn.com
  - www.mywaymail.com

- http://mail.lycos.com
- www.mail.com

Category 3: High School (Ages 15–17)

- Set a family policy of one email account per child and enforce it. If you suspect your child is using multiple accounts, turn on PC Tattletale in stealth mode and analyze their usage. As appropriate, add unapproved sites to the CyberPatrol blocked list to clamp down on violations.
- Parents need to more aggressively monitor what their kids are doing online via email and other tools at this age. There are two options: (1) inspecting email accounts by logging in as them once a week and reviewing files sent and received by navigating folders and their inbox, or (2) using PC Tattletale in stealth mode and reviewing their activity on a more frequent basis. Teenagers are more likely to use data keys in support of school projects. Look for exchanges of inappropriate files (videos, pictures, etc.) via your child's email account and attempts to save them (possibly by renaming the files) to their data key. PC Tattletale provides some insights into what may be going on, but at the end of the day, parents may need to ask for their child's data key and inspect what's on it. If the key contains significant objectionable material, parents have a lot of options that include revoking accounts and access to the Internet in general via CyberPatrol.
- Have frequent conversations with your teenagers about the risks of opening and responding to emails from senders that they don't know. They should *never* respond to an email from someone that they don't know and *never* open a file attachment from unknown senders as well.
- Teach your teenagers to *never* knowingly publish or allow email account names to be published on any public Web site—including a school Web site, which can expose risks of sexual predators to children. If this occurs unknowingly, contact your school's administrator immediately.
- Ensure that the email provider that you select doesn't flood your child's email account with potentially inappropriate spam. If it does, contact the provider and see if they can correct it. If they cannot, switch to another provider that offers a better anti-spam solution that is built into their email offering.
- Block the same set of free email sites/services that are recommended for category 2. Earthlink and AOL are good options for teenagers when com-

pared to the other younger branded email domains recommended in this chapter.

- Use PC Tattletale as you see fit to monitor what they're doing online via email, especially if your child is using a laptop equipped with a wireless networking card. Many of the free email services on the Internet can't be blocked by a port number because they mostly use the http protocol and port 80 or 443 (secured login) to communicate. Thus, parents should review the PC Tattletale logs and block sites where appropriate.

Instant Messaging and Voice-over-IP

For a list of all the ways technology has failed to improve the quality of life, please press three.

—Alice Kahn

IM BASICS AND TOOLS

Instant messaging (IM) tools are very popular, especially with younger computer users up to and including Generation X adults working in businesses, nonprofits, and academic institutions. People of all ages are starting to embrace IM because it has recently expanded into cell phones and PDAs. IM traffic sent over the Internet is expected to eclipse that of email by 2012. IM is essentially a software program that enables real-time communication between users, usually facilitated by an intermediary company and service like America Online, Microsoft, or Yahoo! Compared to email, which can take longer to deliver messages because they are queued by mail servers and log all outgoing and incoming mail, IM is more like a quick online chat between two or more parties. Due to the near real-time capability, IM is faster than email and for that reason alone has become the tool of choice for an individual that wants to instantly send a message to another person connected to the Internet.

IM has some financial benefits for its users as well. The number one monetary benefit that I hear all the time is that it's cheaper to place a phone call using IM than to make a long-distance call to another country via a traditional phone company. I personally know many businesses and individuals using IM tools to make phone calls to friends and colleagues in other countries in an effort to save money. This capability is often referred to as a voice-over-IP (or VOIP) feature within the IM program itself. Although many IM tools have voice capabilities, the quality of phone calls made over the Internet can vary greatly from crystal clear calls to delayed ones with significant static.

IM tools have evolved over the past few years with additional entrants into the marketplace. The following describes the main features of IM tools.

- Users can chat with one another. Chatting is essentially sending small text messages to one another over the Internet. Chatting requires both parties to be connected to the Internet and available using the same IM tool to communicate.
- You can send files and pictures to one another. Essentially, most IM tools have built-in FTP capabilities, but many of these tools don't necessarily use that protocol to send and receive files, making them harder to block.
- You can make voice phone calls over the Internet. Headphones or speakers are usually required.
- You can send off-line messages to friends and colleagues. A few IM programs allow this. This functionality resembles that of email and can also provide an audit trail of what was sent and received.
- You can use Web cameras to conduct real-time video sessions or send prerecorded video files to other users, which is similar to sending a file attachment.

Most IM users communicate with others online that are also accessing the Internet via an IM service. Users typically maintain a buddy list (an address list of all their IM friends) and can readily see when their friends are online. There are a variety of IM programs available, most of them free, but they usually don't work together. Microsoft's IM tool, Windows Live Messenger, recently announced that their tool would work with Yahoo!'s Messenger. For the most part though, one vendor's IM program doesn't interoperate and send messages to another vendor's tool. As an example, AOL Instant Messenger will not work with Google Talk. The following are some of the more popular free IM programs available with advanced features indicated.

1. Google Talk (www.google.com/talk): voice calls, offline IM.
2. AOL Instant Messenger (www.aim.com): broadcast messages to many, voice calls with AIM Phoneline, logging of messages, offline IM.
3. ICQ (www.icq.com): voice calls.

4. Yahoo! Messenger (messenger.yahoo.com): voice calls, IM chat with Windows Live Messenger, offline IM.
5. MSN Windows Live Messenger (get.live.com): voice calls, IM chat with Yahoo! Messenger, Web camera/video capable.
6. Skype (www.skype.com): voice calls, group chat (up to 100 people), video camera integration.

Beyond these popular sites, there are plenty more alternative programs and related freeware Web sites and tools that offer IM features. Many of the other freeware and shareware sites may come with additional risks, such as exposure to viruses and spyware. A popular IM tool available via a number of sites is Trillian (www.ceruleanstudios.com). It allows users to talk to pretty much any IM program.

The core list of popular programs combined with hundreds of lesser known sites is justification to apply an aggressive block and stealth monitoring approach to IM, especially for children in elementary and middle school. Parents can't possibly have the time to keep track of the various IM tools and passwords. A far better use of their time is to use CyberPatrol's capabilities and turn on PC Tattletale stealth monitoring as needed to combat the risks. Interestingly enough, when I blocked IM chat in CyberPatrol, it was effective at blocking most IM-related Web sites (but not all of them). The following represents the IM sites that I was and was not able to get to and download IM software with CyberPatrol's chat Web category set to the highest level of blocking:

- Allowed: Google, Yahoo!
- Blocked: AOL, Skype, ICQ, MSN

So what are the real risks for children using IM? Parents see other kids using IM and text messaging from their PCs and cell phones all the time, and may assume there must not be any risk associated with these products. The following represent my top threats associated with children using IM tools.

1. IM provides an easy way for strangers to contact children.
2. IM users can receive unwanted messages, like email, that could contain links to adult content and other inappropriate content.
3. If configured inappropriately, IM tools allow anyone on the service to see the user's contact name, or screen name, and message them as they see fit. Many children, when installing these products, don't check off the box that only allows their buddies to contact them, thus exposing their

screen name to the world. There are additional preference settings that may expose an IM screen name if one knows the user's email address. This type of connection is what predators look for.

4. Unlike email, IM conversations between parties are not typically logged or recorded, unless the user specifically does so. This provides for unaudited communication between parties that parents can't review to determine if their children are at risk. Without some type of monitoring tool like PC Tattletale, parents don't know who their children are IMing and what they're talking about. That's a significant risk.

5. IM tools allow children to share photos and send files without a log or trace for parents to review.

6. IM screen names are often disclosed in chat rooms along with other forums. Predators look for IM names and email addresses on Web sites, in chat rooms, and in social networking sites then expand their search for more relevant and personal information in preparation for finding their next online victim.

7. Many IM tools provide for nondocumented or logged voice calls over the Internet to people anywhere in the world. No sane parent would let their child randomly call a stranger from another country using their home phone. IM voice features provide one of the biggest risks to children that predators love to expose. VOIP between computers is a predator's dream and the easiest way for them to communicate via voice in stealth and beyond a parent's control.

IM LINGO PARENTS MUST KNOW

For parents to truly understand what their children are doing on the Internet, they need to get up to speed on the IM lingo that's used. This is necessary so that parents and teachers can decode online communications and shorthand to meaningful text. Children, especially teenagers, often talk in "code" using IM and chat tools to elude their parents and tip off their online buddy that a parent or older sibling is near or monitoring their IM conversation. Table 8.1 provides a list designed to help parents walk the walk and talk the talk.

BLOCKING IM: IT'S NOT EASY

For parents and teachers to understand how to block IM for younger children, they need to know a bit more about how IM works (see Figure 8.1). IM programs need to be installed on any computer where the user wishes to use it.

Table 8.1 IM Lingo Translated

Code	Translation	Code	Translation
2NITE	tonight	P911	parent alert
ADR	address	PAW	parents are watching
AEAP	as early as possible	PIR	parent in room
ALAP	as late as possible	POS	parent over shoulder
ASL	age/sex/location	QT	cutie
BRB	be right back	RN	right now
F2F	face to face	RU	are you?
GYPO	get your pants off	RUMORF	are you male or female?
IWSN	I want sex now	SITD	still in the dark
KFY	kiss for you	SMEM	send me an email
KPC	keeping parents clueless	SMIM	send me an instant message
LMIRL	let's meet in real life	SO	significant other
LOL	laugh out loud	SorG	straight or gay
MOOS	member of opposite sex	TDTM	talk dirty to me
MorF	male or female	TOM	tomorrow
MOTSS	member of the same sex	TS	tough shit
NAZ	name, address, ZIP	TTFN	ta-ta for now
NIFOC	nude in front of computer	WUF	here are you from?
OLL	online love	WYCM	will you call me?
OTP	on the phone	WYRN	what's your real name?

Source: www.netlingo.com

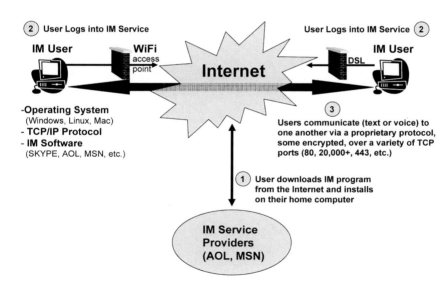

Figure 8.1 How IM Works

The bulk of IM users download their favorite tool from one of the top vendors listed earlier. Once installed, users create a screen name and password that is registered in the IM service provider's directory listing so that other IM users can chat with the new user. Once the registration process is complete, the user can browse from a directory listing of public IM names or simply start building their own buddy list with input from their friends and colleagues. To IM or call someone on the list, users simply double-click the user's screen name and start chatting in real time or send a message to an off-line user.

Most IM products are really hard to block. Many corporations and businesses invest thousands of dollars of time and labor trying to block these tools from their computing environment because they pose security and productivity risks for employers. IM products communicate on various ports, sometimes changing from port to port if a firewall is attempting to block the desired port. There can be literally hundreds of ports that these programs will jump to so as to evade firewalls. Many of the most sophisticated IM products use standard ports that are open for other Web traffic, such as port 80 and port 443, which is used for encrypted traffic. Some IM tools encrypt the communication so that it can't be intercepted across the open Internet and so it can pass through a personal or corporate firewall easily.

Fortunately, there are ways to block IM tools and traffic in the home environment. I've done some extensive testing to confirm that these programs can be effectively blocked. If parents think that just blocking access to the IM Web sites will deter their children from using IM chat clients, they're wrong. Kids are smart. They share downloaded programs with friends and trade installation programs that they can't get access to on the Internet with friends via data keys and CDs. Blocking IM requires the following steps.

1. Block chat in CyberPatrol's tool. Simply set the Web site category chat to maximum block strength and make sure all checkboxes are selected in the ChatGard section under chat programs to monitor.
2. Add additional Web sites listed in the recommendations section of this chapter to block the sites that CyberPatrol doesn't.
3. As needed, use PC Tattletale to monitor and identify other freeware IM tools your children are using and block them in CyberPatrol by using Program Restrictions instead of blocking just the Web site.
4. To close the door on the more difficult IM programs like Skype, parents need to first install the program and then block access to the program itself in CyberPatrol. The following is an example of how to block Skype, but the steps can be applied to any IM tool that you wish to block.

a. Download and install the Skype program.

b. In CyberPatrol, change Program Restrictions access level to Filter instead of Allow All.

c. Select the Customize menu associated with Program Restrictions and then select Customize Programs.

d. Select the Add button, then Find New Programs. I've found that the automatic listing that CyberPatrol doesn't always show all programs installed, which is why I recommend a manual search.

e. Manually locate the Skype program by navigating through the directory structure on the C: or D: drive where the application is installed. To block Skype along with the browser plug-in on the drive, select C:\Program Files\Skype\Phone\Skype and C:\Program Files\Skype\Plug-in Manager\SkypePM.

f. Add both programs to the CyberPatrol program listing.

g. Once added to the list, select each program, one at a time, and click on the access level radio button labeled Deny access at all times.

h. Save your changes for all users or the appropriate user profile.

5. I'd recommend this install and block approach for the Trillian IM tool as well since it's available to download from a lot of Web sites.

The next time a user tries to run Skype, it will be blocked by CyberPatrol and shut down—preventing the user from getting to the Internet using the program entirely. Great stuff!! The combination of the two tools I've recommended in this text (CyberPatrol and PC Tattletale) along with the road map will put parents and educators back in charge of managing their children's Internet experiences.

If parents want to be one step ahead of their kids when they use technology, they need to be tech-savvy and think creatively, like cunning minors often do. Kids, mainly teenagers, use the following activities to hide or conceal what they do on IM.

- Intentionally don't log the conversations, even if the IM tool has the capability.
- Use multiple IM programs.
- Send questionable file attachments with file names intended to not draw attention to them, such as homework1.doc or class-notes.xls.
- Save questionable file attachments to data keys to conceal their contents.

- Delete log files that they have recorded on their computer once the conversation of choice is completed and no longer needed.
- Conduct phone conversations with friends and strangers over the Internet, usually with the aid of a headset.
- Make and send private video clips using IM tools or engage in a real-time video session if the chat client offers that feature.

While I applaud this creativity, it's no match for PC Tattletale, which records all activity and allow parents to play back recorded files, including any of the activities listed above. That's why I recommend using stealth software for challenging middle schoolers and all high school teens that are active on the Internet. Late-night, always-on-the-Internet types of activities are tips for parents that there is something else that may be going on. Homework can't take that long.

CHAT ROOMS: A HANGOUT FOR PREDATORS

Chat rooms, sometimes referred to as online groups, are places for people to discuss just about anything. They are online discussion groups by category where people can login and converse with others. There are thousands of chat rooms on the Internet, hosted by a variety of providers ranging from Yahoo! to MySpace, and of course there are adult chat and video rooms. Top-line chat categories span the gamut and include topics like business, family, government, hobbies, sports, and relationships. A recent search on Yahoo! Groups list revealed the following chat room subcategories of adult content: divorce, extramarital affairs, gay, lesbian, bisexual, and swingers. Each of these categories can then have even more subcategories, getting more specific with each level down. Underneath the category of extramarital affairs, I found a group called *DiscreteDaytimePlaytime* that invites adults to apply for membership in a group that holds daytime orgies starting at noon and running until midnight, at various hotels in California. All a user needs to access a chat room or group like this is an account with the online provider. Thus, to gain access to the myriad of chat/discussion rooms on MySpace, all a child needs is a MySpace account.

Chat rooms or groups are not places for minors to be hanging out. I can think of no logical reason to allow an impressionable young middle school child access to a chat room. *None*! There are too many risks associated with discussing hobbies, likes, dislikes, fetishes, and so on with strangers, some of whom may be sexual predators masquerading as others in the chat room to hone in on their next prey. For children that need special help or someone to talk to, I recommend consulting with your physician or school counselor to get a recommendation for a psychiatrist or psychologist. If you suspect your child is using chat rooms that are not being blocked by CyberPatrol, use PC Tattletale to monitor their online activities and block the services you find offensive.

Online Gaming: Additional Risk

One of the most common ways for kids to chat online is through the use of Internet-enabled computer games. Many parents with an elementary school child that has access to the Internet have heard of the game Runescape. My son used to play this and while seemingly harmless at the surface, it has embedded chat in the game that allows other users to pose questions to someone that they virtually walk up to in the course of playing the game. Kids need to know that games can be dangerous places as well and that they should never give out any personal information, including their real name, to anyone that asks in an online game. If these types of games present problems, simply add the appropriate Web site to the CyberPatrol blocked list, and your risk will be decreased.

MAKING PHONE CALLS OVER THE INTERNET

One of the biggest risks of using sophisticated IM tools is the ability to place phone calls directly over the Internet. Children can use their home computer and IM software to make phone calls to anyone in the world. Predators love this technology because they can use it to develop a more personal relationship with a potential victim and not tip off parents that the call or communication even took place. My recommendation is clear —unsupervised (and unlogged) voice calls over the Internet by children is a significant risk and should be mitigated. Blocking IM and sites that offer these tools is at the top of the list of recommendations in this chapter. Children will be much safer if they use their parent's home phone or their own cell phone to place calls to people they know. If parents allow their child to have a cell phone, they should monitor the call logs from their phone provider and turn off text messaging, especially for younger children.

HOW PREDATORS FIND THEIR VICTIMS

Sexual predators are smart. They know how to develop online relationships with impressionable children, and they definitely know which tools to use and how to do so effectively. There's not a single tool or approach that arms a sexual predator with enough information to exploit a child. They usually piece together bits of information to get additional personal data and then move in using a variety of tools that can include email, IM, chat, and VOIP. Today's kids expose too much information about themselves in a variety of online forums and sites. Figure 8.2 provides an example on how a predator can gain personal information using different tools.

The following approach is just one example of how a predator can get access to enough personal information from a child to be dangerous.

1. Search teen chat rooms masquerading as a teenager, looking for email addresses and IM screen names.
2. Search online member profiles of popular social networking sites for additional information by using a found email address or IM screen name. Search for posted pictures of the child and friends and if need be—cross-reference any information found about their posted friends.
3. Armed with an email address or IM screen name, use a search engine to find any references of a related home or cell phone number.
4. Search online directories for a home address that is affiliated with a phone number.
5. Using mapping and driving direction Web sites, search for a map and directions to the home address.
6. Using other powerful search databases, look up school names and addresses within the proximity to the home address.

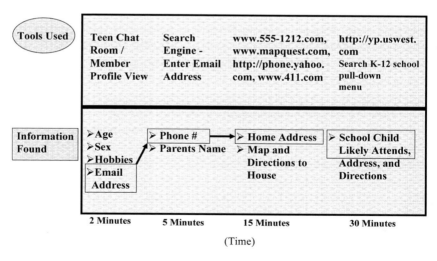

Figure 8.2 How Predators Get Personal Information

Simply put, the tools on the Internet combined with a child or teenager that (unintentionally or intentionally) posts personal content about themselves on the Internet can be found relatively easily by a predator or anybody else. It's the parents' job to help mitigate these risks, and that takes knowledge, tools (like CyberPatrol and PC Tattletale), and the will to do something about it.

RECOMMENDATIONS

The following recommendations are provided to help parents guard against the risks and dangers associated with these technologies.

All Ages

- Lock down children's user accounts on home computers to prevent them from installing new software like IM or peer-to-peer communications programs on your computer.
- Install PC Tattletale on all laptops and enable stealth mode from time to time for middle and high school children. Review usage via the movie play-back feature as needed and remember to delete log files.

Category 1: Elementary School (Ages 8–11)

- Children in this age category should *not* have an IM account and should not be making unsupervised phone calls over the Internet. These tools are even more dangerous than email accounts and are the preferred method of communication by sexual predators. Use CyberPatrol to block chat and the following IM tool sites:

  - www.google.com/talk
  - http://aimexpress.aol.com
  - www.aim.com
  - www.yahoo.com/r/p1
  - http://messenger.yahoo.com
  - http://get.live.com
  - http://login.live.com
  - www.icq.com
  - http://download.icq.com
  - www.adiumx.com

- www.bitwiseim.com
- http://www.ceruleanstudios.com

- Block chat via CyberPatrol using the procedures outlined in this chapter.
- If needed, use PC Tattletale to see what you're kids are doing online and block their preferred IM tools and chat room sites as necessary by adding them to the CyberPatrol blocked list of sites and programs. CyberPatrol is an effective tool at blocking IM tools only after they've been installed on your home computer.

Category 2: Middle School (Ages 12–14)

- Children in this age category should *not* have an IM account and should definitely not be making unsupervised phone calls over the Internet. Duplicate the recommendation on this one from category 1, including the list of blocked sites and programs.
- Block chat and chat room sites via CyberPatrol using the procedures outlined in this chapter.
- If needed, use PC Tattletale to see what you're kids are doing online and block their preferred IM tools and chat room sites as necessary by adding them to the CyberPatrol blocked list of sites and programs.
- If parents do allow their children to use IM, enable PC Tattletale *all the time* and review the logs frequently. Also, teach children to *never* publish their IM screen name on any public Web site or social networking site. Predators use these bits of information to hunt down their next potential victim.

Category 3: High School (Ages 15–17)

- Children in this age category will likely have an IM account to be social and fit in at school. Parents need to reinforce that IM is a privilege and if misused, it can be taken away. Standardize on just one IM tool and monitor your children by using PC Tattletale for inappropriate behavior or use.
- Recommend to your teenager that they do not use away messages with their IM tool. Away messages are popular with teens as they're a way of telling their friends what they are feeling, where they are, and so on. Unfortunately, these type of messages advertise too much information about them and add risk.

- Block chat rooms via CyberPatrol by using a combination of programs and blocked sites. Chat rooms are not for children of any age.
- Expose your mature teenagers to some of the risks associated on the Internet in plain terms. Teach them to *never* publish their IM screen name or favorite chat rooms on any public Web site or social networking site. Predators use these bits of information to hunt down their next potential victim.
- Put in place a family policy of no Internet phone calls and monitor via PC Tattletale. If a teenager break the rules, warn once, then block their IM tool with CyberPatrol's program restriction feature. Unsupervised phone calls with strangers on the Internet should not be allowed for any child, including teenagers.

Cell Phones and PDAs

Technology is dominated by two types of people: those who understand what they do not manage, and those who manage what they do not understand.

—Putt's Law

AN OVERVIEW OF PORTABLE COMMUNICATION DEVICES

Cell phones are the hot tool for most kids, and the devices have evolved to include many of the software components and features on standard computers. Global growth in the adoption of cell phones has exploded in the past decade or so, and is accelerating at an even more rapid rate in developing countries like India and China, where technology is redefining how people interact with one another. Over 1 billion mobile phones were shipped in 2006, a 22.5 percent increase from 2005.[1] Today's cell phones can really be broken down into the following four categories.

1. Child/restricted phones
2. Standard cellular phones
3. PDAs
4. Satellite phones

Child/restricted phones come in a variety of flavors, but all of them greatly limit what the phone holder can do. Most of these phones have a limited number of keys that restrict the number of phone numbers the user can call. They also restrict most other add-ons like downloading games or text messaging. Some of the phone providers in this category have built in global positioning system (GPS) capabilities that allow parents to find out where exactly their children are or where they placed their last call from. (I will discuss vendor and products in more detail later.) These types of phones are really simple phones that children can use to get a hold of a parent, teacher, or guardian in the event of an emergency.

Standard cell phones are what most teenagers and parents currently use. They offer a variety of features and add-ons, but the primary purpose of the device is to make phone calls. Some of the add-ons that are cool but add risk to children include instant messaging, Internet browsing, email, text messaging, cameras, and video camcorders. The majority of standard cell phones have 10-key phone pads that are fine for making calls but clunky for sending text or email messages. Many providers are now integrating MP3 players into their phones as more teenagers opt for listening to music as well as making phone calls.

PDAs (personal digital assistants) are used mainly by working professionals who need voice, email, and integrated calendars, contacts, and address books that are essential to managing their professional career and home environment. I use one of these devices and find it invaluable. The breakdown of features that I use most often on my PDA is as follows: 50 percent email, 30 percent voice calls, and 20 percent calendar activity—all of which is wirelessly synchronized with my email and calendar system at work. These devices are usually much more expensive in terms of initial purchase price and come with higher monthly usage fees for voice and data. Even though teens find PDAs attractive, they should be used for business purposes and are not ideal for children due to the number of features that can add risk.

Satellite phones are the last category of phones. They are the high-end version of communication intended for international travelers who must stay in contact anywhere on the globe. I've used these phones many times in my professional career, mostly to stay in contact with staff and colleagues at work and with family at home from remote locations like Nepal, Bhutan, Africa, and several locations in South America. Satellite phones are very expensive, ranging in price between $1000 and $2000, and require monthly service plans for per-minute usage. These are clearly not for children. Satellite phones are an option for the business elite and professionals that work in far off places with poor in-country communications systems.

Now I'll cover the types of functions that are readily available on phones and PDAs. The following describes the main features. Users can

- make voice calls and access voicemail where necessary
- download and play music (sometimes for a fee)
- download and play games
- browse the Internet
- manage contacts and calendars
- download various ring tones (usually for a fee)
- send and receive email. Many phones and PDAs have email programs built into them, and others allow users to download specialized email program add-ons from vendors like Google.
- send and receive text messages (SMS) to other phones
- push-to-talk two-way radio capability (certain models/networks)
- chat with other users. Chatting is essentially sending small text messages to one another over the Internet. Chatting requires both parties to be connected to the Internet and available using the same instant messaging (IM) tool to communicate.
- take, send, and receive photographs. Some carriers charge separate fees for sending photos via email, while others do not. Don't forget to read the fine print on your contract.
- view video files (downloaded or streamed)
- record video files and send them to other users. Most phone providers that have an integrated camera also provide for users to take short video clips, save them for future viewing, and send them to others as desired.

Considering all of these features, are the risks as high as with these features on a computer? Parents often see kids using text messaging, email, and browsing the Internet directly from their phone, and might assume that there must not be any risk associated with these devices. Because phones are mobile and in many ways used away from one's parents, they are actually *more* risky with a full feature set than similar tools on a desktop or laptop. The following list shows top threats associated with children using cell phones.

1. Cell phones have become the target of advertising with companies peddling their wares via text messages and email to cell phone users. That means getting advertisements for content that may be inappropriate for children.
2. Email accounts on a phone are more difficult for parents to monitor and screen. In addition, anti-spam tools and parental controls on phones are nowhere near as good as the protection available for computers today.
3. Monitoring software hasn't caught up to the mobile environment yet.

There isn't a PC Tattletale version for a phone at the moment, but it may be coming. Parents are at the cell phone provider's mercy when it comes to providing reports and appropriate content filters. The telecommunications industry in general is notorious for being behind on these kinds of technologies. They often roll out trendy new features and then think about security after the fact. It's a revenue game for this industry, not a safety focus.

4. IM software on a cell phone opens up the risk of hidden and nonlogged conversations between friends and potential sexual predators. Remember, IM is the preferred hidden tool of communication because many of the conversations are not logged. As consistent with my recommendation in Chapter 8, just say no to IM on the phone, too.

5. Internet access via a cell phone is a parent's nightmare and a huge risk for children, plain and simple. Most cell phone providers don't have parental controls for phones, and the ones that do have significant disclaimers on their Web site indicating that they may not work well. My tests revealed that most cell phones with Internet access provide an open portal to pretty much any content on the Internet. I even tested my BlackBerry's Internet access and was able to get to adult sites with pictures quite easily.

6. Camera and video capabilities are a risk on a phone if a child misuses the feature. Phones with email or IM capability can also display pictures and videos sent to the user. This means that there's an opportunity that a child may receive an email or picture from a stranger that contains pornography or other inappropriate content.

7. Cell phones and some of the add-ons, like IM and text messaging, can be very expensive for parents and teens if they don't pay attention to how their phone service provider charges for them. Most phone companies have discounted the cost of voice calls to within 2.5 to 5 cents per minute in the United States. At that rate, they're not making much money off of their customer. Thus, they bring in the add-ons. Text messaging can cost 15 cents per message, over 10 times the cost of a one-minute call. Parents need to restrict these types of extra fees and only provide the features their children need to stay in touch.

How Cell Phones Work and Where GPS Fits In

A cell phone is essentially a basic device and radio that contains a low-power transmitter which communicates via a series of towers and base stations.[2] Phones get their signal from the nearest cell tower, and as customers move from one area to another, one tower transfers the signal to the nearest one with a stronger signal.[3] Buildings and confined areas within them, like elevators, can present problems for cell phones because they can't find and connect to a tower and antenna with a strong enough signal. That's why people often drop calls in the center of large buildings or underground subway tunnels—there's no signal strong enough to carry the call through. The only way to guarantee a signal in areas like these is for the provider to install antennas inside those remote areas. Some corporations install such devices to ensure that their staff can get clear phone calls and send and receive email. When you're operating in a wireless environment, the nearest tower is king.

Cell phones with GPS capabilities also rely on radio waves, but instead of looking for the nearest ground-based tower, they look to the sky for the closest satellite orbiting the Earth.[4] Some cell phone service providers (like Sprint) have launched GPS location features with their phone, which allow parents to locate their children with the phone via satellite within a pretty good level of a accuracy—usually 100 to 500 yards.[5] To determine the location of a GPS phone holder, the GPS receiver has to determine the location of at least three satellites and then uses trilateration to determine the exact location, latitude and longitude, of the phone.[6] Some GPS phones use other methods to determine the location of the phone, including the use of satellites in conjunction with information about the cell phone's signal.[7] This is sometimes called enhanced GPS or wireless GPS and can often get a faster fix on the phone than just satellite-based approaches alone.[8] Sophisticated PDAs and cell phones with support for Java programming languages can actually turn them into navigational devices and provide nearly real-time driving instructions.[9] In any event, GPS phones are here to stay and are a valuable tool for parents who want to track their children's location.

Options on the Market Today

In an attempt to slice through the promotional material on phones, I've researched and recommended a number of phones and services that will help parents. I list them for each of the phone categories defined earlier. The following options are available for parents as they decide which technology to let their children use when it comes to phones.

Child/Restricted Phones

1. Firefly (www.fireflymobile.com)
   - $80 purchase price with service plans starting at $9.99/month
   - Five-key phone with no standard keypad, no contract, cancel any time

- Emergency button requires network access and works even if the phone is out of minutes
- Parental controls for incoming and outgoing phone numbers
- No GPS locator capability

2. Tictalk (www.tictalk.com)

   - $99 purchase price with various service plans
   - Download photos
   - Stop watch
   - Learning games included with points system for playing them
   - Parental controls for incoming and outgoing phone numbers

3. Wherifone (www.wherify.com)

   - $99 purchase price with various service plans starting at $20/month
   - World's smallest GPS locator capability and tracking phone
   - Parents can find phone location via the Web or another phone
   - Shows street and aerial maps and can automatically capture locations at preset times and days
   - No games or text messaging
   - 20-number phone book
   - SOS panic/emergency button, requires network access and works even if the phone is out of minutes
   - Parental controls for incoming and outgoing phone numbers

Standard Cell Phone Providers

1. Sprint GPS Locator phones (https://sfl.sprintpcs.com/finder-sprint-family/signIn.htm)

   - $99 and higher purchase price with various service plans for voice and data
   - GPS locator feature allows parents can find phone location via the Web or another phone (30+ phones to choose from)
   - Email, text messaging (SMS)
   - Bluetooth wireless to work with hands-free headsets
   - Push-to-talk two-way radio (on certain models)
   - View videos
   - Sound recorder

- Java capable—allows other types of programs, such as turn-by-turn navigation
- MP3 audio player
- Internet browsing on certain phones

2. Other GPS and non-GPS provider cell phones (AT&T, T-Mobile, etc.)

PDAs (Usually Include Fully Functional QWERTY Keypads)

1. BlackBerry (www.blackberry.com)
2. Nokia (www.nokia.com)
3. T-Mobile (www.t-mobile.com)
4. Sony Ericsson (www.sonyericsson.com)
5. Apple iPhone (www.apple.com)

Satellite Phones

1. Iridium (www.iridium.com)

As you can see from the features list in the standard cell phone category, there are a lot to choose from, complicating a parent's choice and also adding risk to a child or teenager. Most of the phones in this category don't offer GPS capabilities, so if you're interested in a phone service that has a program to track the user via GPS satellite and tower-based services, you need to ensure that the phone you purchase has that function.

Advanced PDAs offer many features and are designed to be good voice phones and excellent email communicators. Many of these devices allow for IM plug-ins so that users can maintain one IM service and screen name, regardless of whether they're communicating from their PDA or their computer. These sophisticated devices also usually have fully functioning Internet browsers and not stripped-down text versions like earlier devices. Email programs supported are also usually productive and some come with slimmed-down versions of Outlook. These are not worth the risk of trying to manage for children and are often too expensive anyway.

One Last Alternative for Pre-Phone Communication

Parents who have children in elementary school they want to keep track of have another slick option available on the market, but it that doesn't quite fit into the cell phone category. Two-way pagers allow parents to keep tabs on their kids within a short distance, usually one to two miles, and may work well when their children are playing outside their home or at a park. Two-way pagers have been around for years and are effective, low-cost devices. They don't however provide GPS tracking capabilities, just instant communication.

A recent newcomer to the two-way radio market is the Wristwatch Communicator from XACT. It's a pretty cool watch with a rugged case and digital screen that comes equipped with a small talk button below the watch dial.[10] The XACT Communicator retails for about $45 (it can be purchased online for about half that), requires no monthly service, is voice activated, and can communicate over a range of 22 channels to a distance reliably within a mile or two.[11] Thus, for parents who don't want to plunk down the cash for a moderately priced kid-friendly phone with service or a more expensive standard cell phone, this is a great option, especially in the early elementary school years. My wife found this device on the Internet in the course of researching less expensive tools for parents.

TEXT MESSAGING: HOW TEENS COMMUNICATE

Ok—time for a reality moment. Teens prefer to communicate via text messaging (SMS) because they think it's cool, discreet (their phone doesn't ring), and they can hide much of what they're saying from their parents. Texting has some risks, and it's an uphill battle for parents to fight. According to the Cellular Telecommunications and Internet Association, the number of text messages sent per month from 2001 to 2005 grew from a little over 14 million to 2.5 billion.[12] Keep in mind that many of the cell phone service providers like AT&T, Qwest, Sprint, and T-Mobile don't just let these messages fly from phone to phone without charging a fee. Fees can be incorporated into the monthly service charge for the phone, charged via a flat fee, say, for up to 200 messages per month, or individually at a high cost, up to 15 cents per message. The reality is that text messages are here to stay. Though not appropriate for younger children, text messaging will be a method of communication for your teenager.

MONITORING CALL LOGS AND BILLS

Because phones are mobile in nature, move in and out of the household, and can be pretty much controlled by the user, then need to be proactively monitored. Tricks teens might use to conceal their phone activities include the following.

1. Deleting sent and received text messages
2. Deleting the list of recent phone calls made
3. Taking photographs or short videos, emailing them to friends, and then deleting the audit trail of the message
4. If enabled, browsing adult-oriented Web sites on their phone and emailing some of the more interesting ones to their friends as links

As stated earlier, monitoring software and controls for computers aren't readily available for cell phones. This will become a growth market, and one that adult consumers will likely drive in the coming years. Today parents are at the mercy of logging and reporting capabilities from their cell phone service providers. I encourage all parents purchasing standard cell phones for their children to inquire about the types of monitoring and usage reports that can be delivered to them before buying the phone. If you're not comfortable with usage reporting (or lack thereof), you should greatly restrict the types of services on your children's phone. The recommendations section of this chapter provides some clear guidance in this area with regard to what features to allow and for what age category.

BROWSING AND IM CHALLENGES WITH PDAs

Children of all ages should *not* have a cell phone with an Internet browser. There really isn't any need for one, and the risks are too great. Cell phones should be used for voice calls, not browsing. I guarantee that they won't be researching web sites for homework on a cell phone with an Internet connection, so why give it to them. Blocking this feature will also keep them out of online chat rooms and social networking sites from their phone, if they are not be blocked by your cell phone service provider. This typically drives up the cost of the monthly service, as most vendors charge a fixed fee per month or by the amount of data , usually in megabytes, that is transferred through the network. In my professional career, I've rarely found a need for an Internet browser on my phone, but there are some businesses that use them to keep their employees in touch with key information via special programs designed for their PDA. Do yourself and favor and sleep better at night by keeping the Internet connections available for your children restricted to computers in your home, school, and libraries, where they can be better protected and monitored.

To close this section out, keep those nasty IM programs off of kid's cell phones, too. Remember, IM is a predator's preferred mode of communication because most of the messages are not logged by the individual users themselves.

Effective cell phones for middle and high school children have the following key features that most kids can live with.

- Voice calls
- Text messaging (for mature teens)
- Email (for responsible teens)
- MP3 players

Everything else comes with risk and isn't necessary.

RECOMMENDATIONS

The following recommendations are provided to help parents be effective with these risky technologies. As with prior chapters, recommendations are broken down by age category.

Category 1: Elementary School (Ages 8–11)

- Children in this age category should *not* have a cell phone. I recognize that there will be some exceptions, so for working parents who feel strongly that their child should have one in case of emergencies, select one of the child/restricted phones with limited services and keys, but ensure that it has GPS and the feature, possibly a locator service, is turned on. GPS can be a helpful tool if kids are missing.

For parents who insist on a cell phone for their elementary school child, follow these recommendations.

- Block text messaging (incoming and outgoing) and IM by contacting the cell phone service provider.
- Block Internet browsing by calling the cell phone service provider. The parental controls for cell phones today are not good, and many don't protect against adult content. *No child* should have a cell phone with Internet browsing. The risks are too great.
- Block email capabilities by contacting the cell phone service provider. This recommendation is consistent with not allowing elementary school children to have an email account.
- Purchase a cell phone that doesn't have a camera. They are unnecessary add-ons, and children in this age bracket will use them as toys.

- An alternative to a cell phones for this age category is a two-way radio or communicator, such as the Wristwatch Communicator from XACT. These devices cost less than cell phones, don't require monthly service plans, and are perfect for parents who want to keep in touch with their child as he or she plays outside with friends. They have a range of about 1 to 2 miles.

Category 2: Middle School (Ages 12–14)

- Purchase a cell phone from the standard cell phones category and ensure that it has a GPS capability that is turned on. I like what Sprint has to offer and believe that they've taken the lead on providing this valuable technology in the marketplace. GPS and locator Web-based and phone-based tracking add-ons can be especially helpful when keeping tabs on active teenagers and can come in handy if a child goes missing.
- I recommend that parents pay for their child's first cell phone, but consider having their children pay for a portion of the monthly usage bill. I've done this with my children and have found that it teaches kids responsibility and that people should work for the things that they want. From my perspective—nothing is free and if it is, it won't last forever.
- If desired, enable text messaging (incoming and outgoing), but review the text logs from time to time by asking to see the phone or calling the service provider and requesting a detailed usage report. Children at this age will likely press their parents for a phone that allows text messaging because it's the preferred way of communication for young teens. If your child receives unsolicited text messages from strangers, consider disabling the feature.
- Block IM by contacting the cell phone service provider. Parents should inspect the phone every few months to ensure that their children haven't downloaded and installed a free IM add-on for their phone. If they have, reinforce the rules with a warning and, if necessary, revoke the phone for repeat offenders.
- Block Internet browsing by calling the cell phone service provider. *No child* should have a cell phone with Internet browsing.
- Block email capabilities by contacting the service provider. For children at this age, email on a phone is a luxury. The primary purpose of a phone is to call someone, especially if there is an emergency. Don't lose sight of that purpose. Because parental controls and anti-spam measures aren't as good on phones as they are on computers, it's not worth exposing middle

school children to those risks. They should be happy with voice calls and text messaging.

- If parents purchase a phone with a built-in camera, they need to have a serious conversation with their child about the risks and acceptable use. Tell them the real life story about how students in New Jersey were expelled for taking pictures of other students and teachers and posting them to the Internet.
- Children at this age should *not* have a PDA. They're more expensive, usually come packed with additional features, and are not suited for children. Leave them to the working professionals.
- Add the following Web sites to CyberPatrol's blocked site list to prevent children from downloading mobile email and IM programs that can work on their phones:

  - http://mobile.google.com
  - http://sms.google.com
  - www.google.com/mobile/gmail
  - http://download.icq.com/download/icq2go
  - *http://mobile.yahoo.com*

Chapter 8 covers how to block Skype, which works for mobile phones as well. Unfortunately, there are too many other free mobile email programs to list in this chapter.

- Look at your child's phone from time to time and see what free add-on programs have been added. PC Tattletale may come in handy because most of these programs have to be downloaded to a computer before they can be installed on a phone. This is one other good reason to *not* allow Internet browsing from the phone itself, as teens can download any programs that work with their phone as they see fit.

Category 3: High School (Ages 15–17)

- Purchase a cell phone from the standard cell phones category and ensure that it has a GPS capability that is turned on. GPS and locator Web-based and phone-based tracking add-ons can be especially helpful when keeping tabs on active teenagers and can come in handy if a child goes missing.
- I recommend that parents pay for their child's first cell phone, but consider having their teenagers pay for a portion (possibly all) of the monthly usage

bill. Teens at this age should also pay for any phone upgrades and accessories. It teaches them responsibility at an appropriate age, and most teens are able to find some kind of work to earn money for the latest styling phone that they've just got to have. These are luxury items, not necessities.

- Enable text messaging (incoming and outgoing), but review the text logs from time to time by asking to see the phone or calling the service provider and requesting a detailed usage report. If your teenager receives unsolicited text messages from strangers, consider disabling the feature.
- Block IM and Internet browsing by calling the cell phone service provider.
- Enable email capabilities by calling the service provider and ensure that the provider turn on anti-spam features. If they don't have an anti-spam offering for their email function, then disable the feature. Spam and the varieties that they come in, including adult content, are not appropriate for any teenager.
- If you purchase a phone with a built-in camera, you need to have a serious conversation with your teen about acceptable use.
- Add the following Web sites to CyberPatrol's blocked site list to prevent children from downloading mobile email and IM programs that can work on their phones:

  - http://mobile.google.com
  - http://sms.google.com

Unfortunately, there are too many other free mobile email programs to list in this chapter.

- Look at your child's phone from time to time and see what free add-on programs have been added. PC Tattletale may also come in handy because most of these programs have to be downloaded to a computer before they can be installed on a phone. This is one other good reason to *not* allow Internet browsing from the phone itself because teens can download any programs that work with their phone as they see fit.
- Children at this age should *not* have a professional PDA. Again, they're best suited for adults, not children.
- Review your child's cell phone bill from time to time to see who they are communicating with, who they call versus who calls them, and how long the calls are. If there are odd or repeating entries, confront your child immediately and ask questions.

A Glimpse into the Future

The best way to predict the future is to invent it.

—Alan Kay

CONVERGING DEVICES

It's already starting to happen. Internet-enabled devices are rapidly proliferating in the marketplace, and vendors are rushing to produce and market products that have wired or wire-free access to the Internet. PCs with access to the Web have evolved to other, smaller, and more personal devices like cell phones, PDAs, and even watches. Television and media companies are also embracing the Internet as they look for alternatives to standard TV and cable programs to get content and advertisements to consumers.

At the end of the day, the devices on the market will converge in terms of features, but they will also expand in numbers of various types. Cell phones will evolve into high-end PDAs and will be fully packed with features, leaving a void of simpler devices for parents to chose from. Innovation and experimentation in today's businesses and academic institutions will result in a more competitive market. Multinational product-based firms with enough cash and market presence will buy up small and innovative companies and build them into their portfolio. There will continue to be rapid acceleration of technical innovations and a reduction in size of wireless devices.

FREE STUFF EVERYWHERE (ADVERTISERS' HEAVEN)

Advertisers are moving from traditional print media and into the electronic space with a focus on any delivery mechanism to get to a customer or prospect. You have undoubtedly seen the advertisements that proliferate most Internet home pages and Web portals. There are very few major Internet portal sites (if any at all) that don't offer some form of advertisements. I just clicked on four such sites: MSN.com, Yahoo.com, CNN.com, and AOL.com, and not one of them came up add free. As I'm writing this, I just got a SPAM email to start a nursing degree as well. What accuracy . . .

One of the problems with advertisements for consumers is that many of them are not targeted toward what the recipient is looking for. Some advertisers use sophisticated analytics and pore over Web site click-stream analysis, like Amazon.com does, to offer up links to content or products that they think are related to ones that the consumer has viewed or previously purchased. Those are the good guys. The bad advertisers use a variety of mediums including email, text messaging, voice calls, Web pages, and direct mail to peddle their wares, many of which are not appropriate for children. Some categorize these vendors as spammers because the unwanted email is just one part of the other electronic media used in these campaigns. Regardless of the current scope of advertising, it's here to stay and will likely get more prevalent as we see more decentralized and personal computing devices tapped into the Internet. That said, parents are cautioned against adopting technologies that don't provide appropriate filters to remove or restrict content from getting to their children.

GLOBAL POSITIONING TAKES OFF

Global positioning systems (GPS) will become a household word with most mobile items that connect to the Internet having some kind of GPS real-time and static locator functionality. In the next decade or so, GPS will be available on such items as cars, bikes, watches, phones, jewelry, and other accessories in an effort to locate and track people and things around the world. Software services to support these items will become mature and will be accessible from a variety of devices, not just computers with Web access. Get ready for a society that tracks everything from customers to criminals via GPS.

BUILT-IN SECURITY FOR FUTURE OPERATING SYSTEMS

Operating systems that control home computers, laptops, and servers will get better at securing the environment and data within. Some of the best operating systems of prior years were more closed in nature and had to be opened via configuration to expose security risks. Today's operating systems are quite the opposite, requiring technology professionals to harden or close them to prevent hackers from exposing weaknesses in them and gaining access to private information or even taking control of the host computer itself.

Tomorrow's operating systems will be better secured and move from a decentralized model back to a centralized model in some form of large hosting on the Internet via a private or public access with encryption playing a key role. Many of the software utilities and add-ons that help secure predominantly Windows-based decentralized computers will be purchased by the largest companies and integrated into the operating system. As a result, the services sector that provides for much of these add-on security services will diminish, and software vendors that stay in business will focus on nonsecurity types of applications instead.

FUTURISTIC WAYS TO STAY CONNECTED

If I had a crystal ball that would help me predict the future, I could help a lot of people and make a lot of money! Unfortunately, there is no such orb that can forecast where we'll end up in 5, 10, and 20 years. What we have to rely on is past information, trend forecasting, and plain old gut feelings based on the types of technology inventions and innovations we think will be introduced and will survive the marketplace. Before I provide some of my predictions, I thought I'd share some from others.

> People's social networks will be richer and more interesting, but the closest parts of those networks won't be numerically larger—we can only take in about 150 people, virtually or in real space. . . . [1] Susan Crawford, professor, Cardozo School of Law/Policy Fellow with the Center for Democracy & Technology/Fellow with the Yale Law School Information Society Project

> By 2014, as telework and home-schooling expand, the boundaries between work and leisure will diminish significantly. This will sharply alter everyday family dynamics. . . . [2]

> It is 2025. Your mobile is now much more than just a communication device— more like a remote control on your life. On a typical day, it will start working even before you wake. . . . [3] Dr. William Webb, head of Research and Development at the regulator Ofcom

> Most access to the Internet will be via wireless networks, especially as cities begin to establish WiFi grids. Just as many Americans are foregoing their land-lines at home for cell phones, I suspect that they will give up their broadband for wireless. . . . [4] A. Halavais, State University of New York at Buffalo

At least one devastating attack will occur in the next 10 years on the networked information infrastructure or the country's power grid.[5]

The following are my own predictions regarding technologies that will impact parents, children, and society in general in the coming years.

By 2010

- Personal privacy on the Internet will continue to erode. More access will be in the form of wireless mechanisms, resulting in more of our activities being captured into some kind of marketing or government database.
- Boundaries between work and home life will continue to blur as a result of technology integration in professional and consumer devices. Societies and countries that embrace this trend the most will be the most productive labor markets on the planet at the risk of increasing health problems resulting from stress and other technology impairments that we haven't determined yet.
- Cell phones and PDAs will fully converge and prices will fall so that almost anyone wanting a full-featured device can have one, leaving very few basic options for consumers. Standard features will include streaming audio/ video, email, IM, text messaging, MP3 player, Internet access, games, voice recorders, calendars, to do lists, and full-function video players. Disk storage systems for these devices will expand from current limitations of 40–80 GB to 500 GB to 1 terabyte, and screen resolution for all activities will be crystal clear and comparable to HDTV.
- Email will become fully integrated with voicemail systems, and users will be able to either read their messages or listen to them via their cell phone. These systems are evolving and available today for business customers, and will be consumer-ready at a relatively low cost in the future.
- Social networking will continue to evolve with an increase in the number of online interactions and a decrease of the quality of those interactions. Today's social networking sites list thousands of friends for each person registered. Those friends aren't really friends by nature, just those wishing to be engaged online in some form or frequency of communication. Trusting online relationships will continue to be low in number and will only increase as real-time video chatting and other more interactive forms of communication improves current forms of interaction like email, IM, and text messaging.
- Miniature external sound-reducing headsets and earphones will become

common, allowing phone users to talk with other background noises almost totally eliminated for the party on the other end. These technologies are just starting to appear on the market and are expected to be fully incorporated in phones and wireless headsets in the mass market shortly.

- Anti-virus, anti-spam, and parental controls will greatly improve for the cell phone industry, allowing parents to adjust with much better granularity the types of content their children see and hear on their mobile device. Current on/off controls will be replaced and driven by software vendors that have developed solutions for laptops and desktop computers.
- Major search engines will consolidate as competition increases for both advertising revenue and unique Web site visitors.
- GPS will become standard in cell phone and mobile device technology as compared to just a select number of devices currently offering GPS location services today.
- The Internet and TV will converge. Viewing programs, watching movies, and accessing the Internet will be done through a variety of devices in the family room and not just via computers and PDAs.
- Intelligent watches with Internet features will begin to emerge again. The initial round of techno-looking devices will be replaced by stylish options from reputable jewelers, not computer manufacturers.
- Productivity office software, like Microsoft Office, will be accessible via an Internet subscription instead of relying on program downloads to individual computers. These applications will be accessible via an Internet portal by users, regardless of the device from which they are connecting, and storage for information will be hosted on the Internet instead of stored within individual decentralized devices.
- The adult pornography industry will be as robust as ever, offering a wide array of content (teaser and subscription) via a variety of Internet-enabled devices. Real-time video camera functionality will evolve from computers to smaller devices like PDAs, enabling mobile interactive sessions and viewing.

By 2015

- IP version 6 will be fully integrated into society, allowing just about any electronic device to have a unique IP address and connect to the Internet.
- A significant percentage of the world will have access to the Internet in

some way. The proliferation of inexpensive portable communication devices will facilitate the increase.

- Security and access to devices and systems will be driven by biometrics instead of character-entered passwords.
- Voice calls over the Internet will merge with traditional phone vendors and wireless offerings. Phones will evolve to accommodate automatically switching between multiple paths to place a voice call, including those that travel over land lines, wireless cell towers, satellites, and Internet connections.
- GPS tracking capabilities will be embedded into much smaller objects such as watches, jewelry, pens, purses, and wallets, giving parents greater control with monitoring and keeping their children safe.
- Brick-and-mortar book and video stores will diminish if not be gone from the marketplace. Customers will be able to purchase and wirelessly transfer content to an Internet-enabled wearable device via a variety of mechanisms, including in a store or from other point-of-purchase portals. Thus, retail stores for electronic media may exist, but they will probably offer virtual products instead of stocking the shelves with physical products. Wireless installations will become the gold standard going forward.
- Email and text messaging will morph toward full voice message delivery via wireless and nearly invisible ear plugs that will replace awkward looking Bluetooth wireless earphones.
- Cell phone QWERTY email keyboards will be augmented by speech recognition software that will allow users to record messages and send/receive them as a voice calls.
- Mobile devices will evolve to controlling other devices in the home and office via wireless applications and add-ons. Capabilities include remote controlling home devices (TVs, DVDs, stereos, etc.) and being able to ubiquitously print documents via built-in wireless printing without additional add-on software.
- Refrigerators and other appliances will have Internet-enabled inventory systems built in and use scanning technology to automatically place orders over the Internet for items that need to be replaced.

By 2025

- Internet bandwidth will increase to homes and businesses by a factor of 100, facilitating the migration away from decentralized devices like PCs to Internet appliances, with information stored away from the actual device.

- Information-gathering activities from vendors for goods purchased, used, viewed, and accessed will proliferate into giant repositories of information that will blur what people intend to keep private and public.
- Advertisements will proliferate every electronic device connected to the Internet and will be served up and driven by what the consumer buys, sees, drives by, calls, emails, samples, and so on. Leading industrialized governments will have access to all of this information as part of a national intelligence program in support of national security. What people do will be tracked in these databases.
- The personal computer as we know it today will cease to exist and will be replaced by numerous consumer and professional devices integrated into the Internet.
- Holograms and three-dimensional graphics capabilities will be integrated into mobile devices for viewing various types of information, such as email, calendars, real-time video conferences, and person-to-person video feeds.

RECOMMENDATIONS

This is a difficult section to write given some of the predictions above. The following is the only advice I have at this point.

- In the next few years, don't fly on the cutting edge of technology, especially for consumer-related devices. They're usually too expensive at their launch and often don't live up to their marketing promise. The difficulty here is that children always seem to want the latest and greatest new gadget— especially if it is computer-related and allows them to communicate with friends. Hold the line or make them pay for it, but only after checking on the security and parental controls for those devices.
- As new kinds of technology come out that provide access to a variety of information, stay focused on what you choose to adopt. Remember that it's always a buyer's market from a technology perspective. Thus, let your children be kids at early ages, and don't rush to get them tech-savvy.
- Technology in the future will be even more decentralized than it is now, with literally thousands of types of products and devices tied to the Internet. As new kinds of services come online, try before you buy and *always* inquire about parental controls. If they don't have any or they're not fully vetted, take a pass and watch to see how others who do take the plunge fare. Early adopters of Internet-related devices might be introducing unknown risk to children—plain and simple.

Talking to Your Kids about Online Risks

Parents were invented to make children happy by giving them something to ignore.
—Ogden Nash

AN INTERNET USAGE CONTRACT

Part of parenting around technology is developing and setting clear expectations and rules. My parents did so, and I've adopted a similar approach with my kids. I can still remember my father's statement to me after I was all grown up:– "I gave you just enough rope to hang yourself." I interpreted that as giving me some freedom, clearly setting expectations, and explaining what would happen if I broke the rules. One summer when I was a kid, many of the teenage boys in my neighborhood started to experiment with taking their fathers' cars out for joy rides. Assuming that I wouldn't get into an accident, I thought through the other potential repercussions. Would my father know? Would he ground me? Would he let me drive when I became the legal age or make me wait for a few months or even a year? After thinking about these types of questions, I realized that he probably *would* know, probably by the way I would have parked his car back in the garage, and I would have gotten in some *serious* trouble. Thus, I never did it.

Only a few months later did I realize I made the right decision. One of the other boys in the neighborhood decided to take his father's car out for a spin. He lost control of the car and flipped it end over end, but fortunately he didn't injure himself. He also didn't get his license when the rest of us did because of his mistake. Parenting is about getting the right mix of love, learning, education, and toughness.

I encourage parents to set up an Internet contract with their children, especially middle school and high school teenagers. A contract signed by each child does three things: (1) clearly spells out expectations, and (2) puts in writing tips to help them stay safe, and (3) discusses repercussions of they break the rules. There are a variety of good contracts available on the Internet from sites like Netsmartz.org. My suggested contract would be a pledge that would be signed by each child and his or her parents/guardian and read like the following.

Internet Safety Agreement

1. **Personal Data**: I will *never* share private information on the Internet, which includes full name, address, Social Security number, phone number(s), school attended/attending, and recent pictures. Exceptions require approval from my parents.

2. **Talking with my Parents**: I promise to tell my parents about any strange things that come up as a result of using the Internet via email, IM, browsing, text messaging, social networking sites, and cell phone calls. If I feel uncomfortable as a result of using the Internet, I will talk to my parents, show them what made me feel strange, and listen to their advice on how to prevent the situation in the future.

3. **Banned Technology**: I promise *not* to use the following technology without first getting my parents' approval: (1) voice calls over the Internet, (2) instant messaging, (3) social networking sites, and (4) video cameras or Webcams. In addition, I will *never* (5) attempt to access adult/pornographic content, (6) enter a chat room, or (7) illegally copy or download material including games, songs, and videos that are not clearly advertised as free to the public.

4. **Dealing with Strangers:** I will *never* respond to an email message, text message, IM request, or phone call from a stranger (or someone that I don't know). I will also *never* agree to meet anyone that I've met on the Internet. I understand that people aren't always who they say they are.

5. **Respecting Others**: I will respect other people on the Internet that I communicate with and treat them as I wish to be treated.

6. **Breaking the Rules**: I understand that if I break these rules, that I may temporarily or permanently lose the right to use Internet technologies including email, browsing, cell phone, and text messaging. These tools are a privilege and not a right.

_____ Child's Signature Date _____

_____Parent's Signature Date_____

Feel free to use this template or mix and match the terms and conditions that work best for your family based on input and agreements from other reputable safety organizations outlined in this text.

WHEN AND HOW TO BE FIRM

Speaking to children about the risks of the Internet, rules of engagement, and repercussions can be difficult. Every child is different and they comprehend information differently at various age groups. The Web site Talk With Your Kids (www.talkingwithkids.org) has some good advice for talking to children about a variety of tough issues. Here are some other ideas.

1. Tell your children what's acceptable and what's *not* acceptable behavior on the Internet.
2. Set clear expectations and spell out penalties if they don't play by the rules.
3. Don't back down if they break the rules. Kids are notorious for wearing down parents.
4. Initiate conversations with your child if you sense something is wrong or if their behavior is changing. Don't wait for them to come to you.[1]
5. Listen to your child before enforcing a penalty. An infraction of the rules may not have been intentional or their fault. When you have all the facts, make the call. Reacting without listening is careless.
6. Be honest and patient. If you're disappointed with their actions, tell them why. If you change the rules or revoke a privilege, spell out the reasons, update their Internet agreement, and get them to sign it.[2]

WHAT NOT TO SAY TO YOUR TEEN

Talking to your kids about the risks of the Internet can be tricky. In addition, when dealing with kids that break the rules outlined in your Internet agreement, it's easy to get angry, express dissatisfaction with their actions, and say things that you may regret later. I offer the following advice on what *not* to say to your child as you implement an Internet safety approach.

- Speak to the age of your children. When discussing the risks of the Internet with your younger kids, be honest, tell them that you care about their safety, and give them examples of the risks. Inform them, don't scare them. Gory scare tactics are not appropriate for younger children. For your middle to high school teenagers, cut to the chase and tell them some of the things that can go wrong and have gone wrong with other kids around the world. Let them know that you're informed about the risks, you know how to handle technology, and that it's your job as a parent to set rules designed to protect them. Young to mature teenagers tend to feel that they're invincible. I remember that feeling well, but then again—we didn't have online predators when I was growing up.

- If they make a mistake or intentionally break the rules of your Internet agreement, keep a cool head. You may greatly dislike what they've done and be disappointed in them, but you're also supposed to be there for them when times get tough. That means keeping your temper in check and clearly explaining the risks of what they've done, and what the repercussions are.
- If they break the rules, stick to your guns and deliver the appropriate punishment, which may result in revoking some of their Internet privileges. A parent I know revoked her daughter's Internet rights when she became aware that her daughter had posted a page on MySpace, which was not allowed. Kids need consistency. Setting clear expectations with defined repercussions is only part of an Internet agreement with your child. Enforcing it is the other part.
- Never tell children that they're stupid as a result of what they've done. They may have done something foolish that puts them at risk, but words like *stupid* can have a different (and potentially devastating) impact.

ADVICE FROM THE PROS (CHILD PSYCHOLOGISTS)

I'm not a child psychologist or psychiatrist and wouldn't think of giving out advice to parents from their perspective. If parents are having difficulties talking to their children about issues, potential harms, or problems associated with the Internet or any other issue for that matter, there are always alternatives to ignoring the problem. Many professionals can help, including law enforcement, school counselors, social workers, family, friends, and, yes, child psychologists and psychiatrists. The Internet can be a great resource when looking for assistance. Use it and get some help from a professional if you sense that your child is in harm's way, involved in risky behavior, not listening, or displaying behavior that isn't consistent or condoned.

I asked Dr. Sam Hackworth, a private practice psychologist and CEO/founder of AskaChildPsychologist.com for some additional advice on how to get through to kids today at various ages in development. The following questions and answers are provided to give parents some additional help and advice from the perspective of a professional doctor.

Question: To what level can children comprehend the risks of going online (sexual predators, graphic pornography, hate materials, violence, kidnapping, etc.) at various age groups (category 1, elementary school; category 2, middle school; category 3, high school)?

Dr. Hackworth: Elementary school (ages 8–11): Very little understanding of online risks, and fleeting at that. Middle school (ages 12–14): Very limited understanding still, and very naive about it. High school (ages 15–18): Limited true comprehension, still with ongoing naiveté and tendency to "forget" the risks impulsively.

Q2: Why?

Dr. Hackworth: The youngest group, ages 8–11, typically don't think at all about what's on the Internet other than what is on the screen right in front of them. Faceless predators or criminals, down the street or around the globe, usually wouldn't cross their minds unless their parents or the news media told them about such possibilities—even then, I doubt that most kids this age would "remember" the risks without constant reminders. The middle school group, in my clinical experience, barely seems to get it. This age group can talk more about the risks and seem to know some real examples of things gone wrong, but they are very naive and expect that nothing could happen to them. They also very easily forget the basics about security, giving out personal information left and right. The high school group does tend to understand the risks to a more comforting level, but even then that varies widely across teens. Some in high school are vigilant and relatively mature, and try to be safe; others routinely operate just as the middle schoolers do—with great naiveté and immaturity. In my clinical experience, if anyone expresses great attraction or interest in any way to a certain subset of high schoolers, then that portion of them will "slip" and do something stupid on the Internet sometime.

Q3: If a child is physically or emotionally harmed as a result of an Internet-related event, how long does it take to complete a healing process?

Dr. Hackworth: That depends on too many variables to really answer. Can be from a short period to years long. If it's from a face-to-face event and involving anything physical, the healing could take years.

Q4: In your opinion, can many online/Internet-related crimes against children be prevented?

Dr. Hackworth: Yes.

Q5: How so?

Dr. Hackworth: By parents repeatedly educating and reeducating their children on the risks and how to be safer. And by monitoring what their children are doing and asking questions about their Internet experiences and contacts. One of the biggest things I think parents can do is continually drive home the fact that anyone could be up to anything on the Internet, telephone, and so on, and that their children should assume anything is possible. Remind them that letting their guard down would be like routinely forgetting to lock the doors at night. I think they know that somewhere in the world (again, down the street or around the globe) there are lots of people who would come in and commit criminal acts if they knew they had the opportunity.

Q6: What recommendations can you give parents regarding how to talk to their children about the risks of using the Internet?

Dr. Hackworth: (1) Even the most honest, responsible, and mature child or teen needs clear expectations about Internet use. Tell them exactly what you expect and exactly what the consequences will be for following through or not. (2) Be straightforward and frank about risks and dangers of putting oneself out there in the world via the Internet. The older they get, the less benefit to anyone to mince words. (3) Teach your child or teen to assume nothing on the Internet—to remember that anything is possible from anyone they (and you) don't know firsthand. (4) Talk with them regularly and frequently, keeping in mind that from elementary through high school a certain degree of repetition is necessary to learn most things. (5) Let them know they can talk with you about anything at any time.[3]

RECOMMENDATIONS

Parents today can make a difference in their children's life and improve their safety if they make an effort. Some adults are scared of technology, and many simply don't know where to begin to make the Internet safer for their children. This book provides parents and teachers with the tools and the road map to get it done.

I offer the Smith Safety Road Map (Figure 11.1), which is an eight-step approach to making your child's experiences on the Internet fun, educational, and safe. The roadmap summarizes some of the major steps and recommendations put forth in this book. Parents and guardians that follow the instructions and the more detailed recommendations within each chapter by age category will greatly reduce the risk of harm to their children. I close with the following recommendations.

START

Talk to Your Kids
1. Use real life stories to get messages across about risk
2. Don't sugar coat the message
3. Keep communication open
4. Talk to them *frequently*

Set Clear Policies
1. Use an Internet agreement
2. Set time restrictions
3. Kids – can't install software
4. Kids - no changing passwords

Use Software to Help
1. Install / configure CyberPatrol
2. Install / configure PCTattletale in *Stealth mode** on all computers in the house

Parents Maintain Accounts
1. Parents control all admin accounts
2. Kids – block software installs

Block Search Engines and Adult Content
1. Set access to safe search sites
2. Block adult content in CyberPatrol

Use Safe Email Programs
1. Eliminate / minimize SPAM
2. Block free email sites
3. Set policy: 1 email account / person
4. Don't forget about anti-virus and anti-spyware software
5. Review email messages (sent and received) via PCTattletale and watch for strange file attachments stored to data keys

Block Social Networking, IM, and Chat
1. If allow IM at older ages, use PCTattletale to capture passwords and review content frequently
2. Learn the IM lingo
3. Block voice calls over the Internet
* Chat should always be blocked

Use Safe Cell Phones
1. Use GPS for younger kids
2. Restrict extra features outside of making calls
3. *Never* allow Internet browsing
4. Avoid PDAs for children

Figure 11.1 The Smith Safety Road Map

- Get up to speed on basic Internet and related technology and stay educated as the technology changes. Treat your knowledge of the Internet like a job—you must always be learning something new to stay ahead and keep competitive.
- Follow the road map outlined in this book. It's easy to do, given the types of technology recommended if you follow the steps, and it will help keep your kids safer.
- Be a technology-savvy parent. Don't make excuses when it comes to keeping your children safe on the Internet.
- The Internet is a really great place, but it's not always safe for children. Don't let kids roam loose. Set clear expectations and use Internet agreements to seal the deal regarding what behavior is acceptable and what's not.
- Set time restrictions for your children when accessing the Internet. Watch out for excessive time spent late at night on their computers. It may be a sign that they're talking to the strangers or accessing content and tools they shouldn't be.
- Use software to help protect your children on the Internet. Parents couldn't possibly protect their kids without the kinds of software like CyberPatrol and PC Tattletale. These programs are designed to make protection easier, especially when used together.
- Don't deprive your children of the Internet entirely. If used appropriately, it can be a great resource.
- Educating your kids is more than just talking about protecting them against the risks of the Internet. Education is about teaching them helpful facts, materials, and life lessons. Technology and the Internet can be an important tool in doing so. Don't leave educating your children to their teachers alone. Educators are important, but at the end of the day, it's a parent's job to raise their children in a safe and nurturing environment.
- If you become aware or suspect that your child has been harmed or abused as a result of using the Internet, call a professional for assistance. Here are some important numbers.

  1. Childhelp USA National Hotline (800) 4-A-CHILD (TDD 800-2-A-CHILD)
  2. National Center for Missing and Exploited Children, (800) 843-5678 (TDD 800-826-7653)
  3. National Children's Alliance, (800) 239-9950

- Never give up.

Notes

Chapter 1

1. DP-1, Profile of General Demographic Characteristics: 2000, U.S. Census, available online at factfinder.census.gov (accessed August 28, 2006).

2. Ibid.

3. Teen Internet Safety Study, Cox Communications and NCMEC, available online at www.netsmartz.org/safety/statistics.htm (accessed July 24, 2006).

4. Ibid.

5. Ibid.

6. Ibid.

7. "ARPA-DARPA: The History of the Name," U.S. Defense Advanced Research Projects Agency, available online at www.darpa.mil/body/arpa_darpa.html (accessed August 28, 2006).

8. Ibid.

9. "A Brief History of the Internet," *Internet Society*, available online at www.isoc.org/internet/history/brief.shtml (accessed August 28, 2006).

10. Ibid.

11. Ibid.

12. Ibid.

13. Ibid.

14. Ibid.

15. Ibid.

16. Ibid.

17. Wayne Rash, "Net Neutrality Advocates Face Off," *eWeek Magazine* (July 24, 2006), p. 20.

18. Kim Hart, "Center Opens to Train New Web Protocol Users," *Washington Post*, September 14, 2006, p. D4.

19. Ibid.

20. "Commodity Computing," Wikipedia, available online at en.wikipedia.org/wiki/Commodity_computing (accessed September 4, 2006).

21. Ibid.

22. "Computer History: History of Microsoft Windows," ComputerHope, available online at www.computerhope.com/history/windows.htm (accessed September 4, 2006).

23. Ibid.

24. "What Are CERN's Greatest Achievements: History of the WWW," CERN, available online at public.web.cern.ch/public/Content/Chapters/AboutCERN/Achievements/WorldWideWeb/WebHistory/WebHistory-en.html (accessed September 4, 2006).

25. "The History of HTML," About, available online at inventors.about.com/library/inventors/blhtml.htm (accessed September 4, 2006).

26. "Web Inventor Wins $1.23 Million Award," MSNBC, available online at msnbc.msn.com/id/4744554 (accessed September 4, 2006).

27. "What Are CERN's Greatest Achievements."

28. Ibid.

29. Ibid.

30. Ibid.

31. Ibid.

32. "Happy Birthday, Altavista!" SearchEngineWatch.com (December 18, 2002), available online at searchenginewatch.com/showPage.html?page=2161421 (accessed September 11, 2006).

33. Company overview, Google, available online at www.google.com/intl/en/corporate/index.html (accessed September 11, 2006).

34. Company profile, Research in Motion, available online at www.rim.com/company/index.shtml (accessed September 11, 2006).

35. "Neutral Net: A Battle for Control of the Web," *Wall Street Journal*, June 24–25, 2006, p. A9.

36. "Worldwide Internet Users Top 1 Billion in 2005," Computer Industry Almanac, available online at www.c-i-a.com/pr0106.htm (accessed September 11, 2006).

37. Ibid.

38. Ibid.

39. Pam Tobey, "Trend Lines: Digital Divide," *Washington Post*, September 10, 2006, p. A2.

40. Ibid.

41. Ibid.

Chapter 3

1. Amanda Lenhart, Mary Madden, Lee Rainie, Pew Internet and American Life Project, *Teens and the Internet—Findings Submitted to the House Subcommittee on Telecommunications and the Internet*, July 11, 2006, p. 2. www.pewinternet.org.

2. Ibid., p. 5.

3. Ibid.

4. Ibid.

5. Ibid., p. 2.

6. "125 Arrested in Child Porn Roundup," CNN.com, available online at www.cnn.com/2006/US/10/18/child.porn/index.html (accessed October 19, 2006).

7. Ibid.

8. Ibid.

9. Ibid.

10. "A Secret Life," *Newsweek* (October 16, 2006), p. 33.

11. Ibid.

12. Ibid.

13. Ibid.

14. Ibid., p. 34.

15. "Ads to Warn Teens about Web Crimes," *USA Today*, August 22, 2006, p. 5A.

16. Ibid.

17. Dana Bash, "Congressman Quits after Messages Sent to Teens Found," CNN.com, September 30, 2006, available online at www.cnn.com/2006/POLITICS/09/29/congressman.e.mails/index.html (accessed October 1, 2006).

18. Amy Satkofsky, "In the Web," Pennlive.com, *Express-Times*, February 25, 2004, available online at www.pennlive.com/specialprojects/expresstimes/index.ssf?/news/expresstimes/stories/molesters4_mainbar.html (accessed November 29, 2006).

19. Excerpts from Panorama BBC1, Canadian Children Rights Council, October 6, 1997, available online at www.canadiancrc.com/female_sexual_predators_awareness.htm (accessed November 30, 2006).

20. Frederick Mathews, "The Invisible Boy: Revisioning the Victimization of Male Children and Teens 1996," 1996, available online at www.canadiancrc.com/The_Invisible_Boy_Report.htm (accessed November 30, 2006).

21. Ibid.

22. "The Ultimate Taboo: Child Sexual Abuse by Women," BBC World Service, October 6, 1997, available online at www.canadiancrc.com/articles/BBC_Child_sexual_abuse_by_women_06OCT97.htm (accessed November 30, 2006).

23. Satkofsky, "In the Web."

24. "Sexual Abuse of Children," Prevent Child Abuse, available online at www.ridalaskaofchildabuse.org/PCAA_CSA.html (accessed November 30, 2006).

25. Senator Leo T. Foley, "S.F. No. 2873—Solicitation of a Child to Engage in Sexual Conduct," State of Minnesota Senate, February 23, 2000, available online at www.senate.leg.state.mn.us/departments/scr/billsumm/1999–2000/SF2873.HTM (accessed November 30, 2006).

26. Jen Stadler, "Online Child Molesters," Netsmartz, available online at www.netsmartz.org/news/onlinemolesters.htm (accessed November 20, 2006).

27. "About Us," Netsmartz Workshop, available online at www.netsmartz.org/overview/aboutus.htm (accessed December 2, 2006).

28. "Statistics—Teen Internet Safety Study," Netsmartz, available online at www.netsmartz.org/safety/statistics.htm (accessed July 24, 2006).

29. "National Mandate and Mission," National Center for Missing and Exploited Children, available online at www.missingkids.com/missingkids/servlet/PageServlet?LanguageCountry=en_US&PageId=1866 (accessed December 3, 2006).

30. Ibid.

31. David Finkelhor, Kimberly J. Mitchell, and Janis Wolak, "Online Victimization: A Report on the Nation's Youth," National Center for Missing and Exploited Children, June 2000, pp. 9, 15, and 16.

32. Ibid.

33. Kimberly Mitchell, David Finkelhor, and Janis Wolak, "The Exposure of Youth to Unwanted Sexual Material on the Internet: A National Survey of Risk, Impact, and Prevention," *Youth & Society*, 2003, 34(3): 330–58, available online at www.unh.edu/ccrc/pdf/Exposure_risk.pdf (accessed September 12, 2006).

34. Ketchum Global Research Network, "Parents' Internet Monitoring Study," National Center for Missing and Exploited Children, Cox Communications, and Netsmartz, 2005, available online at www.netsmartz.org/pdf/takechargestudy.pdf (accessed December 18, 2006).

35. Children's Online Privacy Protection Act of 1998, U.S. Federal Trade Commission, 1998, available online at www.ftc.gov/ogc/coppa1.htm (accessed September 8, 2006).

36. Children's Internet Protection Act, U.S. Federal Communications Commission, 2000, available online at www.fcc.gov/cgb/consumerfacts/cipa.html (accessed December 18, 2006).

Chapter 4

1. Amy Satkofsky, "Technology Provides Anonymous Access to Children," *Express-Times* (February 25, 2004), available online at www.pennlive.com/specialprojects/expresstimes/index.ssf?/news/expresstimes/stories/molesters4_mainbar.html (accessed November 20, 2006).

2. Ibid.

3. "Kacie René Woody," Kacie Woody Foundation, available online at home.alltel.net/rkw/kaciewoody_a.html (accessed November 20, 2006).

4. Ibid.

5. Ibid.

6. Christine Loftus, "Teen Murdered by Man She Met in Chatroom," Netsmartz, available online at www.netsmartz.org/news/dec02–02.htm (accessed November 20, 2006).

7. "Kacie René Woody."

8. Ibid.

9. "Help to Halt Online Predators," CBS News, May 8, 2003, available online at www.cbsnews.com/stories/2003/05/07/earlyshow/living/parenting/main552841.shtml (accessed November 20, 2006).

10. Ibid.

11. Ibid.

12. Jen Stadler, "Online Child Molesters," Netsmartz, available online at www.netsmartz.org/news/onlinemolesters.htm (accessed November 20, 2006).

13. Ibid.

14. Christine Loftus, "12-Year-Old Girl Back Home after Ordeal," Netsmartz, available online at www.netsmartz.org/news/jul03–03.htm (accessed November 20, 2006).

15. Ibid.

16. Ibid.

17. Ibid.

18. Ibid.

19. Ibid.

20. Stadler, "Online Child Molesters."

21. Ibid.

22. Ibid.

23. Ibid.

24. Ibid.

25. "Three Arrested in Internet Kidnapping, Assault Case," USAToday.com, August 14, 2001, available online at www.usatoday.com/news/nation/2001/08/14/netcrime.htm (accessed November 20, 2006).

26. Ibid.

27. Ibid.

28. Ibid.

29. "Life Jail for Minister Who Lured Boys via Internet," *The News* (Portsmouth, UK), July 28, 2006, available online at www.portsmouthtoday.co.uk/ViewArticle2.aspx?SectionID=455&ArticleID=1660093 (accessed November 22, 2006).

30. Ibid.

31. Ibid.

32. Ibid.

33. Ibid.

34. Hilary Hylton, "Another Suit in the MySpace Case?" Time.com, June 22, 2006, available online at www.time.com/time/nation/article/0,8599,1207043,00.html (accessed November 22, 2006).

35. Ibid.

36. Ibid.

37. Ibid.

38. "Man Indicted for Having Sex with Two Boys He Met on the Internet," *Daily News Journal,* July 14, 2006, available online at http://observer.guardian.co.uk/world/story/0,,1833433,00.html (accessed July 30, 2006).

39. "Police Uncover the Depraved World of Supalover666," Buzzle, available online at www.buzzle.com/editorials/7-29-2006-103877.asp (accessed November 27, 2006).

40. Ibid.

41. Ibid.

42. Ibid.

43. Ibid.

44. Ibid.

45. Ibid.

46. Ibid.

47. Ibid.

48. Ibid.

49. Ibid.

50. "Child Rape Suspect Used Internet to Lure Girls," *The Local—Sweden's News in*

English, March 29, 2006, available online at www.thelocal.se/article.php?ID=3408& date=20060329 (accessed November 27, 2006).

51. Ibid.

52. Ibid.

53. Ibid.

54. Wendy Leonard, "Man Charged with Rape of Child," *Deseret News*, Utah News, April 11, 2006, available online at deseretnews.com/dn/view/0,1249,635198653,00.html (accessed November 27, 2006).

55. Ibid.

56. Wendy Leonard, "Orem Man Admits to Phone Porn," *Deseret News*, Utah News, April 28, 2006, available online at deseretnews.com/dn/view/0,1249,635203179,00.html (accessed November 27, 2006).

57. Ibid.

58. Ibid.

59. Eliza Barlow, "Break Came from Two Girls," *Edmonton Sun*, July 29, 2006, available online at www.edmontonsun.com/News/Edmonton/2006/07/29/1708968-sun.html (accessed November 27, 2006).

60. Ibid.

61. Ibid.

62. Ibid.

63. Ibid.

64. Leila Fujimori, "Police Arrest Man Found in Teen's Bed," StarBulletin (Honolulu), February 15, 2006, available online at starbulletin.com/2006/02/15/news/story05.html (accessed November 27, 2006).

65. Ibid.

66. Ibid.

67. "Waikiki Man Arrested for Allegedly Sexually Assaulting Teen Girl," KHNL, March 14, 2006, available online at www.khnl.com/Global/story.asp?S=4627504 (accessed November 27, 2006).

68. Ibid.

69. Ibid.

70. Ibid.

71. "Internet Predator Sentenced for Seducing League City Girl," KHOU, August 4, 2006, available online at www.khou.com/news/local/galveston/stories/khou060804_mh_minorsexsentence.21ba6de.html (accessed November 27, 2006).

72. Ibid.

73. Ibid.

74. "RadioShack Director Quits; Faces Child Porn Charges," CNNMoney.com, November 2, 2006, available online at money.cnn.com/2006/11/02/news/companies/bc.retail.radioshack.reut/index.htm (accessed November 3, 2006).

75. Tony Blais, "Mother Pleads Guilty for Molesting Son for Master," *Ottawa Sun*, May 2, 2006, available online at www.canadiancrc.com/articles/Ottawa_Sun_Mother_guilty_molesting%20_son_02MAY06.htm (accessed November 30, 2006).

76. Ibid.

77. Ibid.

Chapter 5

1. Jonathan Zittrain, "Can the Internet Survive Filtering?" CNET News, July 23, 2002, available online at news.com.com/2102–1071_3–945690.html?tag=st.util.print (accessed September 8, 2006).

2. Ibid.

3. "Government Study: Web 1 Percent Porn," CNN.com, November 16, 2006, available online at http://www.forumopolis.com/showthread.php?t=37593 (accessed November 16, 2006).

4. Ibid.

5. Ibid.

6. Ibid.

7. Ibid.

8. Jessica E. Vascellaro and Anjali Athavaley, "Foley Scandal Turns Parents into Web Sleuths," *Wall Street Journal*, October 18, 2006, p. D1.

9. "Government Study: Web 1 Percent Porn."

Chapter 6

1. "Web Reaches New Milestone: 100 Million Sites," CNN.com, November 1, 2006, available online at www.cnn.com/2006/TECH/internet/11/01/100millionwebsites/index.html (accessed November 1, 2006).

2. Ibid.

3. Ibid.

4. Ibid.

5. "Why on Earth Does the World Need Another Search Engine," *Wall Street Journal*, October 27, 2006, p. B3.

6. "Harvard Criticizes Google's Adult Content Filter," Search Engine Watch, April 16, 2006, available online at searchenginewatch.com/showPage.html?page=2191611 (accessed October 3, 2006).

7. Danny Sullivan, "Hitwise Search Engine Ratings," Search Engine Watch, August 23, 2006, available online at searchenginewatch.com/showPage.html?page=3099931 (accessed January 2, 2007).

8. Danny Sullivan, "Search Engine Sizes," Search Engine Watch, January 20, 2005, available online at searchenginewatch.com/showPage.html?page=2156481 (accessed January 2, 2007).

9. Ibid.

10. Ibid.

11. Danny Sullivan, "Kids Search Engines," Search Engine Watch, April 4, 2005, available online at searchenginewatch.com/showPage.html?page=2156191 (accessed October 3, 2007).

12. Ibid.

13. Testimony of Dr. Mary Anne Layden, "The Science Behind Pornography Addition," U.S. Senate Hearings, Science, Technology, and Space hearing, November 18, 2004, available online at commerce.senate.gov/hearings/testimony.cfm?id=1343& wit_id=3912 (accessed January 1, 2007).

14. Ibid.

15. Ibid.

16. Ibid.

17. Ibid.

18. "Teen Testimonials on Internet Porn and Recovery," Protect Kids, available online at www.protectkids.com/effects/teentestimonials.htm (accessed January 11, 2007).

19. Ibid.

20. Ibid.

21. Yuki Noguchi, "Xanga to Pay $1 Million in Children's Privacy Case," *Washington Post*, September 8, 2006, p. D5.

22. Amanda Lenhart and Susannah Fox, "A Blogger Portrait," Pew Research Center, July 19, 2006, available online at pewresearch.org/pubs/236/a-blogger-portrait (accessed November 5, 2006).

23. Ibid.

24. Ibid.

25. Vauhini Vara, "MySpace Has Large Circle of Friends, But Rivals' Cliques Are Growing Too," *Wall Street Journal*, October 2, 2006, p. B1.

26. Ibid.

27. "Facebook to Open Its Membership Eligibility," *Wall Street Journal*, September 13, 2006, p. D4.

28. "Networking Sites Fight for Fickle Teen Users," *Washington Post*, October 29, 2006, p. A11.

29. Steve Israel, "Strangers in MySpace," Recordonline, February 12, 2006, available online at archive.recordonline.com/archive/2006/02/12/myspace.html (accessed January 9, 2007).

30. Ibid.

31. "Fear and Loathing on MySpace," *Washington Post*, June 27, 2006, available online at www.washingtonpost.com/wp-dyn/content/article/2006/06/27/AR2006062700709.html (accessed July 21, 2006).

32. Ibid.

33. "NJ Students Suspended over Web Postings," 1010wins, available online at www.1010wins.com/pages/24851.php? (accessed January 29, 2007).

34. Ibid.

35. May Wong, "Online Video Boom Raises Risks, Concerns," *Washington Post*, July 9, 2006, available online at www.washingtonpost.com/wp-dyn/content/article/2006/07/09/AR2006070900346.html (accessed July 21, 2006).

36. Ibid.

37. Ibid.

38. "YouTube Blocked in Much of Brazil," CNN.com, January 8, 2007, available online at cnn.com/2007/WORLD/americas/01/08/youtube.brazil.ap/index.html (accessed January 9, 2007).

39. Ibid.

Chapter 7

1. Heinz Tschabitscher, "Top 10 Free Email Services," About, available online at email.about.com/cs/freemailreviews/tp/free_email.htm (accessed January 11, 2007).

2. "Types of Email Service," Emailaddresses, available online at www.emailaddresses.com/guide_types.htm (accessed January 11, 2007).

3. Heinz Tschabitscher, "Top 10 Free Email Programs for Windows," About, available online at email.about.com/od/windowsemailclients/tp/free_email_prog.htm (accessed January 11, 2007).

4. Resource Center, Postini.com, available online at www.postini.com/stats (accessed January 11, 2007).

5. Ibid.

6. Ibid.

7. Ibid.

Chapter 9

1. "By the Numbers," *eWeek Magazine*, February 5, 2007, p. 31.

2. Tracy V. Wilson, "How GPS Phones Work," HowStuffWorks, available online at electronics.howstuffworks.com/gps-phone.htm (accessed February 9, 2007).

3. Ibid.

4. Ibid.

5. Rob Pegoraro, "Watch Out, Kids: With GPS Phones, Big Mother Is Watching," *Washington Post*, April 19, 2006, p. D1, available online at www.washingtonpost.com/wp-dyn/content/article/2006/04/18/AR2006041801604.html (accessed February 9, 2007).

6. Wilson, "How GPS Phones Work."

7. Ibid.

8. Ibid.

9. Ibid.

10. WatchZone Web site, available online at www.watchzone.com/cgi-bin/watchzone.filereader?45cfd6db00046c1c27430a801252064a+EN/catalogs/3412 (accessed February 11, 2007).

11. Ibid.

12. "Learn Kids Codes for Instant Messages," Wesh, May 5, 2006, available online at www.wesh.com/print/4454738/detail.html (accessed October 27, 2006).

Chapter 10

1. Susan Crawford, quoted in "Imagining the Internet: A History and Forecast," Elon University/Pew Internet Project, 2004 Survey, Prediction on Social Networks, available online at www.elon.edu/e-web/predictions/expertsurveys/2004_socialnetworks.xhtml (accessed February 12, 2007).

2. "Imagining the Internet."

3. Dr. William Webb, "Predictions for the Mobile Future," BBCNews, January 10, 2007, available online at news.bbc.co.uk/1/hi/technology/6232243.stm (accessed January 25, 2007).

4. A. Halavais, quoted in "Imagining the Internet."

5. "Imagining the Internet."

Chapter 11

1. "10 Tips for Talking with Kids about Tough Issues," Talk with Your Kids, available online at www.talkingwithkids.org/first.html (accessed February 13, 2007).

2. Ibid.

3. Interview with Dr. Sam Hackworth, January 22, 2007, via completion of a survey.

Bibliography

Journal Articles

"A Secret Life," *Newsweek* (October 16, 2006), pp. 33–34.

"By the Numbers," *eWeek Magazine* (February 5, 2007), p. 31.

Finkelhor, David, Kimberly J. Mitchell, and Janis Wolak. "Online Victimization: A Report on the Nation's Youth," National Center for Missing and Exploited Children, June 2000.

Lenhart, Amanda, Mary Madden, and Lee Rainie. Pew Internet and American Life Project, *Teens and the Internet—Findings Submitted to the House Subcommittee on Telecommunications and the Internet*, July 11, 2006, pp. 2–5.

Rash, Wayne. "Net Neutrality Advocates Face Off," *eWeek Magazine* (July 24, 2006), p. 20.

Newspaper Articles

"Ads to Warn Teens about Web Crimes," *USA Today*, August 22, 2006, p. 5A.

"Facebook to Open Its Membership Eligibility," *Wall Street Journal*, September 13, 2006, p. D4.

Hart, Kim. "Center Opens to Train New Web Protocol Users," *Washington Post*, September 14, 2006, p. D4.

"Networking Sites Fight for Fickle Teen Users," *Washington Post*, October 29, 2006, p. A11.

"Neutral Net: A Battle for Control of the Web," *Wall Street Journal*, June 24–25, 2006, p. A9.

Noguchi, Yuki. "Xanga to Pay $1 Million in Children's Privacy Case," *Washington Post*, September 8, 2006, p. D5.

Tobey, Pam. "Trend Lines: Digital Divide," *Washington Post*, September 10, 2006, p. A2.

Vara, Vauhini. "MySpace Has Large Circle of Friends, But Rivals' Cliques Are Growing Too," *Wall Street Journal*, October 2, 2006, p. B1.

Vascellaro. Jessica E. and Anjali Athavaley. "Foley Scandal Turns Parents Into Web Sleuths," The Wall Street Journal, October 18, 2006, p. D1.

"Why on Earth Does the World Need Another Search Engine," *Wall Street Journal*, October 27, 2006, p. B3.

Interviews

Interview with Dr. Sam Hackworth, January 22, 2007, via completion of a survey.

Web survey of parents about how they protect their children online; 100 surveys completed and used in the analysis. Survey designed by author on September 1, 2006.

Web Articles

"10 Tips for Talking with Kids about Tough Issues," Talking With Kids, available online at www.talkingwithkids.org/first.html (accessed February 13, 2007).

"125 Arrested in Child Porn Roundup," CNN, available online at www.cnn.com/2006/US/10/18/child.porn/index.html (accessed October 19, 2006).

"A Brief History of the Internet," Internet Society, available online at www.isoc.org/internet/history/brief.shtml (accessed August 28, 2006).

"About Us," Netsmartz Workshop, available online at www.netsmartz.org/overview/aboutus.htm (accessed December 2, 2006).

Barlow, Eliza. "Break Came from Two Girls," *Edmonton Sun*, July 29, 2006, available online at www.edmontonsun.com/News/Edmonton/2006/07/29/1708968-sun.html (accessed November 27, 2006).

Bash, Dana. "Congressman Quits after Messages Sent to Teens Found," CNN, September 30, 2006, available online at www.cnn.com/2006/POLITICS/09/29/congressman.e.mails/index.html (accessed October 1, 2006).

Blais, Tony. "Mother Pleads Guilty for Molesting Son for Master." *Ottawa Sun*, May 2, 2006, available online at www.canadiancrc.com/articles/Ottawa_Sun_Mother_guilty_molesting%20_son_02MAY06.htm (accessed November 30, 2006).

"Child Rape Suspect Used Internet to Lure Girls," *The Local*--Sweden's News in English, March 29, 2006, available online at www.thelocal.se/article.php?ID=3408&date=20060329 (accessed November 27, 2006.

"Children's Internet Protection Act," U.S. Federal Communications Commission, 2000, available online at www.fcc.gov/cgb/consumerfacts/cipa.html (accessed December 18, 2006).

"Children's Online Privacy Protection Act of 1998," U.S. Federal Trade Commission, 1998, available online at www.ftc.gov/ogc/coppa1.htm (accessed September 8, 2006).

"Commodity Computing," Wikipedia, available online at en.wikipedia.org/wiki/Commodity_computing (accessed September 4, 2006).

"Computer History: History of Microsoft Windows," Computer Hope, available online at www.computerhope.com/history/windows.htm (accessed September 4, 2006).

Excerpts from Panorama BBC1, Canadian Children Rights Council, October 6, 1997, available online at www.canadiancrc.com/female_sexual_predators_awareness.htm (accessed November 30, 2006).

"Fear and Loathing on MySpace," *Washington Post*, June 27, 2006, available online at www.washingtonpost.com/wp-dyn/content/article/2006/06/27/AR2006062700709_2.html (accessed July 21, 2006).

Foley, Senator Leo T. "S.F. No. 2873—Solicitation of a Child to Engage in Sexual Conduct," State of Minnesota Senate, February 23, 2000, available online at www.senate.leg.state.mn.us/departments/scr/billsumm/1999–2000/SF2873.HTM (accessed November 30, 2006).

Fujimori, Leila. "Police Arrest Man Found in Teen's Bed," *Star Bulletin*, February 15, 2006, available online at starbulletin.com/2006/02/15/news/story05.html (accessed November 27, 2006).

"Government Study: Web 1 Percent Porn," CNN.com, November 16, 2006, available online at www.cnn.com/2006/TECH/internet/11/15/internet.blocking.ap/index.html (accessed November 16, 2006).

"Happy Birthday, Altavista!" Search Engine Watch, December 18, 2002, available online at searchenginewatch.com/showPage.html?page=2161421 (accessed September 11, 2006).

"Harvard Criticizes Google's Adult Content Filter," Search Engine Watch, April 16, 2006, available online at earchenginewatch.com/showPage.html?page=2191611 (accessed October 3, 2006).

"Help to Halt Online Predators," CBS News, May 8, 2003, available online at www.cbsnews.com/stories/2003/05/07/earlyshow/living/parenting/main552841.shtml (accessed November 20, 2006).

"The History of HTML," About, available online at inventors.about.com/library/inventors/blhtml.htm (accessed September 4, 2006).

Hylton, Hilary. "Another Suit in the MySpace Case," Time.com, June 22, 2006, available online at www.time.com/time/nation/article/0,8599,1207043,00.html (accessed November 22, 2006).

"Imagining the Internet: A History and Forecast," Elon University/Pew Internet Project, The 2004 Survey. Prediction on social networks available online at www.elon.edu/-web/predictions/expertsurveys/2004_socialnetworks.xhtml; Prediction on families available online at www.elon.edu/e-web/predictions/expertsurveys/2004_families.xhtml; Prediction about how people go online available online at www.elon.edu/e-web/predictions/expertsurveys/2004_online.xhtml; Prediction on network infrastructure available online at www.elon.edu/predictions/q9.aspx (accessed February 12, 2007).

"Internet Predator Sentenced for Seducing League City Girl," KHOU, August 4, 2006, available online at www.khou.com/news/local/galveston/stories/khou060804_mh_minorsexsentence.21ba6de.html (accessed November 27, 2006).

Israel, Steve. "Strangers in MySpace," Recordonline, February 12, 2006, available online at archive.recordonline.com/archive/2006/02/12/myspace.html (accessed January 9, 2007).

"Learn Kids Codes for Instant Messages," Wesh, May 5, 2006, available online at www.wesh.com/print/4454738/detail.html (accessed October 27, 2006).

Lenhart, Amanda and Susannah Fox. "A Blogger Portrait," Pew Research Center, July 19, 2006, available online at pewresearch.org/reports/?ReportID=36 (accessed November 5, 2006).

Leonard, Wendy. "Man Charged with Rape of Child," *Deseret News*, Utah News, April 11, 2006, available online at deseretnews.com/dn/view/0,1249,635198653,00.html (accessed November 27, 2006).

Leonard, Wendy. "Orem man admits to phone porn," *Deseret News*, Utah News, April 28, 2006, available online at deseretnews.com/dn/view/0,1249,635203179,00.html (accessed November 27, 2006).

"Life Jail for Minister Who Lured Boys via Internet," *The News* (Portsmouth, UK), July 28, 2006, available online at www.portsmouthtoday.co.uk/ViewArticle2.aspx?SectionID =455&ArticleID=1660093 (accessed November 22, 2006).

Loftus, Christine. "12-Year-Old Girl Back Home after Ordeal," Netsmartz, available online at www.netsmartz.org/news/jul03–03.htm (accessed November 20, 2006).

Loftus, Christine. "Teen Murdered by Man She Met in Chatroom," Netsmartz, available online at www.netsmartz.org/news/dec02–02.htm (accessed November 20, 2006).

"Man Indicted for Having Sex with Two Boys He Met on the Internet," *Daily News Journal*, July 14, 2006, available online at dnj.midsouthnews.com/apps/pbcs.dll/arti cle?AID=/20060714/NEWS01/60714002 (accessed July 17, 2006).

Mathews, Frederick. "The Invisible Boy: Revisioning the Victimization of Male Children and Teens 1996," 1996, available online at www.canadiancrc.com/The_Invisible_ Boy_Report.htm (accessed November 30, 2006).

Mitchell, Kimberly, David Finkelhor, and Janis Wolak, "The Exposure of Youth to Unwanted Sexual Material on the Internet: A National Survey of Risk, Impact, and Prevention," *Youth & Society*, 2003, available online at www.unh.edu/ccrc/pdf/ Exposure_risk.pdf (accessed September 12, 2006).

"National Mandate and Mission," National Center for Missing and Exploited Children, available online at www.missingkids.com/missingkids/servlet/PageServlet?Language Country=en_US&PageId=1866 (accessed December 3, 2006).

"NJ Students Suspended over Web Postings," 1010wins, available online at www.1010 wins.com/pages/24851.php? (accessed January 29, 2007).

"Online Victimization of Youth: Five Years Later," Cox Communications and NCMEC survey, available online at www.netsmartz.org/safety/statistics.htm (accessed July 24, 2006).

"Parents' Internet Monitoring Study," National Center for Missing and Exploited Children and Cox Communications, 2005, available online at www.netsmartz.org/pdf/ takechargestudy.pdf (accessed December 18, 2006).

Pegoraro, Rob. "Watch Out, Kids: With GPS Phones, Big Mother Is Watching," *Washington Post*, April 19, 2006, available online at www.washingtonpost.com/ wp-dyn/content/article/2006/04/18/AR2006041801604.html (accessed February 9, 2007).

"Police Uncover the Depraved World of Supalover666," Buzzle, available online at www. buzzle.com/editorials/7–29-2006–103877.asp (accessed November 27, 2006).

"Profile of General Demographic Characteristics: 2000," U.S. Census, available online at factfinder.census.gov

"RadioShack Director Quits; Faces Child Porn Charges," CNNMoney.com, November

2, 2006, available online at money.cnn.com/2006/11/02/news/companies/bc.retail. radioshack.reut/index.htm (accessed November 3, 2006).

Satkofsky, Amy. "In the Web," Pennlive, *Express-Times*, February 25, 2004, available online at www.pennlive.com/specialprojects/expresstimes/index.ssf?/news/express-times/stories/molesters4_mainbar.html (accessed November 29, 2006).

Satkofsky, Amy. "Technology Provides Anonymous Access to Children," *Express-Times*, February 25, 2004, available online at www.pennlive.com/specialprojects/expresstimes/index.ssf?/news/expresstimes/stories/molesters4_mainbar.html (accessed November 20, 2006).

"The Science behind Pornography Addition," testimony of Dr. Mary Anne Layden, U.S. Senate Hearings, Science, Technology, and Space hearing, November 18, 2004, available online at commerce.senate.gov/hearings/testimony.cfm?id=1343&wit_id=3912 (accessed January 1, 2007).

"Sexual Abuse of Children," Prevent Child Abuse, available online at www.ridalaskaofchildabuse.org/PCAA_CSA.html (accessed November 30, 2006).

Stadler, Jen. "Online Child Molesters," Netsmartz, available online at www.netsmartz.org/news/onlinemolesters.htm (accessed November 20, 2006).

"Statistics—Teen Internet Safety Study," Netsmartz, available online at www.netsmartz.org/safety/statistics.htm (accessed July 24, 2006).

Sullivan, Danny. "Hitwise Search Engine Ratings," Search Engine Watch, August 23, 2006, available online at searchenginewatch.com/showPage.html?page=3099931 (accessed January 2, 2007).

Sullivan, Danny. "Kids Search Engines," Search Engine Watch, April 4, 2005, available online at searchenginewatch.com/showPage.html?page=2156191 (accessed October 3, 2007).

Sullivan, Danny. "Search Engine Sizes," Search Engine Watch, January 20, 2005, available online at searchenginewatch.com/showPage.html?page=2156481 (accessed January 2, 2007).

"Teen Testimonials on Internet Porn and Recovery," Protect Kids. available online at www.protectkids.com/effects/teentestimonials.htm (accessed January 11, 2007).

"Three Arrested in Internet Kidnapping, Assault Case," *USAToday*, August 14, 2001, available online at www.usatoday.com/news/nation/2001/08/14/netcrime.htm (accessed November 20, 2006).

Tschabitscher, Heinz. "Top 10 Free Email Programs for Windows," About, available online at email.about.com/od/windowsemailclients/tp/free_email_prog.htm (accessed January 11, 2007).

Tschabitscher, Heinz. "Top 10 Free Email Services," About, available online at email.about.com/cs/freemailreviews/tp/free_email.htm (accessed January 11, 2007).

"Types of Email Service," Emailaddresses, available online at www.emailaddresses.com/guide_types.htm (accessed January 11, 2007).

"The Ultimate Taboo: Child Sexual Abuse by Women," BBC World Service, October 6, 1997, available online at www.canadiancrc.com/articles/BBC_Child_sexual_abuse_by_women_06OCT97.htm (accessed November 30, 2006).

"Waikiki Man Arrested for Allegedly Sexually Assaulting Teen Girl," KHNL, March 14, 2006, available online at www.khnl.com/Global/story.asp?S=4627504 (accessed November 27, 2006).

"Web Inventor Wins $1.23 Million Award," MSNBC, available online at msnbc.msn.com/id/4744554/ (accessed September 4, 2006).

"Web Reaches New milestone: 100 Million Sites," CNN.com, November 1, 2006, available online at www.cnn.com/2006/TECH/internet/11/01/100millionwebsites/index.html (accessed November 1, 2006).

Webb, William. "Predictions for the Mobile Future," BBCNews, January 10, 2007, available online at news.bbc.co.uk/1/hi/technology/6232243.stm (accessed January 25, 2007).

"What Are CERN's Greatest Achievements: History of the WWW," CERN, available online at public.web.cern.ch/public/Content/Chapters/AboutCERN/Achievements/WorldWideWeb/WebHistory/WebHistory-en.html (accessed September 4, 2006).

Wilson, Tracy V. "How GPS Phones Work," HowStuffWorks, available online at electronics.howstuffworks.com/gps-phone.htm (accessed February 9, 2007).

Wong, May. "Online Video Boom Raises Risks, Concerns," *Washington Post*, July 9, 2006. available online at www.washingtonpost.com/wp-dyn/content/article/2006/07/09/AR2006070900346.html (accessed July 21, 2006).

"Worldwide Internet Users Top 1 Billion in 2005," Computer Industry Almanac, available online at www.c-i-a.com/pr0106.htm (accessed September 11, 2006).

"YouTube Blocked in Much of Brazil," CNN, January 8, 2007, available online at cnn.com/2007/WORLD/americas/01/08/youtube.brazil.ap/index.html (accessed January 9, 2007).

Zittrain, Jonathan. "Can the Internet Survive Filtering?" CNET News, July 23, 2002, available online at news.com.com/2102–1071_3–945690.html?tag=st.util.print (accessed September 8, 2006).

Index

Addiction, 24, 46, 105
Addiction, sexual, 104
Add or Remove Programs, 13
Address, 17, 31–32, 52, 58, 61, 76, 81, 108, 133, 138, 143, 163; email, 35, 36, 40, 50, 53, 107, 121, 123, 132, 138, 178; FTP, 109; list, 130; website, 39, 108, 123
Administrative accounts, 16; rights, 16, 22
Administrator user accounts, 31
Adult: porn site, 23; predator, 45
Advanced Research Projects Agency (ARPA), 6
Advertisements, 36, 39, 51, 101, 103, 123, 144, 155, 156, 161
Advertisers, 156
Adware, 36
AIM Mail (AOL), 118, 130, 139
Altavista, 10, 33, 48, 102, 115
Anti-virus, 23–34, 29, 37, 42, 51, 72, 124; controls, 13, 159
AOL Email, 27, 90, 118, 121, 126–27, 139, 156; Instant Messenger, 25, 130, 131; Parental Controls, 67–68, 90, 99, 121; Search, 102, 115–17
Apple, 8–9, 31; iPhone, 148; Safari, 17

Ask.com 23, 30, 33, 48–49, 102, 115, 117
Ask Jeeves for Kids, 44, 103
Assault: cases, 76; sexual, 59, 76–77, 79–80, 108
AT&T, 27, 62, 148–49
Audit trail, 25, 39, 51, 54–55, 87, 121, 130, 150
.au files, 30
Auto-backup, 18
.avi files, 30

Backdoor, access, 24
Back door, program, 32
Bank accounts, 31
BBC News, 52
Berners-Lee, Tim, 9, 25
Blackberry, 10–11, 26–28, 61–62, 145, 148
BlackICE PC Protection, 23, 112, 114
Blackmail, 79–80, 111
Blocking inappropriate content, 65, 111; software, 17, 33, 89–90
Block list, 90; traffic, 23
Blog, 5, 17, 46–47, 60, 67, 101, 103, 105–6

.bmp files, 30
Broadband, 28, 40, 105, 109, 157
Browser software, 9, 42, 44, 86
Browsing, 5, 11, 14, 18–19, 37, 46–48,
    50, 63, 66, 73, 86, 99, 143–44, 148,
    150–54, 163
Buddy list, 78, 130, 134

Cable modem, 18, 37, 41
Cache, 18, 34, 65, 86, 96; directory, 18
Camera add-ons, 40
Cell phones, 5, 38–39, 43, 47, 61,109,
    111, 125, 129, 131, 142–46, 148,
    150–53, 155, 157–58
Chat rooms, 5, 19, 24, 47, 52–53, 60,
    65, 73, 75, 77, 81, 99–100, 107–8,
    117, 132, 136–38, 141, 150
Chatting, 18, 76, 130, 134, 144, 158
Child abduction, 62; exploitation, 53; mo-
    lester, 74; predator, 74; psychologist,
    165; sex abuse, 79; solicitation, 53
Child Online Protection Act (COPA),
    90
Child pornography, 27, 49, 53, 69, 71,
    74, 78–80; distributing, 78
Children, crimes against, 73–74, 90, 166
Children's Internet Protection Act
    (CIPA), 69
Children's Online Privacy Protection Act
    (COPPA), 69, 109
Christie, Christopher J., 50
Clark, Julie, 73
Common file extensions, 30
Computer Industry Almanac, 11
Computer protocols, 6, 15, 17, 27
Confidential information, 31
Configuration setting, 18
Content Advisor, 65, 67, 90
Content filtering program, 19, 87; filters,
    26, 40, 48–50, 66, 87, 90, 95, 99, 145
Control Panel, 13, 95, 114
Cookies, 17, 19, 48, 65
Criminals, 12, 52, 156, 166
CyberPatrol, 92, 94–95, 99–100, 103,
    105, 114–17, 122–23, 126–27, 131,
    134–35, 137, 139–41, 153–54, 169

Cybersex, 19, 20, 67
Cyberspace, 11, 98
CyberTipline, 63, 73

Data key, 20, 23, 30, 33–34, 43, 87–89,
    96, 117, 122–23, 127, 134–35
Death, 75, 78
Defense Advanced Research Projects
    Agency (DARPA), 6, 7
Desktop, 9, 35, 40, 68, 86, 91, 113–14,
    144, 159
Dial-up, 26, 28
Domain name, 20–21, 31–32, 101, 121
DSL modem, 18

Earthlink, 27, 68, 121, 127
Elementary school, 5, 65, 99, 114, 125,
    137, 139, 148–49, 151, 166
Email accounts, 3, 14, 21, 31, 45, 66,
    68, 78, 86, 88, 105, 118–19, 122–23,
    125–27, 139, 144; risks, 120
Email programs, kid-friendly, 121, 125
Encrypted sessions, 21; SSL sessions,
    34
Encryption technology, 18, 34, 40
Eudora, 8, 119–20
Exploited kids, 63

Facebook, 11, 13, 107, 115–16
Face-to-face meeting, 6, 111, 157, 166
Family filters, 48–49; search settings, 33
Family-safe content, 49
Federal Bureau of Investigation (FBI), 50,
    72–73, 75, 80, 107
File attachment risk, 123; attachments,
    50–51, 119–20, 122, 126–27, 130,
    135; sharing programs, 22; transfer pro-
    tocol (FTP), 22–23, 29, 35, 42, 99,
    100, 108–9, 112–14, 116, 130
Filtering software, 16, 22–24, 31, 33–34,
    36, 49, 63, 38, 71, 88–91, 99–100,
    102, 114–16; content, 19, 20, 23, 33,
    72, 86–87, 92, 97, 99, 109, 122
Firewall, 21–25, 27, 34, 37, 43, 68, 109,
    112–14, 116
Flash drive, 20, 43, 87, 89

Foley, Mark, 50–51, 91
Friendster, 6, 60, 105, 107, 115–16
F-Secure, 23, 42, 113–14

Gambling sites, 36
Gamer, 24
Gaming sites, 24, 28, 36
Geek Squad, 27
GIF files, 14, 30
Global Position Systems (GPS), 143,
    145–49, 151–53, 156, 159, 160
Gmail, 118, 126, 153
Google, 10, 23, 30, 33, 36, 48–49, 70,
    90, 102–3, 105, 110, 115, 117–18,
    126, 130–31, 139, 144, 153–54; Talk,
    130; Safe Search, 102
Goowy Mail, 119
Graphic images, 48–49; sexual content,
    33; sexual situations, 19

Hacker, 24, 28, 31–32, 35, 48, 109, 112,
    121, 157
Hackworth, Dr. Sam, 165–67
Hard-core pornography, 3, 13, 21–22,
    30, 33, 104; sex, 23
Harmful content, 34, 43, 49–50, 102,
    105
Help menu, 13
Hewlett Packard, 61
Hi5, 106
High school, 5, 12, 99–100, 107–8, 114,
    116, 118, 121–22, 124, 127, 136,
    139–40, 151, 153, 163, 165–67
High-speed connection, 27
History, 7–10, 12, 17, 34, 39, 65, 86,
    89, 96, 102; of sites viewed, 17
Home computers, 13, 20, 23–24, 28, 31,
    35–37, 40, 42–44, 48, 63–64, 86, 94,
    139, 156; page, 24, 40, 156
Hotmail, 119, 126
Hyperlink, 24
Hypertext Markup Language (HTML), 9,
    25, 38, 103
Hypertext Transfer Protocol (HTTP),
    108, 115–16, 126–28, 139–40, 147,
    153–54

ICQ, 130–31, 139, 153
Identity theft, 47
Illegal files, 22
IM Lingo, 65, 132–133; tools, 21, 25,
    51, 65, 68, 86, 99–100, 129–32, 134,
    136–37, 140
IMAP, 119–20
IMing, 25, 132
Inbox.com, 118, 126
Instant Messaging (IM), 5, 25–26, 30,
    51, 54, 65–70, 72, 81, 86–87, 95,
    99–100, 108, 116–17, 129–40, 148,
    150–51, 154–55, 163
Internet browsing session, 11, 14, 143,
    148, 151–54; cafés, 45–46, 105; child
    grooming, 78; filtering software, 36,
    63, 68, 88, 99–100, 114–16; monitor-
    ing software, 17; predator, 24, 50, 52–
    54, 73, 75, 77, 81; providers, 6, 16,
    27, 88, 100; risk, 4, 47; safety agree-
    ment, 163; safety policy, 69; usage con-
    tract, 162; users, 11, 106
Internet Explorer, 10, 13, 17, 38, 44, 49,
    65, 68, 86, 90, 99
Internet Service Provider (ISP), 18,
    26–29
Inventory, 13–14, 37, 43–44, 123, 160
IP address, 8, 20, 26–27, 31–32, 37,
    159
iTunes, 9, 32

Java, 28–29, 146, 148; applications, 28
JavaScript, 29
Jennycam, 110
JPEG files, 14, 30, 88
JPG files, 13, 30

Kazaa, 22
Keystroke logger, 91, 95
Keywords, 20, 25, 33, 89, 94, 97, 101,
    116–17
Kidnappers, 111
Kidnapping, 47, 59, 76, 166

Laptops, 14, 26, 30, 91, 99, 113–14,
    124, 139, 156, 159

Libraries, public, 70
Library, 14, 46, 59, 64, 71, 102–3
Limeware, 22
Linux, 31, 37, 42
Live.com, 48, 102–3, 115–17, 126, 131, 139
Lycos, 118–19, 127; mail, 119

Mature adult content, 33; content, 48–49, 71
Metatags, 25
Microsoft, 8–10, 17, 23, 27–30, 38, 42, 48–49, 61, 86, 101, 103, 110, 112, 118, 129–30, 159
Middle school, 5, 43, 50, 100, 105, 108, 114–15, 118, 121–22, 125, 131, 136, 140, 152–53, 163, 166
Missing children, 62
Monitor online activity, 61
Monitoring call logs, 149; solutions, 69; tools, 24, 29
.mov files, 30
Mozilla, 17, 120
Mozilla Firefox, 17, 44, 68, 86
MPEG, MPG files, 14, 30
.mp3 files, 30, 33, 112
MP3 format, 32; players, 8, 143, 148, 151, 158
MSN, 25, 33, 90, 102–3, 115–17, 126, 131, 156; mail, 70
MSN Windows Live Messenger, 131
Multimedia, 30
Murder, 47
My Computer, 14, 38, 41, 56, 110
MySpace, 6, 11, 13, 17, 24, 30, 37, 60, 67, 77–79, 88, 105, 107–8, 110, 115–16, 136, 165; unraveled, 116

Napster, 22
National Center for Educational Statistics (NCES), 12
National Center for Missing and Exploited Children (NCMEC), 6, 62–64
National Survey of Risk, Impact, and Prevention, 63

NBC Dateline, 5, 54
Netscape, 9, 44, 68, 70
NetSmartz, 53, 62, 72; workshop, 62, 72
NetSmartz.org, 64, 72, 75, 163
Network activity, 35
Network interface card (NIC), 26–27
Nontechnical parent monitoring, 85, 88
Nudity, 4, 79, 116, 133; photos, 19; pictures, 80, 88

Offline, 152; IM, 130–31
One-on-one meeting, 6, 53
Online activity, 15, 61, 97; chat, 11, 19, 66, 76, 129; chat forums, 11; chat room, 47, 77, 80, 151; communication, 4, 8, 21, 25, 61, 132; conversation, 19, 61, 71, 76, 78, 107, 111; gaming sites, 28; pen pal, 52; predators, 3, 19, 24, 52, 61, 73, 165
Operating system (OS), 8–10, 12–13, 15–17, 23, 28–32, 35, 37, 42, 44, 70, 88, 113, 116–17, 156–57
Outlook, 119–20, 148
Outlook Express, 120

Parental policies, 20, 24
Parent's Internet Monitoring Study, 64
Passwords, 13, 24, 31–32, 34, 36, 42–43, 48, 60, 65, 71, 87–88, 95, 100, 116–17, 119, 121–22, 125, 131, 160
PC Tattletale, 92, 95–100, 108–9, 112–14, 116–17, 119, 122–28, 131–32, 134–37, 139–41, 145, 153–54, 169
PDF, 32, 103
Pedophile, 53, 78
Personal data, 6, 17, 22, 35, 54, 61, 72, 123, 126, 138, 163
Personal digital assistant devices (PDA), 5, 8, 10–12, 14, 26–28, 43, 47, 51, 61, 66, 99, 129, 142–44, 146, 148, 150, 153–55, 158–59, 164
Personal information, 18–19, 24, 29, 31–32, 36, 46, 53–54, 61–62, 69, 76, 81, 98, 106, 111, 120, 132, 137–38, 166; injury, 47

Perverted Justice, 54, 60, 73
Pew Internet and American Life Project
Teens and Parents Survey, 46, 72
Phishers, 32
Phishing, 31, 32, 50, 92; email links, 31;
sites, 31
Phone calls, 3, 40, 130, 137, 139–41,
143, 146, 150, 163; internet, 141
Phone number, 32, 40, 52, 57, 61, 77,
81, 138, 142, 147, 163
Pictures, 6, 11, 13–14, 21, 25, 30, 32,
35–38, 40, 53–54, 63, 79–80, 87, 96,
106, 108–9, 111, 123–24, 127, 130
Piczo, 107, 115–16
Plug-in, 28, 30, 32, 42, 135, 148; files, 32
Podcast, 32–33
POP3, 119–20
Pornographic distributors, 52; films, 53
Pornography, 3, 13, 21–22, 27, 30, 33,
36, 42, 47, 48–49, 52–53, 69, 71, 74,
78–80, 87, 90, 102, 104–5, 120, 145,
159, 166; child, 27, 49, 53, 69, 71,
74, 78–80; graphic, 47–48, 120, 166;
sites, 21, 50; promoting, 79
Port number, 112–13, 128
Port 80, 128, 134
Port 443, 21, 34, 128, 134
Posting, 24–25, 51, 53, 79, 88, 98,
107–8, 110, 153
Private school, 70
Profile, 6, 14, 31, 62, 69, 74, 77–78, 84,
92, 95, 99–100, 106–7, 135, 138;
page, 62, 74, 88, 95; personal, 6, 95;
user, 92, 135
Proxy site, 68, 86
Public school, 17, 69
Public viewing, 17

.qt files, 30
Qwest, 27, 149

Rape, 47, 76–79; statutory, 77
Real-time chat, 24; conversation, 52;
video, 19, 40, 109, 130, 136, 158–59,
161

Recommendations, 4, 5, 12–13, 23–24,
26, 34, 36, 42–44, 71–72, 80–81, 91,
97, 99, 114, 123–24, 134, 137, 139,
150–51, 161, 167
Rename files, 88
Resource for parents and teachers, 73
Results page, 44, 48
Risks of going online, 6, 12, 47, 51, 65,
72, 74, 81, 166; insulating against, 72;
of the Internet, 164, 169
Road map, 24, 47, 123, 135, 167–69

Safe search, 23, 34, 44, 48–49, 102, 105,
115; settings, 34, 105; sites, 34, 115
Safe sites, 103–4
Scammers, 31–32
School: elementary, 5, 65, 99, 114, 125,
137, 139, 148–49, 151, 166; high, 5,
12, 99–100, 107–08, 114, 116, 118,
121–22, 124, 127, 136, 139–40, 151,
153, 163, 165–67; middle, 5, 43, 50,
100, 105, 108, 114–15, 118, 121–22,
125, 131, 136, 140, 152–53, 163, 166
Search button, 14; databases, 33, 138; engine, 10, 23, 25, 30, 33–34, 37, 39–
40, 44, 48–50, 71–72, 86, 90–91,
102–5, 111, 117, 138, 159; filters, 34,
102; tools, 33, 49, 102
Secure Socket Layers (SSL), 34
Semi-private, 17
Services, 35–36, 43, 61, 67, 69–70, 90,
92, 99–100, 106, 112, 118–19, 121,
123–24, 126–28, 137, 146, 148, 150–
51, 156, 159, 161; email, 119, 122,
124, 128; locator, 151; POP3, 119
Setting security, 17
Sex, 3, 19–20, 23, 30, 33, 40, 48–51,
53, 59, 61, 64–65, 70, 73–75, 77–78,
80, 87, 90, 92, 97, 105, 107, 110,
116, 133
Sex abuse, 79; act, 33, 51, 77–79, 111;
addict, 104–5, 156; education, 92;
graphic, 19, 33, 70, 91; offender, 49,
73, 77; sites, 40; slave, 111; toys, 80;
video, 30, 111; with children, 78

Sexual assault, 59, 76, 79; activity, 51, 63, 80; contact, 53; encounter, 59, 78; exploitation, 62; solicitation, 63
Sexual predator, 11, 17, 25–26, 35, 46–47, 50–54, 58–60, 73, 76, 88–89, 104, 107–8, 111, 126–27, 136–37, 139, 145, 166; female, 73
Shortcut, 13, 86–87, 95
Skype, 27, 131, 134–35, 153
Smith Safety Road Map, 167–68
Social networking, 5–6, 11, 13–14, 17, 24, 30, 35, 37, 39, 45–46, 50, 53, 60, 62, 65–66, 68–69, 72, 77, 81, 88, 95, 99, 100–2, 105–8, 110–11, 115–17, 120–21, 132, 138, 140–41, 150, 158, 163; risks of, 35, 108; sites, 5, 11,13, 17, 30, 35, 37, 39, 46, 50, 53, 60, 66, 68–69, 77, 81, 88, 95, 99–100, 105–8, 115, 120, 132, 138, 150, 158, 163
Social Security number, 26, 31, 163
Sodomy, 76–79
Software blocking, 17, 33, 89, 90; filtering, 16, 22–24, 31, 34, 36, 49, 63, 68, 71, 88–91, 99–100, 102, 114–16; protection, 69; stealth monitoring, 72
Sony, 61, 148
Source code, 25
Spam, 13, 32, 35–36, 50, 71, 120–21, 123–27, 144, 152, 154, 156, 159
Spyware, 24, 28–29, 31–32, 36–37, 42, 46–48, 72, 92, 131
Stealth manner, 60; mode, 29, 95, 114, 116–17, 122, 124, 126–27, 139; monitoring, 17, 21, 30, 35, 72, 92, 97, 131; software, 5, 20, 44, 60, 86–88, 98–100, 122, 136; tools, 75
Stop Sexual Predators web site, 50
Subscription fee, 50
Sun Microsystems, 28
Surfing, 5, 14, 28, 32, 37, 44, 48, 63, 70, 86, 101

TCP/IP protocol, 8, 26
Teachers, 17, 47, 53–54, 60–61, 72–73, 88, 91, 97, 99, 105, 108, 111–13, 118, 132, 153, 167, 169

Teasers, 33
Temporary files, 14, 38; internet files, 38, 65, 86, 122
Text messaging, 3, 5, 27, 38, 61, 66–67, 131, 137, 143–45, 147, 149, 151–54, 156, 158, 160, 163
Texting, 38–39, 61, 149
Thumbnail, 23, 123; image, 23
Tomlinson, Ray, 7–8
Transmission Control Protocol/Internet Protocol (TCP/IP), 8, 26, 37
Tricks kids use, 85, 122

Uniform Resource Locator (URL), 32, 39, 42
U.S. Census, 5
U.S. Department of Defense (DOD), 6
U.S. Justice Department, 51
University of New Hampshire, 63
Unix, 8–9, 17, 28, 131
Unwanted exposure to sexual pictures, 63
Unwanted sexual material, 63–64; solicitations, 63
USB port, 20
User IDs, 13, 36, 121; profile, 92, 135

Victim, 17, 47, 49, 50, 52, 54, 59, 62, 73–75, 77–78, 80–81, 107–8, 132, 137, 140–41; female, 52; male, 52
Video camera, 40, 56, 109–12, 131, 159, 163; clip 30, 110–11, 124, 136, 144; file, 14, 23, 130, 144; sharing sites, 110–12
Videocam, 40
Virus, 13, 23–24, 35, 37, 42, 46–48, 50–51, 72, 109, 120, 123, 131, 159
Voice calls, 26, 29, 61, 86, 130–31, 137, 143–45, 150–51, 153, 156, 160, 163
Voicemail, 61, 144, 158
Voice-over-IP (VOIP), 40, 70, 130, 132, 138
Vonage, 27

Wall Street Journal, 11, 91
Walsh, John, 73

.wav files, 30, 33
Web pages, personal, 86
Web-based mail, 21, 119–20, 123
Webcam, 40, 76–80, 111, 163
Websense, 49
Wi-Fi, 41, 46, 113–14
WiMax technology, 41
Windows Media Player, 32
Wired Safety, 72
Wireless access point, 27, 40–41, 113; device, 18, 40, 155; networking cards, 40, 90

World Wide Web, 9, 41
Worms, 47, 109, 120

Xanga, 6, 11, 105–6, 115–16
XuQa, 106, 115–16

Yahoo, 20, 25, 30, 33, 44, 48–49, 66, 86, 90, 102–103, 110, 115–18, 123, 126, 129–31, 136, 139, 151, 156
Yahoo! GeoCities, 86
Yahoo! Mail, 118, 123
Yahooligans, 44, 66, 103

ABOUT THE AUTHOR

GREGORY S. SMITH is Vice President and Chief Information Officer (CIO) of Information Technology at the World Wildlife Fund in Washington, D.C. and Adjunct Professor in the School of Professional Studies in Business and Education Graduate Programs at The Johns Hopkins University. He is an expert in the field of information technology with several technical articles and public speaking engagements to his credit. In addition, he is the author of *Straight to the Top: Becoming a World-Class CIO.*

D1467689

The Art of Naming

The A.B.C

set forthe by the Kynges maiestie
and his Clergye, and commaun=
ded to be taught through out all his
Realme. All other vtterly set apart,
as the teachers thereof tender
his graces fauour.

 A a.b.c.d.e.f.g.h.i.k.l. m.
n.o.p.q.r.z.ſ.s.t.u.v.w.x.
y.z.ɛ.ʒ : Eſt. Amen.

A.B.C.D.E.F.G.H.I.K.L.
M.N.O.P.Q.R.S.T.U.W.
X.Y.

A.B.C.D.E.F.G.H.I.K.
L.M.N.O.P.Q.R.S.T.
U.W.X.

In the name of the Father, and
of the Sonne, and of the holye
Ghoste. So be it.

From a facsimile in Andrew Tuer's *History of the Horn-Book* (London: Leadenhall Press, 1896), vol. 2, p. 203, cut 168. The original was imprinted at London by Wyllyam Powell, ca. 1545–47. Reprinted by permission of the Houghton Library, Harvard University.

Anne Ferry

The Art of Naming

The University of Chicago Press   *Chicago and London*

ANNE FERRY, professor of English at Boston College, is the author of *Milton's Epic Voice: The Narrator in Paradise Lost* and *The "Inward" Language: Sonnets of Wyatt, Sidney, Shakespeare, Donne,* both published by the University of Chicago Press.

THE UNIVERSITY OF CHICAGO PRESS, CHICAGO 60637
THE UNIVERSITY OF CHICAGO PRESS, LTD., LONDON
© 1988 by The University of Chicago
All rights reserved. Published 1988
PRINTED IN THE UNITED STATES OF AMERICA
97 96 95 94 93 92 91 90 89 88   5 4 3 2 1

Library of Congress Cataloging-in-Publication Data
Ferry, Anne.
    The art of naming.

Bibliography.
    Includes index.
    1. Spenser, Edmund, 1552?–1599. Faerie queene.
2. Spenser, Edmund, 1552?–1599—Style. 3. Names in
literature. I. Title.
PR2358.F47 1988   821'.3   88–4826
ISBN 0–226–24464–4

To Marty and Norman Rabkin

Contents

Acknowledgments   ix
Preface   xi
Introduction   1
1   The Verb *to Read*   9
    Definitions   9
    Reading Writing   12
    Reading Speaking   14
    Reading Things   23
    The Narrator as Reader in *The Faerie Queene*   39

2   Parts of Speech   49
    Paired Adjectives and Nouns   49
    Noun Adjectives, Noun Substantives   55
    Shifting Parts of Speech   61
    Words as Names   65
    Names Proper and Improper   69
    A Grammatical Lesson in *The Faerie Queene*   80

3   Translating or Borrowing   83
    Definitions   83
    Places   90
    Metaphorical Epithets   96
    Genitive Metaphors   99
    Transumptive Metaphors   102
    Metaphorical Puns   106
    Metaphors of Identity   112
    Metaphor and Allegory   116
    Spenser's "Way" in *The Faerie Queene*   122

4   Charms, Prayers, Rituals   125
    Magical and Miraculous Language   125
    The "Diuine Breath" of Poetry   133
    Poetry and Prescribed Prayers   137
    Poetry and "Wondrous" Paradox   141

Poetry and Rituals of Naming   144
Contexts of Catalogues in *The Faerie Queene*   148
Afterword   169
Notes   179
Index   201

Acknowledgments

Time to work on this book was provided by a fellowship from the National Endowment for the Humanities in 1984–85, for which I am most grateful.

Along the way I have been generously helped by friends at Boston College. P. Albert Duhamel shared with me his encyclopedic knowledge of sixteenth-century literature, as he has kindly done for almost twenty years. Dayton Haskin listened thoughtfully to many questions and steered me in directions where answers could be found. Andrew Von Hendy agreed to teach a seminar with me on *The Faerie Queene*, where I learned from him many new ways of reading Spenser that are reflected in these pages. Gina Prenowitz, studying the development of the sonnet in the sixteenth century, and Elizabeth Yon, writing about Spenser's *Amoretti*, have discussed so many ideas with me that I can no longer trace with whom they began.

Material from chapters 1 and 2 was presented to the English department Renaissance seminar at the University of Chicago, at New York University to the Poetics Institute, and at Harvard University to the Renaissance seminar of the Center for Literary Studies. Anne Prescott, who read the book in manuscript for the University of Chicago Press, made many suggestions which have been gratefully incorporated.

My husband, David Ferry, has as always been the reader I kept in mind while I wrote. As always, his suggestions were those one might hope from an ideal reader.

Preface

Sixteenth-century writers and their readers generally shared the view inherited from antiquity that the oration was the single most authoritative model of prose composition, even for a piece of writing not spoken to a public audience but intended for readers, like Sidney's *An Apologie for Poetrie*. What made a piece of writing conform to the ideal of an oration was its predetermined shape made up of a certain number of parts of specified kinds and in fixed order. Conformity to such an ideal was the kind of issue about which writers felt very strongly—for instance Thomas Wilson, writing in the mid–sixteenth century about what he calls the "framing, and placing of an Oration in order":

> And the rather I am earnest in this behalf, because I knowe that al things stande by order, and without order nothing can be. For by an order we are borne, by an order we liue, and by an order we make our ende. . . . By an order Realmes stande, and Lawes take force. Yea, by an order the whole worke of Nature, and the perfite state of all the Elements haue their appointed course.[1]

Such a notion of prose composition as the framing of an oration according to a fixed model, which is itself foreign to writers and readers now, is illustrative of the kinds of linguistic issues explored in chapters to follow. It raises questions with far-reaching implications for differences in assumptions about language and its place in the world. For instance, one might ask what would it mean to think of speech as the prototype of all language, even written composition? What would it mean to think that formal speech must follow a fixed model, without particular attention to the subject, or occasion, or experience of the speaker? What would it mean to predicate the proper order of a particular piece of writing on "the whole worke of Nature, and the perfite state of all the Elements?"

In a sixteenth-century oration, what has been said so far would be the introduction, called the *exordium*, followed by the second part, the *narratio* or *narration*. It is typical of sixteenth-century linguistic and literary terms, many of which will be discussed, that even those now still available in English then had meanings closer to Latin than to later usage. An instance is the term *narration*, which, as the name for the second part of an oration, meant something closer to statement of fact than to what would now be meant by it. Yet since such a statement could sometimes take the form of a recitation of events—for example, typically in forensic oratory—it could in those instances be understood to correspond more nearly to a now current meaning of narrative.[2] On the model of that kind of oration, therefore, what follows is the narrative of how the questions in this book evolved, what experiences encouraged them.

In graduate school I chose as my period of specialization what was then and commonly is now still loosely called the English Renaissance. Like all such historical labels, it described boundaries that were partly fictional, since preconceived critical notions as much as historical forces or even simple chronology played a large part in deciding the outlines of the period. The poetry then included in the Renaissance coincided with what recent studies still define as that distinct period of literature, "in England, Wyatt to Milton."[3] What we concentrated on, however, was verse of the 1590s—with some attention to poems by Wyatt and Surrey and by the midcentury plainstylists praised by Winters—followed by a selection of authors writing up to the 1670s, but leaving out other poets of the same time who did not fit the prevailing critical presuppositions about the period.[4] Our attention to sixteenth-century poetry was therefore selective. Most of what we read was chosen to point forward to poetic developments in the next century, and almost all of it with the exception of Spenser's verse we studied in editions which had been wholly or partially modernized.

It was within this framework that I began to write about Shakespeare's sonnets, discussing them in *All in War with Time* in the first of four essays on English Renaissance love poetry, followed by chapters about Donne, Jonson, and Marvell.[5] Placing the sonnets in that sequence invited certain kinds of questions about them but ignored others. Then a growing awareness of these other questions prompted me to begin reading from the 1590s back to the work of contributors to Tottel's miscellany of *Songes and Sonettes*, the chronological span of English verse considered here and in the previous book to which this is a kind of sequel, *The "Inward" Language*.[6] What I learned which has since been the shaping influence on my writing about sixteenth-century poetry is that it is in many fundamental and to me surprising respects radically unlike what came even immediately after it. Instead of being able to respond to sixteenth-century verse with the advantage of literary hindsight, I was reading poetry that seemed to be predicated on sometimes different and inexplicable ways of thinking. This strangeness was brought to my attention not only because I was learning more about earlier and lesser known poets than the selected late Elizabethans usually chosen to exemplify the English Renaissance, but also because I was reading their poems and prose works written in their time in unmodernized texts, often in their sixteenth-century editions. At first they were sometimes barely decipherable, due to unfamiliar aspects of vocabulary, spelling, grammar, and printing (unfamiliar even by contrast with texts printed in the early seventeenth century). Often it was necessary to read a passage aloud to make out the words. Many features of the language and the poems written in it seemed very peculiar: peculiar both in the sense of being puzzling but also in being characteristic of this poetry but not of what was written in the decades even immediately following. It began to seem as if the division between the sixteenth and the seventeenth centuries were not an arbitrary imposition of the calendar to which at the time little notice was given (it did, however, virtually coincide with the momentous end of the Tudor line on the death of Elizabeth) but a major event in linguistic and literary history.

The "Inward" Language explored some of these peculiarities of sixteenth-century verse by reading Shakespeare's sonnets in the context of love poetry which preceded rather than followed them. The focus of my interest then was in discovering what language was available to sixteenth-century poets for writing about experience which they called "inward," and in what ways they used such language. It was not an intention of the study to argue that literary history could or should interpret a distant period by using only its own terms (although I did conduct one minor private experiment by testing what I could learn from writing a book about love poetry without using the anachronistic word *feelings*). Such an intention would have to be predicated on the assumption that literary history investigates "a realm of retrievable fact" from some objective space which would make possible the recognition of "otherness in its pure form."[7] My own recent experience of having approached Shakespeare's sonnets from different directions, of choosing different contexts in which to read them, would in itself have been sufficient to disabuse me of such a notion, even without my having listened to the cogent arguments of recent discussions about literary history. They have been helpful in making historians more conscious and articulate about the fact that their "acts of description are necessarily acts of construction, performed by interpreters of culture who are themselves artifacts of culture."[8] These discussions have provided theoretical arguments to support the recognition that the literary historian who is "a product of his history" must construct the past "always in part through the framework of the present."[9]

These recent discussions of literary history have therefore also supported the informed use of terms for exploring earlier periods which evolved in much later thinking. Michael McCanles states the rationale for this approach in "The Authentic Discourse of the Renaissance":

> The specific codes that a Renaissance text implies, once learned, become no more and no less tainted with twentieth-century thought than do the languages of Amazonian tribes by the field anthropologist who uses modern linguistic tools for formulating such languages' phonological, syntactical, and semiotic components.[10]

Such use of terms and approaches formulated within later frameworks to explore an earlier period can only be validated for the literary historian by familiarity with its language. Yet my unexpected discovery of the radical "otherness" of sixteenth-century poetry, for which neither my own earlier selective reading of it nor any critical studies of it had quite prepared me, led me to believe that this necessary initial stage of historical construction had been slighted. It seemed that by not first recognizing the remoteness of sixteenth-century English from our own, one would be putting oneself in the position of the anthropologist who would use modern linguistic tools to analyze a tribal language he had not first adequately mastered. We would then obstruct what possibilities there might be for historical exploration of sixteenth-century poetry by imposing on it a vocabulary that "answers the question before we ask it."[11] My argument therefore was that before applying modern terms and approaches to analyze Renaissance texts, we must recognize that sixteenth-century writers used an English which in many respects we need to learn as we would the language of a foreign text, before using modern tools for decoding it. Most pertinent to my study was the common application of a number of contemporary disciplines sharing a concern with *the self* (a term which in the sixteenth century meant *itself* or *the same*). An example would be the use of Lacan's psychoanalytic vocabulary to investigate a scene in *The Faerie Queene* in which Britomart sees her "selfe" in her father's mirror (3.2.22).[12] Recovery of a richly detailed linguistic context for Spenser's use of the term seems to me to be a necessary first study for the literary historian, who may then wish to test the capacity of a later vocabulary like Lacan's to illuminate Spenser's passage within that earlier context. To do otherwise would be to treat words as if they had no history.

The attempt to learn the *inward* dimension of sixteenth-century English only heightened my awareness of its unfamiliarity and therefore of the need to measure the distance between it and the later terms with which we may choose to analyze it. It also made me conscious of many related questions around the edges of my earlier study of it, which are the subject of chapters to follow. They are an extension of the exploration begun in *The "Inward" Language*, comparable to the work of the field anthropologist who must first learn the dialect of the tribe, here the language of Elizabethan poets.

What is meant by poetic language in these discussions is quite simply the words and their arrangements to be found in sixteenth-century poems. The choice of this focus is not meant to imply that poetry or literature was either an autonomous or a privileged discourse, notions which recent discussion of literary history has especially singled out as alien to European culture of the Renaissance.[13] Many of the features of poetry considered here are also characteristic of other kinds of writing in this period, examples of which will be examined as well. Yet it is also true that what seem to me among the especially peculiar aspects of this language are sometimes most prominent, are to be found in their most exaggerated or pronounced forms, in poems, and true also that some of these features were thought to be the particular province of poets. It is therefore by focussing especially on poems that the following chapters will explore questions about sixteenth-century language and the assumptions on which it was predicated.

In addition to the poetry, the likeliest sources of illumination on such questions are sixteenth-century writers discussing their own language, and it is a very significant fact about the period that it produced the first literary criticism; rhetorical and logical treatises; grammars; manuals on spelling, pronunciation, and handwriting; handbooks on sermon and letter writing; phrase books for foreigners; book catalogues; and dictionaries in English. These works show new interest in the vernacular and awareness of its possibilities and limitations, analogous to the self-consciousness of the poetry, its experi-

mentation, and its imitation of foreign models. Other treatments of
linguistic issues can be found in dedications and prefatory letters,
controversies about biblical translations, sermons and commentaries
on biblical passages concerning language (especially Adam naming the
animals, the tower of Babel, Pentecost), tracts on education. Also il-
luminating are works where issues about language are involved in discussion of other subjects: etiquette books considering decorum in conversation; treatises on psychology that discuss the image-making
faculty; moral essays on topics like the relation of a good name to good
works; sermons about the priority of public over private prayer or
prescribed over extemporary worship; tracts arguing for or disclaim-
ing the magical powers of language.

   Yet these linguistic discussions also offer their own challenges to
anyone reading them now in search of explanations for uses of language in the poetry of the period. One reason for this is that the
assumptions on which sixteenth-century poetic language was predicated were either so widely held that they were espoused largely
without question or, perhaps as a consequence, they were simply un-
acknowledged. They are therefore rarely made more explicit in writing about language or verse than they are in the poems themselves.
What this means is that where linguistic issues are discussed, the assumptions underlying the writers' explicit statements emerge only
obliquely or indirectly. The writers do not set out to answer the questions that a reader with wholly other presuppositions would ask. Another reason that these linguistic discussions pose their own difficulties for historical exploration is that when Englishmen of the period
write explicitly about language, they often use it themselves in ways
as foreign to our own as do the poets. And of course it is precisely in
its unfamiliar aspects that sixteenth-century writing about language,
like the verse, implies unfamiliar notions that we must search out to
understand.

   The exploration of theoretical writing about language as a tool for
thinking about its uses in poetry in this book can be described by
briefly distinguishing it from some approaches proven useful in other
studies of this period. For example *the places* discussed here in chapter
3 are examined in Rosemond Tuve's *Elizabethan and Metaphysical Imagery.* Her procedure is to summarize statements by sixteenth-century
logicians about what they understood as "the places of Invention" in
order to show how their theories "led to kinds of training which affected habits of framing images." Examples from poems are chosen to

demonstrate her sense that these logical theories find "clear illustration in the formal character of Renaissance images."[14] By contrast, the discussion of the places here in chapter 3 is especially interested in what the theorists' language to describe them implies about usually unstated assumptions which might also be shown to underly uses of language by poets. The linguistic writings are therefore not approached as statements of theories which may be applied to poetic practice but as texts in themselves needing to be excavated, so that some of the presuppositions on which they are predicated may be uncovered. The poems are not quoted as illustrations of theoretical writings but as relevant texts to be explored in the interest of discovering common assumptions which shaped their language in ways specially characteristic of this period. This same approach in chapter 2 to the subject of adjectives in sixteenth-century linguistic theory and in poetic practice therefore makes the discussion of them different in kind from Josephine Miles's classifying studies of their changing nature and frequency in different literary periods.[15] Similarly the discussion in chapter 3 of the richly suggestive vocabularies used by rhetoricians to define transumption has different ends from John Hollander's examination of the trope's "confused but revealing history."[16] The explorations in this book take shape by setting beside one another sixteenth-century poems and discussions of linguistic issues so that they may illuminate some of the shared assumptions unstated but embedded in their language.

The metaphorical vocabulary I have just used to describe the approaches in chapters to follow—"excavated," "embedded," "explored," "uncovered"—signals that like a great many literary historians now studying the Renaissance, I have been in some ways influenced by Michel Foucault's "archaeological inquiry" in *The Order of Things* into the "mode of being of things, and of the order that divided them up before presenting them to the understanding" in the sixteenth century.[17] The subtitle of his book in its English translation, "An Archaeology of the Human Sciences," has been for me a suggestive metaphor to describe approaches to sixteenth-century English designed to dig out assumptions buried in its poetry. These in turn illuminate its differences from seventeenth-century verse, which are as abrupt and thoroughgoing as the larger changes—spanning more than any single country or discipline—charted by Foucault. What my own digging in the much smaller site of Elizabethan England has brought to light, however, is that sixteenth-century thinking about language, and also the ways it is actually used in poetry, are predicated on assumptions often very unlike those ascribed generally to this period by Foucault (the thirty-five footnotes to his chapter on the sixteenth century do not include references to any English texts). The differences between this and the period immediately following in English poetry are therefore described along some lines parallel to his but also in many distinct ways. This relationship is epitomized by the fact that the title *The Art of Naming*, chosen here to characterize Elizabethan poetry, is borrowed from a phrase actually used by Foucault about the classical period to define in his terms its profound differences from the sixteenth century.[18]

As what has been said should make clear, it is not an assumption of this book that linguistic theory was related to the actual practice of poets in monolithic ways. To assume such a notion would be to espouse the myth of some entity called the sixteenth-century mind, or imagination, or world picture which can be hypostasized. Yet works about language, as well as the poems of this period, are in fact remarkably repetitive, in what they say and in their distinctive ways of saying it. This repetitiveness is indeed so striking as to constitute one of the peculiar features demanding exploration for its implied ways of thinking. At the same time it allows possibilities for a later reader who wishes to develop a sense of what were representative concerns, widely held attitudes, even implicit common presuppositions unfamiliar to later ways of thinking. While generalizations here are in no way intended to invoke the fiction of *the sixteenth-century mind* holding a single or unified view of any subject, they are supported by a considerable range of references in the main body of the text and in the notes. Generalizations do not claim wider consensus than is documented here in works by sixteenth-century English writers.

Where translations of contemporary Continental works are quoted, they are treated in the same way as translations from the Bible or from classical authors: as examples of sixteenth-century English, available or familiar to writers and readers of the period. They are not used to document the thinking of their original authors or as grounds for generalizations about languages, periods, or societies other than Elizabethan England. In fact distinctive features of its language, which differentiate it not only from classical languages but from French or Italian of the same period, would preclude such generalizations.

Both poems and prose passages have been quoted from editions with as few modernizations as possible in order to avoid disguising many of the profound differences between English of this period and our own. Printers' marks no longer in use have been somewhat reluctantly altered or omitted, however, in order not to tax the resources of twentieth-century presses and readers unduly.

Introduction

    This book is about some aspects of sixteenth-century English and about some of the ways that poets used it. To prepare for later discussions, the introduction will touch on a series of questions about the state of the language itself, and then on a sequence of poetic devices characteristic of verse in this period. To distinguish the state of the language from poetic practice in such a way is of course to make an arbitrary division (which chapters to follow will largely ignore) among overlapping issues.

    To begin with the simplest element of sixteenth-century writing, letters, it is a measure of the distance between linguistic habits of this and later periods that the word *alphabet*, which entered English in the first quarter of the century, had apparently not become a common word as late as 1611, as is suggested by the objection in an English work of that date to its use as the name for the order of letters in any language except Greek.[1] Other differences from later practices are that letters of the alphabet are often listed out of the strict order now thought of as their fixed sequence, that this order was not followed as an indispensible rule on occasions when it would now be so used, that it was sometimes apparently not understood as an organizing principle. Such practices suggest a relative lack of interest in an established sequence of letters on which later writing and other linguistic systems depend. Yet at the same time letters were thought by many writers, following various ancient and medieval traditions, to be invested with supernatural meaning and power. The most authoritative texts cited to support this view were passages from the Bible, then the ultimate written source and sanction of all verbal significance, where the beginning and end of all things in the divine Word are named *alpha* and *omega*. What is now called the alphabet was an emblem of divine order and a source of power expressed in miraculous or magical uses of language. This cluster of facts suggests a different sense of language even in what would now be considered among its most fundamental components, and one made up of attitudes which might now be thought to cancel one another: a relative indifference to alphabetical sequence juxtaposed with reverence for its divine force. Puzzling paradoxes of this sort, which are themselves also typical of writing in this period, will be explored in the following chapters.

Related to them is a set of linguistic conditions including the comparative freedom by later standards exercised in spelling, an aspect of sixteenth-century language that is frequently masked by modernized texts. The name for what is now called *spelling* (which then meant naming letters or reading out words letter by letter) was a noun variously spelled *orthography, orthographie, ortografy*. As these variants in the spelling of the name for the fixed order of letters in words show, in actual practice spelling was so different from later habits that it must have reflected a sense of language in some ways unfamiliar to us. If the same word could be spelled different ways within a single sentence or in nearly adjacent lines of poetry—the first edition of Shakespeare's sonnets prints in the opening quatrain of Sonnet 18 "Summers day" followed by "Sommers lease"—then words must not only have been experienced differently, but conceived in some ways now unfamiliar.[2] This disparity must reflect a sense of the relation between written and spoken language unlike later notions; it must also imply a different sense of the relations between the poet and his audience, between the reader and the poem. Such differences are discussed in the following chapters.

A parallel aspect of writing in this period is the apparent randomness of some of its punctuation, and the absence of certain marks—apostrophes for possessives are an instance—that in later writing are used to make crucial distinctions. No problem is posed by the lack of an apostrophe in "Summers day," but in Sonnet 126, for example, the state of punctuation allows "Thy louers withering" to be read in several ways including *thy lover's withering* and *thy lovers' withering*, raising the question of whether or not the friend who is addressed is accused of promiscuity. Such freedoms, no longer available, must have allowed poets to think in some different ways about the ambiguous possibilities of their language.

Still another characteristic of sixteenth-century English is the relative fluidity of its grammar. Principal parts of speech seem to have been more readily interchangeable and in some ways that are no longer possible. Such interchanges were particularly common between adjectives and nouns, adjectives and adverbs, verbs and adverbs, but also even nouns and verbs exchanged functions. For instance, in Shakespeare's Sonnet 105 the poet prays, "Let not my loue

. . . as an Idoll show." The grammatical construction makes "Idoll" a noun, "show" a verb. Yet the ear catches a lurking possibility that "show" is a noun and "Idoll" an adjective (which would now invariably be distinguished to the eye by the spelling *idle*), a possibility to which Elizabethan readers might be alerted for reasons to be discussed: that they more often read aloud or experienced words as they sound, and that adjective-noun combinations like *idle show* were a specially prominent feature of this poetry. Such relative freedom in manipulating this basic grammatical distinction between the noun and the verb means that the parts of speech and their functions were in some ways differently conceived, making language seem to be a somewhat different kind of medium.

In sixteenth-century English, radical differences in vocabulary—significantly in ordinary words having to do even with such fundamental linguistic issues as what constitutes reading—also raise questions about the assumptions on which uses of language in poetry were predicated. For example, since the common word *translation* was used both for the transfer of meaning from one language to another, as it is still defined, and for the making of metaphor, then those now differentiated verbal acts may have been thought to overlap in ways significant for the writing of poetry.

A number of more recent as well as older studies have analyzed these characteristics of sixteenth-century language as distinct from later English, but their accounts are more often descriptive than actually exploratory.[3] That is, studies which show how habits of lettering, spelling, punctuation, grammar, vocabulary represent stages in the development of the language or of printing, of education in the vernacular or of lexicography, do not in themselves illuminate what attitudes these habits reflected or encouraged, what cast of mind could accept or work with such relative linguistic fluidity. Or, to phrase the question another way, such linguistic histories do not attempt to answer what conceptions different from our own are embedded in this state of the language. Answers to that sort of question are the interest of the literary historian whose approach could be likened metaphorically to the work of the field anthropologist or the archeologist. Chapters to follow will offer ways of thinking about questions raised by such linguistic conditions, as they are involved in the actual practices both of the greatest poets and of their less gifted contemporaries.

These discussions will therefore also explore other kinds of questions about the peculiar features of this poetry. To illustrate here, the opening of a stanza in *The Faerie Queene* exemplifies various now strange seeming habits of language that abound in the poem:[4]

> Faint, wearie, sore, emboyled, grieued, brent
> With heat, toyle, wounds, armes, smart, and inward fire.
>
>   (1.11.28)

These lines are also very like others to be found everywhere in six-teenth-century verse, for instance in a poem of unknown authorship in Tottel's miscellany of *Songes and Sonettes:*

> Yet haue I felt full oft the hottest of his fire:
> The bitter teares, the scalding sighes, the burning hote
>   desyre.[5]

A couplet from one of Sidney's Arcadian poems follows a similar pat-tern:

> For no thing, time, nor place, can loose, quench, ease,
> Mine owne, embraced, sought, knot, fire, desease.[6]

Yet another instance is from *Godfrey of Bovlogne*, Fairfax's translation of Tasso:

> Soft words, low speech, deepe sobs, sweet sighes, salt
>   teares
> Rose from their breasts, with ioy and pleasure mixt.[7]

The examples are remarkably similar in their ways of using a number of devices: listing, pairing of nouns and adjectives, alliteration, mixed parts of speech, repetition. The combined effect of these devices is to call attention to the highly exaggerated patterning of the lines, which strikes readers now as not only self-conscious but distinctly odd. It is instances of this and other peculiar practices in writing of the period that prompted John Thompson in his indispensible study of it, *The Founding of English Metre*, to say that at times it "can make the modern reader wonder if a kind of idiocy had not descended upon poet and audience alike at that time."[8]

Any reader of sixteenth-century English poetry would recognize these quotations as exemplifying some of its most familiar features, not only habits common to many poets but even particular words and phrases that are endlessly repeated. To say that these characteristics are peculiar to verse of this period in England is of course not to claim that either its verbal patterns or the favorite phrases of its poets are found nowhere in the writing of other periods. To make that claim would be to deny history to poetry, a position as untenable for the literary historian as to deny history to words themselves. Such a claim would also ignore all that recent literary theory has emphasized about the complex relationships among literary texts. One can think of many instances in later poems of the devices common to these quotations. It is obvious, for example, that neither epithets and catalogues nor sighs and tears disappear from poetry after the sixteenth century, but they are not used in later periods with obsessive repetitiveness by poet after poet in all sorts of genres. They do not therefore raise questions about what important ways of thinking in the period are embedded in their use.

Still less unexpectedly, examples of these characteristic features of sixteenth-century verse can be found in earlier poems in English, and in other languages both ancient and modern. Such continuity with past literature would be predictable especially in a period when origins and antiquity were generally revered in theory, when imitation was commonly stressed as desirable in practice for all kinds of writing. Yet even in earlier verse the features most peculiar to sixteenth-century poetry are not present to the same degree or in all of the same forms.

From a present perspective these differences may seem unexpectedly sharp, since with hindsight it has been possible to recognize a great deal of continuity in thought and language between medieval and sixteenth-century literature in English.[9] Yet Sidney, writing *An Apologie for Poetrie* around 1580, expresses a different sense of the distance between himself and Chaucer, a perspective shared by many other writers:

> *Chaucer*, vndoubtedly, did excellently in hys *Troylus* and *Cresseid;* of whom, truly, I know not whether to meruaile more, either that he in that mistie time could see so clearly, or that wee in this cleare age walke so stumblingly after him. Yet had he great wants, fitte to be forgiuen in so reuerent antiquity.[10]

One reason why Chaucer seemed to sixteenth-century writers to belong to an obscure past may have been the many intervening changes in English grammar and vocabulary, which allowed new possibilities in poetry, to be discussed in chapters to follow. Another reason for these writers to assign Chaucer to "antiquity" is that translation and imitation of Italian and French as well as classical poetry had recently encouraged a new kind of self-conscious experimentation in forms and meters which distinguishes the interests and efforts of sixteenth-

century poets. Still another reason why they might have seen themselves at a vast distance from Chaucer is that such writing as existed
about poetry or about language itself in English virtually all began to
appear in the sixteenth century. Both theory and practice in the vernacular therefore achieved a new importance, which may suggest a
reason for Sidney's surprise that Chaucer, without benefit of such
theorizing and example, should "see so clearely" the possibilities of
poetry in English.

The oddity of the lines quoted from the four sixteenth-century
poems can be described by the impression they make that words are
being used in ways that now seem at once arbitrary and predictable.
They seem arbitrary because unfamiliar in practice and inscrutable in
purpose. They seem predictable because elaborately patterned, repetitive, ubiquitous. This paradoxical combination of effects describes
much of Spenser's language throughout *The Faerie Queene* and many
other sixteenth-century poems, making them difficult to discuss in
later critical vocabularies. The apparent arbitrariness may result from
the fact that language is working according to principles or conventions we have not yet rediscovered. Or this seemingly arbitrary poetry may be predicated on the absence of certain later forms of linguistic order which itself reflects some fundamentally foreign notions
of both language and its place in the world. In contradiction of this
effect, the impression of predictability in sixteenth-century verse suggests a self-conscious acceptance of explicitly formulated principles
for the use of language in poetry. All of these possibilities—allowing
the distinct likelihood that quite contradictory assumptions may have
operated at the same time—invite historical investigation.

The elaborate patterning of the quoted lines is created by various
particular devices, beginning with the fact that they all consist of lists.
The catalogues crowd lines of verse with as many words in sequence
as they can contain, following a mode of amplification—"the more
the better"—recommended by some rhetoricians of the day.[11] The
practice of including lists in French writing of this period (modeled
on Rabelais) is attributed by Bakhtin to fascination with new things
and new words to name them.[12] Clearly here in these quotations, although the vocabulary is not new, a strong impulse behind the listing
seems to be to stress the poet's power of proliferating names to express
his matter. Attention is called to the naming function of words by the
prominence given to the device of piling on nouns, enhanced by their
frequent pairing with adjectives bound to them by alliteration: "scalding sighes," "sweet sighes." This function seems to be extended to

verbs when they are enumerated in the same list as nouns and with the same emphasis, so that distinctions among parts of speech are blurred: "For no thing, time, nor place, can loose, quench, ease."

Yet the interest in summoning names does not seem to reflect a search for precision of definition, to present the matter with greater exactitude or particularity. The items in the lists do not specially stand out for the distinctions they make or for the shades of meaning they contribute. Instead they seem chosen more for resembling one another by repetition of sound and metrical stress, so that distinctions among them tend to be minimized. Similarly the predictable pairings of adjectives with nouns also seem to distract from differences, for instance between "Soft words" and "speech" which is "low." The combined effect of these devices is to make the lists less descriptive than incantatory, magical. Each poet seems to be reciting a formula which is enumerative and repetitive. These poetic devices, among others, of listing and repetition will be shown in chapter 4 to be specifically associated with the language of prescribed prayer, which in its outward forms often closely resembles magical formulas. In a catalogue such as these the poet is reciting a kind of incantation, which has a predetermined character. His repetition of it therefore reflects some notions about what poetry is and how it is written which readers no longer share but must rediscover in order to think about the working of such devices.

The impression that the poet is reciting a prescribed prayer in these passages depends on the formulation of the lines themselves but also on the striking similarities among the four quotations. Not only does each adopt the form of a list, but items are also repeated from one list to another: sighs, tears, fire. The resemblances among these examples are especially remarkable because their similar exaggerated form, striking both to the ear and to the eye, appears to be surprisingly indifferent to variations in context. Spenser's list comes in the middle of a battle, Fairfax's at a moment of devotional fervor, the other two in lovers' complaints. In each instance the lines call so much attention to themselves by their rhetorical designs that they seem relatively independent of context, like inserted set pieces, an impression strengthened when they are encountered in poem after poem. This is a feature of sixteenth-century poetry recognizable to readers of it in such ubiquitous instances as the catalogue of trees and the anatomical catalogue or blazon enumerating the lady's parts (types to be discussed in chapter 4). The incantatory formulas in the four quotations are recited by the poets on different sorts of occasions which nevertheless have in

common the fact that they are charged moments, demanding a specially empowered language. By drawing upon it the poet turns the
passage into a kind of invocation. It therefore seems like an inserted
set piece because it seems designed to call attention to its origins outside the poet's mind and apart from its poetic context. It must therefore be predicated on conceptions of poetic inspiration and invention
embedded in the peculiar features epitomized in these quotations.

It has been habitual in discussions of sixteenth-century poetry to
comment on some of its peculiarities by simply saying that they suit
the taste of the time, especially in imitating the exaggerated fashions
prescribed in books on rhetoric.[13] Merely to attribute some seeming
oddities of this poetry to preferences of taste or fashion is not really
to cast light on them, however, as Barthes' different approach to the
significance of the mythologies of modern taste or fashion has made
us especially aware.[14] Behind such nonexplanations merely invoking
taste or fashion as causes are substantive issues about what sixteenth-
century writers conceived devices like the catalogue, or the pairing of
adjectives with nouns, or alliteration to be, what powers they were
thought to have, what moving effects they were intended to work.

It has also been habitual to attribute some characteristics of this
poetry like the dependence of poets on a common store of grammatical
devices, formulaic phrases, and stock figurative expressions to inexperience in the vernacular, or to metrical uncertainty, or simply to
mediocrity.[15] Yet if not only poor writers like the unknown contribu-
tor to Tottel's miscellany, but also great poetic innovators like Sidney
and Spenser shared the habits illustrated by the quoted examples,
then they can no more be explained as ineptitude than as modish
imitation. If an accomplished translator departed from his authoritative original text, as Fairfax does in these lines to exaggerate their
character as a catalogue of alliterated noun-adjective pairings and their
phrasing in familiar formulas, then his choices must be assumed to be
deliberate, to have significance beyond voguishness or clumsiness.
What is more, if representative uses of language in sixteenth-century
poetry seem peculiar to readers now in a variety of respects, their
remoteness from later verbal practices must point to some complex
and far-reaching differences in fundamental assumptions on which
such uses of language are predicated. These will be explored in sixteenth-century English writings where are embedded now unfamiliar
notions clustering around the acts of reading, naming, making metaphors, reciting charms.

1 The Verb *to Read*

Definitions

The historical differences between sixteenth-century and twentieth-century English that have been acknowledged most commonly in our reading of the poetry of this period are differences in the meanings of particular words. Even editions which modernize spelling and punctuation so that the language looks less radically remote from ours than in fact it was, usually gloss words whose meanings have changed as well as those which have dropped from use. Such differences in vocabulary constitute the least problematical kind of historical information about language to recover. It gives answers to the question asked first by any reader of a poem in which vocabulary is unfamiliar or used in puzzling ways: what meanings for this word were available to a poet writing in the sixteenth century?

There is another kind of question to ask about such historical changes in vocabulary when we want to discover assumptions different from our own underlying the language of a poem: what do the available meanings of a word in the sixteenth century imply? That is, what shifts in attitude might be indicated by differences in how a word could be used? This of course is a kind of issue which can only be raised from a later perspective, and is therefore never discussed in any writings of the period. Glossaries and dictionaries—the earliest in English appeared in the sixteenth century—provide some information necessary for exploration of such questions without ever answering them explicitly.

Instances of such shifts in meaning with profound implications surround the verb *to read*. The *O.E.D.* lists about twenty different uses in the sixteenth century, spelled in the given examples as variously as *reede, reade, read, reed, rede*. The citations are from a variety of prose works throughout the century, and from verse by Shakespeare, Sidney, Spenser, and other poets. In English-Latin dictionaries of the period, which preceded those wholly in the vernacular, *to read* is given the same definitions as *lego* in Latin lexicons, typically including "To gather: to read: to passe by: to choose."[1] Yet the verb actually derives

9

not from Latin but from the Old English *raedan*, meaning to advise or explain. This definition was still in use in the sixteenth century along with a noun form meaning advice or counsel. An example of this use frequently heard in English churches is in the first psalm in the translation made by Sternhold and Hopkins: the "man is blest that hath not bent to wicked rede his eare."[2] These meanings were held in respect when a special sanctity attached to origins—in words as in all things—as reminders of unfallen states. The derivation of a word from "our tongue before the *Norman* Conquest" was cherished for its purity by promoters of the vernacular like William Camden, a preference which Spenser and others extended to include archaisms from the less distant past.[3] When Spenser in *The Faerie Queene* praises Chaucer as a "well of English vndefyled" (4.2.32), he subscribes to the then common notion—which sanctified beginnings—that linguistic history consists in the gradual "bringing in of many corruptions that creepe along with the time."[4]

Besides this privileged root meaning, the *O.E.D.* lists six other uses still extant in the sixteenth century that have nothing to do with written language. In dictionaries of twentieth-century English, by contrast, the verb is first and almost exclusively associated with the comprehension of writing. The *American Heritage Dictionary*, for example, numbers nineteen different definitions of reading, all but four of which—the fourth, fifth, seventh, and eighth—explicitly involve comprehending writing.[5] Because this association now has priority in ordinary uses of the verb *to read*, the four interspersed definitions that do not make it explicit are likely to be taken as implying it figuratively. As a result, the phrases illustrating these exceptions, such as "He read her mind" or "read the sky for signs of snow," would seem in the context of the primary definitions to be metaphors comparing the sky and the mind to written texts, so that they may be said to be comprehended through an act similar to reading written words.

In origin, however, the verb was not linked to writing, and many of the definitions current in the sixteenth century identify it with experiences that are not specifically linguistic. Meanings given in the *O.E.D.* include acts of comprehending of many different kinds: to consider, interpret, discern; to guess, make out, or conjecture; to take for something; to discover the meaning of (especially a dream or riddle); to foresee, foretell, predict (especially one's fortune); to see, discern, or distinguish. Only this last definition is cited as rare in the sixteenth century, to be found solely in Spenser's poetry. Yet it shades so easily into other common meanings of the verb that it is hardly

idiosyncratic. Spenser's uses of *to read* in *The Faerie Queene* can therefore exemplify the possibilities inherent in the verb for his contemporaries as well. His ways of working with these generally available
meanings, examples will suggest, may not necessarily consist in either
the kind of punning especially associated with the "fluidity fundamental to the polysemousness of allegory" by Maureen Quilligan, or
the particular "metaphoric activity 'to read'" argued by A. L. De
Neef.[6] Exploration of no longer familiar assumptions underlying
some earlier uses of the verb may show that instances of what these
critics, from a much later perspective, take to be puns or metaphors
might have been differently understood in the sixteenth century.

Multiple meanings of *to read* in *The Faerie Queene* will also show,
along with discussions of other aspects of language, that Spenser's is
less eccentric or unusual in many respects than later criticism has
supposed. In a discussion of grammatical constructions in *The Faerie
Queene* Paul Alpers makes a point which this study will extend to
include other features of language:

> It is to some extent misleading to speak of Spenser's specialized
> sense of language. Loose sentence structure, double syntax,
> and the like are found in much Elizabethan poetry—most no-
> toriously, perhaps, in Shakespeare's sonnets. As a linguistic
> phenomenon, Spenser's ways with sentence structure should
> be regarded as a specialized development of characteristics and
> potentialities that belong to Elizabethan English and Elizabe-
> than verse.[7]

This view has not been stressed as it deserves, at least partly for reasons of ahistorical accident. One is that Spenser's poems are not often
set beside the work of poets whom he studied up to the time of his
first published verse in 1569, or who were writing during the next
two decades before the publication of the first three books of *The Faerie Queene* in 1590. In the context of examples drawn from that body
of writing, Spenser's will be seen to exemplify characteristics and po-
tentialities of much sixteenth-century poetic language. Another reason that his verse has been seen as more specialized or idiosyncratic
in many respects than this study will show it to be is that his poems
are most often read in at least partially unmodernized versions. These
preserve the antique aura he strove to achieve, but exaggerate or dis-
tort it by contrast with the modernized versions in which those poets
with whom he is contrasted are commonly met.[8] Unmodernized examples of their work will show up more clearly many habits of lan-

guage as well as poetic devices that have too often seemed to be Spenser's peculiarities.

Reading Writing

Spenser's uses of the verb *to read*, like his other linguistic habits, concentrate and elaborate practices common in the writing of his contemporaries. Among its more than a hundred occurrences in *The Faerie Queene*, only a small number have its now privileged meaning, the comprehension of writing. There are some instances where reading simply in that sense is intended when the narrator gives the audience directions for following a thread of his story, "As ye may elsewhere read that ruefull history" (3.6.53), or prompts our memories of some former episode, "as earst ye red" (3.11.3). Another time he disclaims knowledge of a detail, "I haue not red" (4.7.7), a device among others to be discussed which claim that the matter of the poem originates outside the mind of the poet who discovers it. The act of reading books, papers, inscriptions, letters is also occasionally demanded of Spenser's characters. At such points the verb is obviously used in its linguistic sense, but almost always in association with occult knowledge: the lost secrets of antiquity, sacred mysteries, or magic charms and spells. Reading is thus linked with opening hidden knowledge, and the matter to be read, the words and letters themselves, are endowed with magical powers (to be explored in chapter 4).

The number of such occasions when the verb *to read* is used simply in the sense of comprehending written words is very small in *The Faerie Queene*. There is one instance, a description of Belphoebe's face, in which this meaning is used explicitly as a term in a metaphorical comparison, making the act of reading language stand for the interpretation of something nonverbal:

> Her iuorie forhead, full of bountie braue,
> Like a broad table did it selfe dispred,
> For Loue his loftie triumphes to engraue,
> And write the battels of his great godhed:
> All good and honour might therein be red:
> For there their dwelling was.
>
> (2.3.24)

Here we can be sure that we are not misapplying later priorities when we interpret the verb metaphorically, because its linguistic reference is pinned down by a pattern of other words—"table," "engraue," "write"—describing Belphoebe's brow as a kind of book. This metaphor is a commonplace in poetry of the period, used to praise the lady's fair face as the written record by some supernatural author of her spiritual beauty. Sidney expands it for this purpose in *Astrophil and Stella* 71:

> Who will in fairest booke of Nature know,
>   How Vertue may best lodg'd in beautie be,
>   Let him but learne of *Love* to reade in thee,
>   *Stella*, those faire lines, which true goodnesse show.[9]

Again it is clear both that reading means the comprehension of writing and that it is here to be understood metaphorically, in the sense that we would tend to take the usage quoted earlier from the dictionary of twentieth-century English: "He read her mind." Yet even in such passages as these by Spenser and Sidney, where the verb is used as a metaphorical term with its linguistic meaning, it has some coloring that has faded from later usage. For the fact is that the activity it denotes—reading a book—has typically become a different experience from what it was in sixteenth-century England in some respects. Then it was a privilege exercised by more exclusive social groups on more special occasions than now. Books both in print or in manuscript—the word *book* was then used for either—were precious possessions in a sense that they are not usually thought to be now. One reason is that only the well-to-do would own even a small number of them, because they were relatively rare and expensive. Another is that more often than now they were elaborately ornamented objects. It is in part this attribute that must have suggested the appropriateness of books as a source for metaphors of praise, for instance in lines by John Heywood about the young Mary Tudor, quoted by Curtius in his discussion of the book as metaphor:

> The virtue of her lively looks
>   Excels the precious stone;
> I wish to have non other books
>   To read or look upon.[10]

Interpreting the lady's countenance may be compared to reading because a book is a physically decorative object in which the invisible beauty of a writer's thoughts is expressed.[11] Awareness of the book as visually pleasing could therefore be part of the definition of reading, although rightly only a part, as Sidney playfully chides in *Astrophil and Stella* 11:

> In truth, ô Love, with what a boyish kind
>   Thou doest proceed in thy most serious wayes:

That when the heav'n to thee his best displayes,
Yet of that best thou leav'st the best behind.
For like a child that some faire booke doth find,
    With guilded leaves or colourd Velume playes,
    Or at the most on some fine picture stayes,
But never heeds the fruit of writer's mind:
    So when thou saw'st in Nature's cabinet
Stella, thou straight lookst babies in her eyes,
In her cheeke's pit thou didst thy pitfould set,
And in her breast bopeepe or couching lyes,
    Playing and shining in each outward part:
    But, foole, seekst not to get into her hart.

Cupid is distracted as if by the appearance of "some faire booke" like those to which Stella's face, or Mary Tudor's, or Belphoebe's "iuorie forhead" are compared. Even when in these comparisons the verb *to read* is used in its linguistic sense, it can therefore involve sensory experiences which we no longer understand it to include when we say we can read a person. The metaphor as we use it is predicated wholly on the assumption that facial expressions, gestures, behavior convey meanings, are susceptible of being comprehended as writing is. The relevant term of likeness between person and book is intelligibility. In present use the metaphor would therefore not include in the comparison a response to any other feature of the book than its verbal character. By contrast, when a sixteenth-century writer uses the verb *to read* in association with a book, even then it may refer to a less strictly linguistic act than we usually understand by it.

Reading Speaking

In *The Faerie Queene*, when the verb *to read* is used for linguistic activity, this most often consists of spoken and heard rather than written language, a priority reflected in other ways everywhere in sixteenth-century writing. In its greatest number of uses in Spenser's poem, it is closer to its Old English origin—to advise or explain—having to do with speech. Such a meaning is given to it when Arthur commands Ignaro: "Aread in grauer wise, what I demaund of thee" (1.8.33). In this line the verb means to answer, as in many other instances where to read is to impart information in response to a question.

The verb also denoted naming of various kinds—"*Belphoebe* red . . . *Amoretta* cald" (3.6.28)—including the assigning of epithets—"False traytour certes . . . I read the man" (2.1.17)—and the recitation of catalogues (3.12.26). In these instances, to read is at once to identify and to describe or explain, for like epithets, names reveal natures: *Belphoebe, Amoret*, or the recipient of Arthur's command, whose "name *Ignaro* did his nature right aread" (1.8.31).[12]

These overlapping definitions of the verb in *The Faerie Queene* which associate reading with speaking, answering, explaining, describing rather than with the comprehension of writing are close to its root in Old English. They therefore reflect Spenser's specially intense reverence for original or antique meanings which embody the ideals celebrated in his fairyland. At the same time, the priority they give to speech rather than to writing is in every way representative of certain fundamental attitudes toward language in sixteenth-century England. There is abundant and various evidence in many kinds of works for this prevailing sense of priority. By contrast, the primacy of writing is now so deeply embedded in our most common definition of the verb *to read* that it is difficult not to impose it retrospectively, as Michel Foucault does in *The Order of Things* when he asserts the "absolute privilege on the part of writing" to be a ruling principle in sixteenth-century thinking. Since Foucault's argument in this part of his book is that the place of language in the world was then conceived to be very different from its position later, and in important ways to be discussed in this chapter, his insistence nevertheless on the priority of written over spoken language is particularly telling evidence of the influence of a more recent order of priority:

> This privilege dominated the entire Renaissance, and was no doubt one of the great events in Western culture. Printing, the arrival in Europe of Oriental manuscripts, the appearance of a literature no longer created for the voice or performance and therefore not governed by them, the precedence given to the interpretation of religious texts over the tradition and magisterium of the Church—all these things bear witness, without its being possible to indicate causes and effects, to the fundamental place accorded in the West to Writing. Henceforth, it is the primal nature of language to be written. The sounds made by voices provide no more than a transitory and precarious translation of it. What God introduced into the world was written words; Adam, when he imposed their first names upon the animals, did no more than read those visible and silent marks; the Law was entrusted to the Tables, not to men's memories; and it is in a book that the true Word must be found again.[13]

Clear and ubiquitous evidence to the contrary will show that in England in the sixteenth century, language was still conceived and experienced primarily as speech and that this predisposition had a shaping influence on many other aspects of linguistic theory and practice
to be discussed. Only when we recognize the existence of this different order of priority from the later one described by Foucault can we
begin to explore its profound ramifications in other fundamental ways
of thinking about language and its uses in poetry.

All the treatises about language that began to appear in the vernacular in this period consider its every component and configuration
chiefly in relation to its oral character. In one of the earliest books
about spelling, John Hart's *The opening of the unreasonable writing of our
inglish toung*, he defines "letters" as "the Images of mannes voice," and
argues that "even as euri bodi is to be resolved into those Elements
wherof it is composed, so everi Word is to be undone, into those
voices onli, wherof it is made."[14] "A voyce," from Latin *vox*, is made
synonymous by Cooper in his widely used bilingual dictionary with
"a sound: a word"; Florio translating Montaigne calls "the name" a
"voice which noteth and signifieth the thing."[15] Other writers also use
voice as a synonym for the whole word even when its transcription in
writing is the explicit subject, as in *The Petie Schole with an English
Orthographie* by Francis Clement. In his definition, "A Word is an
absolute and perfect voice, whereby some thing is ment and signified." William Bullokar describes his own book, which is also a guide
"to print, write, and reade Inglish speech," as a "true picture of voice."
Writing itself "is called of many, a dumb speech," or "*Vox Videnda*.
Which is writing, or the Characters of Mans voice." In a dictionary of
1581, the word "*Language*" is defined as borrowed from the French
but derived from Latin "*Lingua . . .* a tongue. For by the instrument
of our tongue, we vtter our language, or speach."[16]

In treatises on logic, grammar, and rhetoric, the oral character of
language is also given absolute priority. Ralph Lever's *The Arte of Reason*, for example, is predicated on the assumption that "Words are
voyces framed with hart and toung, vttering the thoughtes of the
mynde." The English translator of *The Rvdimentes of P. Ramvs his Latine
Grammar* answers the question "What is *Grammar?*" with the definition that "It is an art to speake well," ignoring the root meaning from
the Greek *gramma*, letter. The rhetorical handbooks that proliferated
in English in the second half of the sixteenth century make the same
claims for their subject. "Rhetorike is an Art of speaking" which aims
to make arguments "gay and delectable to the aere," and "*Composition*"

is the joining of words "in apt order, that the Eare maie delite in hearing the harmonie." Individual rhetorical devices are virtually always defined as a "forme of speaking" in some particular manner: allegory is "straunge speakyng, or borowed speach" in which words "sound one thing, and couertle shew forth an other thing"; proverbs are "sententious speeches"; paradox is "marueilous, or strange speech"; irony is "a mocking speech." Only very rarely is there any reference to language under the aspects of both "speaking or writing," and when such an acknowledgment of written language occurs, the writer lapses at once into terms which ignore it.[17]

The ubiquitous and consistent use of such phrases in all sixteenth-century writing about language is evidence that they were not fossilized remains of obsolete assumptions, as are some such terms in still current linguistic vocabulary, for instance *parts of speech, figures of speech, native tongue*. Other evidence that these attitudes were fully alive in the period is shown, for instance, in the way punctuation is typically described by Richard Mulcaster, Spenser's headmaster at the Merchant Taylors School. Punctuation marks, called "notes," which "we vse in the writing of our English tung," were conceived as aids to "pronouncing," dictating "our breathing, & the distinct vtterance of our speche."[18] This notion of punctuation marks shows clearly that reading itself, even in the sense of comprehending written language, was thought of chiefly as an oral exercise.

Incidental phrasing in all kinds of contexts confirms this fact. A translation of Erasmus's *Prouerbes and Adagies* includes "oure Englishe Prouerbe, which speaketh in this wise." Such wording might be supposed merely to reflect a habit still current now in phrases like *the book says*. Yet this translator's phrasing elsewhere shows more emphatically his assumption that the words of his book will be read aloud or at least experienced as they sound: "The English prouerbe is thus pronounced. Short and swete."[19] With similar implications Thomas Becon, in a discussion of the liturgy, writes that the "*Kyrye*" must have been borrowed from the Greek Church, "forasmuch as the wordes be Greeke and sounde in our English tonge. *Lorde haue mercy vpon vs*."[20] The words are identified with their sound because they were recited aloud by the reader of the printed page as well as by the congregation in church, and also, other evidence has shown, because speaking and reading were not conceived to be activities clearly distinct in kind. The blurring of this now marked distinction is reflected in many uses of language especially characteristic of sixteenth-century writing.

Such practices and notions were ultimately grounded in the primacy granted to "the faculty of speech" with which God endowed man before He gave "letters" designed "to teach his speech."[21] Again respect for origins dictated the ordering of priorities here as in most linguistic matters, which Mulcaster explains in representative terms: "Herevpon in the first writing, the *sound* alone did lead the pen, and euerie word was writen with those letters, which the *sound* did commaund, bycause the letters were inuented, to expresse sounds."[22] Since this order was grounded in biblical authority, it was generally accepted even by writers in vigorous disagreement about other religious beliefs. Sir Thomas More, for example, argued in support of Roman Catholic positions regarding tradition and written revelation that the faith of Adam and his heirs, "longe ere writing began, was taught by the worde of God unwritten."[23] At the same time his opponent William Tyndale, whose life work was to make God's written word readable to every Englishman in his own language, admitted that "God taught Adam greater thynges then to write."[24] To sacred authority Plato's was sometimes added. His *Cratylus* is invoked, for instance by Sir Thomas Elyot, to support this notion of priorities: "Consyderynge (as Plato sayethe) that the name of eyery thynge is none other but the vertue or effecte of the same thinge conceyued firste in the mynde, and than by the voyce expressed and finally in letters signified."[25]

These assumptions about the priority of speech underlie the associations of the verb *to read* with spoken language in *The Faerie Queene* and other sixteenth-century writings. They also help to explain a state of mind which could unquestioningly accept different spellings of a single word. This practice is illustrated in the five versions of the infinitive *to read* in quotations cited in the *O.E.D.*, along with other variants in the spellings of different tenses of the verb to be discussed. If a word was experienced fundamentally as a sound rather than as a visible sequence of letters, then variations in the written approximation of that sound would not alter the essential character of the word. Since words were conceived as images or pictures of sounds, multiple spellings could be compared to portraits.[26] These need not be identical to be recognizable as copies of a single original. Because reading aloud was still common practice, odd or unfamiliar spellings would have been sounded out as a matter of course (a practice to which a twentieth-century reader often has to resort in order to make out writing of this period). By this means their originals could be recognized by ear. Some such habit is implied when Mulcaster explains that in his table of words imported from foreign languages "I sought in it, to write all the words generallie after an English ear."[27]

The relative indifference by later standards to consistency in spelling of most sixteenth-century writers is connected—probably as both cause and effect—to another dimension of their linguistic experience: their handling of the alphabet. An early use of the word *alphabet* itself, cited by the *O.E.D.* from a quotation of 1580, is glossed by the native English word "crosrowe." This was the word most commonly used throughout the sixteenth century (largely replacing the middle-English term *abc*, which more often referred to a category of school-book discussed in chapter 4). The word was variously spelled—in a single work by a critic of what he calls "our Orthographie (or rather Cacographie in deed)"—*crossrowe, crosrow, crosrowe, crosrew.*[28] It derived from the unvarying practice in hornbooks, the first linguistic tools used by children throughout the century, of preceding the sequence of letters by the mark of the cross (with implications to be more fully discussed in chapter 4). The very word *crossrow* suggests primary attention not to a fixed, specific sequence of letters but to the nonalphabetic mark preceding them. At least in the first half of the century, that mark may have directed the pupil to make the sign of the cross before reciting the letters following it. Their commonest word for what we call the alphabet (in accordance with our conception of it as a fixed order of visible linguistic signs) therefore had a different reference. *Crossrow* denoted a row of signs named especially for its nonalphabetic mark, which corresponded to a physical ritual signifying an invisible grace.

Besides the radically different implications of the common word for the alphabet, there are traces of other unfamiliar practices in sixteenth-century England showing differences in the most basic linguistic assumptions. Although boys were required to have mastery of the hornbook and beyond before admission to grammar school, there is evidence that reading was sometimes taught without emphasis on learning the letters in sequence.[29] That seems to be the only possible explanation for a passage in Edmund Coote's treatise of 1596, *The English Schoole-Maister.* His comments are repeated almost word for word by Robert Cawdrey in the first vernacular dictionary of 1604, suggesting that they can be taken to represent some common rather than idiosyncratic concerns. Coote prefaces his table of words illustrating "the true Orthographie" with "Directions for the unskilfull." They explain the new word "Alphabet" and how to use its fixed sequence of letters as a guide to finding words in the table:

If thou hast not been acquainted with such a table as this following, and desirest to make vse of it, thou must get the Alphabet, that is, the order of letters as they stand, without
Booke perfectly: to know where euery letter standeth, as (*b*)
neere the beginning, (*m*) about the middest, and (*v*) toward the
end. Therefore if the word thou wouldest finde, begin with (*a*)
looke in the beginning of the Table, if with (*t*) looke toward
the end: Againe, if thy worde beginne with (*ba*) looke in the
beginning of the letter (*b*) but if with (*bu*) looke toward the end
of that letter, and if thou obseruest the same for the third and
fourth letters, thou shalt finde thy word presently.[30]

The table with these directions for its use comes at the end of the
book, which begins with the alphabet printed in six different type-
faces. The lessons are designed, the author repeatedly says, as se-
quential steps to be followed by anyone desiring to learn how to read
and write. The pupil who arrives at the end of the book must therefore be assumed to have learned to read by recognizing letters without
attention to alphabetical sequence, which he is required to memorize
only in the final lesson, where its usefulness for looking up words is
explained. The explanation itself shows that alphabetical arrangement
was not a system taken for granted as it has become.

Even Coote's own grasp of that order seems incomplete by present
standards, when his table contains such a continuous series as "habit,"
"harmonie," "haleluiah" (spelled "halaluiah" by Cawdrey and listed in
his dictionary after "hale"). Other books of this period which start to
set out matter alphabetically often stray much more widely from the
sequence. Sometimes the deviations result from lack of distinctions
among letters now clearly separate: *u*, *v*, *w*, or *i* and *j* were groups not
often clearly distinguished, although at other times they were assigned to the different categories of vowels and consonants. Elsewhere
the writer simply seems to lose interest in following the sequence and
begins to list words out of alphabetical order, as in Sir Thomas Elyot's
Banket of Sapience in a continuous series of topics such as "Ingratitude,"
"Idlenesse," "Inordinate appetitie," "Cunnyng," "Kynge."[31] At times
an author becomes distracted by some other principle of connection
than the alphabet, or gives priority to it. Father Ong cites an instance
where hierarchical importance takes precedence over alphabetical sequence in a collection of epithets for the use of poets. The section
beginning with *a* starts out of order with "*Apollo*" because, the author
explains, the patron of poetry should head the list.[32] In the first En-

glish dictionary of rhymes, a representative sequence of nouns grouped according to the "alphabet order of the last sillabls," but listed in alphabetical order of the first letter, places "the smart of a wound" after "a warte." It therefore gives priority to sameness of sound (and perhaps also to likeness of meaning, since warts and smarting wounds deface bodies), allowing this interruption of alphabetical sequence.[33] Etymology is a more frequent substitute, as in *A Dictionarie in English and Latin for Children*, which went through many editions starting in 1553. In the section on "Adiectiues belonging some to the bodie, some to the mind," the list of entries beginning with *A* starts out:

> Aboundant, or plentifull, *Copiosus, a, um.*
> Plentie, *Abundantia, & copia.*[34]

These practices parallel and support the habit of approximating the sound of a word by a variety of different spellings. For fixed orders of letters could not then have had the authority given to them once written language came to have the priority over speech embedded in our commonest definition of the verb *to read*. With their different sense of hierarchy, sixteenth-century writers like the poet-musician Thomas Campion held much more inclusively and insistently than would be true of later writers that "we must esteeme our sillables as we speake, not as we write; for the sound of them in a verse is to be valued, and not their letters. . . ."[35]

The authority of etymology and sound over spelling could contribute in other ways to variations in the written formation of a word. As Coote explains in the preface to his treatise:

> Where I vndertake to make thee to write the true Orthographie of any word truly pronounced, I must meane it of those words, whose writing is determined: for there are many wherein the best English men in this land are not agreed. As some write *malicious*, deriuing it from *malice*. Other write *malitious*, as from the Latine *malitiosus*. So some write *German* from the Latine, some *Germain* from the French.[36]

More often variations in sixteenth-century spelling resulted from copying the differences in pronunciation belonging to regional accents, such as "brode North speech and Sowthren smoothednesse." Against the disruptive effects of copying such local accents Coote cautions the pupil who has followed his course in orthography: "I know not what can easily deceiue you in writing, vnlesse it be by imitating

the barbarous speech of your countrie people. . . ."[37] Yet these deviations continued until the spread in the next century of the standard
recommended by Puttenham in *The Arte of English Poesie* of 1589: "the
vsuall speach of the Court, and that of London and the shires lying
about London within lx. myles, and not much aboue."[38]

Rapid historical changes contributed in other ways to the confused
state of English orthography, as they were accepted by some but re-
sisted by writers of more antiquarian taste. Charles Butler complains
of this kind of inconsistency as late as 1634 in *The English Grammar*.
He uses as an example a favorite homonym of poets: *heart:hart* (to be
discussed in chapter 3). What he calls "*heart cor*" was spelled "*hert*" in
"ancient writing" and the "old' Bible," "*hart*" in the homilies, but became "*heart*" in the "nu' mixt writing of *e* and *a*," although pronounced "*hart*."[39] While a small number of linguistic reformers like
Butler devised their own systems aimed to correct (though temporarily contributing to) the vagaries of English spelling, it remained by
recent standards somewhat inconsistent throughout the period. Even
"since printing began, (though printing be the best helpe to stay the
same, in one order)," it was still common to find a word spelled differently in the same sentence or line of poetry, for no apparent reason
other than ultimate indifference to consistency.[40] A telling example is
a sentence in Camden's *Remaines* defending English against attacks on
its unruly spelling:

> This variety of pronuntiation hath brought in some diversitie
> of Orthographie, and heere-vpon Sir *Iohn Price*, to the dero-
> gation of our tongue, and glorie of his *Welsh*, reporteth that a
> sentence spoken by him in *English*, & penned out of his mouth
> by foure good Secretaries, severally, for trial of our Orthogra-
> phy, was so set downe by them, that they all differed one from
> the other in many letters. . . .[41]

Here the subject of the discussion, what would now be called spelling, is printed both "Orthographie" and "Orthography," while Bullokar in his argument for its reform writes of "ortografy."[42]

Besides the relatively casual habits of sixteenth-century writers and
also printers (who were sometimes praised by their contemporaries
for establishing standards and at other times blamed for carelessness),
authors in this period also took deliberate liberties in forming words.
One such conscious practice was to adjust spellings of words—a sixteenth-century writer like Puttenham would describe them as words
"altered in sound"—to make meaningful connections among them, as

examples will show.[43] Although this was said by some rhetoricians to be "lawfull only to Poets," even prose writers sometimes followed it.[44] Puttenham objected to another habit of changing spelling to reinforce rhymes—as for instance in *The Faerie Queene* in the sequence of "dum . . . ouercum . . . mum . . . becum" (4.7.44)—but Spenser and his contemporaries often exercised this liberty as well.[45] These adjustments in the written formation of words are yet another kind of evidence of the primacy given to their audible character, which allowed characteristic freedoms in writing. That difference in priority was itself associated with still other unfamiliar attitudes to be discussed.

Reading Things

At an even greater distance from today's assumptions and usage are the instances in sixteenth-century texts when the verb *to read* refers to acts having nothing to do with language, either written or spoken. Spenser, for example, sometimes makes it literally synonymous with seeing as a physical experience (implying no metaphorical comparison to reading in the linguistic sense):

> Ay me, Deare dame (quoth he) well may I rew
> To tell the sad sight, which mine eies haue red:
> These eyes did see that knight both living and eke ded.
>
> (1.6.36)

This definition is the one found only in Spenser according to the *O.E.D.*, yet it is so closely related as to be sometimes indistinguishable from other common uses of the verb in the sixteenth century which associated it with nonverbal experiences. Such seeing for Spenser, for instance, shades into making a moral observation, a judgment of value:

> But neuer let th'ensample of the bad
> Offend the good: for good by paragone
> Of euill, may more notably be rad,
> As white seemes fairer, macht with blacke attone.
>
> (3.9.2)

These overlapping meanings for reading as seeing, judging, understanding come to be virtually identified in the narrator's description of the Tree of Life:

> There grew a goodly tree him faire beside,
> Loaden with fruit and apples rosie red,

As they in pure vermilion had beene dide,
Wherof great vertues ouer all were red.

(1.11.46)

Since what can be "red" are the "vertues"—the goodness and powers—of the apples, a reader now would tend to understand this as an
act of moral recognition, judgment, discrimination. We do not think
of virtues as being visible in the same way as colors. By this interpretation, the verb would be understood metaphorically. That is, the
virtues would be called readable if the tree is spoken of as if it were a
book. Then its visible properties would be said to be like written characters making up a legible account of its invisible qualities. Yet a different understanding is invited by Spenser's pointed rhyming of the
verb "red" with "red" used as either adjective or noun (the "apples
rosie red" may be rosie and red or of a rosie redness). The rhyme ties
those meanings to seeing: what is visibly colored "red" is directly recognizable as virtuous. That is to say that it can be "red" to be "goodly"
and "faire." To underscore the identity, Spenser chooses the same
spelling over other common variants for the noun and adjective (*redde*,
redd) and the participle (*rad, read, redd, redde*). The link forged by the
rhymed words, identical to eye and ear, points to a possible nonfigurative use of the verb *to read*. For the physical property of redness does
not need to be described metaphorically as if it were writing to be
"red" in these sixteenth-century meanings: to be seen, recognized,
judged.

Most often *to read* in association with nonverbal experiences is used
in *The Faerie Queene* for the act of interpreting in a character's countenance and manner the marks of moral qualities or inward states. The
satyrs who discover Una alone in the wood "feele her secret smart,/
And read her sorrow in her count'naunce sad" (1.6.11). Guyon comes
upon a fallen knight "In whose dead face he red great magnanimity"
(2.8.23). Apollo reaches the conclusion about repining Marinell

That he did languish of some inward thought,
The which afflicted his engrieued mind;
Which loue he red to be, that leads each liuing kind.

(4.12.25)

Studying similar expressions and gestures in Britomart, her nurse
reaches the same interpretation:

Aye me, how much I feare, least loue it bee;
But if that loue it be, as sure I read

> By knowen signes and passions, which I see,
> Be it worthy of thy race and royall sead.
>
> (3.2.33)

Reading the signs of love in a woeful countenance is so familiar in poetry that Sidney, who uses the commonplace often himself, also makes fun of it in Sonnet 31 when Astrophil says he can "reade" a lover's case in the moon's slow steps and wan face.

It is possible that in these instances the verb *to read* is used figuratively, as it was seen to be in the comparison of Belphoebe's forehead to a "table" inscribed by Love where "good and honour might therein be red." The fact that this metaphor is a commonplace, pointing back to medieval writing, in poetry of the sixteenth century would encourage such an interpretation.[46] Yet in these other quoted passages from *The Faerie Queene* where a character's appearance is read, there are no details to associate the act with the comprehension of language. The "signes and passions" therefore need not be understood as terms in a comparison of facial expressions to words. They are visible marks intelligible in their own nature, not only in so far as they may be compared to linguistic signs.

This conception of reading is at work in another instance where a character's face, here Scudamour's, is said to be readable. The act of interpretation is described by a comparison, but not to reading a book. Scudamour's face is described as susceptible to interpretation like a reflection in a mirror:

> Then vp he rose like heauie lumpe of lead,
> That in his face, as in a looking glasse,
> The signes of anguish one mote plainely read,
> And ghesse the man to be dismayd with gealous dread.
>
> (4.5.45)

Such comparisons of interpreting inward states in a face to looking in a mirror are also familiar in poems of this period. Shakespeare, for instance, uses this commonplace in Sonnet 62:

> But when my glasse shewes me my selfe indeed
> Beated and chopt with tand antiquitie,
> Mine owne selfe loue quite contrary I read.

This lover's face, or Scudamour's, is not said to be readable like a page of writing, but like a reflection in a looking glass. The "signes" to be seen in it are not first compared to words and then said to be readable, as they are, for example, in *The life and death of King Richard the Second:*

> Ile reade enough,
> When I doe see the very Booke indeede,
> Where all my sinnes are writ, and that's my selfe.
> Giue me that Glasse, and therein will I reade.[47]

In many other sixteenth-century passages a mirror is used for its own
independent capacity to reflect the signs readable in a person, which
does not depend on a comparison like Richard's of "Glasse" to
"Booke." Often, too, the commonplaces of mirror and book as distinct
but parallel revelations of character are strung together in sequence,
as in these lines from *The Second Part of Henry the Fourth:*

> He was (indeed) the Glasse
> Wherein the Noble Youth did dresse themselues.
> He had no Legges, that practic'd not his Gate:
> And speaking thicke (which Nature made his blemish)
> Became the Accents of the Valiant.
> For those that could speake low, and tardily
> Would turne their owne Perfection, to Abuse,
> To seeme like him. So that in Speech, in Gate,
> In Diet, in Affections of delight,
> In Militarie Rules, Humors of Blood,
> He was the Marke, and Glasse, Coppy, and Booke,
> That fashion'd others.[48]

Assuming a narrower association of reading with the comprehension
of writing, Curtius quotes these lines to illustrate "the metaphor of
'face as book,'" as if they worked in the same metaphorical way as
Richard's speech, when in fact "the Glasse" is more prominent in the
passage, and is not a metaphorical term in comparison with a book.[49]
The commonplaces of mirror and book are linked in similar fashion
in lines from Shakespeare's *Lvcrece.* Again the sequence is not arranged so that the *topos* of reading character in a book comes first as
an introduction to a series of examples then to be understood as comparisons with the act of interpreting writing. Instead mirror and book
are again listed as examples illustrating comparable acts of reading of
another, parallel sort:

> For Princes are the glasse, the schoole, the booke,
> Where subiects eies do learn, do read, do looke.
>
> And wilt thou be the schoole where lust shall learne?
> Must he in thee read lectures of such shame?

VVilt thou be glasse wherein it shall discerne
Authoritie for sinne, warrant for blame? [50]

Both these sets of lines from Shakespeare which catalogue readable objects—"the glasse, the schoole, the booke," "the Marke, and Glasse, Coppy, and Booke"—may be contrasted with an instance of twentieth-century phrasing in Michel Foucault's *The Order of Things*, where he is discussing the sixteenth-century belief in the existence of visible signs on the face of the world. Foucault makes a list comparable to Shakespeare's: "some signature on the plant, some mark, some word, as it were" (*sur la plante une signature, une marque et comme un mot. . . .*).[51] He is compelled to make a consciously figurative comparison of a nonverbal phenomenon to a word in order to make the point that in the sixteenth century the thing, the plant was thought to bear a readable sign. The reason that he does so even here in explaining the more inclusive earlier thinking about what constitutes reading must be that for him it is an exclusively linguistic act: signifying is above all the province of writing. By contrast with his figurative phrasing, in Shakespeare's two quoted lists the nonverbal object, the "glasse" where men "looke," is parallel and equal to the "booke" which they "read." The nonverbal object is not a term in a figurative comparison making it signify in so far as it may be said to be *like a book*. On the contrary, Shakespeare's lists are predicated on the notion that an exemplary human being may equally be compared to a mirror in which faces can literally be read in one sixteenth-century definition of the verb, and to a book in which words are read by a comparable kind of interpretive act. Sidney draws this same parallel in an Arcadian eclogue where he actually uses "glasse" as a verb, synonymous with reading in the sixteenth-century senses of seeing, recognizing, and interpreting:

Me-thinkes I am partaker of thy passion,
     And in thy case do glasse mine owne debilitie. [52]

The noun is used as a verb with these meanings also by other poets, for example by Southwell—"Where saints reioyce to glasse their glorious face"—and by Greville—"While I the Image of my selfe did glasse."[53] Based on the same assumptions, the passages in *The Faerie Queene* where reading faces is not part of a larger pattern of linguistic terms may be understood without recourse to comparison with reading words. That is, what the nurse interprets in Britomart's lovelorn countenance are "signes and passions" such as can be seen in a mirrored reflection. The narrator's statement that they are readable is therefore not a metaphor. The verb *to read* is here used for an act of interpretation which does not need to depend on a comparison with linguistic experience.

A fundamental assumption on which this use of the verb *to read* is predicated is the view which Foucault resorts to metaphor to describe, that objects in the world literally bear signs. Often sixteenth-century writers express this notion by using the commonplace of the creation as "that great booke of the world," "the Book of Gods workes," just as they use the comparison of the human face to a page of writing.[54] Nature is "*a booke*" in which "euery simple man who cannot reade, may notwithstanding spell that there is a God." It is "the *Shepheards Kalender,* and the *Ploughmans Alphabet.*"[55] Yet nature is also called the "Glas of creation"; it is often said that the "whole Frame of Gods Creatures, (which is the whole world,) is to vs, a bright glasse" in which meanings may be read as a face reflected in a mirror is said by sixteenth-century writers to be readable. The ultimate authority sanctioning this commonplace is as always the Bible: "The creation of the world is a glasse, wherein (saith S. *Paul*) wee may behold Gods eternall power and Maiestie. . . ."[56] Sylvester, closely translating Du Bartas, runs through the habitual series of commonplaces describing the world:

> It glads me much to view this Frame; wherein,
> As in a Glasse God's glorious face is seene:
> . . .
>
> The World's a Schoole, where (in a generall Storie)
> God alwayes reades dumbe Lectures of his Glorie:
> . . .
>
> The World's a Booke in *Folio,* printed all
> With God's great Workes in Letters Capitall.[57]

Such catalogues of metaphors to name the world commonly follow the same patterns as those that list objects where human character may be read—"the glasse, the schoole, the booke"—because they are predicated on the same assumptions. By contrast, in a twentieth-century piece of writing these comparisons would more likely be interpreted as granting signifying power to things in the natural world insofar as they may be compared to writing. It is difficult not to impose this understanding retrospectively, as in their different ways both Curtius and Foucault do, because of the priority now given to the act of comprehending written language in uses of the verb *to read.*

The effect of these assumptions on sixteenth-century writing is further illustrated in a passage from a treatise on education combining in a different way this cluster of commonplaces: "A skilful Tutor should frame and mould his Pupils *Imagination* according to the general patterne of the world to make him vniversal, in representing vnto him in his verie childhood, the catholike Countenance of Nature, that al the world may be his book."[58] What seems to be a lax mixing of metaphors—when a face is represented (whether in a mirror or a portrait) it turns into a book—is in sixteenth-century understanding neither loose nor exclusively metaphorical. The "Countenance of Nature," like Scudamour's face, or Marinell's, or Britomart's, can be read in itself because it literally has an inherent "general patterne" of nonverbal signs. Its representation is comparable to the readable reflection of a face in a mirror; both can be seen, recognized, and interpreted. The writer's comparison of the world's "Countenance" to a "booke" is like Shakespeare's parallels of "glasse" and "booke." One is not a metaphorical term for the other, but both name readable creations. The world is intelligible in its own nonverbal terms *before* it is compared to writing. According to John Hoskyns in *Direccions for Speech and Style*, "The order of gods Creatures in themselues is not only admirable & glorious but eloquent," so that "disordered speech is not soe much iniury to the lipps which giue it forth, or the thoughts which put it forth, as to the right pporcion & Coherence of things in themselues soe wrongfully expressed."[59] The repeated phrase "in themselues" stresses that the marks on things do not have to be translated into *words, as it were*, to speak their meanings (an attitude with further ramifications to be explored in discussion of metaphor in chapter 3).

The assumptions underlying these passages are among those implied by the meanings for the verb *to read* available in the sixteenth century: that words are not radically distinct from things by virtue of being intelligible, and that reading is therefore not a specialized linguistic enterprise. These passages also share another assumption implied by the frequent association of reading in *The Faerie Queene* and other texts of the period with nonverbal phenomena. They give priority to the intelligibility of things that have inherent nonverbal meanings, rather than assuming language to be the primary system of signs. The signifying power of "things in themselues" is itself the measure of the truth of verbal signs. For this reason "it followeth that they who will iudge of words," according to Richard Hooker, "should haue recourse to the things them selues from whence they rise."[60]

The ultimate sanction for this view of the order in which God endowed the created world with significance was the story in Genesis of Adam naming the animals, which is repeatedly mentioned in discussions of linguistic issues. It had the unique authority of sacred history in being a divinely inspired account of what literally happened. Richard Mulcaster explains why it was generally held to be the essential text on which all human conceptions of the nature of language and its relation to things must be based:

> We nede not to proue by *Platoes Cratylus*, or *Aristotles* proposition as by best autorities, (tho men be sufficient to proue their own inuentions) that words be voluntarie, and appointed vpon cause, seing we haue better warrant. For euen God himself, who brought the creatures, which he had made, vnto that first man, whom he had also made, that he might name them, according to their properties, doth planelie declare by his so doing, what a cunning thing it is to giue right names, and how necessarie it is, to know their forces, which be allredie giuen, bycause the word being knowen, which implyeth the propertie the thing is half known, whose propertie is emplyed.[61]

What God in this episode demands of Adam is an act of reading in several of its sixteenth-century meanings: to see in the sense of recognizing, to distinguish, to interpret, and finally to confer names. God's creatures are readable in that their "properties" have inherent signifying power, just as His own nonverbal act in presenting them to Adam "doth planelie declare" its meaning without mediation of language. God behaves toward Adam as the ideal tutor in the passage previously quoted, who presents the countenance of nature marked with nonverbal signs. Adam responds as an ideal reader in several sixteenth-century meanings of the verb *to read*, who sees the "properties" of things and confers their "right names" accordingly. Mulcaster's closing generalization drawn from Adam's naming makes clear that he does not believe the conformity of words to things to be the exclusive power of Hebrew, the language of God and Adam, but to be a possibility inherent in words. Their rightness is measured by the signifying power of the creatures themselves which, in Mulcaster's entirely representative interpretation of this episode in Genesis, has the priority of sacred origins and follows the divinely ordained pattern of subsequent history. For as writers on language such as the logician Ralph Lever repeatedly point out, "names are not giuen unto things afore the things themselues be inuented" (with further implications to be discussed in meanings for the verb *to invent*).[62]

This notion of priority is reflected in the order in which Spenser tells of the creation and then the naming of the Tree of Life (1.11.46). Another passage predicated on the same assumption is the description of the slanderous poet who appears to Arthur and Artegall in Mercilla's palace:

> Thus there he stood, whylest high ouer his head,
>   There written was the purport of his sin,
>   In cyphers strange, that few could rightly read,
>   BON FONT: but *bon* that once had written bin,
>   Was raced out, and *Mal* was now put in.
> So now *Malfont* was plainely to be red;
>   Eyther for th'euill, which he did therein,
>   Or that he likened was to a welhed
> Of euill words, and wicked sclaunders by him shed.
>
>   (5.9.26)

One implication here is that the first inscription cannot be "rightly read," in that it cannot be seen or interpreted by all, because it is not a right name for the poet's nature.[63] In addition, the narrator's alternative readings of "*Malfont*" as *he-who-has-done-evil* or *fount-of-evil-words* have implications like those of the shifting grammatical uses of "red" in the description of the Tree of Life. The same word can be an epithet or a metaphor. The same syllable—"*font*"—can be a form of a verb or a noun. Yet all the possible readings are true and identical because they conform to the nature of the thing they describe. The nature of the thing has priority over verbal order.

The biblical story of Adam reading the properties of the creatures was the ultimate sanction for some freedoms with language to be discussed, which are much more typical and central to the workings of language in this than in later periods. Nouns and adjectives and verbs can be allowed to shift and slide in special ways, phrases can more easily make several simultaneous grammatical constructions, spellings can be altered because what finally dictates their rightness is not linguistic order but the primary pattern of nonverbal creatures, which can be read directly, as sixteenth-century uses define that act. It could be said to follow, therefore, that no matter how we use or abuse words, Thomas Wilson asserts in his treatise on logic, "yet the trueth enclosed, is alwaies one, and geuen us of God, vse what termes we liste."[64]

Ultimately the understanding of reading to include seeing and describing things as well as comprehending written language is predicated on a way of thinking which lacks systematic or consistent distinctions between verbal and nonverbal phenomena. Both things and words can be read because both have signifying power, and not of clearly different kinds, though primacy belongs to things before names. Evidence for this cast of mind is abundant in sixteenth-century writing about what we would consider linguistic questions. Often the components of language are referred to as if they were things, objects are compared to verbal signs, and sentences about language slip without distinction into discussion of nonverbal matters.

Demonstration of this blurring of words and things can begin with concepts of letters, said by some theorists to be "first deuised, onelie to resemble, and expresse the sound by their aspectable figur."[65] The literalness of this notion that the actual shapes of letters have signifying power is shown by the visual terms habitually used to describe them. Letters are said by John Hart to be "the Images of mannes voice," so that "what writer doth nearest and most iustly decerne the diuers voices of the speach, he is best able to describe and paint the same with his pen." A reformer of spelling, Hart complains about the imperfections of English orthography, comparing it to bad portraits which do not "so well represent" their subjects "as should the figures of so many Apes, Asses and Beares" portray a human face.[66] This notion that letters have shapes which "describe and paint" sounds conforms to the priority universally given to speech, of which writing is a copy. It also gives a kind of autonomy to letters as being themselves visible objects with the kind of immediate signifying power with which all creatures are endowed: "two V.V. endwise ioyned maketh an X. which is in number 10, the figure of the Law, nature and grace so ioyned togethers, called the law of the tenne commoundementes. . . ."[67]

At the same time the emphasis on the identity of the visible shapes of letters with the sounds they copy made it possible to think of letters as indistinguishable from other sounds in nature, which is to say again that they have autonomous power to signify. In a dictionary of 1581 which went through many later editions, John Baret speculates about the origins of the "common usuall order of letters." He notes that "*A.*" is "the name of the fyrst letter in the crosrowe" in Hebrew, Greek, and Latin, as well as in English:

> But howsoeuer the reast of the letters were driuen to this or-
> der, it is of many supposed that nature hath taught A. to
> stande in the first place, as wee may easilye perceyue by the
> first voyce or confuse crying of yoong infants, which soundeth
> in the eare most like to *A.* being also the first letter in the name

of our great graundfather *Adam*, as *Abba* signifying Father,
which woorde children gladly heare and learne.[68]

A collection of commonplaces cites a variant belief that "*A.*" is the
"foremost" vowel because it is the first cry of "euery man-child . . .
as who would say, Adam, Adam," whereas "*E.*" is the second vowel,
"for that euery female child first cryeth E. E.; as who would say, Eue,
Eue."[69] Distinctions are blurred here among kinds of significance: in
the pronunciation of letters, the nonverbal sounds of things in nature,
and the etymology of Hebrew names. All have signifying powers, not
distinguished from one another. The definitions of letters as both
"seuerall soundes, or names thereof" is also merged, much as their
functions at once to name and to "describe or paint" sounds are commonly undifferentiated.[70]

Words are described as images in much the same way that single
letters are said to "paint" sounds. Sir Thomas More uses this linguistic notion to support a point of theological controversy. Since his op-
ponents honor the name of Jesus "which name is but an ymage repre-
sentynge his person to manes minde and ymaginacion, why and with
what reason can thei dispise a figure of him carued or paynted, which
representeth him and his actes, farre more playne and more ex-
pressely."[71] Because words as well as letters were conceived to be objects also in a physical sense, they too were thought to convey meanings by their shapes. In defending *The Excellency of the English Tongue*,
Richard Carew argues: "Now for significancye of wordes, as euery
indiuiduum is but one, soe in our natiue Saxon language wee finde
many of them suitablye expressed by woordes of one syllable. . . ."[72]
The term *indiuiduum* was used most often in logic, where it meant
particular, so that this argument makes the length or size of monosyllabic words a physical sign identical with the particularity of things.
Sir Thomas Elyot assumes the shapes of words and phrases to have
moral significance in a discussion of the classical imperative *nosce teip-
sum:* "And as concerninge all men in a generaltie, this sentence, knowe
thy selfe, which of all other is moste compendious, beinge made but
of thre wordes, euery worde beinge but one sillable, induceth men
sufficiently to the knowlege of iustyce."[73] Here the attention to the
numbers three and one gives a kind of magical significance to the
physical properties of words and phrases.

Their arrangement into images is an extension of this notion. Most
elaborately pictorial are shaped poems such as Watson's Sonnet 71 of

his *Passionate Centurie of Loue*, which he describes as "this Sonnet following compiled by rule and number, in the forme of a piller."[74] Other types of visual shaping also depend on patterned arrangements of words to represent what they signify. Sylvester departs from Du Bartas in translating a passage designed to imitate pictorially in its arrangement what the marginal gloss calls "the Worlds goodly frame." The translator first inserts the image of the world as a "Ball," and then describes it in lines listing nouns in reversed order (which in the original are repeated without reversal):

> This artificiall, great, rich, glorious Ball,
> Wherein appeares ingrau'n on euery part
> The Builders beauty, greatnes, wealth, and Arte,
> Arte, beauty, wealth, and greatnes, that confounds
> The hellish barking of blaspheming Hounds.[75]

The reversed lists make a kind of circular pattern which is repeated in the last line by the reversed alliteration, another departure from the original French. Gascoigne portrays a lover "toste twixt helpe and harme" by his repeated and reversed placings of alliterated nouns and verbs:

> How should I seeme my sighes for to suppresse,
> Which helpe the heart that else would swelt in sunder?
> Which hurt the helpe that makes my torment lesse?
> One seely harte thus toste twixt helpe and harme,
> How should I seeme such sighes in tyme to charme?[76]

Spenser extends this device to whole phrases depicting Malbecco torn between passion for his wife and his wealth:

> Ay when to him she cryde, to her he turnd,
> And left the fire; loue money ouercame:
> But when he marked, how his money burnd,
> He left his wife; money did loue disclaime.
>
> (3.10.15)

Spenser elsewhere describing the giant who weighs words "Within his ballaunce" to measure "The right or wrong, the false or else the trew," repeats those four nouns in balanced and reversed pairs through a sequence of six stanzas, making a visual pattern depicting what they describe (5.2.44–49). The nouns are therefore treated as tangible objects not only by the giant but in his own way by the poet. Yet even when Spenser here stresses the visible aspect of words, he recalls his readers to the prevailing sense of linguistic priority by giving primacy to their sounds:

> And so likewise of words, the which be spoken,
> The eare must be the ballance, to decree
> And iudge, whether with truth or falshood they agree.
>
> (5.2.47)

Under this aspect, words as well as letters could be thought to correspond to nonverbal sounds in nature. Sylvester translating Du Bartas departs from the original in a line so exaggeratedly patterned by alliteration and assonance that it seems to make a kind of literal equation between the sound of its words and the noise of thunder which it describes: "It roules and roares, and round-round-round it rumbles."[77] The rhetorician Henry Peacham, discussing metaphors that describe man with words usually applied to animals, illustrates them with a list of natural sounds and actions. These are interchangeable with the names for them, again blurring the distinction between the word and the sound for which it is a name:

> The particular properties of the dumbe creatures are very significant, especially in their Verbes and Verbals, for by whining we signifie murmuration and grudging, by stinging secret mischiefe, by crowing proud and arrogant insulting, by swimming possession of abundance, or fruition of great felicitie, by roaring impatient miserie, by hissing terrible threatening, or bitter cursing, by houering attending opportunitie, by deuouring consumption, and by fawning flatterie.[78]

Similarly the signifying power of verbal sounds could be assumed to be one with the "natures" of passions and the meanings of physical gestures like spitting:

> Againe, for expressing our passions, our interiections are very apt and forcible: as findeinge ourselues somewhat agreeued, wee cry *Ah;* yf more deeply, *Oh;* when we pittie, *Alas;* when wee bemone, *Alacke;* neither of them soe effeminate as the Italyane *Deh* or the French *hélas.* In detestation wee saye *Phy,* as if there withall wee should spitt; in attention, *Haa;* i[n] calling, *whowp;* in hallowinge, *wahahowe:* all which (in my eare) seeme to be deriued from the very natures of those seuerall affections.[79]

As these lists show, the correspondence or identity of linguistic sounds and nonverbal phenomena could be thought to exist not only in expressions we would now call onomatopoetic.

Peacham's representative discussion of onomatopeia itself still further blurs distinctions by including more disparate types which would not now be grouped together as examples of that figure. He begins as a writer now might define the term: "First, by imitation of sound, as to say, a hurliburly, signifying a tumult or uprore. . . . Secondly, by imitation of voyces, as the roaring of Lyons. . . ." Then he adds types of onomatopeia more surprising to us. The third type is the formation of a name from its original root, "so *Luds-towne* of *Lud*, and now *London*," which makes derivation of names from similarities of sound a parallel to imitation of physical noises like the roaring of lions. The fourth category of onomatopeia is the composition of compounds: "as to say, Oratorlike, scholerlike: also to call a churle thickskin, a niggard a pinchpeny, a flatterer a pickthanke, a glutton a bellygod."[80] Here links with previous kinds of onomatopeia are provided only by the first two examples which, although they do not themselves imitate sounds, do at least describe imitative behavior: acting like an orator, like a scholar. Fifthly Peacham includes archaisms, the "imitation of ancient speech" (for which he specially commends "the new Shepherds calendar"). Under this category he also cites examples which again describe imitative acts or styles, such as to "Platonize." In his series of categories, then, he includes actually imitating sounds and talking about imitation, without acknowledging differences in kind between the two varieties. Finally, therefore, distinctions disappear between imitation in words or in acts, and between language which actually copies nonverbal sounds and words which instead name or describe acts of verbal imitation.

Elsewhere not the shape or sound of words but their definitions are equated with the significance of acts. Again it is assumed that language and actions express meanings in the same way. Sir Thomas Elyot makes such an identification between the opening movement in a dance, a curtsy or bow, and the name for it, "honour." We are of course still familiar with formalized dances in which acts expressing meanings are given names also expressing those meanings: *curtsy* from *courtesy* is an example. What makes Elyot's sentences different from the way a later description would be likely to work is the ease with which he moves from analysis of the motion of bowing to a sentence where the name "honour" refers to moral states at a great distance from the dance. The focus shifts from the action to the word naming it without acknowledgment, as if their ways of signifying were identical:

> The first meuying in euery daunse is called honour, whiche is
> a reuerent inclination or curtaisie, with a longe deliberation or
> pause, and is but one motion, comprehendinge the tyme of
> thre other motions, or settyng forth of the foote. By that may
> be signified that at the begynning of all our actes, we shulde
> do due honour to god, whiche is the roote of prudence; whiche
> honour is compacte of these thre thinges, feare, loue, and
> reuerence.[81]

Again the numerology of three and one makes almost magical the
identity of words and the actions they name.

Another instance in which a discussion of words slides into interpretation of significant acts without apparent awareness of the shift is
in *The Garden of Eloquence.* Peacham's subject is the places of invention,
meaning here (with implications to be discussed in chapter 3) what a
writer now might call categories of metaphor. The first such category
from which figures are taken is sight:

> Hence it is that a man may say, I see your meaning, I see your
> malice. . . . In like maner by this place we may signifie, by
> looking vp, heauenly meditation, for so doth our Sauiour
> Christ vse it, where he saith, then looke vp for your redemp-
> tion draweth nigh. Also by high lookes is very often signified
> pride and disdaine, by winking parcialitie, by circumspection
> wisdome and prouidence, by looking awry displeasure, by
> looking downe discomfort, and sometime view an suruay, by
> looking vpon due and deliberate consideration.[82]

This list of metaphors drawn from the category of sight shifts from
examples which are verbal formulations to others which are significant acts. Peacham considers the gesture of "looking vp" to "signifie"
in the same way—"In like maner"—as the metaphorical command to
"looke vp for your redemption draweth nigh." His list therefore ignores distinctions between words and nonverbal phenomena.

If words signify as shapes, sounds, and names, those properties
themselves must not have been clearly distinguished. Sometimes even
the pure grammatical form of a word is said to have significance. This
is true of an explanatory note in Lily's Latin grammar, authorized by
King Henry for use in all grammar schools. Directly following the
rule that an adjective "agreeth with his substantiue, in case, gendre,
and numbre" is a sentence which presumably did not strike sixteenth-
century readers as nonsensical: "Here note, that the masculine gendre
is more woorthy than the feminine, and the feminine more worthy

than the neutre."[83] Another instance of the signifying power of grammatical forms is given in an English translation published in 1569 of a
grammar of 1512, cast in the form of an allegorical war between the
noun and the verb. Some effects of the battle are described as alterations in the genders of nouns. "*Balsamum* among all Nounes and trees
abode only a neuter," which grammatical phenomenon is then used to
explain the natural fact that the species is rare. For, being neuter in
gender, the tree—or noun—cannot multiply. In turn that botanical—
or linguistic—phenomenon is used to explain "the cause (as sorrowfull) he yeldeth his fruict all in teares."[84] While a reader now might
assume this little story to be entirely allegorical, it may not be strictly
so. One simple reason is that the neuter pronoun *it* was not yet firmly
established in English, so that "he" in the story need not be exclusively a masculine personification (especially as this "he" is "neuter").
More tellingly, since physical and linguistic spheres—here the botanical fact and its grammatically parallel form—are not clearly distinguished in the passage, the word cannot be considered only as an
allegorical way of speaking about the natural phenomenon.[85] Even the
judicious Hooker assumes the significance of grammatical forms when
he uses parts of speech to make a theological point about faith expressed in good works. God is said "to respect *aduerbs* more then
verbes, because the ende of his lawe in appoynting what wee shall doe
is our owne perfection, which perfection consisteth chiefely in the
vertuous disposition of the minde, and approueth it selfe to him not
by *doing*, but by doing *well*."[86]

This conception of words as objects and sounds in a world full of
other signifying nonverbal things and noises is deeply embedded in
the thinking of writers throughout the sixteenth century. Its persistence and strength is shown by the fact that later grammarians, beginning in the first quarter of the seventeenth century, felt the need to
argue against it. A very clear early example is in John Brinsley's *The
Posing of the Parts*, published in 1612. The issue is raised in his opening
lesson about the noun, always the first part of speech to be discussed
in English as well as Latin grammars:

Q. What is a Noune?
A. A Noune is the name of a thing, that may be seene, felt,
   heard, or vnderstood.
Q. What meane you by that?
A. It is a vvord that signifieth the name by which we cal any
   thing, whatsoeuer may be seen, felt, hard, or vnderstood.
Q. Giue me examples of it.

    A. A hand *manus*, a house *domus*, goodnesse *bonitas*.
    Q. Is a hand a Noune?
    A. A hand it selfe is not a Noune: but the word signifying a
        hand, is a Noune.[87]

Next to the second answer is a marginal gloss stating a rule character-istically ignored by earlier writers: "In Grammar we haue to consider words, not things." The observation of this rule implies assumptions radically different from those on which sixteenth-century English in many fundamental respects was predicated. Its application in the pe-riod following systemized not only "Grammar" but many other as-pects of language, in ways that gave writers new powers while dis-allowing some earlier freedoms. As a corollary, it restricted the reference of the verb *to read*, giving priority to its association with the comprehension of written language.

The Narrator as Reader in *The Faerie Queene*

    Spenser's uses of the verb *to read* in *The Faerie Queene* create a special relationship among the narrator of the story, the characters in it, and its audience, all of whom are called on to perform acts of read-ing of every kind. Explicit phrases draw us all into the common en-deavor of responding to a world full of signs: "which we reed" (4.2.39), "one mote plainely reed" (4.5.45), "full hard to read" (4.9.36), "Who wonders not, that reades so wonderous worke?" (3.2.20). Since the signs to be read are faces, objects, actions, situa-tions as well as words, the activities of reading in which narrator, characters, and audience of the poem are all involved have the ten-dency to blur or dissolve clear distinctions between the poem itself and the world it describes. This effect depends in part on the fact, fully exploited by Spenser, that the same verb could define the re-sponse to things seen as well as read in the linguistic definition. The poet's words, when they are designed to make us see things, call upon us to read in another sense than comprehending language. It is as if we are made to respond to the signifying power of things in them-selves, as they are directly visible to the characters in the poem, not only as those sights are pictured for us through the medium of the poet's words.

    This involvement can be illustrated in one of the many descriptions where the reader is made to see what is visible to the characters as well as the narrator: the presentation of Mercilla to Arthur and Arte-gall as she is seated high on a throne where she "might of all men royally be seene":

All ouer her a cloth of state was spred,
   Not of rich tissew, nor of cloth of gold,
   Nor of ought else, that may be richest red,
   But like a cloud, as likest may be told,
   That her brode spreading wings did wyde vnfold;
   Whose skirts were bordred with bright sunny beams,
   Glistring like gold, amongst the plights enrold,
   And here and there shooting forth siluer streames,
Mongst which crept litle Angels through the glittering
   gleames.

                                                    (5.9.27–28)

In this instance the single use of "red" accumulates meanings succes-
sively. As the last item in a catalogue of regal fabrics, coming after
"cloth of gold," it is first understood as a noun naming another color
signifying majesty. Then the speculative phrasing of "Nor of ought
else, that may be" is completed when "red" is taken as the past participle of the verb, with the meaning of seen and also judged. Combined with the name of the color, these definitions involve Spenser's
audience in precisely the responses to the signs of visible things that
are demanded of his characters. Those responses are then fused with
our distinctive activity of attending to the words of his poem. This
added definition he gives to "red" as a past participle by following it
with the line "But like a cloud, as likest may be told." His poetic
comparison of Mercilla's garment to a cloud is "likest" to the nature of
the cloth, so that we respond to his similitude as a true name for the
material of Mercilla's robe. It is "told" to us by the poet, who then
adds other comparisons to make us read her nature in his words. In
this passage the verb is therefore also to be understood metaphorically: Mercilla's appearance may be interpreted as if it were writing.

The multiple possibilities of "red" in this representative description
help to explain Spenser's extremely numerous and varied uses of the
word. *The Faerie Queene* is in an especially concentrated sense focussed
on responding to the signs of things and also to the language of the
poet describing them. Yet the assumptions about those forms of interpretation are not peculiar to Spenser but are widely held by sixteenth-
century writers, who shared the multiple possibilities understood by
the verb *to read*.

Among its various uses in *The Faerie Queene*, quotations have shown
it to mean both seeing and describing. Many passages of description
in the poem are therefore instances of reading for both the poet and
his audience; his act of describing makes us see the things present also

to the characters in his story. This effect might be supposed to be the aim of any descriptive writing: to give the reader the sensation of seeing what the writer's words depict. Yet if a typical description from *The Faerie Queene* is set beside one from *Paradise Lost*, some distinctive experiences of reading Spenser's descriptive poetry stand out. These effects are predicated on assumptions not only about what constitutes reading, but about the nature of language itself, which he shared with his contemporaries.

In Book 9 of *Paradise Lost*,[88] Milton's narrator tells us what Satan sees when

>   *Eve* separate he spies,
> Veild in a Cloud of Fragrance, where she stood,
> Half spi'd, so thick the Roses bushing round
> About her glowd, oft stooping to support
> Each Flour of slender stalk, whose head though gay
> Carnation, Purple, Azure, or spect with Gold,
> Hung drooping unsustained, them she upstaies
> Gently with Mirtle band, mindless the while,
> Her self, though fairest unsupported Flour,
> From her best prop so farr, and storm so nigh.
>
>   (9.424–33)

Some details when pressed might not be precisely pictorial—"Veild in a Cloud of Fragrance" surrounds Eve with a mysterious sweetness not quite seeable. Still the narrator's language is full of visual effects, so that the reader has an impression of seeing Eve's lovely gestures through a haze of radiant colors.

Visual effects are achieved through parallel means by Spenser in the first of three stanzas describing the daughters of Celia, who appear to Una and the Red Crosse Knight in the House of Holinesse:

> Thus as they gan of sundry things deuise,
>   Loe two most goodly virgins came in place,
>   Ylinked arme in arme in louely wise,
>   With countenance demure, and modest grace,
>   They numbred euen steps and equall pace:
>   Of which the eldest, that *Fidelia* hight,
>   Like sunny beames threw from her Christall face,
>   That could haue dazd the rash beholders sight,
> And round about her head did shine like heauens light.
>
>   (1.10.12)

Again details are given which enable us to visualize what is immediately present to the characters in the scene, the stately movements of

the ladies and the radiance of Fidelia's "Christall face." This detail is
not much more precisely pictorial than Eve's veil of perfume, but creates a comparable effect, giving a visual impression of luminosity and
transparency.

As descriptions—although the lavish texture of Milton's contrasts
with Spenser's restraint—these passages work in many of the same
ways. They begin with an announcement that a narrator is going to
tell us what a character in the scene is looking at. We are therefore
made conscious of our position as an audience for the poem, not immediately present but invited by the poet to attend to his description.
It will allow us to visualize through the medium of his language. Our
situation as an audience for the poem is then kept before us by reminders of the narrator's role in enabling us to experience the scene.

Figures of speech are such reminders. Milton's narrator makes a
comparison of flowery perfumes to a cloud which is like a kind of
bridal veil over Eve's nakedness. The narrator in Spenser's stanza uses
similes comparing Fidelia's radiance to "sunny beames" and "heauens
light" surrounding her head with a mysterious halo. These figures call
attention to the narrators performing what sixteenth-century writers,
following tradition leading back to Aristotle, define as the poet's distinctive art of making comparisons. Something in the scene is described by being likened to something which is not there. Spenser
calls particular attention to this device by saying that Fidelia's brilliance was "like sunny beames . . . That could haue dazd the rash beholders sight." The form of the verb "could haue" insists on the fact
that the likeness is drawn by the poet. Our visual response is not to a
sight that we are told actually did daze Una and the Red Crosse
Knight, who undazed see Fidelia without the mediation of the poet's
language. Our response is to what they "could haue" seen if they had
been privileged to read the poet's simile as we do.

The comparisons in each passage keep the reader aware of the narrator's presence also because they are expressive of his feelings: toward Eve a sense of wonder mingled with tenderness, pity, grief; toward Fidelia a sober admiration and awe touched with fear. The
narrator's feelings are also emphasized elsewhere in these passages,
especially by epithets. This figure was recognized in rhetorical handbooks mainly for use "to praise or dispraise," signaling the writer's
evaluation.[89] Here "fairest . . . Flour," "goodly virgins," "louely wise"
give notice of the poets' presence, calling attention to their language
as the medium through which we experience the scene as the characters present cannot.

The second and third stanzas presenting Celia's daughters do not use descriptive language in quite the same ways. Of course what they consist of is still Spenser's choice and arrangement of words, but here they are so chosen and arranged as to make us experience significance in the scene in a different way. Here the narrator's mode of description may be seen to shift in such a way as to demand what would now be considered two different kinds of acts from us, both of which could then have been literally called reading. This possibility may provide a way of thinking about the seeming peculiarity, the apparent inconsistency of the passage, of a kind critics have found typical of Spenser's poem:

> She was araied all in lilly white,
> > And in her right hand bore a cup of gold,
> > With wine and water fild vp to the hight
> > In which a Serpent did himselfe enfold,
> > That horrour made to all, that did behold;
> > But she no whit did chaunge her constant mood:
> > And in her other hand she fast did hold
> > A booke, that was both signd and seald with blood,
> Wherein darke things were writ, hard to be vnderstood.
>
> Her younger sister, that *Speranza* hight,
> > Was clad in blew, that her beseemed well;
> > Not all so chearefull seemed she of sight,
> > As was her sister; whether dread did dwell,
> > Or anguish in her hart, is hard to tell:
> > Vpon her arme a siluer anchor lay,
> > Whereon she leaned euer, as befell:
> > And euer vp to heauen, as she did pray,
> Her stedfast eyes were bent, ne swarued other way.

> > > > > (1.10.13–14)

Stanza 13 consists almost entirely of a catalogue naming objects—their colors and materials, what they contain, how they are held. They are not described by similes in which the poet likens them to things outside the visible scene, which would be reminders that it is being not only depicted but interpreted or evaluated for us by the poet's words. There are also no epithets expressive of the poet's feelings, or other figures which would also signal that the scene is specially shaped for us as audience by his interpretation of it. The catalogue is presented as a factual account of the contents of the scene such as would be visible to any observer of it who merely notices what is there. One exception might be taken to be the statement that the serpent in the cup "horrour made to all, that did beholde." This line might seem exceptional in the stanza in that it does associate feeling with an object in the catalogue. Yet compared to one from the previous stanza which it parallels, its different way of working is clear. Earlier, we have seen, the narrator compares Fidelia's radiant looks to sunbeams "That could haue dazd the rash beholders sight," had they been visible in the actual scene. Their imagined effect on a hypothetical beholder is asserted by the poet, who therefore tells us more than would be noticed by a spectator present at the scene. This claim, like his choice of comparisons, reveals his own feeling of awe for what he describes, and reminds us that it is his language which enables us to experience it. There we are in the special situation of an audience for the poem, which is not the position of the characters who undazed see Fidelia's face immediately in front of them. By contrast, in the second stanza the serpent, unlike the imagined sunbeams, is actually present to be looked at—by the characters as well as by the poet— along with the other objects. It does evoke a visible response, "That horrour made to all, that did behold," on this occasion Una, the Red Crosse Knight, and the narrator. The response itself is part of the situation, can be seen by any observer of it. Along with the colors, materials, shapes, and positions of objects, this horror in its beholders is recorded as another visible aspect of the scene. The same effect is achieved in the description of the last object in the catalogue of stanza 13, the book "Wherein darke things were writ, hard to be vnderstood." The narrator appears here to include himself among observers for whom the baffling nature of its contents is one among the other qualities noticed about the book; at least he makes no claim to have privileged knowledge of it which he withholds. His language does not tell more about it than could be observed by those who immediately witness the scene.

There is therefore a new kind of reportorial objectivity about the descriptive language in this stanza, so that we are less aware of the presence of the poet choosing words to make us experience the scene as his terms interpret it to us. It is as if we see the objects and actions as they are directly visible, not through the medium of his interpretation, so that we are put in the same position as those that "did behold" it rather than being located, as we were in the previous stanza, in the privileged situation of readers seeing what the characters "could haue" beheld only with the guidance of the poet.

This kind of description extends through the presentation of Speranza in stanza 14. It also consists of a seemingly factual catalogue of objects—their colors, materials, shapes, positions—and of actions. Again there is an apparent exception in a response evoked by another "sight," here Speranza's cheerless appearance:

> Not all so chearefull seemed she of sight,
> As was her sister; whether dread did dwell,
> Or anguish in her hart, is hard to tell.

These lines in a way might be said to interrupt the reportorial description of objects and actions in most of stanzas 13 and 14, because they do call special attention to the presence of the narrator. Yet they do not do so in the same ways as the similes and epithets in stanza 12, which make us aware that a poet's language is the medium through which we experience the scene in a privileged way. Here the reference to the narrator's bafflement in trying to read Speranza's cheerless looks reminds us of his presence as he is again in the act of disavowing the role of poet. His stance is not that of authoritative interpreter who enables us to read the scene, to respond to it and evaluate it in his terms. His claim is merely to be a viewer of it, who can see and know no more than the characters or than we who are presented with the visible objects in the catalogue. Here he says that it is "hard" to read Speranza's appearance, as it was "hard" to understand the dark writings in Fidelia's book (by the repetition suggesting that in both instances his role is that of mere observer). This reminder of his presence therefore does not work against the increasingly reportorial objectivity of the description. As a result, the final details are recorded as if they were sights directly present to us, not effects made visible to us only as readers of the poet's language. Of course we are in fact reading Spenser's words, but here they are chosen and arranged to give the impression that we are experiencing things without the mediation of language. We are in the position of performing a different act of reading by responding, as if we were present at the scene, to the signifying power of what is visible in it. That is, we recognize meanings in the objects and actions catalogued without being told what those meanings are by comparisons or evaluative terms given by the poet to us as audience for his poem. We read the object on Speranza's arm, the "siluer anchor," and her act of leaning on it to signify independently, without a poet's words attributing meanings to them. We understand Speranza's upward gaze the way the narrator does, "as she did pray" (with the simultaneous meanings of as if and while she did pray).

The narrator here disavows authority to interpret for us, and therefore removes us, in midpassage, from the distinctive position of audience for the poem receiving instruction from him beyond what is noticeable by other observers of the scene. Here he is not our interpreter but, like us and the characters, a reader of things in several sixteenth-century understandings of reading. Of course our response to these details in fact depends on Spenser's choice of an emblem—an "anchor"—which has traditional significance—hope—as does the heavenward gaze of her "stedfast eyes," and on his identification of its wearer by the name of "*Speranza*." Yet the narrator merely reports these details as he observes them without interpretive comment. They communicate meanings because they belong to a world of things that have prior and autonomous signifying power not dependent on language used to depict them. Spenser's description is predicated on the same assumptions as Peacham's list of metaphors drawn from sight, which also moves from examples that are verbal formulations to others that describe acts such as "looking vp," by which "we may signifie . . . heauenly meditation."

The way the narrator slides from one kind of descriptive language to another here is typical of many passages in *The Faerie Queene*. Their distinctive mode may be further defined by contrast with the description introducing the bride in Spenser's "Epithalamion." It begins with a kind of invocation—"Loe"—signalling his inspired power to bring what he sees before the reader. He then shapes his description as a catalogue of similes (traditionally associated with the blazon to be discussed in chapter 4) which demonstrate the poet's art of comparison, and concludes by asserting his power to see and name "that which no eyes can see,/ The inward beauty of her liuely spright."[90] The description of Celia's daughters also begins with the invocation "Loe," followed by similes that depict the scene by means of comparisons to what is not part of it, not visible to any observer present to look at it. These verbal devices make us see in terms we would not, were we not the privileged audience for his inspired description, as we are also in the blazon of the bride. Then, however, the devices that demonstrate the poet's special vision are replaced by a catalogue naming the properties of things in the scene about which he speculates like any other viewer.

This shift is the "problem of narration" much discussed by Spenserian critics, whose arguments have been summarized and thoughtfully addressed by Paul Alpers.[91] It is the problem of reconciling the narrator's shifting poetic functions which show up typically in many passages of description such as the one here discussed, where the narrator slides from the position of omniscient authority to the position of one among other observers of the scene described, who are required to interpret the world of appearances. This apparent conflict or discontinuity in modes of narration has seemed strangely inconsistent with Spenser's prevailing habits of using language to accommodate, reconcile, assimilate disparate experiences. Numerous explanations for this apparent discontinuity at the center of Spenser's narrative mode have been proposed, which Paul Alpers, for example, has summarized under the headings of either a dramatic or a rhetorical view of narration.[92] To his discussion might be added some inferences from our exploration of sixteenth-century understandings of what constitutes reading.

In these three stanzas all sorts of details show that they form a closely linked design. This patterning makes stranger the presence of what seems a very marked shift within the passage in kinds of descriptive language, demanding a striking shift in the ways we respond to them. Yet in the context of meanings for the verb *to read* in the sixteenth century, the two modes of description could have seemed less distinct. To comprehend written language and to see the significance of visible objects or actions were both literally defined by the verb *to read*. The first stanza demands one kind of reading, the second and third another, closely parallel kind. The sense of dislocation readers now feel in making the shift may be the result of a stricter understanding of the act of reading, reflecting the priority now given to its association with the comprehension of written language. If for Spenser and his contemporary audience reading included various kinds of acts, then in passages like this he may be characteristically assimilating, accommodating, paralleling experiences rather than distinguishing, contrasting, dislocating them. And if this is so, then the descriptions of the bride in the "Epithalamion" and of Celia's daughters can be seen to work in this fundamentally similar mode of assimilation.

Still, important differences are demonstrably there. They raise the question why the narrator of *The Faerie Queene* shifts between the position of omniscient authority and the position of an observer of the visible scene when the poetic voice in Spenser's other poems does not do so. An answer often given by Spenserian scholars is that *The Faerie Queene* as a whole, and especially Book 1, is centrally concerned with the difficulties of interpreting the appearances of things; that Spenser therefore wants to engage not only his characters but also his readers in acts of interpreting such as we perform when we read the anchor on Speranza's arm to signify hope without any explication from the narrator.

The exploration in this chapter might suggest an additional reason for the use in *The Faerie Queene* of a narrator who acts at times as inspired authority and at other times, even within a single unified passage, as observer or reporter. To return to the "Epithalamion": the invocation "Loe" signals special powers of inspiration by which the poet may see into the meanings of an actual occasion, a bridal day which is identified as the poet's own wedding. The lady described is introduced as his bride. There is no question to be raised about her actuality. In the description of Celia's daughters the poet's invocation "Loe" also summons special powers to interpret, but the matter he interprets is not in the same sense an actual occasion. Fidelia and Speranza and the other persons and scenes of fairyland could be taken to be images chosen by him as inspired poet, like the "sunny beames" and other imagined matter he draws on for comparisons. To establish the existence of fairyland outside his own mind, his narrator's shift to observer of what he sees, but about which he has no privileged knowledge, is a useful device. If he does not know what is in Fidelia's book or what causes Speranza's cheerless looks, then he is not their maker. He has not invented them, by our definition of the verb *to invent*. He can therefore be both inspired poet and observer who tells what he has come upon. In this sense he is an inventor in the root meaning of the verb *to invent* common in the sixteenth century, to find or discover (*in* + *venire*), which Spenser uses literally in this sense in *The Faerie Queene* (3.5.10; 5,2.20).

That is, the poet's shift to the position of observer is a way of validating the origin and existence of his matter outside his own mind. He has not made it up but has found it and described what he has found as if in the act of discovering it. The anchor, the book, the cheerless lady are not images thought up by the poet and self-consciously offered to us in the privileged situation of readers, the way his similes are. Instead they are objects outside his mind and therefore visible to any beholder. For this reason they may be read in one sixteenth-century meaning of the verb *to read*, as his words may be read in another, and in a sixteenth-century meaning of the verb *to invent* as well.

Paired Adjectives and Nouns
The opening sonnet of Spenser's *Amoretti* begins with the adjective "Happy," around which the poem is built:

> Happy ye leaues when as those lilly hands,
>   which hold my life in their dead doing might
>   shall handle you and hold in loues soft bands,
>   lyke captiues trembling at the victors sight.
> And happy lines, on which the starry light,
>   those lamping eyes will deigne sometimes to look
>   and reade the sorrowes of my dying spright,
>   written with teares in harts close bleeding book.
> And happy rymes bath'd in the sacred brooke,
>   of *Helicon* whence she deriued is,
>   when ye behold that Angels blessed looke,
>   my soules long lacked foode, my heauens blis.
> Leaues, lines, and rymes, seeke her to please alone,
>   whom if ye please, I care for other none.[1]

Regular recurrences of "happy" paired with a different noun at the beginning of each quatrain prepare for the recapitulation in the couplet, a structure known as correlative verse (a form to be discussed in chapter 4). The placing of adjectives with nouns creates other predictable effects, especially the rhythmic pattern made by their seemingly inevitable pairings: "lilly hands," "soft bands," "starry light," "dying spright." This design is emphasized by alliteration in such combinations of adjective and noun as "bleeding book," or of double adjectives in "dead doing might" and "long lacked foode." Adjectives and nouns are bound together also by blurrings of grammatical distinctions. In the first pairing, "lilly" is used as an adjective but evokes its different meaning as a noun by being unchanged in form from it. In the several genitive constructions, nouns and adjectives seem closely linked because no apostrophe separates the first nouns, and because the adjectives alliterate with both: "loues soft bands," "harts close bleeding book."

These devices are everywhere in Spenser's poetry, along with other repetitive uses of adjectives relatively unfamiliar in later writing. One is the constant repetition of the same pairings—"loftie towres, "hollow cave," "cole black," above all "wearie way" or "wearie wandring way"—sometimes explained as imitation of older types of formulaic oral poetry.[2] More puzzling is Spenser's practice of joining adjectives with nouns to make combinations that seem to verge on redundancy. Examples in *The Faerie Queene* include unusual pairings such as "safe securitie," "matchlesse paragone," along with others like "rockie stone," "foggie mist," "drowsy slepe," found also in verse by his contemporaries, where either term could be used alone or the pair could be reversed without much change of meaning or emphasis. For instance, Watson's pairing of "stonie rocke" is scarcely distinguishable in effect from Spenser's or Sidney's combination, "rockie stone."[3] In a slightly different way, Spenser's preference for "hollow" above other ways of describing caves tends toward redundancy as it is used over and over in *The Faerie Queene*. For in most contexts in which the pairing appears, the quality of hollowness is not for any apparent reason important to stress specifically, the way the phrase "darksome hole" is essential in the description of Errour's den because the Red Crosse Knight's armor when he enters can make only "A litle glooming light, much like a shade" (1.1.14). The caves described as "hollow" could as pertinently be called "darksome," as are certain others in the poem, or "hideous," to convey a judgment or quality of feeling: "hollow" as opposed to terms of praise like *spacious* or *roomy*, for example. That is, the epithet attaches an ominous gloom to the places that it is used to describe, but not more particularly than would any number of other adjectives used by Spenser to convey a similar impression when combined with other nouns: "dread darknesse," "dongeon deepe," "yawning gulfe" (1.5.44,45,31). The repeated couplings of "hollow" and "cave" cannot therefore be entirely explained as indications of mood, any more than they can be accounted for by particular contexts. Certainly the choice of adjective also cannot be explained as a way of distinguishing caves which are hollow from those which are not, as "hollow eyne" would be differentiated from "watry eyen" (1.9.35,15). It cannot therefore be thought of as a way of specifying.

The combination "hollow cave" so often repeated seems, like "rocky stone," "foggy mist," or still more obviously Googe's "painfull paynes," to be formed on some additional principle not at work in much later poetry.[4] Its recovery can cast light on uses of language that by later ways of thinking seem deliberately to verge on redundancy,

or to be chosen to produce other strange effects. These ways of handling adjectives, along with others illustrated in the opening sonnet of
Amoretti, are prominent features of Spenser's poetry. They will also
be shown to be characteristic of the work of poets he read while his
style was forming, and others who were writing at the same time that
The Faerie Queene and the *Amoretti* were composed.

The following anonymous poem from Tottel's miscellany, "Of his
loue named white," is representative of English poetry in the sixteenth
century, but not of later periods, in its ways of using adjectives:

> Fvll faire and white she is, and White by name:
> Whose white doth striue, the lillies white to staine:
> Who may contemne the blast of black defame:
> Who in darke night, can bring day bright againe.
> The ruddy rose inpreaseth, with cleare heew,
> In lips, and chekes, right orient to behold:
> That the nere gaser may that bewty reew,
> And fele disparst in limmes the chilling cold:
> For White, all white his bloodlesse face wil be:
> The asshy pale so alter will his cheare.
> But I that do possesse in full degree
> The harty loue of this my hart so deare:
> So oft to me as she presents her face,
> For ioye do fele my hart spring from his place.[5]

The most obvious feature of adjectives again here is that there are a
great many of them, especially paired with nouns: within four lines
"lillies white," "blacke defame," "darke night," "day bright," "ruddy
rose," "cleare heew."

While their number is striking, the adjectives do not stand out individually, for several reasons. One is that their pairing with nouns is
so regular as to seem almost automatic, giving them a predictable
rhythm. This in turn prevents them from coming into sharp focus. A
second is that typically they seem chosen for sound effects that blend
them into other heard patterns: "ruddy" alliterates with "rose," "day
bright" is an internal rhyme with "darke night," "harty loue" is
echoed in the repetitions of "my hart." In still other ways the adjectives (in addition to "white" which is the lady's name) seem to have
been chosen for reasons besides elaborating on the meaning of the
noun or conveying a judgment or feeling. Some seem to have been
chosen to make familiar pairings: in the sixteenth century *lilly white*
and *dark night* were combinations at least as firmly embedded in the
language as they are now. Still others seem to be used mainly to create

grammatically ambiguous word play. To illustrate, in the second half of line two the word "white" may be both an adjective and a noun. For the line may say that the whiteness of the lady strives to stain the lilies white to match her, or to stain the lilies' whiteness to make them darker (variants allowed by the absence of apostrophes in possessives).[6] Again in line 10 "asshy pale" blurs grammatical distinctions by pairing what may be an adjective and a noun—as in *asshy paleness*— or a doubling of adjectives like "Fvll faire" and "right orient."

Because these uses of adjectives are not congenial to much later literary taste, and because this example is in no way a distinguished poem, a reader now might attribute them simply to the anonymous author's dependence on stock images and diction to please by making easy word plays and sound effects, and to fill out the metrical line.[7] The poem itself can be dismissed in these ways. It is interesting only as it exemplifies a kind of verse that pleased the editor and authors of Tottel's miscellany and its many readers from its first publication in 1557 through the rest of the century. Yet to say that the effects concentrated in its adjectives reflect prevailing taste in that period is not to understand their use here or by Spenser and many other sixteenth-century writers of unmistakable distinction. The widespread appreciation by the best poets of such uses of adjectives shows that they were not merely fashionable. They must have been predicated on fundamental attitudes accepted by writers and readers of the time. These deeply held assumptions made available a style valued for using language, prominently adjectives, in ways that seem at once oddly predictable and arbitrary. This combination of effects is puzzling now because readers no longer share or even recognize the cast of mind which found these verbal devices congenial and powerful.

The appeal of this style can be taken seriously when its uses are explored at their most effective, as in the opening of Daniel's Sonnet 42 from *Delia:*

> Beautie, sweet loue, is like the morning dewe,
> Whose short refresh vpon the tender greene,
> Cheeres for a time but tyll the Sunne doth shew,
> And straight tis gone as it had neuer beene.
> Soone doth it fade that makes the fairest florish,
> Short is the glory of the blushing Rose.[8]

Another beautiful instance is a stanza from Spenser's description of the Bowre of Blisse:

> The whiles some one did chaunt this louely lay;
>   Ah see, who so faire thing doest faine to see,
>   In springing flowre the image of thy day;
>   Ah see the Virgin Rose, how sweetly shee
>   Doth first peepe forth with bashfull modestee,
>   That fairer seemes, the lesse ye see her may;
>   Lo see soone after, how more bold and free
>   Her bared bosome she doth broad display;
> Lo see soone after, how she fades, and falles away.
>
> (2.12.74)

The resemblance in uses of adjectives among the quoted sonnets and this stanza shows their wide appeal, which was not restricted to any single form such as the sonnet. The deliberateness of choice in the kind and placing of adjectives can in fact be measured particularly in these lines from *The Faerie Queene*, which translate a stanza of Tasso's *Gervsalemme liberata*. For it is chiefly by making use of adjectives in ways characteristic of contemporary poetry in English that Spenser departs here from the Italian original.

Adjectives abound in Daniel's lines and Spenser's stanza, especially coupled with nouns making balanced rhythms. The paired words are also bound together by alliteration—subtly in Daniel's "short refresh," more pointedly in Spenser's "louely lay" (for which there is no parallel in Tasso's lines). Neither poet tries to avoid conventional diction, as they repeat one of the commonest adjectives of this poetry: "faire," "fairer," "fairest." Daniel's "morning dewe" is a pairing as familiar as the anonymous poet's "darke night," while Spenser's coupling of "bashfull" with "modestee" seems to overlap meanings as he does elsewhere in the phrase "shamefast modestie" (1.10.15), words which he actually does use in another place as synonyms (2.9.43). In both these pairings adjective and noun are close enough by definition to be almost reversible, as in Harington's "modest shame," but as they are not to the same degree in others of Spenser's phrases such as "myld modestie" (1.8.26) or "sober *Modestie*" (4.10.51).[9] In its effect the combination "bashfull modestee" seems to approach redundancy.

Both Daniel and Spenser also place adjectives to make grammatical ambiguities. Daniel's "tender greene," for example, can be a doubling of adjectives in which "greene" is the color of young plants, or a pairing of an adjective with a noun, making "greene" the name of a verdant lawn. This double possibility makes the word useful in stock compounds—"Sommers green" and "grassie greene" are familiar in this poetry. Other common pairings work in the same way: "cole blacke," "milk-white," "lillie white," or "rosie red" used by Spenser to describe the apples on the Tree of Life (1.11.46).[10] Daniel's sonnet includes another example of word play with adjectives in the line "Soone doth it fade that makes the fairest florish." The final alliterated pair may consist of an adjective and a noun, or an adjective serving as a noun—meaning the superlative of Spenser's "faire thing"—and a verb. With more emphasis Spenser places the single word "broad" to act as both adjective and adverb: "Her bared bosome she doth broad display." Repeating the sound of "bared," "broad" can be another adjective describing "bosome," while also attaching to the verb to say that the "bold" rose displays herself abroad or broadly.

One more example from poetry of this period illustrates again the pervasiveness and power of such uses of adjectives, the octave of Shakespeare's Sonnet 64. Here adjectives embody in their own patterns the "interchange of state" lamented by the poet:

> When I haue seene by times fell hand defaced
> The rich proud cost of outworne buried age,
> When sometime loftie towers I see downe rased,
> And brasse eternall slaue to mortall rage.
> When I haue seene the hungry Ocean gaine
> Aduantage on the Kingdome of the shoare,
> And the firme soile win of the watry maine,
> Increasing store with losse, and losse with store.

Single and double adjectives are paired with nouns in relentless balance, woven together by complex alliterative patterns, for instance of *r*, *l*, and *s* sounds in line 4. Some make familiar combinations: "loftie towers" are common in this poetry.[11] Some create grammatical as well as other ambiguities. That is, in line 4 "eternall" first modifies "brasse" to make a paradox which is intensified when the adjective is seen also to modify "slaue": what is eternal about brass is its eternal enslavement. In the same line "mortall rage" can mean human rage or rage which is itself subject to mortality.

According to sixteenth-century practice, the phrase "mortall rage" can also mean a rage which is the cause of mortality, in which sense it is a transferred epithet. This use of adjectives is sometimes categorized and condemned by the rhetoricians as "*Hypallage*. . . . The use hereof in *Poesie* is most rife." Elsewhere it is considered to be a type of "*Metonymia*" when "the cause efficient is understood by the effect, as when we say, *Pale death, sorrowfull dread, headlong rage, carelesse wine, vnshamefast night:* wherein is shewed, that dread causeth sorowe, death palenes, wine carelesnes, and so of the rest."[12] Some transferred epithets—in this list " *sorrowfull dread*" and *"carelesse wine"*—derive from the fact that adjectives with certain suffixes could be either active or passive.[13] The others listed along with many stock pairings in six-teenth-century poetry—*weary way* and *wan hope* are favorites to be discussed—must have been formed on the basis of some other prin-ciple.[14] In later writing, adjectives used this way would commonly be understood as personifications, but in the sixteenth century their function was in theory differently conceived. These transferred epi-thets, like other typical combinations of adjectives and nouns—in al-literated phrases, stock formulas, pairings tending toward redun-dancy, reversible syntax—were predicated on assumptions no longer implicit in present English usage. They must therefore be recovered and recognized if its distance from sixteenth-century language and poetic practice is to be measured.

Noun Adjectives, Noun Substantives

A conception of adjectival constructions different from our own is confirmed by the earliest grammars of the English language, such as William Bullokar's of 1586, Paul Greaves's of 1594, Charles Butler's of 1633. They all show that the adjective was not yet considered to be a separate part of speech but to belong, as in Latin, to one of the two categories of noun: *De Adjectivo* or Noun Adjective, as distinct from *De Substantivo* or Noun Substantive. The rhetoricians assumed the same relationship, as is shown in Peacham's discussion of the fig-ure "Scesis onomaton." His examples are described as sentences con-sisting "altogeather of nownes, as when to euery Substantiue and [sic.] Adicatiue, is ioyned."[15] This close identification of the two parts of speech involved fundamental attitudes toward language and its place in the world which are sometimes explicit, more often implied only, in discussions of the adjective by grammarians and rhetoricians. Their assumptions may also be shown to be at work in the practices discussed in the quoted passages of poetry.

Of course such varied uses of language cannot have been predicated on any single conception. It is also important to acknowledge again here that linguistic theory cannot be imagined in a monolithic rela-tionship to the actual practices of poets, even in this period when new interest in theoretical writing in the vernacular about language coin-cided with newly self-conscious experimentation in vernacular poetry. With this caution against simple assignments of causes and effects, it is still possible to show that conceptions of adjectival constructions seem to have played some part in the uses here illustrated, in combination with other pressures on poetic practice that have been recognized. For instance, the fact that Spenser departs from Tasso in the quoted lines must depend in part on differences—about which sixteenth-century writers often commented—between Italian and English. Certainly the greater number of monosyllabic words, valued for their Saxon purity, had a then recognized influence on English verse.[16] Compare, for example, these lines from Tasso with versions of them by Spenser and Fairfax:

> *Cosi trapassa, al trapassar d'vn giorno,*
> *De la vita mortale il fiore, e'l verde.*

Spenser expands the second line into a catalogue of monosyllables (a common feature of this poetry to be discussed):

> So passeth, in the passing of a day,
> Of mortall life the leafe, the bud, the flowre.
>
> (2.12.75)

Fairfax stays closer to the original and yet his lines include only two words of more than one syllable compared to eight in the Italian:

> So, in the passing of a day, doth passe
> The bud and blossome of the life of man.

This feature of English can help to account for many stylistic devices, including the dependence especially by weaker poets on adjectives which can be paired with nouns as an easy way to fill out the metrical line (the list being another ready device for this purpose). Yet more than such a technicality must be involved, for example, in Fairfax's choices when translating Tasso in this characteristic English line: "Soft words, low speech, deepe sobs, sweet sighes, salt teares."[17] The translator's departures here from the Italian—only four pairings stretched over two lines and separated from each other by conjunctions—work in some of the same directions as Spenser's in the previously quoted description of the Bowre of Blisse. Their effects are common also in poems which are not translations and therefore reflect no pressures either to match or to vary an original. An example is a catalogue by Southwell made up of pairings very similar to Fairfax's:

> Prone looke, crost armes, bent knee and contrite hart,
>   Deepe sighs, thick sobs, dew'd eyes and prostrate
>   prayers.[18]

At issue in this and other poetic practices is a sense of adjectival constructions predicated on assumptions also embedded in theoretical writings about the parts of speech.

English grammar books follow their Latin models with very little acknowledgment of differences between the two languages. They draw the distinction between the two kinds of noun on the grounds that "A Noune Adiectiue is that can not stand by him selfe, but requireth to be ioyned" to a substantive. Its description is then commonly phrased as it is by Butler: "An Adjectiv' implyeth a qaliti belonging to a Substantiv'." [19] In rhetorical handbooks, where the adjective is sometimes mentioned in discussions of the epithet—the term *adjective* originated in a Latin translation of the Greek *epitheton*—some of the same wording appears. [20] For example, Peacham writes: "*Epitheton*, called of *Quintillian Appositum*, of others *Adiectiuum:* Is a figure or forme of speech, which ioyneth Adicatiues to those Substances, to whom they do properly belong. . . ." [21] In similar terms Puttenham, discussing "Epitheton, or the Qualifier," defines it as "giuing euery person or thing besides his proper name a qualitie by way of addition." [22] This representative wording points to a fact confirmed everywhere in sixteenth-century writing about language: the grammatical relationship between noun substantives and noun adjectives was thought to express the ontological relationship, understood as Aristotle had defined it, between substance and quality or accident. These were the fundamental categories of being "in the world: for euery thing, whatsoeuer it be, is either a substance, or accident." [23]

Logical treatises, often using terms very similar to those of the grammarians and rhetoricians, argue that qualities or accidents cannot exist apart from substances or subjects, "without the which those accidents haue no being at all." The description which follows is phrased in representative terms in Thomas Blundeville's *The Arte of Logicke:* "Qualitie is an affection, shape, or forme of the minde or bodie, whereof the thing so affected or formed taketh his name: as of wisdome a man is said to be wise, of iustice hee is called iust." [24] The grammatical analogy emerges, for instance, in *The Arte of Reason* in Lever's parallel explanation that a "nowne adiectiue" is "deriued of a nowne substantiue. . . . As of vertue is deriued a vertuous man, a vertuous thing, and vertuously: of health, healthfull, and healthfully." [25] It follows that the logicians often illustrate what they define as qualities by catalogues of adjectives, though without always quite consistently distinguishing them from the other category of noun, as

in this list compiled by Lever: "suche thynges as appertaine to the
qualitie of a man, as wise, folishe, liberall, couetous, learned, igno-
raunt, a runner, lame, sober, hastye, swart, faire, black, foule,
proper, yllfauored or such like."[26]

Along with such descriptions and illustrations of what they call
qualities or accidents, the logicians analyze their function in enabling
us to experience substances. Blundeville, again using representative
phrasing, says that a substance

> is clad with accidents; for otherwise we could not discerne
> with our outward senses, whether it were a substance, or not;
> for we cannot see the substance of any thing with our bodily
> eyes, but onely with the eyes of our minde & vnderstanding;
> but we may see the shape, the quantitie, the colour, and such
> like accidents cleauing to the substance, without the which
> those accidents haue no being at all: and therefore in seeing
> such accidents, we may assure our selues that there is a sub-
> stance sustaining those accidents, which doth alwayes re-
> maine, though the accidents doe faile or change neuer so
> often.[27]

The Aristotelian distinction of substance and accident had been
reflected in European grammatical tradition since the Middle Ages,
but the analogy between the nature and function of accidents and
adjectives seems not to have been generally brought to bear in English
medieval verse.[28] That is, the grammatical practices in sixteenth-
century poems that can be thought to reflect this analogy are not characteristic of Chaucer's poetry, for instance. Lavish uses of adjectives,
especially paired with nouns, as well as other constructions so far
illustrated, are rare in his poetry (and in the work of his followers).[29]
They can be found mainly in a few passages of unusual literary ele-
vation such as the introductory stanzas of *Troilus and Criseyde*, among
his poems the favorite in the sixteenth century, or the catalogue of
trees in the *Parlement of Foules* (shown in chapter 4 to be considered as
an archetype of poetry). These exceptional passages may themselves
have added their influence with other forces contributing to later poetic practices. For not only Spenser but many other English poets of
the sixteenth century took Chaucer for an ideal model in the vernacular. Those passages in which his style is most heightened and literary
may therefore have seemed specially authoritative and exemplary,
though untypical of his poetry. Even in the verse of Lydgate and other
poets inspired by the ideal of the aureate style—"sententiousness and
sonorous ornamentation"—adjectives are not as consistently a prom-

inent feature, nor are they used habitually in the same ways, as in sixteenth-century verse.[30]

At the same time another force contributing to the stylistic patterns especially typical of this poetry may have been that medieval notions of grammar, logic, and the analogies between them were first written about in English in the sixteenth century. The fact that the earliest books in the vernacular on these subjects, as well as on rhetoric, appeared at this time may have extended interest in such concerns or at least perhaps brought them more into the foreground of literary discussion. Their relevance for poetry, which was then also being developed in new ways in the vernacular, could therefore perhaps more readily be absorbed into practice at a time when there was intensified interest in poetic experimentation. Their weakened relevance for later poetry may at least in part be a reflection of revolutionary changes in English thought in the seventeenth century, changes which Alfred North Whitehead directly associates with revised conceptions of the distinction of substance and accident. He argues that whereas sixteenth-century logicians hold that it is the accidents cleaving to substances which make them knowable by our senses, Locke maintains "That by our senses we know nothing of external objects beyond their figure [or situation], magnitude, and motion." This philosophical revolution, according to Whitehead (and to scholars perhaps influenced by his work), had radical implications for language and ultimately for its uses in poetry:

> These sensations are projected by the mind so as to clothe appropriate bodies in external nature. Thus the bodies are perceived as with qualities which in reality do not belong to them, qualities which in fact are purely the offspring of the mind. Thus nature gets credit which should in truth be reserved for ourselves: the rose for its scent: the nightingale for his song: and the sun for his radiance.[31]

In this revolutionary way of thinking, not only the relation of accidents to substances but the expression of that relationship in language is conceived in wholly different terms.

Discussions by grammarians and logicians of the period do cast some light on the distinctive style of sixteenth-century poetry, beginning with the fact that adjectives are linked to nouns with peculiar frequency. Reflecting the importance attached to such pairings, Ascham advocates "the right ioyning togither of substantiues and adiectiues" as the first grammatical lesson after the parts of speech.[32] The

two grammatical forms were thought of as fundamentally bound together in the same way as accidents cleave to substances: the adjective
unable to stand alone, the substance unknowable without it. To borrow Blundeville's wording in his description of quality: it is from the
"Qualitie" or noun adjective that the "thing" or noun substantive "taketh his name," so that the combination of substantive and adjective
could be thought of as a single designation.[33]

This conception may bear some relation also to the nature of these
characteristic pairings, for instance to the fact that many of them now
seem deliberately to verge on redundancy, like Spenser's "bashfull
modestee" or Harington's "modest shame." In a phrase like *inward
heart*, ubiquitous in both prose and poetry, the adjective certainly does
not single out a kind of heart which is inward from hearts which are
not, as the common pairing *constant heart* differentiates that type from
others which are fickle or false.[34] The pair *inward heart* makes up the
name of all hearts, which by nature share the quality of being inward.
Similarly, at times when Spenser in *The Faerie Queene* calls caves "hollow," he may be using the pairing as if it were a single name. The
quality of being hollow which cleaves to any cave by its nature makes
its substance known; the noun adjective *hollow* attaches to the noun
substantive *cave* to which it actually does by nature "properly belong."

This understanding of adjectival constructions may also be associated with other characteristics of poetic language in the quoted examples. The habit of alliterating paired adjectives and nouns was
partly an appeal to readers who recited poetry aloud or in any case
experienced words as they sound. At the same time this practice may
also have been a way of reinforcing the unity of adjective and substantive as a single phrase: "careless cloke," "scalding sighes," "wearie
woe," "hoarie haires."[35] The fact that such stock pairings were tirelessly repeated may also have been supported in part by this conception. For examples have shown that poets often use an adjective in so
familiar a combination that it is sometimes scarcely in focus as a separate word from the noun: "darke night," "morning dewe," "greene
grasse." Such a stock pairing occurs in adjacent lines of Sonnet 30 in
Spenser's *Ruines of Rome* for no clear purpose, unless its parts were felt
to belong together by making up a whole name:

> Like as the seeded field greene grasse first showes,
> Then from greene grasse into a stalke doth spring.[36]

The binding of such pairs is partly due to the rhythm predicted by
the habitual combination, but these conventional pairings may again

reflect the notion that the phrase is a single name, formed by attaching adjective expressing quality to noun denoting substance.

Analyses like Blundeville's of the function of accidents pertain to poetic language of this period in still another way. Thomas Wilson's wording of the same argument points to the relationship: "No Substaunce can be seen with out [sic., for our] yies, but onely the outewarde Accidentes, whereby we iudge and knowe, euery seuerall creature."[37] According to the analogy between the logical divisions of substance and accident and the grammatical distinction of the noun into two kinds, the noun adjective was conceived to have the function of accidents in making us see, know, and judge substances that would otherwise theoretically be invisible, unknowable. The statement posed in theoretical terms is more extreme than the practices of poets and yet may bear some relation to them. For the usefulness of adjectives in their analogy with accidents illuminates their specially lavish pairing with nouns in descriptive writing of this period. Blundeville makes this connection in his definition of *"Description"* as "a speech declaring what a thing is, by shewing the properties and accidents whereby it differeth from other things."[38] Wilson expands on this notion with what amount to directions for writing descriptions: "No one man coulde be knowen from another, neither yet any other thing, if it were not for the Accidentes whiche happen vnto theim. As when I woulde knowe an Herbe, a stone, a beaste, a man, I muste geue the propre Accidentes, declaryng the same to be of this or that coloure, seperatyng all soche by description from all other, aswell of that kinde, as of any other sorte elles."[39]

Shifting Parts of Speech

Noun adjectives used in shifting or reversible grammatical constructions with substantives have been shown to be another feature of poetic language in the examples discussed. Often a single word serves simultaneously as both kinds of noun, for instance in Spenser's "rosie red" or a word which is usually an adjective occupies the place of a noun, as in Shakespeare's Sonnet 18—"And euery faire from faire sometime declines"—where the adjective form "faire" stands in place of *fair thing* and then *fairness*. Adjectives also act as adverbs—Spenser's placing of "broad" is an example—so often as to blur the distinction between these two parts of speech. In *Amoretti* 79 "fayre" is used four times as an adjective, twice as a noun, once simultaneously as an adjective and an adverb. In other instances both words in a pairing of an adjective and a substantive can act as either category of noun in reversible combination. Many stock phrases like *lilly white* and *black night* work in this way, and may have been preferred because they create such word plays. Spenser uses such pairings often and at times constructs others of his own like "vaunting vaine" (3.8.11), a pun allowed by alternate spellings of *vein*. Such devices, though particularly prominent in this period, are of course not unique to it; later poets have used them for special effects, notably Milton. It is, for example, a feature of the inspired narrator's language in *Paradise Lost* to combine adjectives and nouns in unusual or reversible combinations like "vast abrupt" (2.409) or "vast of Heaven" (6.203) to create a style answerable to describe things invisible to mortal sight. The effect is to identify in the narrator's language form and mass, substance and accident in a unity that our fallen grammar divides. Like other verbal devices in the poem, these phrases are designed to seem strange, even strained, at the opposite extreme from commonplace; whereas in sixteenth-century verse reversed and reversible adjective-noun pairings are familiar and easy.

Shifting grammatical categories by the choice and placing of adjectives is one of the most prominent examples of what is—measured by later standards of correctness—the relative linguistic looseness of sixteenth-century English. Such order as existed often seems to be freely ignored. Not only do noun adjectives turn into substantives and adverbs, but even the most basic distinction made by all grammarians (going back to Aristotle) between the two principal parts of speech, the noun and the verb, is often obliterated in practice.[40] Shakespeare, for example, uses a verb in the opening line of Sonnet 18—"Shall I compare thee to a Summers day"—which reappears, without any change of formation, as a noun in Sonnet 21:

> And euery faire with his faire doth reherse,
> · Making a cooplement of proud compare.

A versified experiment among Sidney's Arcadian poems, inscrutable by more recent grammatical standards, makes an entire sonnet out of dissolving the distinction between the noun and the verb. The first stanza sets up the basic pattern followed through all fourteen lines:

> ¹   ²   ³   ¹   ²   ³
> Vertue, beawtie, and speach, did strike, wound, charme,
> ¹   ²   ³   ¹   ²   ³
> My harte, eyes, eares, with wonder, love, delight:

   ¹   ²   ³   ¹   ²   ³

First, second, last, did binde, enforce, and arme,

His workes, showes, suites, with wit, grace, and vow's
    might.[41]

First, second, last, did binde, enforce, and arme,
(1 First, 2 second, 3 last, did 1 binde, 2 enforce, and 3 arme,)

His workes, showes, suites, with wit, grace, and vow's
   might.[41]
(1 His workes, 2 showes, 3 suites, with 1 wit, 2 grace, and 3 vow's might.)

Not only do the lists slide almost imperceptibly from nouns to verbs, but some of the words seem to have been chosen precisely because they have the capacity to act as either part of speech. That is, the last three words of line one are understood to function here as verbs but in another context could be nouns, while the group of three nouns in the second half of line two are as frequently used to act as verbs in other love poems. Here the intervening words "did" and "with" make clear the grammatical functions of the triple groupings, but as the lists accumulate in the poem even those distinctions seem to disappear. An instance is the opening of the sestet:

Then greefe, unkindnes, proofe, tooke, kindled, tought,
(1 Then greefe, 2 unkindnes, 3 proofe, 1 tooke, 2 kindled, 3 tought,)

Well grounded, noble, due, spite, rage, disdaine.
(1 Well grounded, 2 noble, 3 due, 1 spite, 2 rage, 3 disdaine.)

The poem is as tightly patterned as it seems possible for verse to be, but the pattern builds toward dissolution of grammatical order. That very effect in this experiment may be an effort to express the paradoxical nature of passion, at once binding and lawless. The mesmerizing accumulation of lists may here have been intended to represent love's magical power and the lover's possession by it. Yet the fact that manipulation and interchange of grammatical parts is not special to this particular experiment signals that it is a reflection of wider notions than Sidney's particular perception of the lover's case.

Fluidity of grammar is also characteristic of sixteenth-century prose. While this looseness in early Tudor works can partly be explained by inexperience in writing vernacular prose, its continuation even into the beginning of the next century needs further explanation. Some other historical conditions have also been brought to bear to account for the fluid state of English in this period. The most important one for which there is full evidence is that many grammatical forms were still in transition from Middle English. As the inflectional endings, which signalled grammatical relationships, began to decay, differences between parts of speech also weakened or disappeared. Other forms had so recently become obsolete that they were still easily accepted in practice, especially in poetry. Such variations were all the more allowable because no clear conception of the history of the language had yet been formulated, and there were no comprehensive dictionaries to check functional shifts by fixing standard categories of word class.[42]

Another explanation for the relative syntactical looseness in English is supported by rhetorical handbooks of the period. Latin allowed certain freedoms in word order considered desirable for imitation in the vernacular. This impulse was grounded in more than the wish to emulate the styles of revered ancient authors. For, as the grammar books show, English was thought to be virtually identical in construction with Latin.[43] An instance of this thinking in English grammars is that nouns are described as declinable in ways that examples—of both adjectives and substantives—given to illustrate the rule necessarily contradict. Lily's authorized text for all grammar schools, *A Shorte Introdvction of Grammar,* applies definitions to English as well as Latin, illustrated with examples from both. The title of the book and the name for the kind of school where it dominated the curriculum show that grammar meant Latin grammar, which was thought to embody the rules governing the vernacular as well. It must be for this reason that the earliest English grammars have little to say about syntax, and that English grammar was not a subject in the curriculum of English grammar schools. Even the speaking of English in class or at play was sometimes forbidden, for example in the rules for Harrow of 1580, which further explains indifference to vernacular structure in the textbooks of the period; not until the mid–seventeenth century did a grammarian argue against using classical languages as a pattern for English.[44]

Yet many of the characteristic freedoms with verbal order illustrated in earlier quotations from sixteenth-century poems were so persistent and deliberate that neither linguistic evolution nor inattention to the peculiar construction of English can entirely account for them. Even writers about language who sometimes caution against or criticize such liberties taken by poets in their own writings exercise linguistic freedom in parallel ways. Not only explicitly in their pronouncements about language, but more often in their own verbal practices they suggest now unfamiliar assumptions underlying the relative looseness of sixteenth-century English.

A different sense of order in language from our own is implied by the grammarians, rhetoricians, and logicians when their own writing sometimes seems indifferent to distinctions among parts of speech. Often consisting of mixed lists, such sentences ignore grammatical categories in ways paralleling the liberties taken by poets. An example is a list by Thomas Wilson in his work on logic naming accidents belonging to substances: "as mirthe, sorowe, to runne, to sitte, to be well colored." Elsewhere he names qualities that are "rather perceiued by vnderstanding, then knowen by yie sight" in another list blurring the grammatical division between noun and verb: "As nobilitie, powre, fame, aucthoritie. To bee an Officer, a Maior, A Sherief."[45] These lists suggest that grammatical ordering does not have priority in the writer's use of words, for the sentences could easily have been arranged, as they would most likely be in later prose, to make the same logical points without mixing grammatical categories. Even texts where words are said to be arranged according to the parts of speech, presumably to aid order in composition, often stray from their own stated principles. In a widely used dictionary, under the heading "Adiectiues belonging some to the bodie, some to the mind," is the following sequence: "Agreeing, or according," "Agreement," "To accord, to agree."[46]

Words as Names

Some assumptions underlying the sense of language at work in such lists are suggested in a sentence by Richard Sherry in *A Treatise of Schemes and Tropes* about the rhetorical device of amplification: "The first waye of increasyng or diminishing is by chaungynge the worde of the thynge . . . as when we call an euyll man a thiefe, and say he hathe kylled vs, when he hathe beaten vs."[47] To "call" a man by a different word is to give him a new name. The first instance of "chaungynge" here replaces the noun adjective naming him an "euyll man" with the noun substantive naming him "thiefe." The second example of "chaungynge" substitutes for the verb "hathe beaten" another verb, "hathe kylled." The sentence therefore includes adjectives, nouns, and verbs as examples of "chaungynge the worde of the thynge." In doing so it illustrates what Sherry's phrase "the worde of the thynge" itself implies: that not only adjectives and substantives but verbs all stand in the relation to things that grammar books define as the function of the noun. In Lily's authorized Latin grammar a noun is defined to be the "name of a thing that may be seen, felt, heard or vnderstand." In Cooper's dictionary, *nomen* is translated "A name: a nowne," while Blundeville says that the noun adjectives "white or blacke, swift or slow, or such like, is a common name."[48] Yet these standard definitions did not preclude the wider sense that other parts of speech also perform the function of calling things by

[hand-written margin note: hyperbole]

name. In an English translation of *The Rvdimentes of P. Ramvs his Latine Grammar* the question "What is a worde?" is answered, "It is a note by which euerye thing is called."[49]

Not only different parts of speech but rhetorical figures of many kinds are said to be names. Peacham defines onomatopeia, for example, as "a forme of speech whereby the Orator or speaker maketh and faineth a name to some thing, imitating the sound or voyce of that it signifieth. . . ."[50] Puttenham calls this figure the "New namer," antonomasia the "Surnamer," metonymy the "Misnamer," while Peacham writes of catachresis:

catachresis

> By the licence of this figure we giue names to many things which lacke names, as when we say, the water runne, which is improper, for to run, is proper to those creatures which haue feete, and not to water which hath none. By this forme we attribute homes to a snaile, and feete to a stoole, and so likewise to many other things which do lacke their proper names.[51]

This passage again embodies the notion that words belonging to different parts of speech function in the same way as names: here the verb "to run," the noun substantives "homes" and "feete." That assumption in turn must underlie the habit again represented here of shifting grammatical forms in a single list. Poetry as well as prose included many such mixed catalogues (and while they were called catalogues, the term did not come to have its present meaning of a *systematic* list until late in the seventeenth century). Sidney's Arcadian poem "Vertue, beawtie, and speach" is an extreme example. Another instance of this common practice is Spenser's catalogue of virtuous rules given by Charissa to the Red Crosse Knight at Una's request during their sojourn in the House of Holinesse:

> She was right ioyous of her iust request,
>   And taking by the hand that Faeries sonne,
> Gan him instruct in euery good behest,
>   Of loue, and righteousnesse, and well to donne,
>   And wrath, and hatred warely to shonne.
>
> (1.10.33)

Coming in a sequence after "loue" and "righteousnesse," the third item in the list, "well to donne," seems first to be a kind of noun phrase like *good works*, but then to be a verb parallel to the rhymed infinitive "to shonne." As grammatical distinctions in their functions slide, all these nouns and verbs act as names constituting a catalogue of "euery good behest." They can be grouped together, interchanged, reversed in some ways unfamiliar to later readers accustomed to more fixed divisions among parts of speech.

The notion of nouns, adjectives, verbs, adverbs all acting as names may bear some relation also to the very presence of the vast number of lists or catalogues of every sort and length in all forms of sixteenth-century writing. Of course English poets before and after this period also use this device. Chaucer's catalogue of trees (to be discussed in chapter 4) comes to mind, or Milton's description of Satan journeying toward the throne of Chaos:

> Ore bog or steep, throught strait, rough, dense, or rare,
> With head, hands, wings or feet pursues his way,
> And swims or sinks, or wades, or creeps, or flyes.
>
> (2.948–50)

Yet these passages come to mind precisely because they stand out by being special, unusual to the poet's style, whereas listing of all sorts stands out, calls attention to itself in sixteenth-century verse for the opposite reason, because it is ubiquitous.

To recite names, the previous chapter has shown, was conceived as an act of reading not clearly distinct from either describing or interpreting. Such a list could consist of proper names like the ones Spenser recites often in *The Faerie Queene*. His catalogue of rivers, for example, includes so many proper names that the poet

> Cannot recount, nor tell their hidden race,
> Nor read the saluage cuntreis, thorough which they pace.
>
> (4.11.40)

Recitation of names as an act of reading could equally consist of listing common nouns. Such catalogues are everywhere in poetry of this period. Golding, for one, favored them both in his own verse and when translating Ovid:

> In sodaine dropping downe of Dogs, of Horses, Sheepe, and
>   Kine,
> Of Birds and Beasts both wild and tame as Oxen, Wolves,
>   and Swine.[52]

Barnfield writes a similar kind of poetic line, which also sounds like an index of headings in a commonplace book: "In birds, beasts, frute, stones, flowres, herbs, mettals, fish."[53] Gascoigne enumerates nouns naming the cycles of history in a list whose very shape and sounds describe an endless round: "Plentie brings pryde, pryde plea, plea pine, pine peace,/ Peace plentie."[54]

Adjectives are also catalogued, as in Shakespeare's names for "lust" in Sonnet 129: "periurd, murdrous, blouddy full of blame,/ Sauage, extreame, rude, cruell, not to trust." The still commoner practice of listing paired adjectives and nouns is amply represented in lines from Watson's *Passionate Centurie* 18, from which Shakespeare in Sonnet 129 borrowed still other names for lust: "a swollowed bayt" and "very wo." Watson's poem defines "Loue" by listing sixteen such combinations, along with six pairings of substantives in genitive constructions (to be discussed in chapter 3), and one single noun, all naming his subject:

> Loue is a sowr delight; a sugred greefe;
>   A liuinge death; an euerdying life;
>   A breache of *Reasons* lawe; a secret theefe;
>   A sea of teares; an euerlasting strife;
>   A bayte for fooles; a scourge of noble witts;
>   A Deadly wound; a shotte which euer hitts.
> *Loue* is a blinded God; an angry boye;
>   A *Labyrinth* of dowbts; an ydle lust;
>   A slaue to *Beawties* will; a witles toy;
>   A rauening bird, a tyraunt most vniust;
>   A burning heate; A cold; a flattring foe;
>   A priuate hell; a very world of woe.[55]

Verbs, it has been shown, were also thought to act as names, and were recited in parallel fashion. A list of the soul's acts "To knock, to craue, to call to cry to thee" from a poem of uncertain authorship in Tottel's miscellany makes feeble use of this device, later exploited effectively by Donne to describe a sequence of divine actions:

> Batter my heart, three person'd God; for, you
> As yet but knocke, breathe, shine, and seeke to mend;
> That I may rise, and stand, o'erthrow mee'and bend
> Your force, to breake, blowe, burn and make me new.[56]

The principal parts of speech are all appropriate to list alone or in combination because they are all names; to recite them is therefore to read in the sense of describing and interpreting the things they call by name. Neither the demands of translation nor of meter can wholly account for these practices in poetry, for the habit of listing can also be found everywhere in English prose of this period. A vehement rhetorical question by Thomas Becon in *The Reliques of Rome* is typical of this device in the ways that it parallels such uses of language in poetry: "Shall we hope to bee made ryghteous by the obseruances of mennes trifling traditions, croked constitutions, idle inuentions, drousye dreames, fonde fantasyes, antichristian actes, deuilish decrees, etc."[57]

Names Proper and Improper

Other ways of thinking with far-reaching implications in sixteenth-century language are suggested by Peacham's previously quoted definition of catachresis. He says that his examples of the figure—"to run" applied to water or "feete" to stools—are not "proper names." This grammatical term is still used now for a noun designating by name a particular being or thing, as distinct from a common noun that represents one or all of the members of a class. When sixteenth-century writers about language formally define the term, they do so by making essentially this distinction, as Lily does: "A Noun substantiue, ether is propre to the thinge that it betokeneth: as *Eduardus*, is my propre name, or els is commune to mo: as *Homo*, is a commune name to all men."[58] Wilson uses the proposition *Cato est homo* to make the same distinction in equally representative terms: "Cato is the noune propre, whiche belongeth to one manne onely, and manne, is the kinde, whiche is more large, and comprehendeth all menne."[59] In both quotations the defining word "propre" is equated—explicitly by Wilson, by Lily implicitly—with the notion of belonging. It is derived from the noun *property*, meaning here what belongs to oneself, is one's own (the meaning still persisting in definitions of the grammatical term *proper name*).

In sixteenth-century writing about language, as Peacham's description of catachresis will illustrate, this formal distinction between proper names and common nouns is often blurred, when the limiting adjective *proper* is used in a different sense derived from another sixteenth-century definition of the noun *property*. For instance, such a blurring occurs when Peacham argues that "runne" attributed to water and "feete" applied to stools cannot be "proper names." The reason given is not that they are common nouns applying to all members of a class rather than belonging to one particular being, but that they are only "proper to those creatures which haue feete." By implication, therefore, the same words *run* and *feet* could be said to be proper names when used in other propositions: *bulls run, Cato has feet.* Peacham argues this way, ignoring the recognized grammatical distinction between proper and common names, because more funda-

*property or "proneness" vs. possession

mental to his thinking is the notion that the verb "to run" is in a special sense "proper to those creatures that haue feete." Used here the adjective derives from the noun *property* understood as logicians like Wilson define it: "Propretie, is a naturall pronenesse, and maner of dooyng, which agreeth to one kinde, and to the same onely, and that euermore."[60] Since the capacity to run is a property of creatures with feet, the verb naming that property belongs to them, is in that sense a proper name for them. This understanding of property as natural characteristic or quality was often confused with its meaning of possession, since both were said to *belong*. Such mixture of definitions is implied in a simile used to argue a point about biblical translation: "But you by confusion of these sundry names doo seeke confusion of the things: and as theeues are wont to change the markes of thinges which they haue stollen; so you, to make the *Priesthood* of Christ seeme your owne, doo change names, as markes of thinges which they signifie."[61] The notion of property as possession suggests the comparison with robbery; the thieves steal things which *belong* to others. The sense of property as the natural characteristic or quality of things underlies the notion that names *belong* to the things "they signifie." The confusion is often expressed but not acknowledged in discussions of what constitute proper names.

Other writers considering many different linguistic issues use terms like Peacham's. The rhetorician Richard Sherry, for instance, distinguishes between what he calls "proper wordes that belonge to the thinge" and "wordes" which are improper because they do not apply to the "selfe proper thinges."[62] This practice of associating the adjective *proper* not only with names like *Cato* or *London* but with all kinds of words said to belong to the things they designate is widespread. It is therefore evidence that the attitudes on which it was predicated were commonly held. When examined it shows again that in this period other parts of speech were thought to perform the function of naming, even though this function was also described as the distinguishing feature of the noun. Beyond that, other words could be considered to be names understood in a particular way to be proper, that is, names expressing the property of what they designate.

Even more fundamental implications are embedded in a definition of words in *The Logike of the Moste Excellent Philosopher P. Ramus Martyr*, which makes this equation typically without explicit discussion of it: "For wordes are nothing els but notes of matters signified: as Isaac, was so called because his mother laughed at the promise of God made to her."[63] The juxtaposition of statement to example here can be shown to reflect the same assumptions embodied in the term *belonging* associated with all sorts of words said to be *proper.* Here Isaac's name is a word proper to him, so the explanation reads, not for the reason that it belongs to him only rather than to a class of things, but because it signifies a property, laughter, "a naturall pronenesse, and maner of dooyng" belonging to him, as Peacham says the verb "to run" is "proper" to creatures with feet.

Discussions of the signifying power of words are often illustrated this way by Old Testament names which are made of root meanings of words and which, by their sanctity, in themselves lent irrefutable authority to this view of language. Its ultimate sanction, however, was in the New Testament in the metaphor of the church's foundation on "this rocke" derived from the name of "Peter" (Matthew 16:18). Names of medicinable plants were another preferred source from which to draw examples demonstrating the relation between all words and the things to which they properly belong. Ramus turns to this commonplace next after explicating the significances of Hebrew and Greek proper names:

> The phisicions also do geue names to their herbes: to some from the cause: as *Hirundinaria*, from the inuentor: *Filipendula*, from the forme: To other some, from the effecte and working: as *Selfwhole*, and suche lyke: from the subiecte and place: at [sic.] *parietaria*, and *sea trifolie.* From the adiointe and qualitie: as *styncking marubium*, *deade nettle:* from the similitude which they haue with other thinges: as *Mouse eare*, *foxe tayle*, *dogges tonge:* And so forthe from the rest of the places of inuention.[64]

From a later perspective, examples drawn from Old Testament proper names like *Isaac* or common nouns naming a category of plant like "*styncking marubium*" would be special instances, not representative of the way all sorts of words work, or all nouns, or even all proper names. They would be considered atypical in bearing a peculiar etymological relation to what they designate. They signify its property because that significance is built into the name itself, as the Hebrew word for *laugh* is contained in *Isaac.* Abraham gave that name to his son because Sarah laughed at the prophecy of his birth. Physicians call herbs by names made up of words describing their known qualities or accidents. While in later English other common nouns and parts of speech are no longer conceived this way, many sixteenth-century linguistic theorists understood all sorts of words rightly used to be proper names in the sense that they were thought to signify the recognized properties of things and to have been originally chosen and assigned to do so.

Old Testament names were thought by many sixteenth-century writers to be special only in that they belong to the most authoritative class of examples, because Hebrew was believed to be the original language, the only speech before the confusion of Babel. In Hebrew the divinely established relation between property and name is still directly audible: "For, *Adam* (meaneth) made of clay: his wife / *Eua* (translated) signifieth life."[65] The same perfect correspondence must hold true also for the most holy name of Jesus, which caused a problem discussed in some theological commonplace books, because writers were uncomfortably aware that the Lord's name was also borne by mere men. A "mysticall or hid signification of his diuinitie" therefore had to be uniquely attributed to the "diuersitie in the letters" magically distinguishing the name of the only Savior from any other Jesus.[66] It could then be claimed to be proper to the Lord but not to men apparently called by the same name.

In fallen speech the significant relation between name and property can be obscure. Camden makes this common acknowledgment that in languages other than Hebrew sometimes "the truth lieth hidden and is not easilie found, as both *Varro* and *Isidor* do acknowledge." Yet on the same linguistic premises that make the name *Isaac* represent all sorts of words, he argues for the greater power of English before the Norman conquest in aptly expressing the nature of things. Anglo-Saxon was sometimes said to be partly analogous to Hebrew in that it represented a stage of language closer to its origins, when men spoke in purer words and therefore more evidently proper names:

> The holy service of God, which the *Latines* called *Religion*, because it knitted the mindes of men together, and most people of *Europe* have borrowed the same from them, they called most significantly *Ean-fastnes*, as the one and only assurance and fastanker-holde of our soules health.
>
> The gladsome tidings of our salvation, which the *Greekes* called *Evangelion*, and other Nations in the same word, they called *Godspel*, that is, *Gods speech*.[67]

While such interest in etymology was itself predicated on reverence for linguistic origins, where the properties of things may most readily be discovered from the names given to them, even many English words and proper names in current use were also said to retain "like significancy" with Hebrew names: "In *Moldwarp* wee expresse the nature of that beast; in *handkercher* the thing and his vse; in *vpright*, that vertue by a *Metaphore;* in *Wisdome* and *Domesdaye*, soe many sentences as wordes. . . . It may passe allsoe the musters of this significancy that in a manner all the proper names of our people doe importe somewhat. . . ."[68]

This assumption of the bond between name and thing was so widely held that it was shared and cited even by writers whose opinions differed profoundly on many other matters. In *The Svmme of the Conference Betwene Iohn Rainoldes and Iohn Hart*, the Protestant and Catholic apologists are both cited defending their vehemently opposed interpretations of controversial words in theology with the identical argument about the function of those terms as proper names: "For the name openeth the nature of the thing, as *Aristotle* sheweth."[69] To support the same view of language (and without attention to differences between Aristotle and Plato) the *Cratylus* is also sometimes invoked, as by Sir Thomas Elyot, "Consyderynge (as Plato sayethe) that the name of euery thynge is none other but the vertue or effecte of the same thinge."[70] Ultimately, however, the grounds for this theory of language were provided by the episode in Genesis as explicated in the representative passage previously quoted from Mulcaster's *Elementarie:*

> We nede not to proue by *Platoes Cratylus*, or *Aristotles* proposition as by best autorities, (tho men be sufficient to proue their own inuentions) that words be voluntarie, and appointed vpon cause, seing we haue better warrant. For euen God himself, who brought the creatures, which he had made, vnto that first man, whom he had also made, that he might name them, according to their properties, doth planelie declare by his so doing, what a cunning thing it is to giue right names, and how necessarie it is, to know their forces, which be allredie giuen, bycause the word being knowen, which implyeth the propertie the thing is half known, whose propertie is emplyed.[71]

In this view the namings of Isaac and of medicinal plants fairly illustrate the origins of words, which are proper names because they derive their significance from the properties of things. Since Adam conferred names rightly corresponding to those properties, it follows from Mulcaster's argument that fallen man can argue backwards from the name to know the nature of the thing to which it belongs. This conviction was so strong that it caused another difficulty sometimes confronted in theological commonplace books, where it is solved by finding an awkward exception to this notion of proper names in the name of God. The difficulty was that although He does not need "any proper name to be separated therby from others," He nevertheless calls Himself by one when he declares His name to be "Iehouah." This posed a problem to be argued away in order to preserve the unknowable mystery of His nature: "But although that this name do so properly agree vnto god, that it may not be communicate vnto any creature: yet it is not such that therby we mai atteine to know the whole effect and substance of his Maiestie, the knowledge whereof is vtterly incomprehensible."[72] God alone, who is the ultimate source of all words and of their proper significance, can make a supreme exception of his own name. The need to argue this way shows how compelling for some writers was the belief that other words could theoretically be read to reveal the natures of what they name. Authors could therefore choose from this linguistic store such words as sixteenth-century writers about language designated to be proper, that is, whose name and nature are one like the names conferred by Adam: "Such are thought apt wordes, that properly agree vnto that thing which they signifie, and plainly expresse the nature of the same."[73]

Some difficulties for this view of language might be expected to have been posed by the existence of "woordes that vnder one, and the same title, comprehend the nature of many thinges," which were discussed by most linguistic theorists.[74] While their thinking would predict few instances of such words, their examples show that there were many which would not be so categorized in later English. One reason for this difference is that, since words were not always clearly distinguished as belonging to different parts of speech, the sound of "*Graue*," for example, was taken to be a single word with the multiple meanings of "sober, a tombe, and to carue."[75] Another reason is that, since distinctions among possible spellings were also easily ignored, many words were taken as single that are now separated by fixed differences in spelling: "Time noteth bothe the space of houre, daie, and yeare, and also we call an herbe by that name, whiche growth in Gardines."[76] Common examples name as single words others that would now be distinguished both by spelling and by grammatical function: *course, coarse; pray, prey; light, alight.*[77] Discussions of such examples distinguish them from words "which agree in meaning, and differ in sounde" (like "rich, welthie") on the grounds that they "agree in sounde, and differ in meaning."[78] The question of like or unlike spelling is not at issue.

The commonest explanation of how such words came to exist referred them to the confusion of Babel, along with other disruptions of the ontological order in which "name, and nature is all one."[79] Mulcaster accepted their existence as proof of the disparity between the abundance of God's creation and the limits of human speech:

> The number of things whereof we write and speak is infinite, the words wherewith we write and speak, be definite and within number. Whereupon we ar driuen to vse one, and the same word in verie manie, naie somtime in verie contrarie senses, and that in all the verie best languages, as well as in English, where a number of our words be of verie sundrie powers, as, letters, wherewith we write, & letters which hinder: A bird flieth light, wheresoeuer she doth light: and to manie to stand on here.[80]

Biblical interpretations of the origin and history of language, by which so many other linguistic conceptions were sanctioned, therefore also shaped thinking about words naming different things. The very need to explain their diversity of reference shows how strong was the belief in the correspondence between names and the things to which they properly belong. While logicians usually advised writers to avoid such ambiguous words in argument, they were sometimes praised as a "peculiar grace" of English.[81] Among poets they were exploited in combination with other kinds of verbal license allowed by the state of English in the sixteenth century. Spenser, for example, combines multiple meanings with interchangeable parts of speech in lines that sound almost like a counterspell to the enchantments they describe:

> We may not chaunge (quoth he) this euil plight,
> Till we be bathed in a liuing well;
> That is the terme prescribed by the spell.
> O how, said he, mote I that well out find,
> That may restore you to your wonted well?

> (1.2.43)

Other poets commonly used words with double meanings and indistinct spellings in characteristic metaphorical combinations: *hart:heart*, *deer:dear*, *travel:travail* were among the most frequently exploited (in ways to be discussed in chapter 3).

Writers of this period often followed the ideal linguistic model of the Old Testament in giving significant names to their own characters.[82] This practice is most prominent in *The Faerie Queene*, not only because allegory encouraged the naming of characters by what they represent: *Speranza, Gloriana, Mercilla*. It is especially emphasized because Spenser often articulates the principle that proper names rightly read—both conferred and interpreted rightly—reveal the nature of what they designate: "His name *Ignaro* did his nature right aread" (1.8.31); "His name was *Zele*, that him right well became" (1.10.6); "His name was meeke *Obedience*, rightfully ared" (1.10.17); "Her name was *Enuie*, knowen well thereby" (5.12.31).

Sixteenth-century authors also give significant names to characters where they are not needed to sustain the allegorical mode of the work. The name of Sidney's Arcadian hero *Pyrocles* expresses his fiery nature. *Astrophil* is the proper name to identify the lover of starlike *Stella* (as well as an allusion to the name of their author). Shakespeare in Sonnets 135, 136, and 143 makes obscene word plays out of the name *Will* and the meaning of *will* as sexual desire. Also on the same principle articulated by Mulcaster, poets read backwards from proper names to the natures of their bearers, which seems to be the design of the anonymous poem "Of his loue named white." Ben Jonson performs this act of reading in "On Lvcy Covntesse of Bedford" when he praises his subject by comparing her to a star lending influence from his "lucent seat."[83] The compliment carries weight in the poem because it is not frivolous word play. It is supported by a profound belief in the significant interchange between name and nature which is ultimately the subject of Jonson's poem: "My *Muse* bad, *Bedford* write, and that was shee."

This belief in the property of different classes of words as names dictated what was thought to be the right joining and ordering of them. It therefore has some bearing on the way sixteenth-century rhetoricians describe the epithet, for example. Their discussions, in turn, can uncover some of the implications of the ways poets frame and repeatedly use that figure, which Peacham singles out as the most valued: "Among all the forms of eloquution, there is no one eronation either more generall or more excellent then this: for it carrieth alwaies with it, wheresoeuer it be applied a singular grace and maiestie of matter, beside the beautie wherewith it garnisheth the sentence."[84] In his previously quoted definition, Peacham describes the relation of the two parts of the epithet in phrasing closely paralleling the terms used everywhere to describe the proper names that belong to the things they signify: "*Epitheton*, called of *Quintillian Appositum*, of others *Adiectiuum;* Is a figure or forme of speech, which ioyneth Adicatiues to those Substantiues, to whom they do properly belong. . . ."[85] This parallel in wording suggests assumptions underlying some characteristics of epithets in this poetry. For if adjectives have nouns to which they properly belong, "giuing euery person or thing besides his proper name a qualitie by way of addition," then apt pairings copy a relationship established in the nature of things.[86] Right use of language, according to all definitions of the logical and rhetorical term *invention* in this period, must originate in the discovery of this order: "The finding out of apt matter, called otherwise Inuention, is a searching out of things true, or things likely, the which may reasonablie set forth a matter, and make it appeare probable."[87] The same adjective ought therefore to be joined with its proper substantive to reflect the true order in which night is dark, dew falls in the morning, caves are hollow, grass is green. Such common pairings are sanctioned and their repetition recommended by this conception. It may also have encouraged combinations which now seem to be more strangely redundant than merely obvious, like *foggy mist, drowsy sleep, marble stone*, since the prerequisite of belonging implies closeness in the pairing.[88]

The rhetorical handbooks argue from the notion that apt epithets copy a prior ontological order especially when cautioning against epithets "unproperly or peruersly applied." The examples disallowed by Peacham are revealing: "as to say: A valiant Phisitian, a reuerend labourer, a couragious Counseller, which is a forme of speech very vnproper and also very absurd."[89] What makes these pairings improper is that they do not copy "things true" in nature, where the quality of being "valiant" properly belongs to the soldier or where the property of the "Counseller" is to be wise. Puttenham is even more harsh in condemning choices of adjectives which are "disagreable or repugnant" to the substantives they join.[90] His illustrations of them show how "apt and proper" pairings are dictated by a preexisting order which limits and fixes the range of allowable combinations. In illustrating improper epithets he quotes the line "*A dongeon deepe, a dampe as darke as hell.*"[91] He criticizes the choice of "darke" because it names a visible quality, whereas "a dampe being but a breath or vapour, and not to be discerned by the eye, ought not to haue this *epithete.*" The combination "*dongeon deepe*" is allowable, by contrast, because depth is a property of dungeons, much as hollowness is of caves. Their pairing is their proper name, which Spenser uses at least ten times in *The Faerie Queene*.

In practice as well as principle the handbooks encouraged repetition of adjective-noun combinations which reflect the natural order of qualities cleaving to substances. Illustrations of various figures repeatedly use the same examples, which are also rife in poetry. Day lists among approved pairings "wicked guile," "fond fancie"; under metonymy "Pale death"; for hyperbole the epithet "stonie hearte," which occurs in one of Peacham's lists illustrating metaphor, in Spenser's "The Teares of the Muses" and repeatedly in *The Faerie Queene*, in Daniel's *Delia* 13, in Wyatt's "Resownde my voyce," and in many lesser poems.[92] Such examples of epithets and other figures in the handbooks are explicitly recommended for their familiarity. Peacham, for instance, praises "common metaphors," including many still familiar phrases which now would be called clichés (a term introduced in the nineteenth century): "a large field of matter, a mountaine of wealth, a wildernesse of doubts, a denne of theeues, a path of pleasure, a way of error, a vale of miserie."[93]

Besides the encouragement of reiterated illustrations in treatises, repetition of stock epithets and other verbal combinations was reinforced by collections of them drawn from ancient and sometimes also more modern authors (as were the examples cited by authors like Peacham). These were used in schools to furnish matter for compositions. One such, the widely used Textor's *Epitheta*—thought to have been known to Shakespeare—catalogues examples under mythological, historical, and geographical headings, virtues, trees, herbs, and the like.[94] This preference for common phrases often repeated dictated writers' choices in prose as well as poetry. It cannot therefore be explained mainly as a residue or imitation of the formulaic repetitions of earlier oral and epic poetry, although humanists like Ascham hold up Homer and Virgil among models who "do repeate one matter, with the selfe same wordes."[95]

The repetition of ready-made combinations of words also cannot satisfactorily be explained by what would now be thought of as literary decorum. For in the sixteenth century the conception of decorum in works of literature was itself predicated on more than stylistic issues. Certain words, as approved epithets have shown, were thought to make right combinations or to follow the true order because they conform to a prior reality which determines their propriety in an ontological sense. This conception is shown most vividly in discussions by sixteenth-century writers of the fixed order of paired words in commonly spoken phrases, many of which are still frozen in the same order in modern English: "There is also a naturall order, as to saye: men and women, daye and nyght, easte, and weste, rather then backewardes."[96] What Sherry means here by "a naturall order" in certain combinations of words is very different from what would be understood now in an explanation of these fixed phrases. Their origin

would now first of all be said to depend on linguistic issues, on pho-
nological principles and semantic rules. Where these constraints of
language do not explain special cases in the ordering of frozen combinations of words, linguists now may draw on psychological explanations. Examples are the relation of common righthandedness to the
precedence of right over left in verbal combinations, or the priority of
the vertical references in word pairs. The operation of a conceptual
system like the one that orients us to give priority to what is near over
what is far from the prototypical speaker is thought to explain the
order in other fixed phrases, for instance: *up and down, here and there,
now and then, good and bad* (since the prototype considers himself good).
Where no definable relation between modes of perception and verbal
order exists, the more general notions of traditional linguistic and psychological associations are brought to bear, for example to explain
"cases in which the right direction is associated with goodness and
masculinity, the left direction with badness and femininity."[97]

Sixteenth-century writers, by contrast, invoke a "naturall order" to
be followed in verbal combinations such as "the man before the
woman" which is not conceived as linguistic or psychological, or to
be built by tradition. It exists simply in the world from its origins,
prior to the language which copies it and outside the mind of the
writer, who is said to *invent* it in the sense of coming upon or discovering it. The existence and priority of this nonverbal order is so profoundly accepted that it does not have to be explained or defended,
but only invoked to heap scorn, as Wilson does, on writers who violate it: "Some will set the Cart before the horse, as thus. My mother
and my father are both at home, as though the good man of the house
did weare no breches, or that the graie Mare were the better Horse."
Or in the same vein: "Who is so foolish as to say, the Counsaile and
the King, but rather the King and his Counsaile, the Father and the
Sonne, and not the contrary. And so likewise in all other, as they are
in degree first euermore to set them formost."[98]

This fundamental belief that language copies a prior order which
determines its propriety, its power to signify the nature of what it
names, set limits that in certain respects fixed verbal practices. It
therefore contributed to what now seems to be the predictable quality
of much sixteenth-century writing. Simultaneously the same authors
and readers who shared this way of thinking accepted a related idea
that supported the apparently loose and relatively arbitrary uses of
language in this period. This is the notion that nouns, adjectives, adverbs, and verbs can all function as names for the things which make

up that prior order. The combined effects of these simultaneously held beliefs, predictability and arbitrariness in language, now seem puzzling to readers because the grounds on which they are predicated are unfamiliar, unrecognized. In the sixteenth century they were so deeply familiar that they were unquestioned, and for that reason operated all the more powerfully on both writers and their audiences in acts of reading understood in all the available meanings of the verb *to read*.

A Grammatical Lesson in *The Faerie Queene*

One of the many lessons in reading visible signs in *The Faerie Queene* becomes also a lesson in grammar. This is the curious episode in the house of Alma when Guyon's powers as a reader of appearances are tested by the sight of a blushing lady. At the end of the episode Guyon's instructress delivers its message in phrasing that closely follows the grammatical discussions distinguishing adjectives and substantives as they are analogous to accidents and substances: "You shamefast are, but *Shamefastnesse* it selfe is shee" (2.9.43). The passage as a whole therefore not only illustrates in its descriptive style the functions of adjectives discussed in this chapter. It actually seems to make them part of its subject, reflecting the notion that grammatical order in itself has signifying power.

The lady is introduced only as a "Damsell" whose name is not given until the end of the episode, after she is elaborately described so that the reader is able to visualize what Guyon can actually see. The language is therefore designed to put us in the same position as Guyon of reading the damsel's looks as if directly from her visual appearance:

> So long as *Guyon* with her commoned,
>   Vnto the ground she cast her modest eye,
>   And euer and anone with rosie red
>   The bashfull bloud her snowy cheekes did dye,
>   That her became, as polisht yuory,
>   Which cunning Craftesmans hand hath ouerlayd
>   With faire vermilion or pure Castory.
>   Great wonder had the knight, to see the mayd
> So straungely passioned.
>
> (2.9.41)

The description draws on the characteristic resources of language illustrated in this chapter. Adjectives are present in lavish abundance, in pairings sometimes reversible, often alliterated, and in familiar

combinations such as the ubiquitous "rosie red." They make available
to the reader the possibilities for interpreting the lady's blushes that
are immediately present to Guyon, but like us he is incapable of reading them:

> She answerd nought, but more abasht for shame,
>   Held downe her head, the whiles her louely face
>   The flashing bloud with blushing did inflame,
>   And the strong passion mard her modest grace,
>   That *Guyon* meruayld at her vncouth cace.

He remains baffled

> Till *Alma* him bespake, Why wonder yee
>   Faire Sir at that, which ye so much embrace?
>   She is the fountaine of your modestee;
> You shamefast are, but *Shamefastnesse* it selfe is shee.

Alma's speech identifies the moral content of the episode as a lesson
in the virtue of "*Shamefastnesse*," and in the value of knowing one's self
as well as in reading others' characters. Yet the wording of the speech
calls attention to its own grammar in such a way as to make that part
of the episode's subject as well. It becomes also therefore a lesson in
reading itself. It makes us reflect on our experience of the passage, so
that the adjectives which we first respond to as they depict the lady's
appearance are now brought into focus *as adjectives*, as they are distinct
in function from her name.

By evoking the distinction between substance and accident, Alma's
words express the notion that the blushing lady's visual appearance—
her "rosie red," "bashfull bloud," "flashing bloud"—is composed of
accidents or qualities enabling Guyon to read her in the senses of
seeing, knowing, and judging her substance. At the same time, by
invoking the analogy between substance and noun substantive, accident and noun adjective, Alma's speech embodies the conception that
the pairings of adjectives with nouns in the description which enable
the reader to visualize the damsel's "rosie red," "bashfull bloud" are
analogous to the visible blushes that Guyon is supposed to read. This
is yet another instance where words are likened to nonverbal phenomena, as this allegorical episode makes their function identical. Blushes
and noun adjectives which name them render "*Shamefastnesse*" visible
and knowable to the properly instructed reader—of both things and
words. And they do so in the same way. The grammatical lesson
taught by this episode is itself therefore ultimately grounded in assumptions discussed in the previous chapter: that words are not con-

sistently distinct from nonverbal things; that reading is not clearly differentiated from seeing.

Embedded in Alma's grammatical instruction—"You shamefast are, but *Shamefastnesse* it selfe is shee"—is a more particular lesson in reading allegory. It makes Guyon, the main character in the narrative, analogous to both accident and adjective. In that capacity he (or it) would be understood to make visible the substance he represents in the allegory of this episode. At the same time Alma's words would seem to make the lady, who is also a character in the allegory, analogous to substance and noun, while her blushes would—like the figure of Guyon—be parallel to accident and adjective. Such an equation would invite the question why one character in the allegorical narrative has a different ontological—and therefore grammatical—status from another. It is of course possible that this contradiction is simply unresolved in the episode, for logical consistency rarely seems to be an ultimate concern in the poem. Yet the way Guyon comes to comprehend the blushing lady's nature, and our comparable experience of reading the stanzas about his doing so, suggest a different understanding of the lesson in reading allegory. The figure of the damsel functions in the same way as the adjectives that describe her appearance up until the point in the episode where she is given her proper name. When Alma calls her "*Shamefastnesse*," the figure of the lady becomes analogous to that noun naming her, which is a substance. This possibility, that figures in the allegorical narrative can shift in status from accident to substance, corresponds to our experience of the passage, where adjectives heaped up in the description are replaced by a noun substantive naming what underlies them. Relationships among parts of speech as reflections of ontological order here support allegorical meanings to make possible an experience of reading both things and words.

3 Translating or Borrowing

Definitions

The opening of Shakespeare's Sonnet 18—"Shall I compare thee to a Summers day?"—is not a real question but belongs to the category which in the nineteenth century came to be called a rhetorical question. The speaker does not expect or pause for an answer because he is not asking permission to "compare." He is declaring it his intention, which in sixteenth-century literary vocabulary is a way of announcing that he is about to recite a poem. The sonnet made out of his figurative comparison is a demonstration of the poet's talent for making it, and an argument for the godlike power of metaphorical language which here "giues life" eternal to its mortal subject.

This radiant celebration of poetic comparison reflects a traditional judgment deriving ultimately from Aristotle. He is the authority for the view that the greatest gift of the poet, the sole power which must be granted and cannot be taught, is the perception of resemblances, expressed in the making of metaphor.[1] By calling attention to the sonnet as a comparison, which the poet carries through to the triumphant conclusion of the couplet, he lays claim to possessing that unique art. In Sonnets 21 and 130, Shakespeare again identifies poetry with comparing, boasting of the speaker's superiority to other writers in his rejection of the "proud compare" and "false compare" of poetic convention. This claim is itself a commonplace which Spenser, for example, develops in *Amoretti* 9. It begins also with the poet's declared intention to make a poem out of comparison:

> Long-while I sought to what I might compare
>   those powerfull eies, which lighten my dark spright.

The body of the sonnet assimilates a series of familiar comparisons by rejecting them (as Shakespeare does in Sonnet 21) in favor of his own discovered similitude in the couplet:

> Then to the Maker selfe they likest be,
>   whose light doth lighten all that here we see.

The equation of poetic art with the expression of perceived resemblances often seems to be reflected also in the work of much lesser sixteenth-century writers, who appear to have assumed that a string of similitudes would guarantee their compositions to be recognizable as poems.

To compare is one verb associated—more often in poems themselves than in writing about poetry—with the use of figurative language thought to be based on resemblance. This category of language included metaphor, which is "nothing but a similitude contracted into one word," and allegory, which "is none other thing, but a Metaphore, vsed throughout a whole sentence, or Oration."[2] In the handbooks the formation of figures involving likeness is called "mouynge and chaungynge," "putting ouer," "tournyng" or "wresting" words. The writer who uses such figures is said to "fetch" or "transport" words which have been "taken" from their "places," and which "goe beyond the significacion of things."[3]

Use of metaphors and especially spatial terms to describe figurative language is of course habitual with us still, the word *metaphor* being itself metaphorical, derived from its root meaning referring to change of location (Greek *metapherein*, to transfer: *meta*, involving change + *pherein*, to bear).[4] At least one of these particular verbs used earlier for metaphor making still exists in fossilized form in our habit of describing strained comparisons by the term *far-fetched*, used by sixteenth-century writers as the opposite of "nigh."[5] Yet their linguistic vocabulary implies some fundamental attitudes no longer alive in our thinking. These can best be recognized if we begin by exploring uses of the two verbs most often chosen to describe the act of making figurative comparisons: *translating* and *borrowing*.

The two terms often occur together because at the time their available meanings had more overlapping implications than in later English. They do, for example, when John Hoskyns uses them in this definition: "A *Metaphore* or Translacion is the friendly & neighborly borrowing, of one word to expresse a thing with more light & better note: though not soe directly & proplie as the naturall name of the thinge meant would signifye. . . ."[6] The word "Translacion," from the Latin name for metaphor used in the sixteenth century, *translatio*, still had one meaning derived from this root, making it virtually synonymous with transporting. In this sense, then, it shared with "borrowing" the suggestion of a transfer which fills up a space, specifically a lexical lacuna. Since the time of Aristotle this was thought to be the origin of figurative language, or what rhetoricians like Abraham Fraunce call tropes (from the Greek root meaning turn):

> A Trope or turning is when a word is turned from his naturall signification, to some other, so conuenientlie, as that it seeme rather willinglie ledd, than driuen by force to that other signification. This was first inuented of necessitie for want of words, but afterwards continued and frequented by reason of the delight and pleasant grace thereof.[7]

A word said to be *translated* in the root sense of the verb would be equivalent to a word "turned" or "ledd" from its "naturall significa-tion" to fill a different linguistic space, either by replacing another word or by fulfilling a lack, as we borrow what we need but do not own. The playful phrasing in Hoskyns's definition of metaphor mak-ing as "friendly & neighborly borrowing" suggests some transaction like the proverbial transfer of a cup of sugar from lender to needy borrower. These verbs were used to name actions which could be understood "in a sorte" as actual physical motions. That seems, at any rate, to be the only way to interpret a sentence in Richard Carew's *The Excellency of the English Tongue:* "Lastly our speech doth not consist only of wordes, but in a sorte euen of deedes, as when we expresse a matter by Metaphors, wherin the English is very frutefull and forc-ible."[8] What he means by "deedes" would seem to be the acts of bor-rowing or transporting to make metaphors. This is therefore yet an-other instance where words are not clearly distinguished from the acts they name, nor are uses of language separated into what would now be called literal and figurative.

At the same time, the verb *to translate* could also name the specifi-cally linguistic exercise we now mean by it, the transfer of meaning from one language to another. This definition of translating over-lapped with the implications of borrowing in the sense that many words taken from other languages were assimilated into English. Chapman uses wording almost identical with Hoskyns's definition of metaphor making to describe this "good neighbourly borrowing" of terms "farre fetched" from other languages. These were sometimes called "foren" or "ouer-sea" words—therefore literally transported from a distance—while native words used metaphorically were also known as "forraine."[9] They had a function in common with metaphor to fill a space where English was thought to be deficient, a practice heatedly argued in discussions of language such as the dedicatory

epistle to *The Shepeardes Calender:* "which default when as some en-
deuoured to salue and recure, they patched vp the holes with peces
and rags of other languages, borrowing here of the french, there of
the Italian, euery where of the Latine. . . ."[10]

Sir Thomas More, discussing the possibility of translating native
words into Latin equivalents, describes a transferal to fill up a linguistic space in much the same terms as those that defined the making of
metaphors as borrowing or translating: "For that nowne knowledging,
and that verbe knowledge, hath in our tong theyr proper place . . .
where this latyne woorde *agnosco,* or *agnitio* maye stand in the place if
they talked in latine."[11] In religious controversy, transferals of meaning both in this kind of translation and in figurative uses were passion-
ately disputed in the same terms.

These overlapping possibilities in the vocabulary of borrowing and
translating words seem to be at work but unexamined in a passage
where Sir Thomas Elyot describes an instance of actual translation in
both the concurrent senses of assimilating vocabulary from other languages and of making metaphors. He defends his introduction into
English of a word borrowed from Latin to make a name for "an excellent vertue where unto we lacke a name in englisshe":

> Wherfore I am constrained to usurpe a latine worde, callyng
> it *Maturitie:* whiche worde, though it be strange and darke, yet
> by declaring the vertue in a fewe mo wordes, the name ones
> brought in custome, shall be as facile to understande as other
> wordes late commen out of Italy and Fraunce, and made den-
> izens amonge us. . . . *Maturum* in latine maye be enterpreted
> ripe or redy, as frute when it is ripe, it is at the very poynte to
> be gathered and eaten, and euery other thinge, whan it is redy,
> it is at the instante after to be occupied. Therefore that worde
> maturitie is translated to the actis of man. . . . for the neces-
> sary augmentation of our language.[12]

The Latin word "*Maturum*" borrowed to fill a need is in the linguistic
sense translated into an English equivalent, which is then said to be
"translated to the actis of man." In this phrase, "translated" means
that the word has been turned from its natural signification, the ripening of fruit, to become a borrowed or metaphorical name for man's
moral growth.

A similar overlapping of implications surrounds the verb *to borrow*
as it is used for the making of figurative comparisons. In addition to
the notion of a transfer to fill a space, it suggests other assumptions in
Hoskyns's representative phrasing when he writes that a borrowed

word—a word used metaphorically—does not express a thing "soe directly & proplie as the naturall name of the thinge meant would signifye," which is the original word for it.[13] In this sense a borrowed word is one that does not belong to the thing it denotes, is not its proper name. "*Maturitie*" is the natural name belonging to the ripening of fruit from which it is borrowed to name a stage of human growth, much as "*Maturum*" is a word native to Latin, from which it is translated into English.

This is the commonest sense in which a figurative expression is said to be *taken* or *borrowed*, typically with no clear distinction between whether the source to which it originally belongs, from which it is then borrowed, is a linguistic or a nonverbal phenomenon. For instance, in his discussion of metaphor Peacham suggests both possibilities without acknowledgment. He writes that "From certaine Substantiues, very apt and pleasant *Metaphors* are taken," but then "From the earth are borrowed these and such like translations." The first statement asserts the source from which metaphors are borrowed to be words, nouns, with the example immediately given: "Thy word is a lanterne to my feete, and a light unto my pathes." In this metaphorical sentence the nouns "lanterne" and "light," "feete" and "pathes" are borrowed, it would seem, from some hypothetical sentence in which they are used as names having their proper or natural—we might say literal—signification: *This lantern shows me where to put my feet, and is a light to make visible the paths where I walk.* Yet in Peacham's second statement metaphors are seemingly said to be taken from the external world. That possibility depends on the notion that to each part of the creation a word belongs as its proper name, from which it may be turned to name something else, making such metaphors as these recommended by Peacham to be borrowed from the "earth": "a large field of matter, a mountaine of wealth, a wildernesse of doubts, a denne of theeues, a path of pleasure, a way of error, a vale of miserie."[14] The terms *proper* and *natural* for what would now be called *literal* uses of words confirm the suggestion here that the original source from which metaphors are taken could be thought of as outside language, someplace in the external world. Since it was generally agreed that there are "moe things, then there are words to expresse things by," these sources could be considered hypothetically as inexhaustible.[15]

In still other instances, words borrowed to make metaphors are said to belong to a speaker who properly uses them with their natural significance. Fraunce argues from this notion in preferring the native

word "Reasoning" over its more usual latinate equivalents to "expresse the Nature of Logicke," because it is a proper rather than a
translated or borrowed name:

> For the word, disputing, which commeth of *disputare*, it is Met-
> aphoricall, as *Varro* reporteth, and so is *disserere:* the one being
> borrowed of the Winemayster, the other fet from the sower:
> for as the first cutteth off superfluous branches in his Vine,
> which is properly *disputare*, so the other disperseth his seed in
> diuers places, and not confusedly throweth all in one heape,
> which is the natural signification of this woord, *disserere*. [16]

Here the rejected terms are said to be "borrowed," with unexamined
overlappings of meaning for that term. Each "commeth" from Latin
and in that linguistic sense is translated; both are also "fet" from
speakers who would use them in their original sense to describe actual
physical operations. Figures involving extended comparisons—allegories, similitudes, parables, proverbs, riddles—could also be described as belonging to whatever speaker would use them in their
proper signification. Tyndale assumes this in defining such a figure:
"And Allegory is as much to say as straunge speakyng, or borowed
speach. As when we say of a wanton child, this sheepe hath magottes
in his tayle, he must be annoynted with byrchin salue, which speach
I borow of the shepheardes." [17] Shepherds who tend maggoty sheep
are the proper owners of this "speach" originally describing them.

   This conception of making figures out of words or phrases originally used in their proper sense by some archetypal speaker shares
implications with the assumption that words are proper names belonging to things in the external world, outside of language, from
which they may be taken to make metaphorical names for other matter. For such speakers as the winemaker, the sower, and the shepherd
are parts of that wider world. The notion of borrowing from their
ways of talking still more closely parallels the concept of translating
metaphors from a hypothetical sentence in which words are used literally. For both ideas imply that language preexists in a formulated
state outside the mind of the speaker or writer in the act of using it.
This view presupposes some hypostasized original of which the user's
figurative phrasing is a translation. It would then be said to be borrowed in almost a precisely parallel sense that a writer like Ascham
can say that he has "borrowed" a similitude from another author's writings:

> Euery man sees, (as I sayd before) new wax is best for print-
> yng: new claie, fittest for working; new shorne woll, aptest for
> sone and surest dying: new fresh flesh, for good and durable
> salting. And this similitude is not rude, nor borowed of the
> larder house, but out of his scholehouse, of whom, the wisest
> of England, neede not be ashamed to learne.[18]

The actual writings of this unnamed author are a source for borrowed
language analogous to the speech of the archetypal shepherd or
farmer. What is implied is that the similitude or other figurative comparison has been "sayd before," either actually or theoretically, and is
copied anew from some specific or hypothetical model.

Also underlying the vocabulary for metaphor making is the assumption that this original is always usage which would now be called
literal, but in sixteenth-century English would be said to be proper or
natural. At the time the term *literal* was applied almost exclusively in
biblical exegesis. It was the vernacular word for the medieval Latin
literalus, the name for the one sense of Scripture distinguished from
the other (typically three since the time of Augustine) allegorical
senses.[19] In this application the term seems to have had loosely related
but imperfectly distinguished meanings, even though it was the subject of intense interest and debate. A passage where Hooker argues
for the "literall" sense shows one such use:

> I hold it for a most infallible rule in expositions of sacred scrip-
> ture, that where a litterall construction will stand, the farth-
> est from the letter is commonly the worst. There is nothing
> more dangerous then this licentious and deluding arte, which
> changeth the meaning of words, as Alchymie doth or would
> do the substance of metals, maketh of any thing what it listeth,
> and bringeth in the end all truth to nothing.[20]

The commonly used phrase "litterall construction," like the equally
familiar synonym "lyterall cense," could in different contexts have one
of two meanings which seem not to have been separated. It could
mean the way the passage is constructed, the arrangement of the
words in the text, or it could refer to the way the reader construes it,
either his grammatical analysis of it or his interpretation, his understanding of it.[21] Hooker here applies "literall" and "letter" to the explicit "meaning of words" in the text.

These terms also had a more significantly different use in the sixteenth century, which is represented when Tyndale writes: "that

which the prouerbe, similitude, redell or allegory signifieth is euer the litterall sense."[22] Here the phrase does not clearly refer either to the actual arrangement of words or even that construction in combination with the reader's interpretation of them. Instead the "litterall sense" seems to preexist outside, beyond, or behind the "figuratiue speches vsed in the scripture."[23] It is therefore comparable to the absent term for which a borrowed or translated word is substituted. For example, in Tyndale's "borowed" allegory of the maggoty sheep, the absent term "wanton child" would correspond to the "litterall sense" or what the "allegory signifieth." It is not until later that the term *literal* is regularly extended to apply to words used in their etymological sense, for which the *Q.E.D.* gives 1597 as the earliest citation. This is an exception to the otherwise common practice of calling such uses *proper* or *natural*, terms reflecting a cast of mind different from our own which both I. A. Richards and Paul Ricouer associate with belief in the magic of names (to be discussed in chapter 4).[24] For they unite name and thing in an ontological identity which is excluded from the later more strictly linguistic term.

Places

Not only the act of making figurative comparisons, but the sources from which they may be *taken*, where they may be *found*, are described in vocabulary—especially spatial terms—used we would say both literally and figuratively. Commonly there is no acknowledgment of this distinction. Metaphors are said to be borrowed from *places*, often so unspecified, or *the places*. In *The Garden of Eloquence* Peacham discusses them in a passage where he follows a common practice of the rhetoricians by first describing his subject and then illustrating it in the formation of his own sentences. Here it is the art of making metaphors, which he demonstrates by using the traditional comparison—a variant of his book's title—of the "places" where metaphors may be found to "fields," the figures taken from them to "flowers." This is an example of a translation taken from the earth, like his illustration of metaphor quoted earlier, "a large field of matter": "The places from whence translations may be taken, are infinite, notwithstanding there be certaine that be verie vsuall, readie, apt and pleasant, which I purpose hereafter to obserue and note, as the most plentifull fields, yeelding such profitable and pleasant flowers."[25] By first saying here that such places from which metaphors may be drawn "are infinite," he seems to be thinking of them as generalized locations in the natural world. For God created it in unimaginable abundance, believed to extend vastly beyond the boundaries of language, as Mulcaster states: "The number of things whereof we write and speak is infinite, the words wherewith we write and speak, be definite and within number."[26] The earth with its bountiful fields luxuriant with flowers, its mountains, wildernesses, dens, paths, ways, vales is only one among the inexhaustible sources of metaphor in God's creation.

Yet when Peacham next writes in the same passage that there are some places which are "verie vsuall, readie, apt and pleasant," he seems to be thinking of them in a different, more limited and specialized sense, not infinite but regulated by custom and easy access. Here he must be thinking of what tradition originating in antiquity called *topoi* in Greek, *loci communes* in Latin, in English "common places or heads of Inuention."[27] These were headings, topics, seats of arguments, even passages stored in the mind or memory, from which figures and all sorts of other verbal matter might be taken. In this sense a place was not thought of as an external geographical space—like the earth or the sky—but as a metaphorical "storehouse" in the mind of the speaker, or in his memory. Yet even in this use they could also be thought of as physiological areas of the brain or memory, sometimes described as a "chest" or "vessell" capable of containing limited quantities of matter stored in defined areas.[28] This conception is shown, for example, in an argument that things memorized but not understood "doo more harme then good, because that the places in the same memorie, which are possessed with such things, cannot be filled with other more profitable knowledge."[29]

At other times "place" refers to whatever external object—like the head or body—or area—a house, church, "or other roume"—serves as a mnemonic device to which mental images are attached.[30] These were not mutually exclusive conceptions of what constituted the places, but were often held simultaneously and without differentiation, as Peacham's sentence illustrates. Wilson sums up without acknowledging the confusion in this definition: "A place is called any roume, apt to receiue thinges."[31]

Again without clear distinctions the places might be actual sections in commonplace books, also called "storehouses." These were referred to as if they were containers capable of being "opened" by the writer, or holes into which "he falleth" unless "passage is made from one place to another."[32] Such books were collections of written material divided under headings such as "The Earth, with that belongeth to it." Each would characteristically contain such jumbled catalogues of figurative sayings and proper names for things as this continuous se-

quence: "Clay," "Swine are delighted, or loue dyrt and mire," "A vile
and filthie person," "A filthie and vile harlot," "A mud wall," "To spot
or beray."[33] These compilations substituted for mind and memory by
containing and arranging matter to furnish the orator or writer with
ready metaphors and other verbal constructs taken from such places.

One book by John Withal intended for this purpose was first published in 1553. It became one of the most widely used texts in the
second half of the sixteenth century, republished and revised in augmented editions at least a dozen times by 1634. The heading and list
quoted above are from the edition of 1602 edited by Clerk. It also
contained such useful material as seven pages devoted to "Trees, with
that pertaineth to them," "The parts of the trees," "The names of
trees," followed by five more pages headed "Fruites," including matter
pertaining to what may be found in "orchards." A poet who wished
to compose a catalogue of trees, and there were many (as discussion
of this commonplace in the next chapter will show), could find ample
material under these headings. Listed are not only names but facts
associated with trees—such as the production of "Turpentine"—and
stock phrases describing their parts—an instance is "The mast of the
Oke tree." Both these details, for example, appear in Sylvester's translation of a catalogue of trees in Du Bartas's *La Sepmaine* (quoted in the
following chapter). This part of the collection also includes myths and
moral lessons associated with trees, as in verses under the heading
"The Apple tree":

> The originall of all euill and sinne,
> at an apple tree did begin.[34]

The pages of such commonplace books may be referred to by Sidney in *Astrophil and Stella* 1, where he pictures the frustrated poet "Oft
turning others' leaves" in search of "inventions fine."[35] Or Sidney may
have meant those pages to belong to volumes of poetry which, there
is varied evidence, were also often treated as if they were collections
of commonplaces from which to borrow. Harington's translation of
Ariosto's *Orlando Fvrioso*, for example, was printed (as were rhetorical
handbooks and other manuals of style) with marginal glosses pointing
out where to find a particular kind of figure such as a "Sentence" or
"Simile. This is taken out of Catullus, but greatly bettered," or announcing a topic like "The praise of women."[36] Presumably these
glosses were aids to any writer in Astrophil's situation. Sidney dis-
misses such "far-fet helpes" in *Astrophil and Stella* 15, yet in actual
practice there are many examples of poets treating the poems of others

as compilations of commonplaces to be borrowed. A strikingly clear instance is Sonnet 51 from Watson's *The Tears of Fancie* which, Paul Alpers has pointed out, transcribes lines only slightly altered from a catalogue of trees in *The Faerie Queene*.[37] The fact that similar metaphorical names were given to commonplace books such as Erasmus's *The flowers of sencies*, to rhetorical handbooks like *The Garden of Eloquence*, and to verse or poesy itself (for which a common pun was *posie*) is further evidence of similarities in the way they were all conceived for use.[38] One of the standard definitions of the verb *to read* in Latin dictionaries, *to gather*, supports the commonplace repeated, for example, in the statutes for Westminster School of 1560. The teaching of figures was based on readings in classical authors from which "the boys shall gather the flowers, phrases or idioms, also antitheses, epithets, synonyms" and so on.[39]

In the 1602 edition of Withal's collection, the prefatory explanation of its arrangement shows representative overlapping of meanings or blurring of distinctions associated with the notion of places as sources for verbal matter of all kinds, including figurative comparisons:

> And though it leadeth not, as do the rest, by way of *Alphabet*, yet hath it *order*, and *method* both, and the fittest *order*, and the fittest method for yong beginners: for Example, he that would find the *Sunne*, the *Moone*, the *Starres*, or any such other such excellent creatures aboue, he may looke for the *Skie:* that is more readie here, for his capacitie, and that is their place, and there they be readie for him in *English*, and *Latine* both: or so many of them at the least, and more, than be commonlie talked of.[40]

The true order and method here is not linguistic, by alphabetical sequence, but natural, spatial. What the compilation contains are "creatures," not clearly distinct from the names proper to them. These are disposed according to their place in the world, not in the alphabet; the reader may "find" them just as he would in the order of nature. Their "place" in the book is dictated by their physical location in the world, and is somehow identical with that geographical "place."

Like the vocabulary of borrowing or translating words to make figurative comparisons, these various uses for the term *places* as the sources where metaphors may be found again reflect the deep-rooted assumption that language exists in some space external to itself and to the mind of the writer. This assumption in turn encouraged the notion that verbal formulations preexist to be borrowed. The act of

drawing from this repository of places, however variously understood, is described by the term *invention*, with its commonest sixteenth-century meanings of finding, discovering, coming upon. This
usage further confirms conceptions implied by the vocabulary for
metaphor making.

These implications bear on some uses of metaphor in this poetry
that seem strange by later standards. An instance is in one of Gascoigne's poems which includes lines comparing the complaining lover
to a storm-tossed vessel. This was a traditional comparison recently
made famous in England by Wyatt. His sonnet translating it from
Petrarch was printed in Tottel's miscellany and was therefore familiar
to later poets, including Gascoigne. The latter's poem resembles the
sonnets of his predecessors insofar as it uses (in somewhat confused
combination with other similitudes) the commonplace comparison, "I
am the ship my selfe":

> Me thought I was a loft, and yet my seate full sure:
> Thy heart dyd seeme to me a rock which euer might endure.
> And see, it was but sand, whome seas of subtiltie
> Haue soked so with wanton waues, that fate was forst to flye.
> The floodes of ficklenesse haue vndermined so
> The first foundation of my ioy, that myrth is ebb'd to wo.
> Yet at lowe water markes I lye and wayte my time
> To mend the breach, but all in vaine, it cannot passe the
>   prime.
> For when the prime flood comes, which all this rage begoon,
> Then waues of wyll do worke so fast, my piles are ouer
>   roon.[41]

Here each aspect of the lover's case is given a metaphorical name
borrowed from an element in a stormy seascape; his beloved's heart is
not a "rock" but "sand," which is "soked" with "seas of subtiltie,"
"wanton waues," while "flooddes of ficklenesse" undermine his "piles"
with "waues of wyll," and so on. Although a place of common origin—the ocean itself or such a heading in a commonplace book—
connects these metaphorical terms, each borrowing of a word seems
to have been thought of separately, then joined by independent reference back to that place, and by alliteration. Gascoigne's repeated
uses of "waues" in the metaphorical pairings "wanton waues" and
"waues of wyll" show something like this procedure. In the first
phrase the metaphorical term "waues" is a substitute name for some
word like *wiles* and refers to the fickle lady's schemes. In the second
"waues" seems to be a translation of some noun like *desire* and names

the lover's passionate longings (a common meaning for the noun *will* in this poetry). Both are taken from the same place, the stormy sea, but are otherwise kept separate in the poem. For instance, nothing is made of the use of the same word to name attributes of both the lover and the lady. What is more, the nonmetaphorical words, "wanton" and "wyll," express the essential meanings, which are not much affected by their pairings with the borrowed word, "waues." That contributes a suggestion of engulfing power which it does not further particularize in either phrase.

This passage seems to confirm that some sixteenth-century formations of metaphor were dominated by a fundamental assumption that language somehow preexists outside the mind of the poet or the actual lines of his verse, in some place from which it may be borrowed word by word. An important corollary that follows from this notion is that verbal combinations could be imagined to be based on the nature of the places from which they were originally borrowed, rather than on relations among the actual words of the poem. Details in Gascoigne's comparison of the lover's case to the seascape seem to work on that assumption, as do metaphors in Shakespeare's Sonnet 24:

> Mine eye hath play'd the painter and hath steeld,
> Thy beauties forme in table of my heart,
> My body is the frame wherein ti's held,
> And perspectiue it is best Painters art.
> For through the Painter must you see his skill,
> To finde where your true Image pictur'd lies,
> Which in my bosomes shop is hanging stil,
> That hath his windowes glazed with thine eyes:
> Now see what good-turnes eyes for eies haue done,
> Mine eyes haue drawne thy shape, and thine for me
> Are windowes to my brest, where-through the Sun
> Delights to peepe, to gaze therein on thee
> > Yet eyes this cunning want to grace their art
> > They draw but what they see, know not the hart.

Stephen Booth is correct in saying that the poem is based on the convention that a lover can see his own face reflected in his beloved's eyes, and he is helpful in suggesting that "some sanity may be retained if one holds on to the idea of two people looking into one another's eyes."[42] To develop this traditional situation then, Shakespeare borrows his metaphors from the painter's trade, or from such a heading in a commonplace book like Withal's, which contains sections pertaining to various occupations which "haue their titles in this worke with

their appurtenances." For the same purpose the poet could have consulted a source like Thomas Newbery's *A booke in Englysh metre*, an
immensely long verse catalogue of occupations including those of "Al
Grauers, Caruers, and Paincters of clothes," with their "wares and
Implementes, in this world contayned."[43]

Some such procedure is suggested in the sonnet by the proliferation
of metaphors borrowed from painting. For some of the connections
among them can be explained more by their derivation from a place
of common origin than by their relationships within the poem. To
illustrate, the lover's heart is compared to a "table" on which the beloved's portrait is painted. It follows that the lover's body can be said
to be its "frame," since it encases his heart as a frame surrounds a
picture. But then his bosom is the "shop" where the picture hangs.
This comparison can be consistent with the first metaphor—
table:heart—but not with the second—*frame:body*—since the frame
would now have to contain the shop where the picture hangs (presumably framed). In such an elaborately worked out—or perhaps playfully overworked—metaphorical scheme, this kind of incompatibility
between particular details suggests the possibility of a different principle of connection than might be applied now. Since picture, frame,
and shop may be found with many other details of the sonnet in the
place of the painter's trade, they may have been borrowed separately
(like Gascoigne's "waues" from the seascape) and yet be understood to
cohere because they belong together in their place. The kind of thinking that described the art of comparison as an act of translating or
borrowing from places may therefore have encouraged such uses of
language illustrated in Shakespeare's sonnet and Gascoigne's lines.
They seem to have been predicated on the sense that there is an available body of language extending even beyond the tradition of written
sources such as were preserved in commonplace books, because existing somehow in the external world, and in some formulated order.

Metaphorical Epithets

Other ways of thinking embedded in sixteenth-century discussions of metaphor may also suggest presuppositions reflected in some
of its uses. One shown in passages already quoted is that all figures
conceived as based on resemblance were thought to consist in single
words. These could then be strung together in consecutive speech,
for instance in allegory which is described as "a continued Metaphore"; more recent thinking that metaphorical meanings depend on
sentence or context therefore had virtually no part in this view.[44]

What is more, quotations have shown that the single words out of which these figures were made were said to be names belonging to things. To change the words from proper names to metaphors, the writer must disturb this natural order. As Puttenham describes the process: "Single words haue their sence and vnderstanding altered and figured many wayes, to wit, by transport, abuse, crosse-naming, new naming, change of name."[45] To invent or "transport" a metaphor—Puttenham's list also refers to his epithets for other figures, such as catachresis and onomatopeia—is to take a name from one thing and apply it to another (a process now commonly associated with metonymy as distinct from metaphor).[46] The fitness of the new name is determined by the ontological order which made it originally proper to one thing but now figuratively apt to denote another which has some affinity with it. The new name either denotes a thing which has no proper name, or stands in place of its original name. This view does not recognize another attribute associated with metaphor in more recent thinking: that metaphor consists of two parts—I. A. Richards' terms *tenor* and *vehicle* will serve in this discussion—which are simultaneously present in some juxtaposition, tension, or interaction with one another.[47]

The very different conception of metaphor as a single word constituting a change of name encouraged some practices which now seem peculiar both in the sense of being strange and of especially characterizing writing of this period but not later poetry. One is the preference previously discussed for pairings where an adjective is used in a metaphorical sense in combination with a nonfigurative noun to make a phrase or epithet considered in itself to be a single name. It should be said again that the use of epithets is of course not unique to sixteenth-century writing, nor are the particular epithets, which in fact were often chosen precisely because they could be found in biblical, classical, and medieval texts. What is special in writing of this period is the seemingly obsessive repetition of such epithets.

Peacham gives familiar examples of this common sort of phrase in his discussion of metaphors translated from the place of "things without life to things hauing life": "A stonie heart, a greene head, a leaden wit, raw youth. Also a bitter people, a crooked nation, a sharpe iudge, a glorious prince, the blossome of tender age, the mist of memorie. In these examples . . . is signified . . . by stonie heart crueltie, by leaden wit a mind of small capacitie, etc."[48] If at least in theory such a metaphor as the favorite of complaining poets, a "stonie heart," could be thought of as simply a translation of *cruel heart*, then it was not thought to invite detailed response to what might be suggested about the lady's heart by associating it with the properties of a stone: impenetrable surface, bruising hardness, changeless shape, heaviness, the unresponsiveness of a lifeless thing. Simple paraphrase, like Peacham's, of figurative comparisons was characteristically recommended to readers in marginal glosses. These pointed to examples (sometimes even by a printed hand with outstretched forefinger) and gave substitute words to show their proper meanings. Abraham Fleming performed this service in a collection of letters translated from Cicero. For example, the "danger of shipp racke" he glosses "By translation, for hazard of life & goods, a phrase very usuall." Often such paraphrases call attention to the process of reducing the figure to its proper meaning. Fleming does this in retranslating an extended satirical comparison: "Wherein hee deserued as much to be laughed at, as if hee had put uppon him the attyre of a Gyant, and had spoken his words with a feigning voice like a Gyant, to the end men might beleeue he was indeede a Gyant. . . ." His marginal comment defends its simplification as a recovery of the full original meaning: "By this Allegorical speach he meaneth nothing else, but that Long. [Christopher Longolius] tooke more vpon him, then he was able to performe in imitating Tullie."[49] These acts of retranslation are offered both as explanations of how metaphors work and as models of the way a reader should interpret them.

In actual poetic practice, such a metaphorical pairing as "stonie heart"—the same could be said of its virtual synonyms "flintie hart," "frosen heart," "hard hart"—is used so often and typically with so little development that the properties of being "stonie" are scarcely suggested more than they would be by calling the heart of the scornful mistress by its proper name, *cruel.*[50] The result is to make such pairings predictable, because they appear together regularly in this poetry (for one reason, because they were specifically recommended by rhetoricians like Peacham). Yet at the same time they are in a sense arbitrary. That is, they are seemingly chosen without much attention to the range of expressive possibilities opened up by the choice of one adjective over another roughly equivalent, since other metaphors or even the nonfigurative phrase for which they substitute have nearly comparable effect. When Wyatt complains "Oh stony hart . . . So cruell," or Spenser describes a sorrow "That could haue made a stonie heart to weep" (a line almost identical with an example given by Day to illustrate hyperbole), they are making a metaphorical comparison that perfectly conforms to the sixteenth-century theoretical model set forth quite consistently by the rhetoricians, of figures based on resemblance.[51] They are translating or borrowing, as that performance was then understood, which is paradoxically an act closer to what we now mean by translating—substituting one word for a different one with the same meaning—than it is to more recent ideas about the creation of metaphor.

Genitive Metaphors

Another kind of figure characteristic of this poetry also seems to have been encouraged by these assumptions embedded in the contemporary vocabulary for comparing. Instances are in a series of metaphorical pairings in lines from *Passionate Centurie* 91 by Thomas Watson. They are built into the ubiquitous comparison of the lover's state to a sea voyage:

> Ye captiue soules of blindefolde *Cyprians* boate
> Marke with aduise in what estate yee stande,
>   Your *Boteman* neuer whistles mearie noate,
>   And *Folly* keeping sterne, still puttes from lande,
>   And makes a sport to tosse you to and froe
>   Twixt *sighing windes*, and surging *waues of woe*.
> On *Beawties* rocke she runnes you at her will.[52]

Following the familiar adjective noun combination "*sighing windes*" are two pairings of nouns in genitive constructions, "*waues of woe*" and "*Beawties* rocke." Again, as is true of phrases in Gascoigne's passage taken from the same place, there seems to be more interest in their connectedness as borrowings from a single *locus* (seascape, room in the memory, or section of a commonplace book) than in their relations within the poem or in the combined effects within each pairing. "*Beawties* rocke," for instance, invites translation into some phrase like *the threat of beauty* without allowing much more immediate or detailed attention to the way beauty may be associated with a rock. (There might be such an association if the phrase is read as an allusion to the myth of the sirens, a reference which itself would typically be included in the same place in a collection of commonplaces.)

Such metaphorical combinations of nouns in genitive constructions are a common form of figurative comparison in sixteenth-century poetry. Peacham, in his list quoted earlier of metaphors like "stonie heart" pairing noun adjectives with substantives, also includes without distinction examples of this type: "the blossome of tender age, the mist of memorie." The grammatical function of the linking word *of* makes it virtually synonymous with *which is like* to form metaphorical comparisons: *tender age which is like a blossom, memory which is like a mist.*

Ralegh makes a line again based on comparison of the lover's state to a stormy landscape by doubling such combinations: "The wynde of woe hath torne my Tree of Truste."[53] The pairing of "wynde of woe" chosen it would seem partly for the alliteration which binds the two nouns together, derives from the conventional association of "woe" in a complaint with the lover's sighs, recalling Watson's "*sighing windes.*" These can be perceived as bearing some likeness to winds, since both are gusts of air with threatening power (sighs were believed to waste the breath of life).[54] Ralegh's pairing is understood this way when "woe" is translated into *sighs* to make a comparison: *woeful sighs which are like the wind.* It therefore works in the same way as Watson's metaphorical pairing of "*waues of woe,*" with its similarly conventional equation of the lover's sufferings with his weeping. Once "*woe*" here is translated into *tears*, it allows a comparison: *woeful tears which are like waves.* It therefore points in a rather unemphatic way to their shared property of engulfing wetness.

Ralegh's second genitive construction in this line, "Tree of Truste," seems to put still less emphasis on the possible connections between the paired nouns other than that they alliterate (the distance between them is bridged by the even closer resemblance in sound between "Tree" and "Truste" than between "wynde" and "woe"). Trust could be likened to a tree for, among other possibilities, its height, strength, roots, cyclical growth, capacity to shade, but because Ralegh's pairing is not elaborated in any way, such detailed resemblances are scarcely evoked. Nor does his pairing clearly point to an identification of the tree with the lover's perilous state, such as Spenser spells out in a detailed comparison in *Amoretti* 56:

> Fayre be ye sure, but proud and pittilesse,
>   as is a storme, that all things doth prostrate:
>   finding a tree alone all comfortlesse,
>   beats on it strongly it to ruinate.

Ralegh's unelaborated pairing "Tree of Truste" seems to be justified more by the fact that trees may be found in a landscape swept by winds strong enough to uproot them, and by alliteration, than by possible connections between the paired nouns, to which it scarcely calls attention.

A place of common origin seems also to be the main justification for a pairing of nouns in Shakespeare's Sonnet 64:

> When I haue seene the hungry Ocean gaine
> Aduantage on the Kingdome of the shoare.

The link of "Kingdome" with "shoare" extends the military metaphor embedded in "gaine / Aduantage" but does not invite much attention to likenesses between the two grammatically joined terms. Like metaphorical pairings of adjective and noun—for instance *stony heart*—such combinations of nouns in genitive constructions—*heart of stone* is one of the most common—are figures which conform to the notions of metaphor making as acts of translating or borrowing. For although they work as comparisons—*heart which is like a stone, beauty which is like a rock*—they do not evoke detailed connections between the terms, but instead invite translation into such phrases as: *heart which is cruel, beauty which is threatening*. The juxtaposition, tension, interaction between tenor and vehicle associated with metaphor in later thinking are relatively slight in these common sixteenth-century types of figure, in which the borrowed noun—*stone, rock*—is thought of quite strictly as a substitution for the absent word. Theoretically, therefore, but also in actual effect, there seems to be some distance between them.

The workings of these commonly used types of phrases can better be understood if they are set beside comparisons from one of Sidney's Arcadian poems, in which the apparent distance between terms is much more extreme. Here the name of an object, the absent beloved's "glove," is associated with radically unlike metaphorical terms, "starre" and "Anker":

> Sweete glove the wittnes of my secrett blisse
> (Whiche hyding didest preserve that beawtie's light,
> That opened furthe my seale of compforte is)
> Be thow my starre in this my darkest night,
> Nowe that myne eyes their cheerefull sunn dothe misse
> Which dazeling still, dothe still maynteine my sight;
>   Be thow, sweete glove, the Anker of my mynde,
>   Till my frayle barke his haven agayn do fynde.[55]

Whereas we can recognize a relation between winds and sighs or even between beauty and a rock (if not as an allusion to the sirens, then because poetry has so richly associated female beauty with danger and unyielding power), it seems difficult to think of a glove as a star unless some quite thoroughgoing process of conceptualizing takes place. If the word "starre" is taken as a translation of a phrase such as *source of comfort* (parallel to "cheerefull sun" which names the absent beloved), then the two terms can be drawn into some kind of connection. If the word "Anker" is a substitute for a phrase like *secure hope*, it can be seen as comparable to the glove (itself identified with the lover's "secrett blisse"), with which it is associated but which it does not resemble. The actual words "glove," "starre," "Anker" have to be retranslated into the originals—names of things to which they belong—from which they have been borrowed in order for the figure to be intelligible. Sidney's comparisons seem to demand almost explicitly to be read as conforming strictly to the sixteenth-century definition of metaphor as translation in the sense of the substitution of one word for another that has the same meaning. Yet in less extreme form this effect, examples have shown, is shared not only by figures that rhetoricians like Puttenham would call "abuse" of words, or words "far fet," in which category Sidney's might be included. It is also characteristic to a degree of commonly used kinds of figurative comparisons and even particular phrases favored by poet after poet, which must therefore have been thought to be not only intelligible but especially effective.

Transumptive Metaphors

Confirmation of more differences from later attitudes can be inferred not only from Sidney's comparisons but from more typical examples previously discussed when they are explored in the context of other sixteenth-century writing about figurative comparisons. In the vocabulary of the handbooks, Sidney's metaphors and also perhaps Watson's "*Beawties* rocke" and Ralegh's pairings would be said to belong to the category of rhetorical figure rather confusedly discussed under the name of metalepsis or transumption. This form of metonymy was traditionally distinguished as the substitution of one word for another which is itself figurative. A classic example cited by the rhetoricians is a line from Virgil: *Post multas mea regna videns mirabor aristas*. Puttenham translates it "Thus in English":

> *After many a stubble shall I come*
> *And wonder at the sight of my kingdome.*

"By stubble the Poet vnderstoode yeares, for haruests come but once euery yeare, at least wayes with vs in Europe. This is spoken by the figure of farre-fet. *Metalepsis*."[56]

According to Peacham's analysis of the same Virgilian example, an extra step between what would now be called vehicle and tenor is required to trace the full meaning of the figure: "*Virgil* by eares of corne signifieth sommers, and by sommers yeares."[57] Watson's phrase can be read according to this paradigm, when the reader recognizes that in complaints comparing the plight of lovers to a sea voyage, "*Beawties*" is a conventional substitute name for cruel mistresses who have stony hearts. Spenser explicitly works out this set of connections in a similitude in *Amoretti 56*:

> Fayre be ye sure, but hard and obstinate,
>   as is a rocke amidst the raging floods;
>   gaynst which a ship of succour desolate,
>   doth suffer wreck both of her selfe and goods.

As Watson joins them, both nouns in the phrase "*Beawties* rocke" can be recognized as substituted or borrowed names and then retranslated into their originals to make some such sense as *the dangerous power of a beautiful lady who is cruel*. This act of interpretation, similar to the kind of reading demanded by Sidney's associations of glove with star and anchor, fits some sixteenth-century descriptions of metalepsis or transumption.

Definitions of this figure in the earliest English rhetorical treatises are so often obscure and self-contradictory that there seems to have been no inclusive understanding of it by sixteenth-century writers. Even so, their treatments of it are richly suggestive for our purposes because the characteristic terms—especially the spatial metaphors—they use in discussing it, along with their analyses of examples, are revealing of then commonly held but now unfamiliar assumptions. These cast some light on the way not only Sidney's far-fetched comparisons but also less extreme metaphors were thought to work, or how they came to be made.

Certain suggestive phrases recur in definitions of metalepsis or transumption which are sometimes expanded or illustrated in discussions of it. Puttenham calls it the "*farfet*, as when we had rather fetch a word a great way off then to vse one nerer hand to expresse the matter aswel & plainer." Wilson's definition also involves motion: "Transumption is, when by degrees wee goe to that, which is to be shewed." Here the starting point seems to be the vehicle—in the translation from Virgil "eares of corne"—from which we move by stages back to the tenor—"yeares." Day defines this figure also as a kind of movement, but with a somewhat different course. It begins from the tenor and reaches past it by stages to arrive at the vehicle: "when by a certaine number of degrees we go beyond that wee intend in troth, and haue meaning to speake of."[58] In Peacham's definition the motion entailed by the figure is a kind of measurement by degrees

of the space between the vehicle and the tenor: "It is a forme of speech
by which the Orator in one word expressed, signifieth another word
or thing remoued from it by certaine degrees." His caution about
abuses of transumption is grounded in the same spatial metaphor:
"when the word expressed and the thing signified stand too far asunder, that is so many degrees, as the meaning can not be vnderstood."
After giving a definition of the figure, Peacham expands it, typically
concluding with a comparison of his own to illuminate it. Here by
announcing that he is doing so—"it may well be compared"—he
shows a kind of awareness of his own metaphor that neither he nor
other rhetoricians usually signal in their use of spatial terms to explain
transumption:

> This figure is a kind of *Metonimie*, signifying by the effect a
> cause far off by an effect nigh at hand: yet it is a forme of
> speech seldome vsed of Orators and not oft of Poets, yet is it
> not voyd of profit and vtility, for it teacheth the vnderstanding
> to diue downe to the bottome of the sense, and instructeth the
> eye of the wit, to discerne a meaning farre off. For which prop-
> erty it may well be compared to an high prospect, which pre-
> senteth to the viewe of the beholder an object far distant by
> leading the eye from one marke to another by a lineall direc-
> tion, till it discerneth the thing that is looked for.[59]

Here the distant hill seems to be the vehicle, for which the reader
must substitute a series of translations to arrive at the tenor, the "thing
that is looked for." Wilson's different but equally representative example of the figure illustrates the same process: "Transumption is,
when by degrees wee goe to that, which is to be shewed. As thus.
Such a one lieth in a dark Dungeon: now in speaking of darknesse,
we vnderstand closenesse, by closenesse, we gather blacknesse, & by
blacknesse, we iudge deepenesse."[60] The revealing assumption common to all these passages is that interpretation of a figurative comparison can be described as a kind of movement "by degrees" in a "lineall
direction."

This wording shows how strongly and in what ways the definition
of a metaphor as a translated name dominated some thinking about
how it worked. Granted that transumption involves added stages of
translation, still they illustrate the essential motion thought to be demanded in some form by all figurative conparisons. First, descriptions
of the process allow no interaction between tenor and vehicle, for they
are thought of as occupying spaces at an unchanged distance from one
another. They are not described as simultaneously present; the eye of

the beholder in Peacham's explanatory metaphor cannot keep them both in sight at once. The result of the process must therefore be conceived quite strictly as substitution rather than interaction. Second, the act of translation seems to string together what might now be called the connotations of words into "lineall" sequence, one replacing the other rather than clustering, overlapping, colliding, modifying.

These assumptions may be brought to bear in an effort to discover the presuppositions underlying Sidney's combinations of "glove," "starre," and "Anker," and also the examples of more common types of sixteenth-century metaphors. For they seem relatively indifferent to the paired effects of the words themselves, as if they had no interfering connotations present along with the single point of resemblance to which the translated word gives a new name. The habits of mind informing such figures sometimes seem to be at work even in similes, which explicitly point to the resemblance between the two terms. In formal definitions of this figure, emphasis is also on likeness in a single quality, without attention to other effects which might augment, complicate, modify, or contradict it: "Similies: that is, when two things or moe then two, are so compared, resembled, and conferred together, that they in some one propertie seeme like. . . ."[61]

Spenser focusses on such a single point of likeness in an elaborately extended simile used to praise the bride in his marriage hymn:

> Bvt if ye saw that which no eyes can see,
> The inward beautie of her liuely spright,
> Garnisht with heauenly guifts of high degree,
> Much more then would ye wonder at that sight,
> And stand astonisht lyke to those which red
> Medusaes mazeful hed.[62]

In a poem so perfectly controlled as the *Epithalamion*, this similitude calls attention to the poet's power to compare, his divine gift of perceiving a point of resemblance in the shared effect—here the capacity to astonish—of sights otherwise radically unlike. Yet the response demanded by the combination of terms in the similitude in some ways parallels the process set in motion by the examples of what was then called transumption. For it fixes attention on the point of likeness that ignores extreme and obvious differences, as the metaphorical combinations of glove with star or anchor are indifferent to their wholly dissimilar properties. It is characteristic of writing of the period that this practice could exist simultaneously with, and in partial contradic-

tion of, the belief that the origin and fundamental property of all metaphors is the perception of resemblance.

Metaphorical Puns

Also common in sixteenth-century poetry are comparisons
made out of double meanings for a single word, a type more congenial
with later poetic practices. This use of language in some obvious ways
differs from the kinds of metaphor so far discussed. In their differences these comparisons also seem to depart from the theoretical
understanding of metaphor, accepted by all writers about language in
this period, as borrowed or translated speech. How this is so can be
shown in an instance of this kind of comparison compressed in a single
word in one of Wyatt's sonnets: "Wherwith loue to the hartes forest
he fleeth."[63] Perhaps at least partly under the influence of this well-
known sonnet, its identification of *hart:heart* became one of Shakespeare's preferred puns, second only to his favorite, *deer:dear.*[64] Daniel, among others, also repeated it in the lover's complaint of *Delia* 5:
"Which turn'd my sport into a Harts dispaire, / Which still is chac'd."
This common comparison of a lover's heart to a hart seems to work
very differently from such a pairing as *stony heart*, where the figurative
term *stony* acts largely as a substitute for an absent word like *cruel.* In
Wyatt's line neither term can be said to be absent, so that neither can
be translated or substituted for the other. That is, what would now
be called the vehicle—*hart*—and the tenor—*heart*—are both equally
present in the single noun, since sixteenth-century spelling did not
clearly distinguish them as two different words, one of which could
substitute for the other. Neither term therefore requires to be translated, as the "rocke" linked by Watson to "*Beawties*" invites translation
to mean danger, threat.

There is also another way to understand what is different about the
kind of metaphor represented by "the hartes forest." Unlike Watson's
comparison, or Gascoigne's borrowing of "waues" to link with the
lady's wantonness and the lover's desire, the association of hart and
heart does not derive originally from some connections between
things in a place outside the poem's language from which names are
borrowed. On the contrary, the relationship between the seat of the
lover's passion and the gentle but untamed woodland creature originates in the double meaning of the single word itself, which is an
example of what Blundeville in *The Arte of Logicke* calls "Equiuokes by
chance": "when one selfe name is giuen to many things by chance,
and not for any likenesse that is betwixt them, as in English this word

Hart signifieth as well the Hart of a man or beast, as a certayne beast called a Hart in the Forrest."[65]

The metaphorical possibilities of such "woordes of double understandyng," often combined with other devices allowed by the relatively fluid state of sixteenth-century English, invited some of the most frivolous word play in this poetry.[66] An example is Sidney's comparison in *Astrophil and Stella* 9 of Stella's eyes to glossy black stone: "Of touch they are that without touch doth touch." They also encouraged comparisons as powerfully effective as Wyatt's combination, "the hartes forest," or of other multiple meanings held together in the word "Diere" in his sonnet "Who so list to hounte."[67] There the likeness is of the lover's unattainable dear to a deer which he chases, and also (with characteristic shifting between noun and adjective) to an object which is dear in the sense of being costly, priced beyond his reach. Spenser, in *Amoretti* 67, compares his beloved to the "gentle deare" chased by the huntsman but captured by her own "will" (with the double meaning of choice and desire).[68] Jonson, heralding the completion of a friend's journey, exploits another favorite source of comparisons, the identical spellings for what would later be distinguished as two separate words, *travel* and *travail:*

> This is that good *Æneas*, past through fire,
> Through seas, stormes, tempests: and imbarqu'd for hell,
> Come backe vntouch'd. This man hath trauail'd well.[69]

These comparisons differ in formation from the types that have been shown to fit more precisely the definition of metaphor as translation. The way they actually work, they seem to contradict the sixteenth-century conception of metaphor as the substitution of a borrowed word for a proper name, since both terms are present simultaneously. Yet there are no contemporary acknowledgments of this apparent contradiction despite the fact that words with more than one meaning are elaborately discussed by many writers about language as violations of the natural, proper relationship between word and thing. What is more, there is no common or generally used name in sixteenth-century English for such words, comparable to *pun* or *quibble*, both introduced in the next century. This fact is surprising since punning, rare in earlier English verse, came to be one of the prominent features of this poetry, enjoyed by the greatest writers as well as those who relied for interest solely on word play of all kinds.

Since metaphorical punning was not differentiated by being named as a use of words combining meanings in a special way, it was probably somewhat differently understood in theory. Rhetoricians of this period sometimes illustrate uses of words with multiple meanings under the heading of antanaclasis. Peacham defines this figure in representative terms: "*Antanaclasis* is a figure which repeateth a word that hath two significations, and the one of them contrary, or at least, vnlike to the other." The examples which follow focus on the feature of repetition:

> An example: Care for those things which may discharge you of all care. Care in the first place signifieth to prouide, in the last the solicitude and dread of the minde. Another: In thy youth learne some craft, that in thy age thou mayst get thy liuing without craft. In this example craft in the first place signifieth science, occupation or trade; in the second, deceit and subtiltie.[70]

Typically the examples keep the two meanings separate in different sentences or clauses, stressing their unrelatedness. Peacham emphasizes this aspect also explicitly by commenting that in his example the figure "uniteth" them by "sounde" but "distinguisheth them asunder by the diuersity of their sense." Puttenham calls antanaclasis the figure of "Rebounde," which "playeth with one word written all alike but carrying diuers senses."[71] These are usually separated in illustration, and again the chosen example stresses the unrelatedness of meanings in accidentally like sounds:

> To pray for you euer I cannot refuse,
> To pray upon you I should you much abuse.

It is in fact the distance between meanings which Peacham says makes the figure effective in provoking "a most pleasant kind of ciuile mirth."[72] Elsewhere the rhetoricians classify what would later be called puns under the figure of paranomasia or agnomination, along with other types of repetitions in words or syllables with similar but not identical sounds. What these discussions in the handbooks show is that the priority of sound in virtually all considerations of language dominated some thinking about words with more than one meaning. Many of the rhetoricians seem to have conceived of them almost as a species of rhyme rather than as a source of metaphorical combinations. This is also the way they sometimes seem to be used in poetry, as in Sidney's jingling repetitions of "touch," with its multiple meanings as both noun and verb.

Logicians at the same time suggest another way of thinking about puns which they regularly use for illustrations of such categories of language as "Equiuokes," "*Homonymia*," "Fallacians."[73] Blundeville chooses to illustrate an "Equiuoke or doubtfull word" by dividing the "manifold significations" of "this word Wolfe"

> into a man hauing that name, into a foure-footed beast, into an vlcerous sore, and into a certaine fish, each one called by the name of Wolfe: which kind of distinction or diuision is very necessarie, to auoid ambiguitie of speech, which ambiguitie causeth many times great errour.[74]

This represents one type of homonym analyzed by sixteenth-century logicians. Wilson's discussion begins with a definition that could fit an instance of the same type as Blundeville's "name of Wolfe": "*Homonymia*, whiche maie be called in Englishe, the doubtfulnesse of one woorde, when it signifieth diuersely, is a maner of subtletie, when the deceipte is in a woorde that hath mo significations then one." Yet the actual example of a homonym given by Wilson is in our way of thinking a word used metaphorically rather than a word with more than one meaning like Blundeville's "name of Wolfe." Wilson gives two sentences, each containing a word "drawen from this place of doubtfulnesse": "Euery arme is a substaunce made of fleshe, bloude, bones, sinues, and veines. God the father hath an arme."[75] The first use of "arme" is what would now be called literal, the second figurative, for as Wilson says, "it signifieth by a Metaphore the power, strength, or might of God." Lever illustrates "woordes of double understandyng, whiche haue one sounde of letters . . . expressing sundrie substances" with another instance of figurative language: "The Woodcocke hath let my woodcocke flye away." The first use is a borrowed name making an insulting epithet for "an vnwittie man"; the second is the proper name for "a bird haunting the woods, and making his flyght of pleasure onely in the twylight."[76]

Although the logicians discussing puns did not take into consideration the ways some poets actually used them, the theorists did conceive of them on two grounds as belonging to the same category of language as metaphor. One way of considering the connection between homonyms and metaphors is suggested by Abraham Fraunce in *The Lawiers Logike*, where both are listed among departures from ordinary speech: "unusuall and upstart woordes . . . woordes as were quite worne out at heeles and elbowes long before the natiuitie of *Geffrey Chawcer* . . . doubtfull and ambiguous woords . . . Metaphorical woords."[77] Fraunce's position associates him with a tradition of linguistic theory descending with some variations from Aristotle, who conceived of metaphor as a form of deviation from current usage. By including homonyms and metaphors in a list with neologisms and archaisms, Fraunce links them in offense against the decorum of general use. This Aristotelian norm of ordinary speech combined with but did not contradict the later standard of proper or natural language, from which sixteenth-century logicians considered both metaphors and words with more than one meaning to be deviations.[78] In this thinking, what a homonym and a word used metaphorically have in common is that each is constituted of a single word signifying more than one thing, for which reason they are to be excluded from argument: "Therefore this ought euermore to be marked that all woordes be well noted according to their Natures, that the rather we maie escape erroure. Those are onely to be receiued and vsed for the maintenaunce of all trueth, whose name, and nature is all one. . . ."[79]

While figurative comparisons made from puns seem to contradict the standard notion of metaphorical uses as substitutions for absent terms, nevertheless this classification of words with more than one meaning and metaphors under the same category conforms to the view of linguistic history which supported most thinking about metaphor. That is, both puns and borrowed words were conceived as deviating from the archetypal model of proper usage, Adam's naming of the creatures. Wilson, in a marginal gloss on his discussion of homonyms, implies this way of thinking by making them the cause of man's fallen condition: "The mistes of woordes haue blinded all our blisse."[80]

The logicians' accusations of "subtletie," "deceipte," "doubtfulnesse" against words with more than one meaning were sometimes carried over to what the rhetoricians called "figuratiue speaches." According to Puttenham these work by "duplicitie" or "dissimulation," drawing the mind "from plainnesse and simplicitie to a certaine doublenesse, whereby our talke is the more guilefull & abusing."[81] Although this kind of vocabulary about metaphors and words with more than one meaning was familiar to poets, their propensity to use such language might seem to ignore the theoretical cautions against it. Shakespeare, above all, fully explored the possibilities of metaphorical punning. Yet in Sonnet 138 he exposes it as a form of "false speaking" in much the same vocabulary used by writers about language to warn against double meanings:[82]

When my loue sweares that she is made of truth,
I do beleeue her though I know she lyes,
That she might thinke me some vntuterd youth,
Vnlearned in the worlds false subtilties.
Thus vainely thinking that she thinkes me young,
Although she knowes my dayes are past the best,
Simply I credit her false speaking tongue,
On both sides thus is simple truth supprest:
But wherefore sayes she not she is vniust?
And wherefore say not I that I am old?
O loues best habit is in seeming trust,
And age in loue, loues not t'haue yeares told.
    Therefore I lye with her, and she with me,
    And in our faults by lyes we flattered be.

The poem is built out of the fact that the word *lie*, the proper name for "false speaking," is a pun which makes a metaphorical association of lying with words and lying with lovers. The poem dwells on the word by repeating it, surrounding it with words related in meaning and similar in sound, and with other key words also carrying more than one meaning—"vainely," "Simply"—or making a metaphorical pun—"loues best habit." The word *lie* itself, as both verb and noun, performs the linguistic act that it names by suppressing the truth about another act for which it is the proper name, "to lie with" other lovers. In one sense, then, the poem is a brilliant demonstration of its subject, "false speaking." It calls attention to its own exploitation of words which by their very nature tell lies, as if without the complicity of the "simple" speaker. Read this way, it is a bitter confirmation of the suspicions about such words expressed by Shakespeare's contemporaries writing about double meanings. They use terms in those discussions identical with many in his sonnet. In another sense the poem is a vicious example of truth-telling. For the metaphorical comparison built into the pun on *lie* names truths about these lovers, who "lie with" one another in both senses of the word. For them in both these acts "is simple truth supprest," so that the same word is equally fitting as the proper name for both. In this reading, the poem is a radically perverse confirmation of the view that words conform to the nature of the things to which they properly belong. The clash of these fundamental sixteenth-century attitudes toward language may be the most bitterly cynical implication of the poem. Their collision may signal Shakespeare's awareness of these attitudes and of their overlapping, inconsistent, sometimes even contrary assumptions about the nature and power of metaphor and its workings in poetry.

Metaphors of Identity

Another kind of metaphorical construction common in writing of this period, and one that also conforms to orderings familiar in later writing, is a pairing of nouns in an assertion of identity, a category described by William Empson in the formula "A is B." He uses a classic example from *Lycidas* for his exploration of the way this kind of metaphor works:

> 'Fame is the spur which the clear spirit doth raise . . . to scorn delights'; here 'is' introduces a complex relation, but *spur* is a straightforward metaphor, and the function of the following clause is to give the other terms of the proportion scheme (not very definitely perhaps, but *raise* makes the horse jump). However the fact that the parallel can be pursued does not prevent the main point of it from being obvious at the start; the flat way to take it is 'Fame is like a spur, because . . . ' whatever proportions come in later.[83]

Milton's "Fame is the spur" and Empson's paraphrase of it therefore conform to the sixteenth-century concept of all metaphors as the expression of perceived resemblance, since identity here is understood as comparison.

The example of "Fame is the spur" follows the order of terms to be expected in such a metaphorical statement: the formula Empson sets up as "the tenor is the vehicle."[84] This is the customary order in such a construction for reasons besides that it is traditional. For, as Empson explains, the tenor is normally first in this type of statement because it is the subject, the given which is "already known"; the vehicle is the predicate, "what is being said about" the tenor.[85] The order therefore reflects the sequence of thought as it ordinarily occurs in such a statement of identity. Another example of this type of formula, the closing couplet of Donne's "A Lecture upon the Shadow," illustrates the same pattern:

> Love is a growing, or full constant light;
> And his first minute, after noone, is night.[86]

The subject or tenor is modified by the predicate or vehicle in an implied comparison which is then elaborated.

Even in a statement where the first term is not an unembodied entity like "Love" or "Fame," it is typically less concrete in the sense that we now commonly use the term *concrete* as distinct from *abstract*. An instance is a metaphorical equation of the same order in Shakespeare's Sonnet 3:

> Thou art thy mothers glasse and she in thee
> Calls backe the louely Aprill of her prime.

Here the subject named as the tenor is a particular man, not an abstraction like "Love" or "Fame," but still it is the vehicle, his "mothers glasse," that specifies those of his attributes pertinent to the equation. That is to say, the vehicle, the figurative term, acts in a more adjectival way which we might describe as more concrete.[87]

In the sixteenth century the term *concrete* was used by logicians to distinguish qualities or accidents from substances or subjects:

> *Abstractum* is the bare shape of any subiect separated by imagination from the same, as the whitenesse or blacknesse of a wall, or any other thing that is either white or blacke, which abstract cannot be properly spoken of his subiect; for it were no proper speech, to say, that this wall is whitenesse: wherefore we must vse the adiectiue called *Concretum*, signifying the shape, together with the subiect, as when wee say, This wall is white.[88]

Drawing the analogy between ontological and grammatical orders, they explain the distinction in these linguistic terms:

> as if I should say of valiantnesse, *Peter* is said to be valiant; here valiantnesse is the Denominator, valiant the Denominatiue, and *Peter* the Denominated: for *Peter* is the subiect whereunto the Denominator doth cleaue. The Grammarians doe call the Denominator *Abstractum*, that is, a substantiue, and the Denominatiue *Concretum*, that is, an Adiectiue.[89]

In the statement "Thou art thy mothers glasse," what could now be called the vehicle, the more concrete term, sixteenth-century writers would describe as the borrowed or translated name. Yet their discussions of the functions of metaphor sometimes suggest that they thought of a word used in this way as having something more precisely like an adjectival function, and therefore of approaching what would now be meant by concreteness.

This notion is implied in the phrasing of definitions such as one quoted earlier from Hoskyns: "A *Metaphore* or Translacion is the friendly & neighborly borrowing, of one word to express a thing with more light & better note. . . ."[90] His own metaphor—"with more light"—implies what is often stated explicitly. A borrowed word is used to make a thing more visible, Tyndale says, "as it were to paynte it before thyne eyes." Peacham expands on this function in an extended version of Hoskyns' figure: "As a *Metaphore* may be compared to a starre in respect of beautie, brightnesse and direction: so may an *Allegorie* be . . . likened to a signe compounded of many stars, which of the Grecians is called *Astron*, and of the Latines *Sidus*, which we may call a constellation, that is, a company or coniunction of many starres."[91] If a borrowed term makes the thing to which it is compared brighter, more visible, then it must be somehow associated with qualities or accidents, by which substances may be seen and known. To name them "we must vse the adiectiue called *Concretum*," or a borrowed word which works in a similar way. Since various parts of speech were often interchanged, the borrowed name in some other grammatical form could share the adjectival feature of concreteness.

The examples from Milton, Donne, and Shakespeare stating that "A is B" conform to orderings familiar to later readers. For this reason they can serve as a measure of instances in sixteenth-century poetry where figurative assertions of identity work differently, in ways that violate the expectations we would now bring to them. An example is the opening line of an Arcadian poem spoken by Musidorus, one of Sidney's courtly lovers disguised as a shepherd. His make-believe occupation is the place from which his metaphors are borrowed: "My sheepe are thoughts, which I both guide and serve."[92] Everyone to whom I have quoted this line has responded to it as I do, calling it backwards. What this means is that it violates present expectations about the usual order of terms in such a metaphorical equation. For the formula they predict—*the tenor is the vehicle*—is reversed. The assertion of identity here states that *the vehicle is the tenor*. For this reason, the line feels uncomfortable in the context of present expectations, but it is by no means an isolated instance, either in this poem or in sixteenth-century verse. It will also be shown to resemble the workings of other commonly used figures of different sorts.

The formula stated in line one sets up a pattern repeated elsewhere in Sidney's poem:

> My sheepe are thoughts, which I both guide and serve:
> Their pasture is faire hilles of fruitlesse Love:
> On barren sweetes they feede, and feeding sterve:
> I waile their lotte, but will not other prove.
> My sheepehooke is wanne hope, which all upholdes:

My weedes, Desire, cut out in endlesse foldes.
What wooll my sheepe shall beare, whyle thus they live,
In you it is, you must the judgement give.

The way words are arranged in the opening line is repeated, for example, in "My sheepehooke is wanne hope." Here again the terms are
in reverse of the order we expect: *wan hope is my sheephook*. The prose
narrative gives a cause for the speaker's statements: Musidorus recites
the poem to hint what kind of shepherd he is, no shepherd in fact but
a courtly lover of high degree who in reality tends no sheep.[93] The
context therefore puts rhetorical stress on "My," to distinguish his
metaphorical "sheepe" from the kind belonging to actual shepherds.
In this sense it makes an exception of his claims in the poem. They
pertain to his peculiar situation, in contrast to the ordinary state of
shepherds whose sheep are animals that eat grass, bear wool, and get
maggots in their tails.

At the same time, in the context of sixteenth-century linguistic vocabulary Musidorus' claims may be seen as representative rather than
exceptional. What they represent, however, is the poet's language by
contrast with the shepherd's. For the narrative calls attention to the
fact that the words in the poem are not natural or proper to the
courtly speaker but are taken by him from the shepherd's world,
much as the disguised lover's "sheepehooke" is part of a borrowed
costume. To borrow words in this fashion is to be a maker of metaphors, suggesting that Musidorus is a type of the poet. He uses figuratively words that a hypothetical shepherd would speak in their natural or proper sense. The narrative explanation that he is not actually
a shepherd therefore calls attention to his performance of this quint-
essential poetic act within the "song" as pointedly as Marlowe makes
"The Passionate Shepherd to His Love" a figure of the poet by his
claim to "make . . . posies" (a common pun on the term *poesy*).[94] Musidorus's statements in his "song" are therefore, as the narrative explains, unrepresentative of the speech natural to shepherds. Yet for
the same reason, as an expression of fundamental linguistic assumptions, his statements are an embodiment of the true language of poetry, which is borrowed or translated speech. In this way of thinking
the metaphorical assertions in Sidney's song, which seem special, peculiar to readers now, are offered as representative, typical, as models
of the art of comparison. Rather than violating expectations of poetic
performance, Musidorus is fulfilling them. He is announcing his true
identity as a poet, by freely borrowing from the infinitude of places
existing in creation to make new names for "thoughts"—as Sidney

does again in the same kind of metaphor of identity in *Astrophil and Stella* 49, where "The raines . . . Are humbled thoughts"—or any other subject.

Wilson gives the theoretical justification for this exercise: "There is nothing in all the worlde, but the same may haue the name of some other worde, the which by some similitude is the like vnto it."[95] In this thinking either term in an assertion of identity may be used to name the other. The poet need only be sure that "the same be not vnlike that thing wherevnto it is applied." Such a resemblance is not obvious in Sidney's actual assertion of identity, "My sheepe are thoughts," as Empson says it is in "Fame is the spur," but must be explained in the rest of the line, "which I both guide and serve," before it can be understood and worked out by other figures borrowed from the same place.

Though equally justified by sixteenth-century notions of metaphors as new names made from borrowed or translated words, Sidney's inversions do create a different kind of figure from "Fame is the spur." For an assertion that "A is B" in the usual order would normally be understood as: *the vehicle is like the tenor, wan hope is like my sheephook*. Here, however, the second term does not describe the first by making it more concrete because it is the name of an abstract entity. It does not therefore work to specify attributes of something that is itself named by the less concrete term. As a result, instead of primarily expressing resemblance—*my sheep are like thoughts, my sheephook is like wan hope*—Sidney's equations can actually be better understood to express a somewhat different relation between terms: *my sheep stand for thoughts, my sheephook represents wan hope*, much as the "siluer anchor" on Speranza's arm in Spenser's description of her stands for or represents a hope which is not wan (1.10.14).

Metaphor and Allegory

Sixteenth-century discussions about allegory (the word derived from Greek *allos* + *agoreuein*: other + speak openly) sometimes describe the relationship between its terms in a vocabulary that might distinguish "My sheepe are thoughts" from a metaphor like "Fame is the spur." An instance is Edward Fairfax's explanation of "The Allegorie of the Poem" accompanying his translation of *Gervsalemme liberata*.[96] In it he describes the way a concrete person, place, or action in the narrative is "vnderstood for," "stands for," is in "lieu of" what is meant, an abstraction (his terms are "Imitation" for the "outward" sign, and "Allegorie" for the "inward" significance). The meaning intended by the representation is said to be "signified," "figured," "showed," "shadowed," "noted" by it. This vocabulary implies a relation between terms in allegory which may perhaps originate in some perceived resemblance, but which ultimately expresses a somewhat different kind of correspondence, like that between Sidney's "sheepe" and "thoughts," Spenser's "anchor" and hope.

The representative vocabulary in Fairfax's description of the relation between allegorical terms is close to the wording English writers in the sixteenth century use to describe the relation between sign and significance in the sacraments. The standard definition of allegory, "when we shew one thing in wordes and signifie another in meaning," sounds very like typical sentences about the extraordinary signifying power of the sacraments: "There is in them seene one thyng, and understanded an other thyng. That whiche is seene hath a bodely kinde and shape, that which is understanded, hath a spirituall frute."[97] Yet although writers like Fairfax sometimes describe allegory in these slightly different terms from their typical vocabulary about metaphor, there is no evidence that he or other writers of the time theorized much about this distinction. Puttenham, for example, begins with a definition of allegory that ignores the "affinitie or conuenience" which he finds in metaphor between the "right signification" of a word and its figurative use. In defining allegory he emphasizes instead the distance between them "when we speake one thing and thinke another, and that our wordes and our meanings meete not." Yet at the same time he defines allegory in wholly representative wording as "a long and perpetuall Metaphore."[98] A similar indifference to distinctions is everywhere in sixteenth-century commentaries on actual figures, such as the metaphorical comparisons in these lines from "Febrvarie" of *The Shepheardes Calender:*

> For Youngth is a bubble blown vp with breath,
> Whose witt is weakenesse, whose wage is death,
> Whose way is wildernesse.[99]

The gloss describes them as "A verye moral and pitthy Allegorie of youth, and the lustes thereof, compared to a wearie wayfaring man." Here the verb for the relation between terms in an "Allegorie" is that they are "compared," while elsewhere the absent term in a metaphor is said to be "signified" by the borrowed name, as in Peacham's statement that by "stonie hart" is "signified" cruelty. Nowhere are these sets of terms systematically distinguished to identify different modes of language, so that when sixteenth-century writers like Puttenham discuss figurative language, they make no theoretical distinction between allegory and metaphor: "But properly & in his principall vertue *Allegoria* is when we do speake in sence translatiue and wrested from the owne signification, neuertheless applied to another not altogether contrary . . . and this manner of inuersion extending to whole and large speaches, it maketh the figure *allegorie* to be called a long and perpetuall Metaphore."[100]

Discussions of these figures usually follow tradition by treating metaphor first because of the elevated status granted it since Aristotle, and because most writers agreed with Fraunce that "That there is no trope more florishing than a *Metaphore.*"[101] The fact that it provided many of the terms to define allegory suggests that it was generally understood to be the more inclusive figure, as well as the more common and illustrious. Yet at the same time the fact that the names for the two tropes were often used interchangeably has slightly different implications. For it shows that allegory was not thought to be a particularly specialized mode of language. Puttenham names it "the chief ringleader and captaine of all other figures," and illustrates it with examples that might then by some other writers be categorized as metaphors: "As for example if we should call the common wealth, a shippe; the Prince a Pilot, the Counsellours mariners, the stormes warres, the calme and [*hauen*] peace, this is spoken all in allegorie. . . ."[102] Other discussions of it show by their chosen examples different reasons why allegory was not set apart as a clearly distinct and more specialized use of language. It was identified not only with metaphor but, by virtue of its extension, also with "prouerbe, similitude, redell," favored in all kinds of speech as well as poetry. Day's discussion both claims and illustrates everyday familiarity:

> *Allegoria*, a kinde of inuerting or change of sence, as when we shew one thing in wordes and signifie another in meaning, a Trope most usuall amongst us euen in our common speaking, as when we saie. *Bow the With while it is greene*, meaning to correct children whilest they bee yong: or *There is no fire without smoake:* meaning that there is no ill conceipt without occasion: or, *I smell a Rat*, that is, I know your meaning. . . .[103]

Since these extended uses of figurative language were all thought to express some likeness among the things from which names were taken, in theory they all reflected the same ontological pattern of resemblance. This in turn was the common understanding of all borrowed or translated words discussed by writers about metaphor and boasted of by poets as their distinguishing art of *compare*.

Another explanation for these interchangeable vocabularies is that not only traditional emblems like Spenser's "anchor," but ultimately all nouns, adjectives, and verbs could be thought of as names for things having meaning in themselves, which therefore pointed beyond themselves to other things and meanings. In that way they would be held to work like sacramental signs as they are typically described in sixteenth-century writing. At the same time, the fact that the acts of making both metaphor and allegory were defined as borrowing or translating can suggest another reason why these modes were not theoretically distinguished except by length. Any translated or borrowed name, in prevailing sixteenth-century theory, acts according to Fairfax's description of allegorical representation: it can be "vnderstood for," it "stands for," or is "in lieu of" the proper name. Conceived this way, the figurative term in a metaphor could be thought to represent, signify, or denote its subject, like a sacrament, or an emblem in an allegory. For this reason, the various kinds of sixteenth-century metaphors discussed in this chapter might have been thought to conform to the same theoretical model.

Along with "My sheepe are thoughts" and other instances of this kind of metaphor of identity in Sidney's song are figures belonging to different types of metaphor previously discussed. An instance is the pairing of adjective and noun in the phrase "wanne hope." Like *stony heart*, this is a familiar epithet; it is a conventional description of the lover's plight, as is Gascoigne's metaphor, "waues of wanhope." Because the pairing is so familiar and in Sidney's song so undeveloped, it works in fact more like a simple translation than like a personification of hope as a man "pale and wan" (another pairing commonly used to describe the languishing lover) with despondency.[104] Sidney's figure "faire hilles of fruitlesse Love" follows the same genitive construction as metaphors already discussed by Watson, Ralegh, and Gascoigne (binding the adjective-noun pairs together by alliterating their matched parts but adding the slight complication of the pun "fruitlesse"). Shifts in the relation between terms such as these in Sidney's song—*the vehicle is like the tenor, the vehicle stands for the tenor*—were common in figurative language of this period. They were probably encouraged by the same assumptions embedded in the interchangeable vocabularies used to describe the workings of allegory and metaphor, as well as in other definitions of figurative language.

The possibility of such shifts or interchanges in figurative language seems to be the chief interest of *Astrophil and Stella* 9, which opens with a line set up so that either term can be understood as tenor or vehicle: "Queene *Vertue's* court, which some call *Stella's* face."[105] Of course the subject is the lady being praised, but the poem makes a kind of game out of questioning which reading of the line makes it more complimentary to her: *some makers of comparison liken Queen Virtue's court to Stella's face; some liken Stella's face to Queen Virtue's court.* The poem keeps the riddle going by making the terms have sometimes equal and sometimes alternating prominence:

> Queene *Vertue's* court, which some call *Stella's* face,
>> Prepar'd by Nature's chiefest furniture,
>> Hath his front built of Alabaster pure;
> Gold is the covering of that stately place.
> The doore by which sometimes comes forth her Grace,
>> Red Porphir is, which locke of pearle makes sure:
>> Whose porches rich (which name of cheekes endure)
> Marble mixt red and white do enterlace.
> The windowes now through which this heav'nly guest
> Looks over the world, and can find nothing such,
> Which dare claime from those lights the name of best,
>> Of touch they are that without touch doth touch,
>> Which *Cupid's* selfe from Beauties's myne did draw:
>> Of touch they are, and poore I am their straw.

Explicit references—"which name of cheekes endure," "Which dare claime . . . the name of best"—draw attention to the fact that one term of comparison or "name" can stand for the other, as is also assumed about "sheepe" and "thoughts" in Sidney's song or what in sixteenth-century vocabulary about allegory would typically be called the *outward* sign and the *inward* significance. It is partially in such interchange that catalogues of praise like Sidney's find their grounds of compliment. The treasures of creation—alabaster, gold, porphyry, pearls—are enriched by comparisons with the lady's parts, as her forehead, hair, lips, teeth are in turn adorned by these associations.

Another kind of blurring of figurative modes was especially sanctioned by common use in religious texts translating mixed phrases from the Bible or imitating their construction. An instance is in the lesson translated from the Epistle to the Romans, read in English churches on the first Sunday of Advent: "Let vs walke honestly, as it were in the day lyght: not in eating and drinking, neither in chambering and wantonnesse, neither in strife and enuying: But put ye on the

Lorde Iesus Christ. . . ."[106] What we understand as the opening metaphor compares the way a true Christian should live to a man who
walks in the open, where he may be seen, with nothing to hide. This
metaphor includes two borrowed terms—"walke" from *live*, "day
lyght" from *open*—to make up a sentence intelligible in a literal sense,
like "*There is no fire without smoake*," but understood as a whole to be
metaphorical in this context. The borrowed word "walke" then carries over grammatically as the verb in the next three clauses, but it
can no longer work in the same way as it does in the opening metaphor. Here instead the borrowed verb "walke" stands for the proper
or natural word for which it is a translation, while the noun with
which it is paired is not borrowed but proper, so that the whole clause
cannot make literal sense, nor can it be taken as wholly figurative. A
man cannot be said to walk in wantonness as he can be described as
walking in daylight. As we understand the later clause, what we have
done is to retranslate the borrowed verb, replacing it with the absent
word as is explicitly done for us elsewhere in the prayer book in
phrasing from the Epistle to the Hebrews: "the new and liuing way,
which he hath prepared for vs through the vaile (that is to say) by his
flesh."[107] Here the explicit retranslation of the borrowed word "vaile"
into the proper word "flesh" is a demonstration of what is done by the
reader to understand Saint Paul's lesson about Christian living. The
sentence in the Epistle shifts midway from metaphor to mixed phrasing which demands a different mode of reading. Sixteenth-century
translations made such biblical passages familiar in English and available as models; writers could take for granted their accessibility to
readers. By contrast, the translators of the Revised Standard Version
of the Bible appear to have thought that the mixed phrasing of Saint
Paul's lesson on the duties required of a Christian would cause difficulties for their readers. To avoid such problems they chose to substitute a nonfigurative verb—"conduct"—for the metaphorical use of
"walke" (in both the prayer book and the Geneva Bible): "let us conduct ourselves becomingly as in the day, not in reveling," making the
whole sentence what would now be called literal.[108]

Connections between such mixed phrasing and theoretical notions
of metaphor are suggested by Wilson's treatment in *The Arte of Rhetorique* of the last-quoted clause of the lesson: "put ye on the Lorde Iesus
Christ."[109] Instead of reading the verb metaphorically in the same way
as we understand the comparison of Christian living to walking in the
daylight, he turns the borrowed verb back into some proper or natural
phrasing for which it was thought to be a substitute (as "vaile" is for

"flesh"): "Put vpon you the Lord Jesus Christ, that is to say, be in liuing such a one as he was." The only hypothetical alternative according to his thinking about metaphor would be to translate the name of Jesus into some term for which it is a substitute, such as "the armour of light" which Saint Paul urges Christians to "put on" in the preceding sentence of the Epistle. To do this would be to take the Lord's name as the borrowed name for a prior reality, perhaps a substitution Wilson wished to avoid. His interpretation of the imperative can therefore be understood in the light of thinking about metaphor in this period: the verb is taken as a translated term substituting for a name or thing outside the actual words of the passage. The same process is demanded by similar phrases everywhere in religious writing: "put on loue," "walke in loue," "such good woorkes as thou hast prepared for vs to walke in," "walke" in his "Commaundementes," "bow the knees of your hearts," "knees of my heart will fold."[110]

Spenser's "Way" in *The Faerie Queene*

Because the language of the Bible was the most authoritative model, it justified the use in sixteenth-century poetry of figurative phrasing apparently copied after such sacred examples. These phrases occur often in *The Faerie Queene*, for example: "her tongue did walke/ In foule reproch" (2.4.5); "pourd out his idle mind/ In daintie delices, and lauish loyes" (2.5.28). They represent in little the relations between modes of figurative language in the larger patterns of Spenser's poem, where any number of details can illustrate the way similar wording occurs in allegorical narrative and in metaphorical comparisons. For example, the story of Book 2 can almost be summarized by these lines from its opening canto:

> Then *Guyon* forward gan his voyage make,
> With his blacke Palmer, that him guided still.
> Still he him guided ouer dale and hill.
>
> (2.1.34)

Here the character in the narrative who "guided" the hero on his journey through the landscape of fairyland is (in Fairfax's terms for allegorical representation) "vnderstood for," "stands for," is "in lieu of" that inward force which directs Guyon's moral conduct. Using a different kind of figurative language, Spenser epitomizes the more perilous story of the Red Crosse Knight in these lines:

> The true *Saint George* was wandred far away,

Still flying from his thoughts and gealous feare;
Will was his guide, and griefe led him astray.

(1.2.12)

Here the metaphorical assertions in the final line follow what Empson
describes as the usual pattern of "A is B": *the hero's will was like a guide.*
That is, his inner quality was like Archimago or some other wicked
character met in the course of his adventures along the way, a false
"guide" who, like "griefe" here, "led him astray" into dangerous
places. In the first instance the character of the Palmer is the concrete
term, the vehicle, representing Guyon's inward virtue, an abstract
entity which is the tenor: *the vehicle stands for the tenor.* In the second
passage the tenor is the hero's "Will," compared to a tempter who is
the vehicle: *the tenor is like the vehicle.* In Spenser's poem and in writing
of his contemporaries these modes could be interchangeable.

Where such guides lead in *The Faerie Queene* is along or away from
what in its first occurrence is simply called "the way" (1.1.10), later
"the wearie way" (1.10.36; 5.2.29) or "the wearie wandring way"
(1.9.39). Like so many uses of language in Spenser's poem and other
sixteenth-century writing, "the way" is charged with powerful suggestions by associations with its innumerable appearances in the
Bible, often in particular passages evoked by other supporting details
in Spenser's language. It is a specially rich term also because in these
biblical sources it combines meanings which sixteenth-century definitions of allegory would call *outward*—path, road, direction—and
inward—moral tendency or progress. The word itself therefore offers
possibilities for interchange between allegory and metaphor, also accomplished by the uses of "guide" as either tenor or vehicle. Spenser
builds on these possibilities for "the way" by surrounding it with
other devices previously shown to be allowed by features of sixteenth-
century English.

In the allegorical narrative, characters along "the way" are repeatedly said to "travell" or "traveill," another biblical term favored by
poets of this period for its simultaneously present *outward* and *inward*
meanings. These are made possible by unfixed spelling, which also
allowed double meanings to the noun forms—now distinguished as
travel and *travail*—making the journeying character "The wearie
Traueiler, wandring that way" (2.5.30). These metaphorical puns
sometimes describe the actual movements of characters in the allegorical narrative, elsewhere the metaphorical journey of the human soul
"Who trauels by the wearie wandring way" (1.9.39).

Quotations have already shown another device for charging Spenser's "way" with various kinds of figurative possibilities. The noun, with its own geographical and spiritual meanings, is surrounded by varied groupings consisting not only in "travell" as both verb and noun, but also "wearie," "wander," and "wandring." Sometimes it is a character who is described as "A wearie wight forwandring by the way" (1.6.34), "this faire virgin wearie of her way" (1.12.1). Elsewhere it is the path, road, direction itself which is described as "the wearie way" (1.10.36; 5.2.29; 6.7.39). In sixteenth-century rhetoric this kind of transferred epithet—"wearie way" was a common one used, for instance, by Gascoigne and Breton—would not be categorized as a metaphor personifying the noun as a traveller worn by the journey.[111] It would be taken as a kind of metonymy naming the noun substantive "way" as the cause of the accident described by the adjective: "wearinesse . . . of the way" (4.7.3) is the familiar state caused in Spenser's characters by the travail of their travelling, and expressed in repeated epithets.

The repetition of verbal formulations is itself a device associated with special powers (to be discussed in the following chapter). In the instance of the repeated cluster of words with multiple figurative possibilities surrounding "the way," the almost mesmerizing effect is to bind *outward* and *inward* meanings, to weave allegory and metaphor into a kind of seamless web, much as particular words are blended together by alliteration in "the wearie wandring way." Since both "way" and "traueiller" are "wearie" and "wandring," distinctions between the landscape of fairyland and the inner state of the characters tend to dissolve in Spenser's narrative in ways analogous to the blurring of distinctions between allegory and metaphor shown to be characteristic of much theoretical writing about these modes in Spenser's time.

4 Charms, Prayers, Rituals

Magical and Miraculous Language

In Book 1 of *The Faerie Queene* are two matched and contrasting episodes which involve reading in the sense of interpreting a book. The first takes place when Una and the Red Crosse Knight follow an "aged Sire" to his "little lowly Hermitage" beside a "holy Chapell," where they pass the evening with "faire discourse," entertainment said to be enjoyed by minds content with the humble, contemplative life (1.1.29–35). The characters and at first also the narrator are taken in by these appearances of piety:

> For that old man of pleasing wordes had store,
> And well could file his tongue as smooth as glas;
> He told of Saintes and Popes, and euermore
> He strowd an *Aue-Mary* after and before.
>
> (1.1.35)

Even without prior knowledge of Spenser's Protestant affiliations, the reader is now warned of what should have been recognizable earlier when the hermit first identified himself as a "Silly old man, that liues in hidden cell/ Bidding his beades all day" (1.1.30).[1] His piety is as false as his artful language, by which his visitors have been deceived. While they sleep unawares, the identity of their host is revealed to us in his secret acts, which truly predict his name—Archimago:

> He to his study goes, and there amiddes
> His Magick bookes and artes of sundry kindes,
> He seekes out mighty charmes, to trouble sleepy mindes.
>
> (1.1.36)

Here reading unleashes language with dangerous powers:

> Then choosing out few wordes most horrible,
> (Let none them read) thereof did verses frame,
> With which and other spelles like terrible,
> He bad awake blacke *Plutoes* griesly Dame,
> And cursed heauen, and spake reprochfull shame

Of highest God, the Lord of life and light;
A bold bad man, that dar'd to call by name
Great *Gorgon*, Prince of darknesse and dead night,
At which *Cocytus* quakes, and *Styx* is put to flight.

(1.1.37)

Spenser makes a close connection in the hermit's language between "Magick bookes," "wordes," "verses," "spelles," names, and Catholic prayers "strowd . . . after and before." This association was common in Protestant polemics of the period, when the word *spells* first became a common synonym for occult charms. This use was perhaps a response in some way associated with the recent invention of printing, sometimes described as a "mysticall Science."[2] The currency of the word was also a measure of intensified interest in occult studies, to be discussed. At the same time the word *charm*—from *carmen*—was used as in Latin for song, verse, incantation, oracular response. It was also the name for objects and signs worn to ward off evil or to bring good. Like other practices, the wearing of charms was interpreted as having suspect magical power or truly miraculous efficacy, judgments depending on the context and reflecting the sympathies of the writer. For instance, the "signe of the crosse" as protection "from euils present, past, and to come, inward and outward" was dismissed by English reformers as a "papisticall charme," yet Spenser's Protestant Saint George wears a cross on his breast which is blasphemously scorned—or superstitiously read—as a "charme" by Sansfoy (1.2.18).[3]

In *The discouerie of witchcraft* of 1584 Reginald Scot sets out to prove that "all popish charmes, coniurations, exorcismes, benedictions and curses" are indistinguishable from the "charmes" of witches and other practitioners of black magic. To make his point Scot likens examples of various occult rituals to "papisticall charmes," allowing the only difference between them that Catholics practice them "without shame openlie," while magicians work "hugger mugger secretlie," like Archimago. One representative example taken according to Scot from a sixteenth-century primer promises: "To all them that afore this image of pitie deuoutlie shall saie fiue *Pater nosters*, fiue *Aues*, and one *Credo*, piteouslie beholding these armes of Christs passion, are granted thirtie two thousand seuen hundred fiftie fiue yeares of pardon."[4] Even more than such numerical repetitions of prayers, the canon of the Mass was the object of Protestant attacks on its claims for the supernatural power of language. Christ's blessing of the bread and wine is said to be superstitiously turned into a magic ritual of consecration, "with a

coniuring of murmuring and force of words." The priest is called a
"sorcerer" whose language, marked with as many "crosses as a con-
iurers circle," claims magical power to transubstantiate the elements
into the body and blood of Christ.[5] Spenser's hermit is such a magician-priest, whose words are at once false and dangerous. The narrator both disbelieves them and fears them. He cautions his readers not
to be deceived by them and yet warns "Let none them read," as if
even the knowledge of their falsity could not protect us from their
"mighty" power.

When Una brings the Red Crosse Knight to the House of Holinesse, we are invited to view the episode as a parallel and contrast to
their stay in the house of the aged hermit.[6] This retreat is presided
over by Celia, a "matron graue and hoar," whose devotions are a Protestant reformation of the hermit's:

> All night she spent in bidding of her bedes,
> And all the day in doing good and godly deedes.
>
> (1.10.3)

There Una asks a daughter of the house, Fidelia, to instruct the Red
Crosse Knight in her "heauenly learning" and "words diuine":

> And that her sacred Booke, with bloud ywrit,
> That none could read, except she them did teach,
> She vnto him disclosed euery whit,
> And heauenly documents thereout did preach,
> That weaker wit of man could neuer reach,
> Of God, of grace, of iustice, of free will,
> That wonder was to heare her goodly speach:
> For she was able, with her words to kill,
> And raise againe to life the hart, that she did thrill.
>
> (1.10.19)

Like Archimago's books, which he pores over in secrecy, Fidelia's "sacred Booke" contains mysteries hidden from Una and the knight. Like
the magician's secrets, they endow her with supernaturally powerful
"speach":

> And when she list poure out her larger spright,
> She would commaund the hastie Sunne to stay,
> Or backward turne his course from heauens hight;
> Sometimes great hostes of men she could dismay;
> Dry-shod to passe, she parts the flouds in tway;
> And eke huge mountaines from their natiue seat
> She would commaund, themselues to bear away,

> And throw in raging sea with roaring threat.
> Almightie God her gaue such powre, and puissance great.
>
> (1.10.20)

By contrasting the supernatural power of Fidelia's commands with Archimago's, Spenser makes a familiar Protestant distinction between scriptural demonstrations of miraculous language—sometimes called "Art Magicke"—like those attributed to Fidelia, and the "magical mumbling" of the priest in the rite of consecration, or the mechanical repetition of prayers such as Archimago's sprinkled *Ave Marias* or Corceca's mutterings.[7] For Corceca is another parallel figure encountered by Una whose superstitious devotions contrast with Celia's Protestant worship:

> Where that old woman day and night did pray
> Vpon her beades deuoutly penitent;
> Nine hundred *Pater nosters* euery day,
> And thrise nine hundred *Aues* she was wont to say.
>
> (1.3.13)

This distinction embodied in Spenser's pattern of contrasts is argued in representative terms by Scot: "For where words haue had miraculous operation, there hath beene alwaies the speciall prouidence, power and grace of God vttered to the strengthening of the faith of Gods people, and to the furtherance of the gospell: as when the apostle with a word slue *Ananias* and *Saphira*."[8] The emphasis in Scot's argument is on the "speciall" infusion of supernatural efficacy, which circumscribes its miraculous force. Yet the granting of such efficacy means that the argument between Protestants and Catholics was not so much about the capacity of words to cause supernatural effects as it was about the origin and occasion of their empowerment. What this means in turn is that, within circumscribed limits encouraging caution in belief, Protestant writers in the sixteenth century did share with those they attacked the fundamental assumption that words can work in mysterious ways to perform wonders. This mode of thinking made their distinction between miraculous and magical language clearer on theological grounds than it sometimes was in actual use in their verbal rituals. These often seem versions of each other, as Spenser's carefully paralleled episodes point out.

The association between words and supernatural power is built into the very word for the alphabet in sixteenth-century English, *crossrow*, which largely replaced the Middle English name, *abc*. The earliest use of *crossrow* cited by the *O.E.D.* is 1529; it was apparently a variant of a term in earlier use, *christcross* or *crisscross*. Both derived from a practice that seems to have become common in the fifteenth century: teaching the letters by means of hornbooks, rather than as earlier by a large cloth stretched on the wall. In these and other primary reading books, the letters were always preceded by the sign of the cross (sometimes even the book itself was in that shape).[9] The signs alone and also the whole sequence including the cross and the letters following were both called *christcross* and later more often *crossrow*—sometimes "Christes cross rowe" even in the last quarter of the sixteenth century. The usage shows how closely the two different kinds of sign were conceived to be bound together.[10]

Still another name for the cross at the head of the alphabet is given in a late-fourteenth-century English translation of *Bartholomaeus de Proprietatibus Rerum*:

> Crosse was made all of red
> In the begynning of my boke,
> That is callyd god me sped
> In the fyrste lesson that j toke
> Thenne j lerned, a, and b,
> And other letters by her names
> But always God spede me.[11]

The cross on hornbooks was "callyd god me sped" probably because that prayer was said by the pupil reciting the letters to sanctify the performance (or to ensure that he would get safely through it). It seems likely that the mark also directed the speaker to cross himself for further divine remembrance and protection as he said the formula. This practice would probably have been discouraged if not discontinued in schools when the printed mark corresponding to the signing of the cross by the celebrant was suppressed except in the baptismal service in *The Boke of Common Prayer* of 1552 (which also condemned the belief that the sound of consecrated bells, often inscribed with the crossrow, had power to drive away devils).[12] The suppression was vital to the Protestant purge of what reformers called popish charms. It was an attack at large on prayers which encouraged belief in the mechanical efficacy of repeated formulas and crossings such as one quoted by Scot, beginning:

> Omnipotens ✠ Dominus ✠ Christus ✠ Messias ✠ with 34.
> names more, and as many crosses. . . .[13]

More particularly the reform was directed against what polemicists like Scot called the conjuring of priests in the Mass. It therefore de-

manded the removal in 1552 of the crosses in the words of consecration as they had been printed in *The Booke of Common Prayer* of 1549:

> and with thy holy spirite and worde, vouchsafe to bl✠esse and
> sanc✠tifie these thy gyftes, and creatures of bread and
> wyne. . . .[14]

Yet the mark of the cross, typically printed this way as it had been
here and in other passages of the first Edwardian prayer book, continued to be set at the head of the crossrow in hornbooks and other
lessons. In addition, even after the removal of the crosses from the
printed rite of communion, the act of making the sign of the cross
during the service, along with kneeling and other physical gestures of
devotion, was left to the discretion of the individual Christian.[15] The
persistence of these practices, as well as verbal rituals to be discussed,
suggests that reformation of doctrine and liturgy may not at least for
some time have much altered the profoundly held assumptions closely
associating language with supernatural power expressed in ritual.

This likelihood is confirmed by memories of religious practices in
the Elizabethan church recorded by Augustine Baker, a Benedictine
monk born in 1575, in his autobiographical treatise. In his account the
"change" to Anglicanism was for many churchgoers scarcely noticeable:

> And indeed at the first, and for some years after the said
> change made by Queen Elizabeth, the greatest part even of
> those who in their judgments and affections had before bin
> Catholickes, did not well discern any great fault, novelty, or
> difference from the former religion, that was Catholick, in this
> new sett up by Queen Elizabeth; save only change of language,
> as bringing in service in the English tongue, in lieu of that
> which had bin in the Latin; in the which difference they con-
> ceived nothing of substance or essence to be. And so eas-
> ily digested the new religion and accomodated themselves
> thereto. . . .[16]

Despite Protestant rejection of magical verbal formulas, what the evidence of hornbooks and other reading lessons will show is that not
only the sacred and (to the unlearned) mysterious language of the
Latin Mass, but also the vernacular was thought to be charged with
power even in its most elemental features. This conception may have
contributed to its acceptance in place of Latin in the ritual of the
English church. The mark before the letters of the crossrow in read-

ing lessons may also have been intended to recall biblical passages encouraging reverence for learning, such as "The beginning of wisdome is the feare of the Lord" (Psalm 111:10). Since the sequence of letters began with the sign of the cross and ended with *Est. Amen* (perhaps a remnant of the formula closing the Latin Mass, *Ite missa est. Amen*), the lesson of the crossrow may especially have brought to mind the words of John: "I am α and ω, the beginning and the ending, saieth the Lord, Which is, and Which was, and Which is to come, euen the Almightie" (Revelation 1:8).[17] Still another religious lesson in the lettering and recitation of alphabets is recorded by a seventeenth-century collector of commonplaces looking back at this "old time": "They vsed three prickes at the latter end of the crosse row, and at the end of their bookes, which they caused children to call tittle, tittle, tittle; signifying, that as there were three pricks, and those three made but one stop, euen so there were three persons, and yet but one God."[18] Such close association of the crossrow with religious practices was further strengthened by the fact that on hornbooks the alphabet was always followed by the Lord's Prayer, while in the A.B.C. books and in the primers, the second and third linguistic tools used in schools, the crossrow was printed as if it were the first in a sequence of sacred lessons, which constituted its contents. A primer of 1538 makes precisely that identification in a colophon: "Thus endeth the .A B C translated out of Laten to to [*sic.*] Englysshe with other deuoute Prayers."[19] Immediately after the alphabet and several sequences of vowels and syllables are printed various prayers in both English and Latin. The identification of these schoolbooks with formal prayer is even fixed in the name still used for the place in London where they were printed, Pater Noster Row.

Their importance for religious teaching is most clearly shown by the fact that, along with the prayer book, the homilies, and Lily's Latin grammar (which preceded its lessons with a prayer), they were authorized in standard editions and dictated for use by the Crown. In 1545 King Henry issued not only a prescribed primer but an A.B.C.: "The A. B. C set forthe by the Kynges maiestie and his Clergye, and commaunded to be taught through out all his Realme. All other vtterly set apart as the teachers thereof tender his graces fauour."[20] It contained the crossrow—the mark of the cross and the letters following it—in three different types, the Lord's Prayer, the Hail Mary, the Creed, the Ten Commandments, graces, psalms, and various other devotional formulas. Lines by Skelton cited in the *O.E.D.* as the earliest use of the term *crossrow* suggest that this order reflected an established practice of reciting the alphabet as if it were the first in a sequence of prayers:

> In your crosse rowe nor Christ crosse you spede,
> Your Pater Noster, your Ave, nor your Crede.[21]

The ultimate sanction for this view of the alphabet was found in Scripture in the example of God's "holy & blessed worde in the same order" of alphabetical arrangements in psalms, the Lamentations of Jeremiah, and the Proverbs.[22] Persistent use of the term *crossrow*, along with these conventions of recitation and printing throughout the sixteenth century, show continuity in the association of letters with supernatural power expressed in religious practices.

This habit of mind was for some Englishmen encouraged in complicated forms by revived or newly imported occult studies which are known to have interested Sidney, Spenser, Harvey, Marlowe, Harington, Nashe, Bacon, and Shakepeare, among other writers.[23] The various strands of Neoplatonism, Hermeticism, Cabalism that attracted serious attention among scholars and writers in the sixteenth century systematized belief in the supernatural power of letters—especially the Hebrew alphabet—as well as numbers and hieroglyphs. Rituals were developed using them in incantations and other formulas, many of them taken from the spurious fourth book of Agrippa's *De occulta philosophia*, which was widely known in England in the sixteenth century.[24] Scot gives examples to prove how closely parallel were the "Alphabeterie or Arythmaticall diuinitie" of Cabalists and other esoteric cultists to Catholic devotions, illustrating these by describing a ritual of marking church floors with a cross between the Latin and Greek alphabets to drive away the devil.[25] Ceremonies similar to some performed by respected students of the occult were also enacted by practitioners of more suspect types of magic. Shakespeare portrays such a figure in the fortune-teller who uses the power of letters to predict the future of the king in *The Tragedy of Richard the Third*:

> He hearkens after Prophecies and Dreames,
> And from the Crosse-row pluckes the letter G:
> And sayes, a Wizard told him, that by G,
> His issue disinherited should be.[26]

Yet not only magicians, occultists, and Catholics shared this kind of association of letters with supernatural powers. Protestants also applied it for their own uses. Henry Smith in *Gods Arrow Against Atheists* makes the standard identification of the Pope with Antichrist by the familiar device of opening an alphabetical mystery in Revelation, where the Hebrew word for *"Romanus, a man of Rome . . .* doth in those Hebrew letters containe the iust number of 666, which is the number of the name of that Antichristian beast."[27] With respect to belief in the supernatural power of letters, occult studies mainly elaborated and overlaid with systems what were presuppositions underlying attitudes toward language held by many writers and readers with less special interests. Their shared beliefs were that "God made the world by worde, and the worde is to the world sentence"; that "God was the first Author of letters"; that God's language was Hebrew, "whose Elements/ Flow with hid sence . . . points with Sacraments"; that God gave this "sacred Dialect" to Adam, who used it to confer right names on the creatures.[28]

Adam's speech therefore represented the ideal of language because it was closest to the divine Word which commanded the creation, and because God gave it to him "in signe of maistrie" over the creatures.[29] By conferring names Adam left his mark on them, "for howsoeuer the man named the liuing creature, so was the name thereof" (Genesis 2:19). This biblical episode as it was usually interpreted sanctioned belief in the power of words over nature. By extension it could then be used to make Adam's right naming available as an analogy for the poet's divine force of language.

The "Diuine Breath" of Poetry

Sidney builds on the analogy between Adam and the poet or "maker" in *An Apologie for Poetrie*, a work held in special respect for his authorship, which in turn therefore could add authority to the interpretation:

> Neyther let it be deemed too sawcie a comparison to ballance the highest poynt of mans wit with the efficacie of Nature: but rather giue right honor to the heauenly Maker of that maker, who, hauing made man to his owne likenes, set him beyond and ouer all the workes of that second nature, which in nothing hee sheweth so much as in Poetrie, when with the force of a diuine breath he bringeth things forth far surpassing her dooings, with no small argument to the incredulous of that first accursed fall of *Adam:* sith our erected wit maketh vs to know what perfection is, and yet our infected will keepeth vs from reaching vnto it.[30]

Sidney's claim here for the poet to exert force analogous to Adam's "ouer all the workes" of nature through the "diuine breath" of his language could seem "sawcie" to the point of blasphemy. For the view of poetry implied here is more compatible with pagan notions of poetic inspiration than with a Christian understanding of creation—which Sidney elsewhere expresses without acknowledging inconsistency or contradiction—and in this passage shows its derivation from ancient definitions of the poet as "maker." Yet habits of assimilation in sixteenth-century ways of thinking made it possible to accommodate such a view of poetic language within a biblical framework, by making Adamic naming its archetype.

Also legitimizing this argument is its compatibility with the distinction claimed by Protestants as theirs exclusively, which Sidney assumes, between divinely empowered language and the false claims of magic arts: "The Poet neuer maketh any circles about your imagination, to coniure you to beleeue for true what he writes."[31] In his discussion of ancient notions about poetry as the utterance of a "Diuiner, Fore-seer, or Prophet," he first attempts to distinguish it from the "very vaine and godles superstition . . . that spirits were commaunded by such verses—whereupon this word charmes, deriued of *Carmina,* commeth—so yet serueth it to shew the great reuerence those wits were helde in." Although elsewhere Adam's example is used to differentiate the view of poetry as a gift of divinely empowered language from superstitious notions of magical spells, here the distinction becomes somewhat blurred. For as the passage continues, occult charms are likened in form to verses "proper to the Poet": "And altogether not without ground, since both the Oracles of *Delphos* and *Sibillas* prophecies were wholy deliuered in verses. For that same exquisite obseruing of number and measure in words, and that high flying liberty of conceit proper to the Poet, did seeme to haue some dyuine force in it."[32] This passage shows that currents of thought encouraging accommodation of pagan and biblical attitudes reinforced fundamental assumptions about language associating it with supernatural power. Throughout *An Apologie for Poetrie* Sidney calls the art "a diuine gift" of "hart-rauishing knowledge" containing "many mysteries" and accompanied by the "well inchaunting skill of Musicke."[33] Sixteenth-century poetry itself, both explicitly in its claims and implicitly in many of its forms, shows the continued strength of these assumptions.

Shakespeare's Sonnet 18 claims the force of divine breath for the language of the poem in terms close to Sidney's. Their assertions of power are predicated on the same assumptions:

Shall I compare thee to a Summers day?
Thou art more louely and more temperate:
Rough windes do shake the darling buds of Maie,
And Sommers lease hath all too short a date:
Sometime too hot the eye of heauen shines,
And often is his gold complexion dimm'd,
And euery faire from faire some-time declines,
By chance, or natures changing course vntrim'd:
But thy eternall Sommer shall not fade,
Nor loose possession of that faire thou ow'st,
Nor shall death brag thou wandr'st in his shade,
When in eternall lines to time thou grow'st,
   So long as men can breath or eyes can see,
   So long liues this, and this giues life to thee.

As the opening line points forward to the comparison which constitutes the poem, the final boast—that "this" lives and gives life—brings to the foreground the completed poem as a figure in its own design. It becomes as much an actor as the poet himself, as much a part of his subject as the person the poem promises to immortalize. By such means Shakespeare not only asserts the miraculous power of his language but calls attention to its particular workings. That is, he not only says what he has achieved in this sonnet but points to how he has brought about his triumph. He has made a new nature, where the beloved will flourish to the end of time, and this has come to pass in the poem because words have demonstrated their power over things. By the poet's art of comparison they have transformed mortal life into an "eternall Sommer," and the friend into a plant made to grow in "eternall lines."

The process it demonstrates makes the sonnet's claims to power over nature parallel to another description of the poet's art in *An Apologie for Poetrie:* "Nature neuer set forth the earth in so rich tapistry as diuers Poets haue done, neither with plesant riuers, fruitful trees, sweet smelling flowers, nor whatsoeuer els may make the too much loued earth more louely. Her world is brasen, the Poets only deliuer a golden."[34] Again a parallel between the poet and Adam is suggested, since the mythological golden age restored by the poet's language is a commonplace analogy for the unfallen world. If the passage also implies a comparison of the poet to the alchemist, whose art transmutes baser metals into gold (a commonplace which Shakespeare uses to make poetry suspect in Sonnets 33 and 114), it again attributes to language power over nature which makes it hardly distinguishable in its operations from magic. Among rhetoricians the alchemist was a familiar type of the poet, but to Protestant writers bent on purging religion of superstitious rituals, the practitioners of "Alcumysterie" were devisers of magic charms to deceive the uninitiated, like priests, witches, and conjurers:

> For what plaine man would not beleeue, that they are learned and iollie fellowes, that haue in such readinesse so many mysticall termes of art: as (for a tast) their subliming, amalgaming, engluting, imbibing, incorporating, cementing, ritrination, terminations, mollifications, and indurations of bodies, matters combust and coagulat, ingots, tests, etc. . . . This science (forsooth) is the secret of secrets; euen as *Salomons* coniuration is said among the coniurors to be so likewise. [35]

Yet it is precisely the strength of the association of poetic "art" with "mysticall termes" that makes the comparison of the poet to the alchemist acceptable to Sidney in disregard of such Protestant arguments, and despite the fact that it blurs the distinction he makes elsewhere between the divine power of poetry and the "godles superstition" of magic.

Shakespeare's claim of miraculous force for poetry is most triumphant in Sonnet 18. He makes it again as explicitly though less confidently in Sonnet 65, where the power of the poet's language offers the only hope of rescuing his beloved from the natural world:

> Since brasse, nor stone, nor earth, nor boundlesse sea,
> But sad mortallity o'er-swaies their power,
> How with this rage shall beautie hold a plea,
> Whose action is no stronger then a flower?
> O how shall summers hunny breath hold out,
> Against the wrackfull siedge of battring dayes,
> When rocks impregnable are not so stoute,
> Nor gates of steele so strong but time decayes?
> O fearefull meditation, where alack,
> Shall times best Iewell from times chest lie hid?
> Or what strong hand can hold his swift foote back,
> Or who his spoile of beautie can forbid?
>   O none, vnlesse this miracle haue might,
>   That in black inck my loue may still shine bright.

The reference to "this" in the couplet, here as in Sonnet 18, makes the poem itself a figure in its own design, a part of its subject. It announces a demonstration of the way the poet's language may act upon things. It may alter the laws of nature by working a "miracle" which is defined in the last line. We are therefore directed not only to hear what it may claim, but to notice how it works to make any such claim believable in the face of the poet's accumulated images of destruction in the natural world. The last line creates a paradox which states a truth in contradiction of the laws of nature. The poet's "loue," metaphorically transformed into a "Iewell" in line 10, may "shine" in the "black inck" of the poem. If this is possible it is because words may have power that transforms the natural world, a "might" that can make light shine out of darkness, like the divine Word.

These two sonnets base their claims to make miracles on demonstration of devices—specifically metaphor and paradox—representing how the poet's words exert power over nature. By doing so they suggest that the pervasive association of words with supernatural force included closer, more particular links between poetic and religious language. The existence of such connections may in part explain the original appeal of some verbal practices especially characteristic of poetry in this period. It can also give a reader with a very different later perspective a context in which to think about the ways these devices were used and repeated—as it seems obsessively—by the best as well as the least interesting poets of the sixteenth century.

Poetry and Prescribed Prayers

In Sonnet 35 Shakespeare associates his own metaphors with religious language by describing the act of making them in echoes of the Lord's Prayer: "Authorizing thy trespas with compare." In the octave of Sonnet 108 he makes an extended comparison between his poetic practices and prayer:

> What's in the braine that Inck may character,
> Which hath not figur'd to thee my true spririt,
> What's new to speake, what now to register,
> That may expresse my loue, or thy deare merit?
> Nothing sweet boy, but yet like prayers diuine,
> I must each day say ore the very same,
> Counting no old thing old, thou mine, I thine,
> Euen as when first I hallowed thy faire name.

The association of poetry with formal devotions is embedded in his language, for praising the beloved is again like repeating the Lord's Prayer: "Euen as when first I hallowed thy faire name."[36] Here the repetition has become mechanical "Counting." The poet's words have lost the force of divine breath they claimed in Sonnet 18. They are themselves "old," and so their efficacy to work on the mortal world must be worn out. For this reason the claims in the sestet for the power of "eternall loue" to renew life sound like a willed imitation or perhaps even parody of parallel claims in Sonnets 18 and 65:

> So that eternall loue in loues fresh case,
> Waighes not the dust and iniury of age,
> Nor giues to necessary wrinckles place,
> But makes antiquitie for aye his page,
>   Finding the first conceit of loue there bred,
>   Where time and outward forme would shew it dead.

At this stage of the sequence the poet cannot sustain his belief in the force of language to work miracles. Yet he still associates it (whether wishfully or parodically) with divine empowerment. Love which belongs to the "eternall" realm inspires poetry expressed in the "outward forme" of prayer.

Another poem from this part of the sequence, Sonnet 105, develops the same comparison between the language of the poet's "songs and praises" and prescribed prayers.[37] Like Sonnets 18 and 65, though without confidence or energy, it bases its claim to miraculous power, "wondrous scope," on demonstration of how the poet's language works to achieve it. The sonnet therefore calls attention to particular devices shared by poetic language with other forms of ritual, which it here imitates or again perhaps parodies:

> Let not my loue be cal'd Idolatrie,
> Nor my beloued as an Idoll show,
> Since all alike my songs and praises be
> To one, of one, still such, and euer so.
> Kinde is my loue to day, to morrow kinde,
> Still constant in a wondrous excellence,
> Therefore my verse to constancie confin'de,
> One thing expressing, leaues out difference.
> Faire, kinde, and true, is all my argument,
> Faire, kinde and true, varrying to other words,
> And in this change is my inuention spent,
> Three theams in one, which wondrous scope affords,
>   Faire, kinde, and true, haue often liu'd alone,
>   Which three till now, neuer kept seate in one.

Repetition, what the sonnet sardonically praises as "constancie," is the most obvious feature of its language, and in all its aspects. Alliterative patterns, syllables, words, phrases, grammatical constructions, rhythms, figures are repeated over and over.

This habit, equally prominent in so much other sixteenth-century verse, has already been amply demonstrated in quotations illustrating different dimensions of poetic language. Elaborate repetition appears everywhere in the smallest linguistic patterns. For instance, alliterated pairings of nouns with adjectives and words repeated in different grammatical forms have already been shown to be features characteristic of this poetry. Repetition also controls its larger designs. Additive stanzas with identical openings and refrains are typical of songs of the period. Poems in which the speaker is answered by an echo, another preferred model, make repetition both their design and central image. Poets also favored verse forms structured by rhymes or end words repeated in prescribed patterns, of which the most brilliantly ambitious example is Sidney's double sestina, "Yee Gote-heard Gods."[38] Other poems depend on stock sequences of rhymes often repeated within a single poem, especially the ubiquitous series of rhymes with *heart*. Wyatt provided a model in Tottel's miscellany of a poem built out of this familiar grouping. He makes explicit the association of its form with religious language by calling his poem "mortall prayer":

> Go burning sighes vnto the frosen hart,
> Go breake the yse which pities painfull dart.
> Myght neuer perce and yf that mortall prayer,
> In heauen be herd, at lest yet I desire.
> That death or mercy end my wofull smart.
> Take with thee payn, wherof I haue my part,
> And eke the flame from which I cannot start,
> And leaue me then in rest, I you require:
> Go burning sighes fulfil that I desire.
> I must go worke I see by craft and art,
> For truth and faith in her is laid apart:
> Alas, I can not therfore assaile her,
> With pitefull complaint and scalding fier,
> That from my brest disceiuably doth start.[39]

The poem by Petrarch from which Wyatt's may be at least partly adapted has only three words repeating the sound of the opening rhyme word, *core*, while Wyatt's "hart" belongs to a scheme of eight rhymes. This exaggerated patterning turns repetition into a form for which "prayer" is again here the suggested model.

In Shakespeare's Sonnet 105, in addition to minute repetitions, the reiteration of the phrase "Faire, kinde, and true" becomes a structural principle which creates a version of correlative verse. This form, practiced also by Gascoigne, Sidney, Daniel, Spenser and many other poets, repeats key words used earlier in the poem in a final recapitulation, making them into a formula and giving the poem itself a clearly defined shape which is predictable. An example is Sonnet 11 from Daniel's *Delia:*

>   Teares, vowes, and prayers win the hardest hart:
>   Teares, vowes, and prayers haue I spent in vaine;
>   Teares, cannot soften flint, nor vowes conuart,
>   Prayers preuaile not with a quaint disdaine.
>   I lose my teares, where I haue lost my loue,
>   I vowe my faith, where faith is not regarded;
>   I pray in vaine, a merciles to moue:
>   So rare a faith ought better be rewarded.
>   Yet though I cannot win her will with teares,
>   Though my soules Idoll scorneth all my vowes;
>   Though all my prayers be to so deafe eares:
>   No fauour though the cruell faire allowes.
>   Yet will I weepe, vowe, pray to cruell Shee:
>   Flint, Frost, Disdaine, weares, melts, and yeelds we see.

Like Daniel here, Shakespeare uses a correlative structure in Sonnet 105 as another form of repetition linking his poetic recitations with the language of prayer. Opening with words of petition—"Let not"—it ends with a repeated triad "Faire, kinde, and true." This resembles triple formulas printed after portions of the order of service in the English liturgy:

>   Glory be to the Father, and to the Sonne: and to the holy
>   Ghost.
>   As it was in the beginning, is nowe, and euer shal be: world
>   without ende. Amen.[40]

The way prayers open with petitions and end with such formulas gives them a fixed and predictable shape, which correlative verse resembles. The echo of such a liturgical closing also in line 4 of the sonnet—"To one, of one, still such, and euer so"—further insists that forms of repetition in the poem are shared with prescribed "songs and praises." In doing so it may reflect awareness of the controversy between the established church and its puritan critics, against whom Hooker defended ritually repeated prayers. He questions whether the puritans were right to judge God "by our owne bellies, and to imagin that he doth loath to haue the selfesame supplications often iterated, euen as we do to be euery day fed without alteration and change of diet. . . ."[41] Writers on both sides of this controversy closely identified prayer and repetition, as Shakespeare does also in Sonnet 76. Again both are associated with poetry which echoes the formulas of prayer: "Why write I still all one, euer the same."

Poetry and "Wondrous" Paradox

Another device prominently displayed in the language of Sonnet 105 is paradox: "Three theams in one, which wondrous scope affords." Again there is a connection with Sonnet 65, where the poet's hope to effect a "miracle" is grounded in his creation of a paradox: "That in black inck my loue may still shine bright." Sidney associates "miraculous power" with the paradoxical brightness of Stella's black eyes in *Astrophil and Stella* 7; Spenser ponders the "miraculous" paradox that his flaming desire can "harden yse," the lady's frozen heart, in *Amoretti* 30. Cawdrey's *Table Alphabeticall* defines "paradoxe" as "marueilous, or strange speech," while Puttenham nicknames it "the Wondrer," and Day describes it as "a kinde of maruelling or woondering." Protestant polemicists associated the term especially with Catholic claims that the words of consecration in the Mass effect "a miracle in the Sacrament, and that Christ is there miraculously," which they condemn as "This monstrous paradoxe of transubstantiation."[42] Yet of course since paradox is at the very heart of Christian doctrine, it was habitual in the ways of thinking of sixteenth-century Protestants as well as Catholics. It was therefore woven into their uses of language and their conceptions of its nature and workings. Even the smallest linguistic unit, the letters of the crossrow themselves, was thought capable of expressing the miraculous power of paradox to transcend the laws governing things in nature. This assumption is illustrated in a commonplace based, like Sonnet 105, on the doctrine of the triune God: "A is thought to bee the first letter of the row, because by it we may understand Trinity and Unity: the Trinity in that there bee three lines, and the Unity, in that it is but one letter."[43] Paradox is a demonstration of the divine power over nature which writers claim for language by reflecting its supernatural origins in forms and uses.

In Sonnet 105 the paradox of three in one repeated and recapitulated constitutes a poetic ritual as it does also in stanzas of *The Faerie Queene* where Spenser tells the story of three brothers whose destinies are united by the power of their mother's magic:

> Their mother was a Fay, and had the skill
>   Of secret things, and all the powres of nature,
>   Which she by art could vse vnto her will,

And to her seruice bind each liuing creature,
Through secret vnderstanding of their feature.

(4.2.44)

The spell binding the fates of her three sons into one is reenacted by the poet's language in paradoxes repeated and recapitulated in correlative verse:

Amongst those knights there were three brethren bold,
Three bolder brethren neuer were yborne,
Borne of one mother in one happie mold,
Borne at one burden in one happie morne,
Thrise happie mother, and thrise happie morne,
That bore three such, three such not to be fond;
Her name was *Agape* whose children werne
All three as one, the first hight *Priamond*,
The second *Dyamond*, the youngest *Triamond*.

(4.2.41)

The triad of names—themselves alluding to the numbers one, two, three—is then repeated and rearranged in other combinations which create a kind of magic circle:

Stout *Priamond*, but not so strong to strike,
Strong *Diamond*, but not so stout a knight,
But *Triamond* was stout and strong alike:
On horsebacke vsed *Triamond* to fight,
And *Priamond* on foote had more delight,
But horse and foote knew *Diamond* to wield:
With curtaxe vsed *Diamond* to smite,
And *Triamond* to handle speare and shield,
But speare and curtaxe both vsd *Priamond* in field.

(4.2.42)

More exaggerated than Shakespeare's imitation or parody of prayers in Sonnet 105, the chanting repetitions in these stanzas sound like the magical incantations and popish charms reviled by Scot. Yet the poetic devices associating both the sonnet and Spenser's stanzas with supernatural power are very similar in kind to language in the prayer book repeated in church by all members of the English church in the sixteenth century. An example is a passage from what was known as the Athanasian Creed stating the doctrine of the Trinity. In the first prayer book of Edward VI the order for evensong contains the directive: "In the feastes of *Christmas, Thepiphanie, Easter, Thascencion, Pentecost,* and upon *Trinitie* Sonday, shalbe song or sayd immediatly after

Benedictus this confession of our christian fayth."[44] To those required performances the revision of 1552 adds seven saint's days when the creed must also be repeated, a directive retained in the prayer book throughout the century.

This recitation of beliefs necessary for salvation consists of a long list of affirmations and negations about the central Christian paradoxes of first the Trinity and then the Incarnation. The definition of the triune God is made in twenty-five statements framed with an opening declaration of the faith and the conclusion "Hee therefore that will bee saued: must thus thinke of the Trinitie." The catalogue begins:

> And the Catholike faith is this: that we worship one God in Trinitie, and Trinitie in vnitie.
>
> Neither confounding the persons: nor diuiding the substance.
>
> For there is one person of the Father, another of the Sonne: and another of the holy Ghost.
>
> But the Godhead of the Father, of the Sonne, and of the holy Ghost, is all one: the glorie equal, the maiestie coeternall.
>
> Such as the Father is, suche is the Sonne: and such is the holy Ghost.
>
> The Father vncreate, the Sonne vncreate: and the holy Ghost vncreate.
>
> The Father incomprehensible, the Sonne incomprehensible: and the holy Ghost incomprehensible.
>
> The Father eternall, the Sonne eternall: and the holy Ghost eternall.
>
> And yet they are not three eternalls: but one eternall.
>
> As also there be not three incomprehensibles, not three vncreated: but one vncreated, and one incomprehensible.
>
> So likewise the Father is almightie, the Sonne almightie: and the holy ghost almightie.
>
> And yet they are not three almighties: but one almightie.
>
> So the Father is God, the Sonne is God, and the holye Ghost is God.
>
> And yet they are not three Goddes: but one God.
>
> So likewise the Father is Lord, the Sonne Lord: and the holy Ghost Lord.
>
> And yet not three Lords: but one Lord.

The catalogue continues in the same pattern of repeated and balanced triads recapitulated in a final verse which restates the opening paradox:

So that in all things, as is aforesaide: the vnitie in Trinitie,
and the Trinitie in vnitie is to be worshypped.[45]

Since this creed was sung or said in every English church on the principal feasts of the Christian year, its language must have resonated in the memories of writers and readers. Such recitations could then be models for sixteenth-century poets when they wanted to charge their language with special power.

Poetry and Rituals of Naming

Reiteration in Sonnet 105 of "Faire, kinde, and true" calls attention to another device previously discussed as characteristic of poetry of this period, listing. Whole lines were often made out of lists, such as Drayton's "My Zeale, my Hope, my Vowes, my Prayse, my Pray'r."[46] Even entire poems consisted of such catalogues, as Shakespeare claims his to be: "Faire, kinde, and true, is all my argument." His Sonnet 66 is in fact a catalogue. Correlative verse, examples have shown, lists words or phrases in the body of the poem and then strings them all together again in the conclusion. Fletcher associates this pattern explicitly with prayer in the conclusion of a correlative poem, Sonnet 36 of *Licia:*

Thus sighes, and teares, flame, griefe, shall plead for me,
So shall I pray, and you a goddesse be.[47]

A parallel in the English liturgy for this kind of listing was the portion of matins known in the prayer book throughout the century as the *Benedicite omnia opera domini domino* (attributed in the Apocrypha to the singers in the fiery furnace). It consists of thirty-two invocations of the works of the Lord, including heavenly bodies, seasons, times of day, and more particular locations and creatures of the earth:

O ye mountaines and hilles, blesse ye the Lorde: praise him and magnifie him for euer.
O all yee greene things vpon the earth, blesse yee the Lorde: praise him and magnifie him for euer.
O ye wels, bles ye the Lord: praise him & magnify him for euer.
O ye seas and floods, blesse ye the Lord: praise him and magnifie him for euer.
O yee Whales and all that moue in the waters, blesse yee the Lord: praise him and magnifie him for euer.
O all ye fowles of the aire, blesse ye the Lord: praise him and magnifie him for euer.

> O all ye beasts and cattell, blesse ye the Lord: praise him
> and magnifie him for euer.

The catalogue continues to invoke six categories of righteous men, and then concludes with a triad of names for the "thre holie children" in "the hote fyrie fornace" (The song of the thre children):

> O Ananias, Azarias, & Misael, blesse ye the Lorde: praise
> him and magnifie hym for euer.[48]

Such sequences of nouns were common in sixteenth-century poetry, as were lists of proper names. Spenser's magical trio is an example. Noun adjectives like "Faire, kinde, and true" also often made up lists, of which a line from Sonnet 31 of Griffin's *Fidessa* is an instance: "Loulie, faire, gentle, wise, vertuous, sober, sweete."[49] Still others were composed of mixed parts of speech such as Daniel combines in *Delia* 11 in its final line of recapitulation: "Flint, Frost, Disdaine, weares, melts, and yeelds we see." All of these grammatical forms, earlier discussions have shown, could be thought of as names, and naming was considered to be the essential function of the language God empowered Adam to invent. "Hauing made Nownes, his Verbes he also wrought," and bestowed them upon the creatures.[50] This divinely sanctioned use of language in conferring names on the works invoked in the *Benedicite* was an archetypal image of verbal power over nature. It is in keeping with that interpretation that metaphor making, said to be the most distinctive feature of the poet's art and the one thought to be a divine gift, was defined as the bestowing of a new name.

This configuration of beliefs suggests that the device of listing or naming in poetry of this period was one of the verbal patterns ultimately associated with supernatural power expressed in religious ritual. It is Shakespeare's repeated triad of names—"Faire, kinde and true"—which he says gives his poetic language its "wondrous scope." That claim, however doubtfully or cynically made, is grounded more specifically in the association of his list with the triple formula repeated everywhere in the liturgy of the English church: "In the name of the father, and of the sonne, and of the holy gost."

This sacred triad is pronounced, for example, in the sacramental ceremony when Christians receive new names "in token" that by baptism they are made new creatures. In the first Edwardian prayer book the administration of the sacrament is elaborately described:

> *Then, the prieste shall take the childe in his handes, and aske the name.*
> *And naming the childe, shall dyppe it in the water thryse. First*

> *dypping the ryght syde: Seconde the left syde: The thyrd tyme dip-*
> *ping the face towarde the fonte: So it be discretly and warely done,*
> *saying.*
>
> I Baptize thee in the name of the father, and of the sonne, and
> of the holy gost. Amen.[51]

Beginning with the prayer book of 1552, the directions for immersion
are simplified to one *"dippe,"* but the triple formula is retained and
"Then the Priest shall make a crosse upon the chyld's forehead."[52] Protestants
differentiated their ceremony on theological grounds from Catholic
claims for the magical efficacy of name and sign, but its outward performance even in revised form did not wholly dissociate it from that
belief. A list invoking in turn by more elaborate titles the three persons of the Trinity followed by a recapitulation—"O holy, blessed,
and glorious Trinitie, three persons and one God"—opens the litany
which was said or sung by the priest with responses repeated by the
congregation.[53] In Sonnet 105 the poet performs both parts.

Earlier sixteenth-century primers contained many prayers consisting in lists of titles for the Son of God and other supernaturally powerful names. One such, which Scot likens to the "coniurations" of
magicians, is a long list alternating the sign of the cross with "holie
names" like "alpha & omega" or with single letters said to be written
"with Gods finger" on the side of Jesus upon the cross.[54] A particularly popular prayer attributed to Saint Bridget strung together a series of fifteen invocations of the name of Jesus, each beginning with
"O," and was therefore "called commonly the .XV. oos." Printed with
it in earlier sixteenth-century primers were promises of its supernatural efficacy: "who so say this a hole yere he shall delever .xv. soules
out of purgatory of hys next kyndreed: and converte other .xv. syn-
ners to gode lyfe and other .xv. ryghtuouse men of hys kinde shall
persever in gode lyfe. And what ye desyre of god ye shall have yt, yf
it be to the salvacyon of your sowle."[55]

It was in part to suppress such belief in the magical efficacy of
repeated lists of names that an authorized primer was issued, purged
of such prayers and promises. Yet the fifteen o's appeared in a Protestant collection of private prayers (to be recited at home rather than
in church) in English, published in 1590 by the printer of the authorized primer, and reprinted in at least three more editions.[56] The vol-
ume was embellished with an engraving of "Elizabeth Regina" kneeling in her bedroom at a priedieu with a book open upon it. The
version of the fifteen o's included in this collection, along with anonymous prayers and some attributed to Saint Augustine and to John

Foxe, was theologically corrected with the promise of efficacy and
Saint Bridget's name omitted. Yet it retained virtually the same incantatory form that provoked Scot's comparisons to conjuring, and with
some justification. For the rituals practiced by students of the occult,
based on the magic of verbal formulas, often consisted of long sequences invoking supernatural powers by various sorts of naming. An
example is a planetary incantation to Venus by Giordano Bruno,
whose works were well known among Englishmen interested in the
occult, including the courtiers and writers of Sidney's circle. Bruno's
charm, adapted from an incantation in Agrippa's *De occulta philosophia*,
begins:

> *Venus alma, formosa, pulcherrima, amica, beneuola, gratiosa, dulcis,
> amena, candida, siderea, dionea, olens, iocosa, aphrogenia, foecunda,
> gratiosa, larga, benefica, placida, deliciosa, ingeniosa, ignita, concil-
> iatrix maxima, amorum domina. . . .*[57]

While reformed theology rejected claims of miraculous power for
the recitation of names, many writers with strongly Protestant affiliations were nevertheless interested in occult studies, which seem to
have gained in respectability in the later part of the century. The rep-
utation of the English astrologer John Dee is an instance. Dee was
attacked as a "great Conjurer" in the 1563 edition of John Foxe's *Actes
and Monuments*, but then all hostile references were suppressed in the
edition of 1576, a sign of official protection given to some forms of
what even at the time were considered magical practices.[58] The studies of such occultists could be assimilated more easily perhaps, even
by Protestants particularly committed to religious reform, because
some private prayers authorized by the English church and even some
parts of its public worship, we have seen, continued to resemble rituals based on belief in the supernatural power of naming. Saint Paul's
exaltation of the name of Jesus occupied a position of special prominence by being read as the lesson on the Sunday before Easter:

> Wherefore God hath also exalted him on high, & giuen him a
> Name, which is aboue all names, that in the name of Iesus
> euery knee should bowe, both of things in heauen, and things
> in earth, and things vnder the yearth, and that all tongues
> should confesse that Iesus Christe is the Lorde, vnto the praise
> of God the Father.[59]

This text was the sanction for the Protestant revival of Saint Bridget's
fifteen invocations of the "sweet" and "healthfull name" of "O Good
Jesu, O sweet Jesu. . . . O louing Jesu. . . . O moste mercifull Jesu

. . . O moste sweet Jesu . . . O Jesu."⁶⁰ In form the prayer could be justified according to the model of the repeated invocations of the persons of the Trinity in the beginning of the litany, all preceded by "O," like the thirty-two verses naming the works of God in the *Benedicite*.

Naming in the form of extended lists is also everywhere in sixteenth-century poetry. The device was sometimes called a *catalogue* from the Latin *catalogus*, translated in Cooper's dictionary as "A rehearsall in wordes, or table in writing of the number of things: a roll: a bill." The term was defined by Cawdrey as a "beadroole, or rehearesall of words, or names."⁶¹ Originally *beadroll* was the word for a list read out in church naming the living and the dead to be prayed for by the parish. The ceremony, which was revised several times by the English church in this period, was known as the "Bidding of the Bedes" (from the Middle English verb for praying, *bidden*).⁶² The word *beadroll* was also the name for actual strings of beads used by Catholics in the recitation of prayers. These concurrent meanings explain why Spenser could describe both Archimago's popish charms and Celia's Protestant devotions as "Bidding . . . beades" (1.1.30; 1.10.3). The priest-magician conjures by mechanical telling of the rosary. The true Christian repeats the prayers naming the faithful according to the form authorized by the English church. The fact that Spenser uses the same wording to describe both practices points to their resemblance in outward form, which is expressed also in other detailed parallels between the contrasting episodes. Gradually both *beadroll* and *catalogue* came to mean any long sequence of names. Spenser uses the liturgical term with this meaning in a tribute to his poetic master:

> Dan *Chaucer*, well of English vndefyled,
> On Fames eternall beadroll worthie to be fyled.
>
> (4.2.32)

Although the commonplace of a book of Fame in which the names of immortal poets are inscribed is pagan in origin, Spenser's term for it still retains some echo of its meaning in church ritual, with which it associates poetry.

Contexts of Catalogues in *The Faerie Queene*

The first catalogue in *The Faerie Queene* is introduced at the earliest possible opportunity, in the beginning of the opening episode.⁶³ When a storm overtakes Una and the Red Crosse Knight, they seek shelter in a "shadie groue." The narrator gives warning of danger in the place because its "loftie trees yclad with sommers pride" spread branches that "heauens light did hide" (1.1.7). Yet the characters are heedless of this sign, "And foorth they passe, with pleasure forward led" into the wood:

> Much can they prayse the trees so straight and hy,
> The sayling Pine, the Cedar proud and tall,
> The vine-prop Elme, the Poplar neuer dry,
> The builder Oake, sole king of forrests all,
> The Aspine good for staues, the Cypresse funerall.
>
> The Laurell, meed of mightie Conquerours
> And Poets sage, the Firre that weepeth still,
> The Willow worne of forlorne Paramours,
> The Eugh obedient to the benders will,
> The Birch for shaftes, the Sallow for the mill,
> The Mirrhe sweete bleeding in the bitter wound,
> The warlike Beech, the Ash for nothing ill,
> The fruitfull Oliue, and the Platane round,
> The caruer Holme, the Maple seeldom inward sound.
>
> (1.1.8–9)

The warning given before these lines and their ominous closing note connect the catalogue to the narrative by identifying the place as the "wandring wood" where the knight will fight with Errour. The opening of the catalogue, "Much can they prayse the trees," links it also to the allegory by declaring that the list is an expression of the inward state of the characters, whose passive indulgence in "pleasure" makes them ignore the signs of danger in their surroundings. Yet the actual effect of this passage is to separate it from the movement of the canto as a set piece with a distinct shape and function.

The presence of such set pieces, seemingly inserted passages which have a special kind of apparent autonomy, is another characteristic of sixteenth-century poetry. It must have derived at least in part from the notion of the places as sources of invention, which then encouraged borrowing passages either from collections like Withal's or from poems treated as such compilations. Spenser, for example, here assimilates details from Chaucer and Ovid, as well as other medieval and ancient authors.

A more particular reason why Spenser's catalogue of trees has the effect of an inserted set-piece is that although these lines are supposed to be "prayse" of the place spoken by the characters, the passage does little to invite the reader to keep this in mind. For Spenser makes no

effort to associate the names imposed on nature with the characters'
particular perspective, although poems of this period are often designed to reflect such reciprocity between the inward state of the observer and the landscape. An example where that reflection is stressed
is a passage from one of Sidney's Arcadian eclogues. It consists of a
catalogue of trees in which the poet-lover sees his "estate represented":

> Pine is a maste to a shippe, to my shippe shall hope for a
> maste serve?
> Pine is hye, hope is as hie, sharpe leav'd, sharpe yet be my
> hope's budds.
> Elme embraste by a vine, embracing fancy reviveth.
> Popler changeth his hew from a rising sunne to a setting:
> Thus to my sonne do I yeeld, such lookes her beames do
> aforde me.
> Old aged oke cutt downe, of newe works serves to the
> building:
> So my desires by my feare, cutt downe, be the frames of her
> honour. [64]

Nothing like this kind of matching is attempted in the catalogue of
trees attributed to Una and the Red Crosse Knight. For although it is
framed by phrases describing their submission to the pleasant distrac-
tions of the place—"with pleasure forward led," "Led with delight"—
the actual lines do not reflect that inward state (though the argument
has been advanced that the act of naming itself is in a different way
distracting). [65] Their disparity can be seen if these lines are set beside
a correlative catalogue of "pleasaunce" (from which Watson transcribed lines in Sonnet 51 of *The Tears of Fancie*) experienced by Guyon
in Phaedria's island: [66]

> No daintie flowre or herbe, that growes on ground,
> No arboret with painted blossomes drest,
> And smelling sweet, but there it might be found
> To bud out faire, and her sweet smels throw all around.

> No tree, whose braunches did not brauely spring;
> No braunch, whereon a fine bird did not sit:
> No bird, but did her shrill notes sweetly sing;
> No song but did containe a louely dit:
> Trees, braunches, birds, and songs were framed fit,
> For to allure fraile mind to carelesse ease.

> (2.6.12–13)

This passage lists nouns and adjectives paired to reflect the pleasing effects of the place on the senses of characters present to see its "painted blossomes," to inhale its "sweet smels," and to hear its birds "sweetly sing." The first catalogue of trees is shaped to a different end. Rather than reflecting what its framing phrases call "pleasure" or "delight" in the impression made by the shady grove on its observers, it expresses satisfaction in a kind of abstract order. Rather than passive immersion in the agreeable effects of a place into which their sensual indulgence has "led" the characters, the epithets (until the last) express a beautifully austere appreciation of the beneficent reciprocity between nature and society. Such assignments as the laurel to conquering heroes and poets, or the "Sallow for the mill," are detached and judicious rather than self-indulgent. The recitation of trees named with epithets in balanced pairs—"The fruitfull Oliue, and the Platane round"—is as formal and generalized as an established ceremony publicly reenacted in a prescribed form, which Spenser's sixteenth-century audience would have recognized the catalogue to be. It is therefore mainly intended to have a special function that makes appropriate its nearly autonomous effect as an inserted set piece.

Even more than later readers aided by editorial commentary, Spenser's first audience would have identified this passage with the voice of the poet in *The Faerie Queene*. Coming at the beginning of the narration, the catalogue calls attention to the presence of Spenser, associating himself with his master Chaucer, with Virgil, Ovid, and with the whole tradition of poetry. The "prayse" recited in the catalogue is unmistakeably the poet's more than the characters', and its subject is poetic tradition itself more than the pleasing aspect of a landscape or even the order in nature and society. This is another reason why the passage detaches itself from the canto as a set piece rather than seeming to be integrated into the narrative by describing a setting where characters will take part in its action.

Coming at the beginning of the opening episode, this catalogue is an announcement of the poet's presence and an invocation to literary tradition. By repeating a poetic ritual of naming, Spenser summons its divine power over the natural world to inform his language. This force is demonstrated in the verbal order of the catalogue. Its balanced rhythms are created by judiciously matched epithets, which show the poet's authority to confer right names. The lines reflect his supernatural art in the creation of a new nature, like Shakespeare's in Sonnet 18, by summoning a series of imaginative categories. "The fruitfull

Oliue" is not *a* tree or *this* tree but an ideal that transcends the particular. "The Laurell, meed of mightie Conquerours" is a symbol more
than a bush. "The Mirrhe sweete bleeding in the bitter wound,"
whatever the botanical properties of the species, evokes myths more
than it describes a plant.

Above all, the passage lays claim to the divine force of poetry by
invoking the presence of poets whose voices inhabit all the other catalogues of trees echoed here at the beginning of Spenser's poem. Their
presence is registered in a kind of subliminal catalogue of immortal
names which the passage recalls, like "Fames eternall beadroll" in
which Chaucer's name is elsewhere said to be inscribed. Spenser's
recitation of his list of trees adds his own name to that mysteriously
heard though unspoken catalogue. It is entered in a list stretching
back into the ancient time of Orpheus, archetypal figure of the poet
whose name was etymologized "best voice."[67]

Spenser—or any other poet who recites a catalogue of trees—re-
enacts the transformation of nature wrought by the magic art of Orpheus, whose "voyce," Sidney says, "had force to breathe" life
"Through pores of senceless trees, as it could make them move."[68] In
Ovid's account translated by Golding

> There was a hyll, and on the hyll a verie levell plot,
> Fayre greene with grasse. But as for shade or covert was
>   there not.
> As soone as that this Poet borne of Goddes, in that same
>   place
> Sate downe and toucht his tuned strings, a shadow came
>   apace.[69]

The magic art of Orpheus set in motion a procession of trees that
gathered around him to make a new nature. Ovid's catalogue then
describes the procession, imitating that order by the supernatural
force of his language, which is in turn recreated in the catalogues of
trees recited by other poets.

The power of Orpheus made him a pagan archetype of the poet.
His authority derived in part from the generally held notion that he
was one of the most ancient writers next to Moses. Among students
of the occult the Orphic hymns attributed to him, which were
thought to prefigure Christ, were used for their magical efficacy as
incantations.[70] Sidney compares them "in antiquitie and excellencie. . . .though in a full wrong diuinitie" to the Psalms of David, Solomon's "song of Songs," and other biblical hymns.[71] Spenser draws a

parallel between the "godlike" power of Orpheus's "siluer Harpe" and the "heauenly notes" of the "celestiall Psalmist" in *The Faerie Queene* (4.2.1–2).

Like the ideal poet in *An Apologie for Poetrie* who returns the brazen world to a golden age, Orpheus is typically praised by writers about language for using his eloquent and learned tongue to restore civilization and manners lost to the fallen world. The belief that Orpheus was the first poet and a priestly interpreter of the gods was known in the middle ages in Horace, but was revived in the sixteenth century under the influence of Ficino.[72] Francis Clement in one of the earliest English spelling books expands on this commonplace:

> *Amphion* and *Pindarus* were two excellent among the *Græcians*, but *Orpheus* his tongue surmounted all other, so sweete, so smooth: so fayre, so filed: so gallant, so goodly: so passing, so pleasant: so leading, so learned. It entised, and procured: it delited, and allured: it moued, and rauished: it pearsed, and pleased: it persuaded, and preuayled with men, that in those dayes were in maner of brute beastes, wildely sparpled abrode in fieldes, forestes and woody places, wandryng vagabondes, and peragrant pesantes, liuying by rapine and raw flesh, who hauing resigned reason, and standying to their strength, were now as rigorous as rockes, as mouelesse as mountaynes, as sturdy as trees, as lawlesse as Lyons, as brutishe as beastes.[73]

When Spenser begins his narrative by reciting a catalogue of trees, he is invoking the eloquence of Orpheus.

As Orpheus is a traditional figure of the poet, the catalogue of trees is the prototype of all catalogues, and of poetry itself, which is the art of naming. Its special force is expressed in each repetition, for which some writers found ultimate sanction in the opening chapters of Genesis listing the creative acts of God's Word. Direct connection between the poetic commonplace of the catalogue of trees and this scriptural archetype is made in Du Bartas's hexameral poem, which Spenser and other poets could have known in the original French, published in 1578. Sylvester's close English translation of the passage shows the association of the literary tradition of the catalogue of trees with Genesis very clearly. In Sylvester's lines, which also resemble Spenser's catalogue of trees, God's Word is

> No sooner spoken, but the loftie Pine
> Distilling pitch, the Larche yeeld-Turpentine,
> Th'euer-greene Boxe, and gummie Cedar sprout,
> And th'Airie Mountaines mantle round about:

> The Mast-full Oake, the vse-full Ashe, the Holme,
> Coate-changing Corke, white Maple, shadie Elme,
> Through Hill and Plaine ranged their plumed Ranks.
> The winding Riuers bord'red all their banks
> With slice-Sea Alders, and greene Osiars small,
> With trembling Poplars, and with Willowes pale,
> And many Trees beside, fit to be made
> Fewell, or Timber, or to serue for Shade.[74]

Moses, believed to be the human interpreter of this divine catalogue, was a biblical archetype of the poet to whom many writers granted even greater antiquity as well as authority than Orpheus.[75] To occultists like John Dee, associate of Sidney's family and literary circle, Moses was a magus instructed in the secret *"wisdome of the Ægyptians"* which gave him magical *"power in both his wordes, and workes."*[76] The force of his language could be claimed to empower the acts of naming recited by poets in their repetitions of the catalogue of trees.

In the second episode of *The Faerie Queene* the "charmes" and "spelles" of Spenser's magician-priest "call by name" spirits of darkness to do his wicked work. While one is sent on an errand to the underworld, the other participates in a second ritual performed by Archimago:[77]

> Who all this while with charmes and hidden artes,
> Had made a Lady of that other Spright,
> And fram'd of liquid ayre her tender partes
> So liuely, and so like in all mens sight,
> That weaker sence it could haue rauisht quight:
> The maker selfe for all his wondrous witt,
> Was nigh beguiled with so goodly sight:
> Her all in white he clad, and ouer it
> Cast a blacke stole, most like to seeme for *Vna* fit.
>
>   (1.1.45)

In Book 3 a witch who is another practitioner of magic "art" performs the same kinds of rituals. Her first act is to "coniure" spirits who then aid her in making another "counterfet" lady, "So liuely and so like, that many it mistooke" for the real Florimell:

> The substance, whereof she the bodie made,
> Was purest snow in massie mould congeald,
> Which she had gathered in a shadie glade
> Of the *Riphoean* hils, to her reueald
> By errant Sprights, but from all men conceald:
> The same she tempred with fine Mercury,

> And virgin wex, that neuer yet was seald,
> And mingled them with perfect vermily,
> That like a liuely sanguine it seem'd to the eye.
>
> Instead of eyes two burning lampes she set
> In siluer sockets, shyning like the skyes,
> And a quicke mouing Spirit did arret
> To stirre and roll them, like a womans eyes;
> In stead of yellow lockes she did deuise,
> With golden wyre to weaue her curled head;
> Yet golden wyre was not so yellow thrise
> As *Florimells* faire haire: and in the stead
> Of life, she put a Spright to rule the carkasse dead.
>
> (3.8.6–7)

The conjuring of spirits was an actual practice illustrated in sixteenth-century examples collected by Scot, who gives among many one which invokes this power by "the holie names of thy sonne; to wit, A and Ω, and all his other names."[78] Similarly the Cabalists claimed power to create artificial beings by magic naming. One sixteenth-century master was reported to have brought to life such a creature by inscribing the secret name of God on the forehead of a clay figure, a magical version of the rite of holy baptism.[79] The charms of Spenser's magicians may therefore allude to actual or rumored contemporary practices. Certainly their language is associated with demonic powers.

These passages also refer in design and in many specific details to examples of a particular kind of verse catalogue, the anatomical list of the lady's parts, recited by the narrator in *The Faerie Queene*. These paralleled catalogues again point to contrasts, as do the paired episodes describing the devotions of Archimago and Celia. Again the matched passages represent rituals which seem to be versions of one another by virtue of resemblances in their outward forms. The charms of Archimago and the witch, which are magical perversions of poetic recitations by the narrator, also resemble the anatomical catalogues attributed in Sylvester's translation of Du Bartas to the "wanton & lasciuious Poets of our Time":

> Those learned Spirits, whose wits applied wrong,
> With wanton Charmes of their inchanting song,
> Make of an old, foule, frantike *Hecuba*,
> A wondrous fresh, faire, wittie *Helena*:
> Of lewd *Faustina*, that loose Emperesse,
> A chaste *Lucretia*, loathing wantonnesse.[80]

The passage is unusual in the degree to which it expands on and departs from the parallel lines opening the second day of *La Sepmaine:*

> *Tovs ces doctes esprits, dont la voix flateresse*
> *Change Hecube en Helene, & Faustine en Lucresse.*[81]

Behind Sylvester's variant, which turns the accusation of flattery into an attack on the magic "Charmes" of poetry, may be the same English Protestant attitudes which moved Spenser to portray conjurers as demonic poets, makers of a kind of ritual of naming known as the blazon.[82]

Shakespeare uses the term "blazon" in Sonnet 106 to name the kind of poem that praises the beauties "Of hand, of foote, of lip, of eye, of brow." The emphasis on listing the lady's parts in this line suggests he is referring to the type of poem he makes fun of in Sonnet 130, which catalogues as it rejects a number of comparisons seemingly inevitable in this genre:

> My Mistres eyes are nothing like the Sunne,
> Currall is farre more red, then her lips red,   .
> If snow be white, why then her brests are dun:
> If haires be wiers, black wiers grow on her head:
> I haue seene Roses damaskt, red and white,
> But no such Roses see I in her cheekes,
> And in some perfumes is there more delight,
> Then in the breath that from my Mistres reekes.
> I loue to heare her speake, yet well I know,
> That Musicke hath a farre more pleasing sound:
> I graunt I neuer saw a goddesse goe,
> My Mistres when shee walkes treads on the ground.
>   And yet by heauen I thinke my loue as rare,
>   As any she beli'd with false compare.

In Sonnet 106 Shakespeare calls the anatomical catalogue "old rime," implying that it is exhausted like his other repeated "songs and praises" in the sonnet just before, and in Sonnet 108. Elsewhere, however, there is evidence that, while Spenser and other poets also associated this type of catalogue with religious language, for them it was still charged with special force.

Spenser's catalogue naming Belphoebe's fair parts, a model of the genre which Archimago and the witch pervert and which Shakespeare makes fun of, calls attention to the presence of the poet as much as does his opening catalogue of trees, and for many of the same reasons. Here again these have to do with its established form and content, repeated by poet after poet. It interrupts the narrative, here for ten stanzas, with another set piece consisting of an extended list following a pattern established in poetic tradition. In a parodic elegy, "Loves Progress," Donne questions the prescribed order of the blazon: "How much they stray that set out at the face."[83] Spenser follows that convention here:

> Her face so faire as flesh it seemed not,
>   But heauenly portraict of bright Angels hew,
>   Cleare as the skie, withouten blame or blot,
>   Through goodly mixture of complexions dew;
>   And in her cheekes the vermeill red did shew
>   Like roses in a bed of lillies shed,
>   The which ambrosiall odours from them threw,
>   And gazers sense with double pleasure fed,
> Hable to heale the sicke, and to reuiue the ded.
>
> In her faire eyes two liuing lamps did flame,
>   Kindled aboue at th'heauenly makers light,
>   And darted fyrie beames out of the same,
>   So passing persant, and so wondrous bright,
>   That quite bereau'd the rash beholders sight:
>   In them the blinded god his lustfull fire
>   To kindle oft assayd, but had no might;
>   For with dredd Maiestie, and awfull ire,
> She broke his wanton darts, and quenched base desire.
>
> Her iuorie forhead, full of bountie braue,
>   Like a broad table did it selfe dispred,
>   For Loue his loftie triumphes to engraue,
>   And write the battels of his great godhed:
>   All good and honour might therein be red:
>   For there their dwelling was. And when she spake,
>   Sweet words, like dropping honny she did shed,
>   And twixt the perles and rubins softly brake
> A siluer sound, that heauenly musicke seemd to make.
>
>   (2.3.22–24)

The catalogue continues in the direction prescribed at least since the thirteenth century from the top of the head downwards—Donne's proposal is to reverse and "Rather set out below"—naming parts in more or less descending order: "eyelids," "brows," "snowy brest," "daintie paps," "legs," but concluding with a stanza devoted to "Her yellow lockes crisped, like golden wyre," making a circle back to where such catalogues begin.

Not only the order and shape of the blazon but its enumerated details were tirelessly repeated. Puttenham shows the compelling force of its formulas in his own choice of examples when he describes the "imagerie" of this kind of verse: "And this maner of resemblaunce is not onely performed by likening of liuely creatures one to another, but also of any other naturall thing, bearing a proportion of similitude, as to liken yealow to gold, white to siluer, red to the rose, soft to silke, hard to stone and such like."[84] The range of detail in the blazon seems narrowly fixed to a reader now, since not only their order but their matter is endlessly reiterated: the lady's yellow hair is inevitably like gold, the red in her cheeks like the rose. Belphoebe, Britomart, Serena, Spenser's bride in his marriage hymn, the lady in *Amoretti* 64 and 81 all have virtually interchangeable parts, typically described in comparisons used also to praise beauties celebrated by other poets. Gascoigne, in his *Certayne Notes of Instruction* for the writing of good poetry, is critical of these formulas: "If I should vndertake to wryte in prayse of a gentlewoman, I would neither praise hir christal eye, nor hir cherrie lip, etc. For these things are *trita et obuia.*"[85] Yet this sort of dismissal was itself a commonplace tracing back at least as far as the thirteenth century, when Geoffrey de Vinsauf in his treatise *Poetria nova* follows several pages prescribing how to praise a lady's beauty (in precisely the sorts of phrases condemned by Gascoigne) with a comment on the triteness of such description.[86] Gascoigne, in a blazon of his own, clearly felt no obligation himself to avoid the obvious when he catalogues the lady's "haire of golde, hir front of Iuory," "Her teeth of Pearle, lippes Rubie, christall eye."[87] The most famous sixteenth-century example in English of the blazon was Sidney's Arcadian poem "What toong can her perfections tell," which survives in a number of versions showing more frequent revision than his other work. It was also copied, quoted, printed, and imitated more often than any of his other poems, proving the imaginative appeal of the form to Sidney and his contemporaries.[88] Sidney's catalogue typically follows the same pattern as Spenser's blazon of Belphoebe, beginning with "Her haire fine threeds of finest gould," and praising in "downward" order "fore-head," "browes," "brests," and so on. It too makes a circular return in its conclusion, which repeats the opening couplet in a device parallel to the way correlative verse makes a final recapitulation. His imperative to repeat, "As I began, so must I ende," sounds like Shakespeare's "I must each day say ore the very same" in Sonnet 108, likening the blazon to a prescribed form which has religious associations.

For sixteenth-century poets the predetermined shape and detail of the blazon must therefore have seemed rich rather than restricted. This may have been the expression of beliefs previously discussed, which hallowed repetition itself as a verbal device closely linked with prayer. This association is made explicit in a type of blazon shaped as a catalogue of petitions often sounding like phrasing in the English prayer book. Sir Arthur Gorges strings together such a series in imitation of Du Bellay's sonnet 91 from *L'Olive:*

> Restore agayne that colloure to the golde
>   that garnishte hath those haires like golden streames
> And lett those eyes so heavenly to beholde
>   resigne unto the Sonn their borrowed beames
> And let those lyppes whose smyles so much delight
>   unto the corrall yeelde their lyvely hue
> And let those rancks of pearles retorne of ryghte
>   unto the Oryente whereas first they grewe
> And lett that snowe which shadoweth so her breste
>   dissolve it selfe and unto dropps distyll
> And lett that mynde which honoreth all the reste
>   surcease to use Mynervas sacrede skill
> And let that harte off hardened flynty stone
>   returne unto the rocks from whenc it came
> And then (oh love) if thow wilte heare my mone
>   teach me withall how to foregett her name.[89]

Daniel, beginning in the same vein in *Delia* 18—"Restore thy tresses to the golden Ore"—varies the formulas of petition in imitation of prayer: "Yeelde . . . Bequeath . . . Yeelde . . . Restore . . . Let . . . giue back . . . restore . . . Yeelde."

The power associated with blazons derived also in large part from the example of their archetypal model, which Spenser acknowledges in a borrowed similitude describing Belphoebe's legs:

> Like two faire marble pillours they were seene,
>   Which doe the temple of the Gods support,
>   Whom all the people decke with girlands greene,
>   And honour in their festiuall resort.
>
>   (2.3.28)

The comparison is borrowed directly from a characteristic catalogue in the Song of Solomon, which the Geneva Bible glosses by identifying the bride who recites it with the church. "She describeth Christ to be of perfite beautie, & comlines":

My welbeloued is white and ruddy, the chiefest of ten thousand.

His head is as fine golde, his lockes curled, & blacke as a
rauen.

His eyes are like dooues vpon the riuers of waters, which
are washt with milke, & remaine by the ful vessels.

His chekes are as a bed of spices, and as swete flowres, &
his lippes like lilies dropping downe pure myrrhe.

His hand as rings of golde set with the chrysolite his bellie
like white yuorie couered with saphirs.

His legges are as pillers of marble, set vpon sockets of fine
golde: his countenance as Lebanon, excellent as the cedres.

(Canticles 5:10–15)

The introduction of Belphoebe is an especially charged moment in
The Faerie Queene because she is a representation of Queen Elizabeth.
The recitation of the blazon, by far the most extended of this kind in
the poem and one of its longest catalogues, elevates and ceremoni-
alizes the moment. It works like the opening catalogue of trees as an
invocation, a summoning of divine force to empower the poet's language. Working in the same way as the association—made explicitly
in Du Bartas's widely read hexameral poem—of naming with the catalogue of God's works in Genesis, the blazon announces Spenser's
lineage as a descendent of a succession of poets echoed in endless repetitions again tracing back to a biblical examplar, here King Solomon.
For he was believed to be "the Holy-ghosts Poet" who penned what
is called by a "Title giuen vnto it by the holy Ghost" in the Geneva
Bible: "An Excellent Song which was Salomons."[90] These epithalamic
verses, admitted into the biblical canon in the first century A.D., were
the archetype of the blazon in particular.[91] Their description of the
"fayre" church epitomized the genre: "This beautie is declared by
numbring vp of all the partes, vnder a continued similitude of a
Woman, set forth in the proper beautie and comelines of her partes."[92]
Another title by which these verses were widely known, "the song of
Songs" as Sidney calls them when comparing them to other sacred
hymns, shows that they were at the same time an archetype of all
poetry. The blazon was therefore associated, like the catalogue of
trees, with the divine force of poetic language. For this reason Spenser, who is believed to have made a translation of the Song of Solomon
now lost, found the form fitting to introduce Queen Elizabeth, as he
also used it to usher his bride into the "temple" at the beginning of
the "sacred ceremonies" of his marriage hymn.[93]

If catalogues demonstrate the poet's art of naming, the anatomical catalogue is an occasion also to display more particularly the divine gift of comparison. Solomon was sometimes said to be especially endowed with this power because his "knowledge of the natures of all creatures" enabled him to use "similitudes . . . aptlie drawne from them" to make divine mysteries plain.[94] His gift is amply illustrated in the Song of Songs in such catalogues as the blazon attributed to the bride of Christ or another headed in the Geneva Bible "The beautie of the Church in all her members":

> How beautiful are thy goings with shoes, ô princes daughter: the iointes of thy thighs are like iewels: the worke of the hand of a cunning workeman.
> Thy navel is a rounde cuppe that wanteth not lickour: thy belly is as an heape of wheat compassed about with lillies.
> Thy two breastes are as two yong roes that are twinnes.
> Thy necke is like a towre of yuorie: thine eyes are like ye fishpooles in Heshbon by the gate of Bath-rabbim: thy nose is as the towre of Lebanon, that loketh toward Damascus.
>
> (Canticles 7:1–4)

Like the other quoted catalogue, this is characterized by an abundance of opulent comparisons drawn from the riches of nature and civilization with a free range that seems almost magical. This effect derives in part from the lavish heaping of names for precious and exotic things and places, as if all nature, human art, and language itself were at the poet's command to praise a beloved whose beauty is commensurate with those infinite resources. Spenser, Sidney, even Shakespeare in his playful rejection of the blazon, draw on the same treasury.

The effect of remarkable power in these biblical catalogues depends also on the way the verses expand similitudes beyond their declared point of likeness, assimilating further richness with a lordly disregard for irrelevant differences. Spenser's borrowed description of Belphoebe's legs follows the pattern of such comparisons. The first two lines establish the resemblances discovered by the poet. Belphoebe's limbs are like "faire marble pillours," white, smooth, straight, strong: they support her body which is a chaste temple. By the authority invested in him as the maker of the comparison, he can then develop it in the next two lines, which describe the temple with details applicable to it but not to Belphoebe's legs. For they cannot be imagined hung with garlands by "all the people" like a public building.[95] By freely developing the similitude in this way, the poet displays the power to perceive resemblances beyond the ordinary, after the model of King Solomon: "thy nose is as the towre of Lebanon, that loketh toward Damascus."

Such similitudes are not remarkable merely as hyperbole (although Puttenham makes blazons an exception in his cautions against this figure, allowing poets to "ouer-reach a little by way of comparison" when "we fall a praysing, specially of our mistresses vertue, bewtie, or other good parts").[96] In sixteenth-century theory, comparisons associated especially with the blazon are distinguished as the perception of an essential likeness that strips away accidental differences. A 1557 translation of Beza's commentaries on "the Canticle of Canticles" explicates chapter 1, verse 8—in the Geneva Bible "I haue compared thee, ô my loue, to the troupe of horses in ye charets of Pharoah"— by focussing on one point of resemblance extracted from dissimilarities:

> So likewise in this place the spirite meaneth not to compare his church vnto an horse or a mare. But because one of the principall bewties of a woman is this tall and streight feature of body, with a comely countenance, as it is also specified, *Psal*. 144.12. where the daughters are compared to *high & straight pillers of great Pallaces:* the holy ghost meaning to represent vnto vs by these corporall thinges, the excellency of the church of the Lord when shee keepeth herselfe to her true Pastours, hath chosen this similitude, in opposing it vnto the former desolation, in the which the spouse went as it were hanging downe her head.[97]

The same process of pivoting on a single point of resemblance might also describe similitudes in another blazon in *The Faerie Queene*, which praises Serena's "daintie parts" in lines echoing the Song of Songs in the Geneva Bible:[98]

> Her yuorie necke, her alablaster brest,
>   Her paps, which like white silken pillowes were,
>   For loue in soft delight thereon to rest;
>   Her tender sides, her bellie white and clere,
>   Which like an Altar did it selfe vprere,
>   To offer sacrifice diuine thereon;
>   Her goodly thighes, whose glorie did appeare
>   Like a triumphall Arch, and thereupon
> The spoiles of Princes hang'd, which were in battel won.
>   (6.8.42)

Sixteenth-century blazons, we have seen, not only follow the example of the Song of Songs by heaping similitudes drawn from nature's riches. Some also actually echo or imitate specific passages of the biblical catalogues, as Spenser does or Sidney in "What toong can her perfections tell," which makes similar extended comparisons (often drawn from the same riches of nature enumerated in the Song of Solomon such as "gould," "Marble," "Saphir," "Doves," "lillies," "milke," "Cedars"):

> Her shoulders be like two white Doves,
> Pearching within square royall rooves,
> Which leaded are with silver skinne,
> Passing the hate-spott Ermelin.[99]

Sometimes these borrowings and imitations achieve the boldness as well as the opulence of the biblical model, but too often the sanction to make comparisons that ignore accidental differences encouraged hyperboles absurd in their indifference to the distance between the lady's anatomy and what is used for comparisons to describe it. Gascoigne, for example, in praising the lady's jewelled speech likens her jaws (inadvertently one supposes) to a hazardous ship's channel:

> Since that her sugred tongue the passage breakes,
> Betweene two rockes, bedekt with pearles of price.[100]

Watson compares his lady's brow to the inevitable tablet or polished surface of ivory, which then turns into what seems to be a kind of dance floor:

> Her Forehead smooth and white as *Iuory*,
> Where *Glory*, *State* and *Bashfullnes* held handes.[101]

Because special latitudes were allowed them, the comparisons in blazons often seem elegantly silly to later readers, but even some writers of the period were apparently aware of this risk. Gascoigne, for example, follows his correlative catalogue of the lady's "Rubie, Christall, Iuory, Pearle, and Golde" parts with a hint that it might "offend in the superlatiue."[102] In a handbook of epistolary models by William Fulwood, an anatomical catalogue is given the heading:

> One writes in earnest, or in iest:
> As then shall like his Ladie best.

The blazon which follows begins soberly enough where such poems properly start, "To shew her glittering golden haire,"-and proceeds in

the prescribed direction downward to final details which seem a mild
burlesque of the tradition:

> Her pretie toes, her inch broad heele,
> her foote scarce cracke an egge.[103]

The heading for the poem suggests that not only later readers could
be uneasy about how the comparisons of some blazons were to be
taken, whether "in earnest, or in iest." Clearly they were not all directly imitative of the Song of Songs—Watson claims that his copies
Ronsard—or intended to evoke religious associations. Yet the recognized existence of a biblical model, however distant from the poem's
surface, sanctioned the poet's exercise in the blazon of the divine gift
of comparison in a daring display of its power. For, as it has been
shown, it was the consistent practice of sixteenth-century writers to
justify any use of language—from alphabetical sequence to particular
figures of speech—by referring to scriptural precedent.

   In addition to its echoes of the Song of Songs, Sidney's "What
toong can her perfections tell" suggests also a classical model for the
blazon, following the common pattern of paralleling a sacred and a
pagan source:

> Yet never shall my song omitte
> Those thighes, for *Ovid's* song more fitte;
> Which flanked with two sugred flankes,
> Lift up their stately swelling bankes;
> That *Albion* clives in whitenes passe:
> With hanches smooth as looking glasse.[104]

The reference pays tribute to the ancient poet of amorous verse most
favored among sixteenth-century writers, while it may also allude
specifically to the story of Pygmalion from the tenth book of the *Metamorphosis*. Golding's translation of it tells how "by wondrous Art an
image he did grave" of a maiden so lifelike that the artist himself could
scarcely tell "if the woork that he had made/ Were verie flesh or Ivorye
still." Next the story describes how the artist for "his counterfetted
corse conceyveth love in hart"; how he brought "gorgeous garments,"
"rings," and "perles" to "decke" her; how in supplication to Venus he
"did cause three tymes at least/ The fyre to kindle and to spyre thryse
upward in the ayre"; how that charm caused the statue to come to
life, melting the ivory into flesh as if it were a "peece of wax made
soft ageinst the Sunne."[105] Pygmalion was therefore an archetype of
the maker whose charms could invoke supernatural power to give life
to his art. More specifically he represented the figure of the poet-lover,

in sixteenth-century verse typically said to deck or adorn his lady with praise described as ornament. These connotations are assumed, for example, in a poem of uncertain authorship in Tottel's miscellany called "The tale of Pigmalion with a conclusion vpon the beautye of his loue":

> Of Yuorie white he made so faire a woman than:
> That nature scornd her perfitnesse so taught by craft of man.
> Welshaped were her lyms, full cumly was her face:
> Eche litle vayn most liuely coucht, eche part had semely
>   grace.
> Twixt nature, & Pygmalion, there might appeare great
>   stryfe.
> So semely was this ymage wrought, it lackt nothyng but life.
> His curious eye beheld his own deuised work:
> And, gaysing oft thereon, he found much venome there to
>   lurke.
> For all the featurde shape so dyd his fansie moue:
> That, with his idoll, whom he made, Pygmalion fell in loue.
> To whom he honour gaue, and deckt with garlandes
>   swete,
> And did adourn with iewels riche, as is for louers mete.[106]

Jonson's blazon "On Lvcy Covntesse of Bedford" makes the association between Pygmalion and the catalogue of praise part of the argument of the poem:

> This morning, timely rapt with holy fire,
>   I thought to forme vnto my zealous *Muse*,
> What kinde of creature I could most desire,
>   To honor, serue, and loue; as *Poets* vse.
> I meant to make her faire, and free, and wise,
>   Of greatest bloud, and yet more good then great;
> I meant the day-starre should not brighter rise,
>   Nor lend like influence from his lucent seat.
> I meant shee should be curteous, facile, sweet,
>   Hating that solemne vice of greatnesse, pride;
> I meant each softest vertue, there should meet,
>   Fit in that softer bosome to reside.
> Onely a learned, and a manly soule
>   I purpos'd her; that should, with euen powers,
> The rock, the spindle, and the sheeres controule
>   Of destinie, and spin her owne free houres.
> Such when I meant to faine, and wish'd to see,
>   My *Muse* bad, *Bedford* write, and that was shee.[107]

Jonson's catalogue is partly a criticism of the bejewelled and sometimes prurient style of blazons—later parodied in Marvell's "To his
Coy Mistress"—which it pointedly avoids.[108] It makes fun of their
rituals by its own announced intention to enact a triad of prescribed
rites: "To honor, serue, and love; as Poets vse." It is in part also a joke
about the view of poetry as the art of naming, for the Muse glibly
assumes that is all there is to writing verse. Yet at the same time the
playfulness of the poem does not exclude from it a serious claim for
the power of the catalogue which constitutes it. The poet who sets
out to "forme" a "creature" that he can "honor, serue, and love" is
prefigured by Pygmalion. His declarations of the ways he "meant to
make her" perfect do indeed create his ideal. The fact that it is
matched in the reality of nature and society confirms the poet's capacity for true invention. The actual lady designated by the name of
Countess of Bedford and the "creature" fained by the poet are the
same "shee."

The "charmes and hidden artes" of Archimago and the witch,
when they create "counterfet" ladies, are vicious parodies of Pygmalion's art, as they are magical perversions of Spenser's when he adorns
Queen Elizabeth with a catalogue of praise.[109] Spenser insists on this
reading in the pseudo blazon that animates the false Florimell:

> In stead of eyes two burning lampes she set
> In siluer sockets, shyning like the skyes.
>
> (3.8.7)

These "lampes" are then said to become "like a womans eyes." The
name of the object chosen for comparison—what sixteenth-century
writers would call the borrowed word—has usurped the place of the
proper word in the true blazon of Belphoebe:

> In her faire eyes two liuing lamps did flame,
> Kindled aboue at th'heauenly makers light.
>
> (2.3.23)

The same disruption of the relation between the proper name and the
borrowed word linked by comparison occurs in the inevitable description of the hair. The poet describing Belphoebe devotes a whole
stanza to praising "Her yellow lockes crisped, like golden wyre"
(2.3.30). The witch decks the false Florimell with what only looks like
the hair of a lady in a true blazon:

> In stead of yellow lockes she did deuise,
> With golden wyre to weaue her curled head;

> Yet golden wyre was not so yellow thrise
> As *Florimells* faire haire.

> (3.8.7)

Because the witch violates the prescribed form followed in a true blazon, her charms do not have the force of poetry, or of Pygmalion's art, to breathe life into her creation. The conclusion of the catalogue describing her black art points to that failure, for "in the stead/ Of life, she put a Spright to rule the carkasse dead."

By contrast the blazon of the bride in Spenser's marriage hymn is a triumphant declaration of the poet's power. First he invokes her presence like a vision—"Loe where she comes"—and then gathers the world's riches to deck her in traditional comparisons: "Her long loose yellow locks lyke golden wyre," her "eyes lyke Saphyres," "Her forehead yuory white," "Her paps like lyllies,"

> Her snowie necke lyke to a marble towre,
> And all her body lyke a pallace fayre.[110]

This climactic line in the anatomical catologue reverberates with an echo of Psalm 144 as translated by Sternhold and Hopkins: "Our doughters as carued corner stones, / like to a pallace faire."[111] It therefore infuses the hymn also with the sacred authority of David. The Psalmist is named by Sidney as poet in a familiar comparison with Solomon; along with the Song of Songs, the Psalms were another source for the kind of similitude associated with the blazon.[112] Since the translation by Sternhold and Hopkins was printed with the prayer book to be sung in church, Spenser's allusion to it here emphasizes the liturgical character of the passage, in keeping with its place in the celebration of the marriage ceremony. The biblical epithalamion is also evoked by many of the similitudes in this blazon as in others, previously discussed, by Spenser and Sidney. Inspired by these hallowed sources, and having brought the bride before our sight by his display of the poet's divine art of comparing, Spenser finally declares his power to see what sixteenth-century writers repeatedly say is visible only to God:

> But if ye saw that which no eyes can see,
> The inward beauty of her liuely spright,
> Garnisht with heauenly guifts of high degree,
> Much more then would ye wonder at that sight,
> And stand astonisht lyke to those which red
> Medusaes mazeful hed.[113]

The poet's vision gives him the power to see and name the "liuely spright" which breathes into this lady the life no black "art" can grant to the false Florimell.

The appeal of catalogues for sixteenth-century poets and readers was ultimately grounded in some still widely held belief in the efficacy of naming which, like other assumptions about the nature and power of language, survived the efforts of theological reformers to change aspects of this way of thinking. At the heart of the Protestant atttacks on the Mass was the charge that Catholics saw "no difference betweene calling and making." They therefore were accused of failing to recognize that Christ's words—"This is my body, and this is my bloud"—confer names on the bread and wine which then "represent" or "signify" what they are named. Protestants insisted that the names themselves have no power, as Catholics were accused of claiming, to transubstantiate the elements "into the verie bodie of Christ by a miracle."[114] No Protestant writers would have disagreed with this theological position, and yet the very assumptions it attacked remained embedded in linguistic theory and poetic practice throughout the sixteenth century.

Afterword

In *An Apologie for Poetrie*, Sidney defends the Roman name for the poet—"*Vates*, which is as much as a Diuiner, Fore-seer, or Prophet"—by attaching it to the Psalmist, often referred to by sixteenth-century writers as one of the "secretaries" of the Holy Ghost:

> And may not I presume a little further, to shew the reasonablenes of this worde *Vates*? And say that the holy *Dauids* Psalmes are a diuine Poem? If I doo, I shall not do it without the testimonie of great learned men, both auncient and moderne: but euen the name Psalmes will speake for mee, which, being interpreted, is nothing but songes. Then that it is fully written in meeter, as all learned Hebricians agree, although the rules be not yet fully found. Lastly and principally, his handeling his prophecy, which is meerely poetical. For what els is the awaking his musicall instruments; the often and free changing of persons; his notable *Prosopopeias*, when he maketh you, as it were, see God comming in his Maiestie; his telling of the Beastes ioyfulnes, and hills leaping, but a heauenlie poesie, wherein almost hee sheweth himselfe a passionate louer of that vnspeakable and euerlasting beautie to be seene by the eyes of the minde, onely cleered by fayth?[1]

Sidney here identifies what is "meerely poetical" in the Psalms first with their believed composition in meter, and then at length with their use "often and free" of rhetorical ornaments. When Sidney translated the first forty-three psalms into English verse, probably at about the time that this praise of them was written, he may have thought of the work as both a pious and a literary effort to rescue them from the monotonous meter and rhetorical plainness of the version by Sternhold and Hopkins, frequently printed both with the prayer book and the Bible for use in church. It may also have been a patriotic attempt to do in English what Marot had accomplished by translating the Psalms into French verse. Some such intentions may be hinted in the final sentence of the quoted paragraph praising the poetry of David:

> But truely now hauing named him, I feare mee I seeme to
> prophane that holy name, applying it to Poetrie, which is
> among vs throwne downe to so ridiculous an estimation: but
> they that with quiet iudgements will looke a little deeper into
> it, shall finde the end and working of it such, as beeing rightly
> applyed, deserueth not to bee scourged out of the Church
> of God.[2]

The versification of the Psalms by Sternhold and Hopkins may have
seemed a scourge of a kind to Sidney for the restrictions, designed to
suit it for congregational singing, of its rigid meter and unadorned
style. In Sidney's own English translation he combines a different
stanza form and rhyme scheme shaped to the sense of the words in
each psalm, a marked contrast to the unvarying stanzas of alternating
eight and six syllables used throughout the standard version.[3]

Equally pointed is Sidney's elaboration of verbal devices characteristic of his own and other sixteenth-century poetry, which are here
designed to match the richness he ascribes to the "meerely poetical"
style of David: adjective and noun pairings; interchangeable parts of
speech; puns and paradoxes; mixed metaphorical constructions; lavish
repetition of sounds, words, and phrases. These habits of language,
which preceding chapters have shown to be characteristic of sixteenth-century poetry, are also especially prevalent in it by contrast
with later writing. The change can be seen in epitome when we set
examples from Sidney's translations of the first eight psalms beside
Milton's versions of them, done in 1653.[4]

In making Psalm 1 into an English poem, Sidney uses many of the
devices shown to exemplify sixteenth-century verse. Most noticeable
are the sixteen pairings of adjectives with nouns in twenty-two lines:

1   He blessed is, who neither loosely treads
         The straying stepps as wicked Counsel leades;
     Ne for bad mates in way of sinning waiteth,
         Nor yet himself with idle scorners seateth:
2   But on God's law his heart's delight doth bind,
         Which night and day he calls to marking mind.

3   He shall be lyke a freshly planted tree,
         To which sweet springs of waters neighbours be,
     Whose braunches faile not timely fruite to nourish,
         Nor withered leafe shall make yt faile to flourish.
     So all the things whereto that man doth bend,
         Shall prosper still, with well succeeding end.

4   Such blessings shall not wycked wretches see:
            But lyke vyle chaffe with wind shal scattred be.
5   For neither shall the men in sin delighted
            Consist, when they to highest doome are cited,
        Ne yet shall suffred be a place to take,
            Wher godly men do their assumbly make.

6   For God doth know, and knowing doth approve
            The trade of them, that just proceeding love;
        But they that sinne, in sinfull breast do cherish;
            The way they go shal be their way to perish.[5]

Many of the combinations are bound together by alliteration of
the most obvious sort—"straying stepps," "marking mind," "sweet
springs," "wicked Counsel"—while at least one pair—"wicked
wretches"—combines likeness of sound with overlapping meanings
tending toward redundancy. The fact that several of the adjectival
terms are formed from verbs—"straying," "marking," "planted,"
"well succeeding"—shows how easily Sidney could have rearranged
the grammar of his translation, had he wished to avoid the predictable
effects of these pairings coming as they do in so many lines, sometimes reinforced in sound by alliteration with other words in the line:

    Whose braunches faile not timely fruite to nourish,
        Nor withered leafe shall make yt faile to flourish.

Instances of such reinforced pairings occur often in the translations,
as in Psalm 3: "My causeless wrongs hast wroken."[6] The insistence of
this dominant pattern gives prominence to nouns as well as to the
adjectives with which they are bound, associating poetry especially
with naming, the divinely instituted function of language.
    Milton avoids this grammatical design in his version of the first
psalm:

    Bless'd is the man who hath not walk'd astray
    In counsel of the wicked, and ith' way
    Of sinners hath not stood, and in the seat
    Of scorners hath not sate. But in the great
    Jehovahs Law is ever his delight,
    And in his Law he studies day and night.
    He shall be as a tree which planted grows
    By watry streams, and in his season knows
    To yield his fruit, and his leaf shall not fall,
    And what he takes in hand shall prosper all.
    Not so the wicked, but as chaff which fann'd

> The wind drives, so the wicked shall not stand
> In judgment, or abide their tryal then,
> Nor sinners in th' assembly of just men.
> For the Lord knows th' upright way of the just,
> And the way of bad men to ruine must.[7]

In these sixteen lines there are only four combinations of adjective and noun. Where Sidney names "sweet springs of waters" Milton says "wat'ry streams," and he uses "just men" where Sidney has "godly men" (perhaps to predict the sound of "God" in the next line). Milton's other pairings—"upright way," "bad men"—which occur in the last two lines have no equivalent combinations in Sidney's last stanza:

> For God doth know, and knowing doth approve
>   The trade of them, that just proceeding love;
> But they that sinne, in sinfull breast do cherish;
>   The way they go shal be their way to perish.

Instead of binding adjectives to nouns here, Sidney makes other kinds of links by repeating words in different grammatical forms and functions—"know," "knowing," "sinne," "sinfull"—as he often does elsewhere, for instance in Psalm 8: "Of glorious Croune, and crouning honour."[8] The effect is to blur distinctions between parts of speech, and to create combinations that can be thought of as a pair acting like a single name—*crowning crown*, *sinful sin*—rather than as a redundant descriptive phrase. Here again, therefore, the priority given to naming is embedded in stylistic choices.

In the last line Sidney repeats "way," as does Milton in his final couplet, but the repetitions work quite differently. Milton's makes a grammatical parallel between the "way of the just" and the "way of bad men" in order to point to the contrast between the rewards awaiting the upright and the ruin impending for the wicked. This is how "way" is repeated at the end of the first psalm in the Geneva Bible. Sidney, however, changes the meaning of the line in his translation: "The way they go shal be their way to perish." He seems to do this in order to play a metaphorical use—"The way they go" would have been described as wording borrowed from the place of a journey— against a natural or proper use—"their way" or their means leading them to ruin. The word play turns the line into a condensed version of an episode such as we have found in *The Faerie Queene*, and does so by using language shown to typify Spenser's allegory. For the line shifts between figurative and literal uses, as Sidney does again more radically in a metaphor in his version of Psalm 5. It has no equivalent in Milton's translation or in the Geneva Bible, but belongs to a type of figure previously shown to be common especially in religious writing: "And in they feare knees of my heart will fold."[9] The mixture of what were then called borrowed and proper words cannot make what would now be termed literal sense, nor can be taken as wholly figurative. It must, according to sixteenth-century theory, be partly re-translated to be interpreted. Reflected are the previously discussed assumptions embedded in sixteenth-century linguistic vocabulary about the relation between things and the names belonging to them, between words and the places from which they are taken.

In the last stanza of Psalm 1 Sidney creates another opportunity for word play in the line "The trade of them, that just proceeding love." For "proceeding" can be read simply as a noun equivalent to procedure, or as a present participle parallel to "knowing" in the line before, making "just" an adverb synonymous with simply, solely. The possibility is underscored by the pattern of words in shifting grammatical forms in the lines just above and below this one. Some of these word plays exploit multiple meanings as well as alternative spellings (as in "mutter murmures vaine" of Psalm 2, punning on *vein* which Sidney does also in *Astrophil and Stella* 6).[10] Others merely depend on repeated sounds along with different forms of repetition, creating effects which work less like puns than like rhymes. An instance is a particularly jingling line from Psalm 7: "Now brought abed, hath brought nought foorth, but nought."[11] What appears as trivial word play, or a facile appeal to the ears of an audience accustomed to hearing poetry read aloud, is also a way of binding words together in their common nominal function.

These verbal devices are to be found everywhere in Sidney's psalms as well as in the rest of his poetry and that of other sixteenth-century writers. The fact that he makes the common association of such poetic practices with religious expression, suiting them especially to imitate the "heauenly poesie" of David, is clearly shown in the style of his translations as exemplified in his version of Psalm 4:

1   Heare me, O heare me when I call
         O God, God of my Equity,
         Thou sett'st me free, when I was thrall,
         Have mercy therfore still on me,
         And hearken how I pray to Thee.

2   O men, whose Fathers were but men,
           Till when will ye my honour high
           Staine with your blasphemys? till when
           Such pleasure take in Vanity,
           And only hunt, where lyes do ly?

3   Yet know this too, that God did take
           When He chose me, a godly One:
           Such one I say, that when I make
           My crying plaints to him alone,
           He will give good eare to my moane.

4   O tremble then with awfull will:
           Sinne from all rule in you depose,
           Talk with your hearts, and yet be still:
           And when your chamber you do close,
           Yourselves yet to yourselves disclose.

5   The sacrifices sacrify
           Of just desires, on justice stayd,
           Trust in that lord, that cannot ly,
           Indeed full many folkes have said,
           From whence shall come to us such ayd?

6   But, lord, lift Thou upon our sight
           The shining clearness of thy face:
           Where I have found more heart's delight
           Than they whose stoare in harvest space
           Of grain and wine fills stoaring place.

7   So I in peace, and peacefull blisse
           Will lay me down, and take my rest:
           For it is thou lord, Thou it is,
           By power of whose only brest,
           I dwell, layd up in safest neast.[12]

All the uses of language illustrated in Psalm 1 are present again here
in lavish abundance, along with the central paradox in the exact
middle of the poem: "Talk with your hearts, and yet be still." It articulates what perhaps seemed, to a worshipper accustomed to common
prayer repeated aloud according to prescribed forms either in church
or in private houses, to be the paradoxical nature of silent devotions—
at once inward and expressed. For this figure there is no precedent in
the Geneva Bible or in the paraphrases of Calvin and Beza consulted
by Sidney.[13] There is also no parallel in Milton's version. Sidney's
placing of it in the center of the poem gives it importance reflecting

the association of paradox with supernatural power and therefore with its invocations in prayer and poetry.

Contributing to this association are Sidney's uses in Psalm 4 of repeated sounds—"awfull will," "full many folkes"—and repetition of words in different grammatical forms—"lyes do ly," "sacrifices sacrify," "just . . . justice," "peace . . . peacefull." These are given added prominence by the presence of another form of repetition epitomized in the opening stanza:

> Heare me, O heare me when I call
> O God, God of my Equity,
> Thou sett'st me free, when I was thrall,
> Have mercy therfore still on me,
> And hearken how I pray to Thee.

Formulas of prayer like those repeated in the first two lines recur throughout the translation—"O men," "O tremble," "For it is thou lord, Thou it is." This impression of predictable form is enhanced by the relatively simple rhyme words coming in endstopped lines, and by the metrical regularity, here especially in lines 3 and 5. The combined effects can be measured against the opening of Milton's version, which is made to seem more like what he calls "Unmeditated" prayer in *Paradise Lost* (5.149) than Sidney's ritualistic language:

> Answer me when I call
> God of my righteousness;
> In straits and in distress
> Thou didst me disinthrall
> And set at large; now spare,
> Now pity me, and hear my earnest prai'r.
> Great ones how long will ye
> My glory have in scorn
> How long be thus forborn
> Still to love vanity,
> To love, to seek, to prize
> Things false and vain and nothing else but lies?
> Yet know the Lord hath chose,
> Chose to himself a part
> The good and meek of heart
> (For whom to chuse he knows)
> Jehovah from on high
> Will hear my voyce what time to him I crie.
> Be aw'd, and do not sin,
> Speak to your hearts alone,

Upon your beds, each one,
And be at peace within.
Offer the offerings just
    Of righteousness and in Jehovah trust.
Many there be that say
Who yet will shew us good?
Talking like this worlds brood;
But Lord, thus let me pray,
On us lift up the light
    Lift up the favor of thy count'nance bright.
Into my heart more joy
And gladness thou hast put
Then when a year of glut
Their stores doth over-cloy
And from their plenteous grounds
    With vast increase their corn and wine abounds.
In peace at once will I
Both lay me down and sleep
For thou alone dost keep
Me safe where ere I lie
As in a rocky Cell
    Thou Lord alone in safety mak'st me dwell.[14]

Like Sidney in line 26, Milton in his corresponding line 29 follows
the original in asking God to lift the light of his countenance on a
collective petitioner. In other ways, however, he mainly avoids the
devices that in Sidney's version imitate the effects of prescribed
prayer. Repetitions such as prominent alliterative patterns are suppressed—as "O tremble then with awfull will" is replaced by "Be
aw'd"—and shifting grammatical forms are eliminated—as "lyes do
ly" becomes "nothing else but lies." He also largely avoids the formulaic patterns that Sidney establishes in his opening lines. Milton's
corresponding stanza, for example, repeats no phrases, lessens the
prominence of rhyme by using more polysyllabic words at the ends
of lines that are not endstopped, and by these combined devices imitates a voice meditating in prayer more than a public recitation of a
liturgy.

The changes illustrated in translations of psalms by these two poets
must of course be traced in part to revolutionary transformations of
thought and practice within English Protestantism in the seventy
years between Sidney's translations of psalms and Milton's. These
movements clearly are not the subject of explicit discussion in this
book. Yet since the characteristics of Sidney's language in his versions

of psalms have been shown to be representative of sixteenth-century verse, their radical differences from Milton's must be understood also in the light of changes in conceptions of language and in the most fundamental assumptions on which it is predicated. These altered ways of thinking dissolved the close association of poetry with the art of naming, making less accessible and appealing, even to poets writing not long after, the uses of language which in sixteenth-century English verse embodied this association. Its unravelling caused a profound division in kind between poetry written in the first and second halves of the period of literary history called the English Renaissance.

Notes

Preface

1. Thomas Wilson, *Wilson's Arte of Rhetorique 1560*, edited by G. H. Mair (Oxford: Clarendon Press, 1909), 156–57.

2. Edward Corbett, *Classical Rhetoric for the Modern Student* (New York: Oxford University Press, 1982), 4.

3. For a recent use of this definition of the English Renaissance see Thomas Greene, *The Light in Troy* (New Haven: Yale University Press, 1982), 4.

4. Ivor Winters, "The 16th Century Lyric in England," in *Elizabethan Poetry*, edited by Paul Alpers (New York: Oxford University Press, 1967), 93–125; reprinted from *Poetry* 53 (1939): 258–72, 320–35; 54 (1939): 35–51.

5. Anne Ferry, *All in War with Time* (Cambridge, Mass.: Harvard University Press, 1975).

6. Anne Ferry, *The "Inward" Language* (Chicago: University of Chicago Press, 1983).

7. Jean Howard, "The New Historicism in Renaissance Studies," *ELR* 16 (1986): 23.

8. Louis Montrose, "A Poetics of Renaissance Culture," *Criticism* 23 (1981): 358.

9. Howard, "New Historicism," 23.

10. Michael McCanles, "The Authentic Discourse of the Renaissance," *Diacritics* (1980): 86.

11. Richard Helgerson, *Self-Crowned Laureates* (Berkeley: University of California Press, 1983), 4.

12. Kenneth Gross, *Spenserian Poetics* (Ithaca: Cornell University Press, 1985), 146–51.

13. Stephen Greenblatt, "As They Like It," *The New Republic* (10 Nov. 1986): 45.

14. Rosemond Tuve, *Elizabethan and Metaphysical Imagery* (Chicago: University of Chicago Press, 1961), 327, 309.

15. Josephine Miles, "Major Adjectives in English Poetry," *University of California Publications in English* 12 (1946): 305–64.

16. John Hollander, *The Figure of Echo* (Berkeley: University of California Press, 1984), 133.

17. Michel Foucault, *The Order of Things* (New York: Vintage, 1973), xxii. Evidence of the pervasive influence of this work is that it is cited as a "prime text" for the study of sixteenth-century English poetry in a recent critical introduction for students of the period by Gary Waller, *English Poetry of the Sixteenth Century* (London:

Longman, 1986), 289. The index lists twenty pages containing references to Foucault.

18. See Foucault, *Order of Things*, 43; *un art donc de nommer, Les mots et les choses* (Paris: Gallimard, 1966), 58.

Introduction

1. The *O.E.D.* cites this objection with the added information that it is removed from the second edition of the work in 1632, suggesting that the word had become familiar by that date.

2. William Shakespeare, *Shakespeare's Sonnets*, edited by Stephen Booth (New Haven: Yale University Press, 1978). All quotations from the sonnets are taken from this edition and are cited by number in the text only.

3. Among more recent studies are: Charles Barber, *Early Modern English* (London: André Deutsch, 1976); G. L. Brook, *The Language of Shakespeare* (London: André Deutsch, 1976); Margreta De Grazia, "Shakespeare's View of Language: An Historical Perspective," *Shakespeare Quarterly* 29 (1978): 374–88; Jane Donawerth, *Shakespeare and the Sixteenth Century Study of Language* (Urbana: University of Illinois Press, 1984); Marion Trousdale, *Shakespeare and the Rhetoricians* (Chapel Hill: University of North Carolina Press, 1982); Richard Waswo, *Language and Meaning in the Renaissance* (Princeton: Princeton University Press, 1987). Older studies include: Owen Barfield, *History in English Words* (London: Faber and Faber, 1954); Albert Baugh, *A History of the English Language* (New York: Appleton Century, 1935); George Gordon, *Shakespeare's English* (Oxford: Clarendon Press, 1923); Hilda Hulme, *Explorations in Shakespeare's Language* (London: Longmans, 1962); George McKnight, *English Words and Their Background* (New York: D. Appleton, 1923); Robert Peters, *A Linguistic History of English* (New York: Houghton Mifflin, 1968); Margaret Schlauch, *The English Language* (London: Oxford University Press, 1964); H. C. Wyld, *A History of Modern Colloquial English* (London: T. Fisher Unwin, 1921). Other such studies are cited elsewhere with reference to particular aspects of linguistic history.

4. Edmund Spenser, *The Faerie Queene*, in *The Works of Edmund Spenser. A Variorum Edition*, edited by Edwin Greenlaw, et al. (Baltimore: Johns Hopkins University Press, 1932–38). All quotations from the poem are taken from this edition and are cited by book, canto, and line number in the text only.

5. *Tottel's Miscellany*, rev. ed., edited by Hyder Rollins (Cambridge, Mass.: Harvard University Press, 1965), 1:121.

6. Sir Philip Sidney, *The Poems of Sir Philip Sidney*, edited by William Ringler (Oxford: Clarendon Press, 1962), 84.

7. Edward Fairfax, *Godfrey of Bovlogne* (London, 1624), book 3, stanza 6, p. 40.

8. John Thompson, *The Founding of English Metre* (New York: Columbia University Press, 1961), 65.

9. For a recent discussion of this continuity, see A. C. Spearing, *Medieval and Renaissance in English Poetry* (Cambridge: Cambridge University Press, 1985).

10. Sir Philip Sidney, "An Apologie for Poetrie," in *Elizabethan Critical Essays*, edited by G. G. Smith (London: Oxford University Press, 1950), 1:196.

11. Abraham Fraunce, *The Arcadian Rhetorike* (1588), edited by Ethel Seaton (Oxford: Basil Blackwell, 1950), 105.

12. Mikhail Bakhtin, *Rabelais and His World*, trans. by Helen Iswolsky

(Bloomington: Indiana University Press, 1984), 455–56.

13. For a classic statement of this view see Sir Sidney Lee's "Introduction" in *Elizabethan Sonnets*, edited by Sidney Lee (New York: E. P. Dutton, n.d.), 1:xlix–lxxxv.

14. See especially Roland Barthes, *Mythologies* (New York: Hill and Wang, 1977).

15. For a typical example, see remarks about Arthur Golding's verse by C. S. Lewis, *English Literature of the Sixteenth Century* (Oxford: Clarendon Press, 1954), 251–53.

Chapter One

1. Thomas Cooper, *Thesavrvs Lingvae* (London, 1584).

2. Thomas Sternhold and John Hopkins, *The Whole Booke of Psalmes* (London, 1586), psalme i.

3. William Camden, *Remaines* (London, 1605), 18.

4. George Puttenham, *The Arte of English Poesie*, edited by Gladys Willcock and Alice Walker (Cambridge: Cambridge University Press, 1936), 144.

5. *The Heritage Illustrated Dictionary of the English Language*, edited by William Morris (Boston: Houghton Mifflin, 1979), 2:1085.

6. Maureen Quilligan, *The Language of Allegory* (Ithaca: Cornell University Press, 1979), 288, and see also pp. 258–60; A. Leigh DeNeef, *Spenser and the Motives for Metaphor* (Durham, N.C.: Duke University Press, 1982), 154. DeNeef's discussion on pp. 142–56 consistently treats the verb as used in *The Faerie Queene* as a metaphor or "metaphoric conceit" (p. 146).

7. Paul Alpers, *The Poetry of "The Faerie Queene"* (Princeton: Princeton University Press, 1967), 90.

8. For example, see Stephen Greenblatt, "A Note on Texts" explaining that in his study all texts are modernized except Spenser's poetry, out of respect for his "attempt to cast the glow of antiquity upon his work," *Renaissance Self-Fashioning* (Chicago: University of Chicago Press, 1980).

9. Sir Philip Sidney, "Astrophil and Stella," in *The Poems*. All quotations from this sonnet sequence are taken from this edition and are cited by number in the text only.

10. Ernst Curtius, *European Literature and the Latin Middle Ages*, trans. by Willard Trask (New York: Pantheon, 1953), 332.

11. Ibid., 335.

12. Angus Fletcher, *The Prophetic Moment* (Chicago: University of Chicago Press, 1971), 100–103.

13. Foucault, *Order of Things*, 38.

14. John Hart, "The opening of the unreasonable writing of our inglish toung" (1557), in *John Hart's Works*, edited by B. Danielsson (Stockholm: Almquist and Wiksell, 1955), 1:118.

15. Cooper, *Thesavrvs Lingvae;* Michel de Montaigne, *The Essayes of Montaigne*, trans. by John Florio (New York: Modern Library, 1933), 560.

16. Francis Clement, "The Petie Schole with an English Orthographie" (1587), in *Four Tudor Books on Education*, edited by Robert Pepper (Gainesville: Scholars' Facsimiles and Reprints, 1966), 59; William Bullokar, "A short Introduction or guiding to print, write, and reade Inglish speech" (1580), in *The Works of William*

Bullokar, edited by B. Danielsson and R. C. Alston (Oxford: for The University of Leeds, 1966), 1:ii; Pierre de la Primaudaye, *The French Academie*, trans. by T. Bowes (London, 1586), 132; Robert Robinson, *The Art of Pronuntiation* (1617), (Menston: Scolar Press, 1969), heading for the section on writing; John Baret, *An Alvearie or Quadruple Dictionarie* (London, 1581).

17. Ralph Lever, *The Arte of Reason* (1573), (Menston: Scolar Press, 1972), 1; Peter Ramus, *The Rvdimentes of P. Ramvs his Latine Grammar* (Menston: Scolar Press, 1971), 1; Fraunce, *Arcadian Rhetorike*, 3; Leonard Cox, *The Arte or Crafte of Rhetoryke*, edited by Frederic Carpenter (Chicago: University of Chicago Press, 1899), 48; Wilson, *Art of Rhetorique*, 166; William Tyndale, "The obedience of a Christen man" (1528), in *The Whole workes of W. Tyndall, Iohn Frith, and Doct. Barnes* (London, 1573), 166; John Bodenham, *Politeuphuia* (London, 1598), 166; Robert Cawdrey, *A Table Alphabeticall of Hard Usual English Words* (1604), edited by Robert Peters (Gainesville: Scholars' Facsimiles and Reprints, 1966), 92, 76; Henry Peacham, *The Garden of Eloquence* (1593), (Gainesville: Scholars' Facsimiles and Reprints, 1954), 15; unless otherwise specified all references to this work are to this edition.

18. Richard Mulcaster, *Mulcaster's Elementarie* (1582), edited by E. T. Campagnac (Oxford: Clarendon Press, 1925), 167; quoted by Walter Ong, "Historical Backgrounds of Elizabethan and Jacobean Punctuation Theory," *PMLA* 59 (1944): 355. For discussion of the shift from oral to silent reading habits, see Walter Ong, *The Barbarian Within* (New York: Macmillan, 1962), 175.

19. Desiderius Erasmus, *Prouerbs or Adagies, gathered out of the Chiliades of Erasmus*, trans. by Richard Taverner (London, 1569), 46, 64.

20. Thomas Becon, *The Reliques of Rome* (London, 1563), fol. 123.

21. Joseph Hall, "A Commendatory Preface," in John Brinsley, *Lvdvs Literarivs: or, The Grammar Schoole* (London, 1612), 1.

22. Mulcaster, *Elementarie*, 73.

23. Sir Thomas More, "The Confvtacion of Tyndales Avnsvvere" (1532), in *Th workes of Syr Thomas More*, edited by William Rastall (London, 1557), 445.

24. Tyndale, "An aunswere vnto Syr Thomas Mores Dialogue" (1530), in *Whole workes*, 255.

25. Sir Thomas Elyot, *The Boke named The Gouernour* (1531), edited by Henry Croft (London: Kegan Paul, Trench, 1883), 2:227.

26. Hart, "Opening of the unreasonable writing," 1:123.

27. Mulcaster, *Elementarie*, 246.

28. Baret, *Alvearie*, introduction to E.

29. A Monroe Stowe, *English Grammar Schools in the Reign of Queen Elizabeth* (New York: Teachers College, Columbia University, 1908), 104–10.

30. Edmund Coote, *The English Schoole-Maister* (1596), (Menston: Scolar Press, 1968), 72–73. The passage is repeated by Cawdrey, "To the Reader," *Table Alphabeticall*, 8.

31. Sir Thomas Elyot, *Banket of Sapience* (London, 1546), 51–53. For an account of the development of alphabetization, see Lloyd Daly, *Contributions to a History of Alphabetization* (Brussels: Latomus Revue D'Études Latines, 1967).

32. Walter Ong, *Interfaces of the Word* (Ithaca: Cornell University Press, 1977), 169.

33. Peter Levens, "To the right worshipful M. Stanley," in *Manipvlvs Vocabvlorvm* (1570), (Menston: Scolar Press, 1969).

34. William Clerk, *A Dictionarie in English and Latine for Children* (London, 1602), 324. This edition by Clerk was revised and augmented from earlier editions starting in 1553 by John Withal et al.

35. Thomas Campion, "Observations in the Art of English Poesie" (1602), in *Elizabethan Critical Essays*, 2:352.

36. Coote, "The Preface for direction to *the Reader*," in *English Schoole-Maister*.

37. "Arthur Golding to the reader," prefixed to Baret, *Alvearie*; Coote, *English Schoole-Maister*, 30.

38. Puttenham, *Arte of English Poesie*, 145.

39. Charles Butler, *English Grammar* (1634), (Halle: Max Niemeyer, 1910), 29.

40. William Bullokar, "Bullokars Booke at large" (1580), edited by J. R. Turner in *The Works*, 3:2. For discussions of the rise of printing and its influence on language, see Elizabeth Eisenstein, *The Printing Press as an Agent of Change* (Cambridge: Cambridge University Press, 1979); Hereward Price, "Grammar and the Compositor in the Sixteenth and Seventeenth Centuries," *JEGP* 38 (1939): 540–48; D. G. Scragg, *A History of English Spelling* (Manchester: Manchester University Press, 1974), 64–87. Accusations against printers are cited by E. J. Dobson, *English Pronunciation 1500–1700* (Oxford: Clarendon Press, 1954), 136.

41. Camden, *Remaines*, 23.

42. Bullokar, "Bullokars Booke at large," 2.

43. Puttenham, *Arte of English Poesie*, 161.

44. Henry Peacham, *The Garden of Eloquence* (1577), (Gainesville: Scholars' Facsimiles and Reprints, 1954), Dj. An example of adjusted spelling in prose is the substitution for *art* of "hart" in a description of women using cosmetics to make literal blazons of themselves translated from Annibale Romei, *The Courtiers Academie* (1598), 29: "making their haire like the shining colour of gold, the cheekes like to white lillies and red roses, the lips to rubies, the teeth to orient whitenes of pearle . . . kindling by such hart, in the harts of men amarous flames." For discussion of the blazon, see chapter 4.

45. Puttenham, *Arte of English Poesie*, 82.

46. Curtius, *European Literature*, 337.

47. William Shakespeare, *The life and death of King Richard the Second*, in *Mr. William Shakespeares Comedies, Histories, & Tragedies*, edited by Helge Kökeritz (New Haven: Yale University Press, 1954), 4.1.344. All passages quoted from Shakespeare's plays are taken from this facsimile edition and are cited by act, scene, and page number in the notes.

48. William Shakespeare, *The Second Part of Henry the Fourth*, 2.3.383–84.

49. Curtius, *European Literature*, 336–37.

50. William Shakespeare, "Lvcrece," in *The Poems: The New Variorum Edition of Shakespeare*, edited by Hyder Rollins (Philadelphia: J. B. Lippencott, 1938), 171.

51. Foucault, *Order of Things*, 27; *Les mots et les choses*, 42. The same assumption is at work in the argument that Spenser's uses of *read* warn us that "all observations are metaphoric acts of reading," made by DeNeef, *Spenser and the Motives for Metaphor*, 147.

52. Sidney, *Poems*, 60.

53. Robert Southwell, *The Complete Poems of Robert Southwell*, edited by Alexander Grosart (New York: AMS Press, 1971), 27; Fulke Greville, *Poems and Dramas*

of Fulke Greville, edited by Geoffrey Bullough (New York: Oxford University Press, 1945), 1:98.

54. Samuel Daniel, "A Defence of Ryme," in *Poems and a Defence of Ryme*, edited by Arthur Colby Sprague (Cambridge: Mass.: Harvard University Press, 1930), 139; Sir Francis Bacon, *The Tvvoo Bookes of Francis Bacon. Of the proficience and advancement of Learning, diuine and humane* (London, 1605), 6. For discussion of this metaphor, see Curtius, *European Literature*, 337.

55. John Boys, *An Exposition of Al the Principal Scriptvres Vsed in our English Liturgie* (London, 1610), 34.

56. John Dee, "Mathematicall Præface," in *The Elements of Geometrie of the most auncient Philosopher Evclide*, trans. by Henry Billingsley (London, 1570), bij; Boys, *An Exposition*, 34.

57. Joshua Sylvester, trans., "The first Day of the first Weeke," in *Bartas His Deuine Weekes and Workes* (London, 1605), 6–7.

58. James Cleland, *The Institvtion of a Yovng Noble Man* (Oxford, 1607), 59.

59. John Hoskyns, "Direccions for Speech and Style," in *The Life, Letters, and Writings of John Hoskyns*, edited by Louise Osborn (New Haven: Yale University Press, 1937), 116.

60. Richard Hooker, *Of the Lawes of Ecclesiastical Politie. The fift Booke* (London, 1597), 30.

61. Mulcaster, *Elementarie*, 188. For recent discussions of linguistic theories in the *Cratylus*, see: Thomas Bestor, "Plato's Semantics and Plato's 'Cratylus,'" *Phronesis* 25 (1980): 306–30; Gail Fine, "Plato on Naming," *Philosophical Quarterly* 27 (1977): 289–301; W. K. C. Guthrie, *A History of Greek Philosophy* (Cambridge: Cambridge University Press, 1978), 5:1–31; Richard Ketchum, "Names, Forms and Conventionalism: Cratylus, 383–395," *Phronesis* 24 (1979): 133–47. For distinctions between Plato and Aristotle on this issue, see R. H. Robins, *A Short History of Linguistics* (Bloomington: Indiana University Press, 1968), 18–19.

62. Lever, "The Forespeache," *Arte of Reason*.

63. For discussions of this passage, see DeNeef, *Spenser and the Motives for Metaphor*, 133, 144; A. Bartlett Giamatti, *Play of Double Senses* (Englewood Cliffs: Prentice-Hall, 1975), 117. For discussions of etymologies in *The Faerie Queene*, see Martha Craig, "The Secret Wit of Spenser's Language," *Elizabethan Poetry*, 447–72; Fletcher, *Prophetic Moment*, 100–103; A. C. Hamilton, "Our new poet: Spenser, 'well of English undefyld,'" in *A Theatre for Spenserians*, edited by Judith Kennedy and James Reither (Toronto: University of Toronto Press, 1973), 105.

64. Thomas Wilson, *The Rule of Reason*, edited by Richard Sprague (Northridge: San Fernando State College, 1972), 8.

65. Mulcaster, *Elementarie*, 115. Elsewhere, on p. 72, he argues that there is a conventional rather than a natural relation between the spoken and the written word: "for what likenesse or what affinitie hath the form of anie letter in his own natur, to answer the force or sound in mans voice?"

66. Hart, "opening of the unreasonable writing," 1:118, 123–24; "An Orthographie" (1569), in *John Hart's Works*, 1:170–71.

67. Stephen Batman, *The Golden Booke of the Leaden Goddes* (1577), (New York: Garland Publishing, 1976), 22–23.

68. Baret, *Alvearie*, introduction to A.

69. Thomas Johnson, "A New Booke of New Conceits" (1630), in *The Liter-*

ature of the Sixteenth and Seventeenth Centuries, edited by James Halliwell (London, 1851), 211.

70. Baret, *Alvearie*, introduction to E.

71. Sir Thomas More, "A Dialogve of Syr Thomas More Knyghte" (1528), in *The workes*, 114.

72. Richard Carew, "The Excellency of the English Tongue," in *Elizabethan Critical Essays*, 2:287. For discussion of the term *indiuiduum*, see Ferry, *The "Inward" Language*, 33–39.

73. Elyot, *Gouernour*, 2:212.

74. Thomas Watson, *Poems*, edited by Edward Arber (London, 1879), 116. For discussion of shaped poems, see Martin Elsky, "George Herbert's Pattern Poems and the Materiality of Language," *ELH* 5 (1983): 245–60.

75. Sylvester, "First Day of the first Weeke," in *Bartas*, 5.

76. George Gascoigne, *The Complete Poems of George Gascoigne*, edited by William Hazlitt (London: Roxburge Library, 1869), 1:400.

77. Sylvester, "First Day of the first Weeke," in *Bartas*, 5.

78. Peacham, *Garden of Eloquence*, 8.

79. Carew, *Excellency of the English Tongue*, 2:287.

80. Peacham, *Garden of Eloquence*, 14–15.

81. Elyot, *Gouernour*, 1:241–42.

82. Peacham, *Garden of Eloquence*, 4–5.

83. William Lily and John Colet, "The Concordes of latine speche, The Seconde Concorde," in *A Shorte Introdvction of Grammar* (1549), (Menston: Scolar Press, 1970).

84. Andrea Guarna, "Bellum Grammaticale," trans. by W. Hayward, in *A Collection of Scarce and Valuable Tracts*, 2d ed., edited by Sir Walter Scott (London, 1809), 1:551.

85. In medieval theory a noun reflects the thing it represents and its gender according to Marjorie Boyle, *Erasmus on Language and Method in Theology* (Toronto: University of Toronto Press, 1977), 34.

86. Hooker, *Lawes of Ecclesiastical Politie*, 146.

87. John Brinsley, *The Posing of the Parts* (London, 1612), 2–3.

88. John Milton, "Paradise Lost," in *The Works of John Milton*, edited by F. A. Patterson (New York: Columbia University Press, 1931), 2:275. All references to *Paradise Lost* are to this edition and are cited by book and line in the text only.

89. Peacham, *Garden of Eloquence*, 146.

90. Edmund Spenser, "Epithalamion," in *The Minor Poems*, vol. 2 of *The Works of Edmund Spenser*, edited by C. G. Osgood and H. G. Lotspeich (Baltimore: Johns Hopkins Press, 1947), 246.

91. Paul Alpers, "Narration in *The Faerie Queene*," *ELH* 44 (1977), 19–39.

92. Ibid.

Chapter Two

1. Edmund Spenser, "Amoretti," in *Minor Poems*, 2. All quotations from this sonnet sequence are taken from this edition and cited by number in the text only.

2. For examples of these and other lists of epithets quoted elsewhere from *The Faerie Queene*, see *A Concordance to the Poems of Edmund Spenser*, edited by Charles Osgood (Washington: Carnegie Institute, 1915). For discussion of them, see Ong,

Interfaces of the Word, 195; John Webster, "Oral Form and Written Craft in Spenser's *Faerie Queene*," *SEL* 16 (1976): 75–93. This habit is dismissed as "unimaginative" by A. C. Partridge, *The Language of Renaissance Poetry* (London: André Deutsch, 1971), 65.

3. See for example: Sidney, *Poems*, 331, 59; Arthur Golding, trans., *The .XV. Bookes of P. Ouidius Naso, entytuled Metamorphosis* (1567), edited by John Frederick Nims (New York: Macmillan, 1965), book 1, line 317, p. 12; *Tottel's Miscellany*, 1:159; Watson, *Poems*, 44.

4. Barnabe Googe, *Eclogs, Epytaphes, & Sonettes*, edited by Edward Arber (London: English Reprints, 1871), 101.

5. *Tottel's Miscellany*, 1:145.

6. For discussion of the apostrophe, see Barber, *Early Modern English*, 198.

7. For a typical instance of this kind of accusation, see Nims, "Introduction," *Metamorphosis*, xxii–xxiii.

8. Samuel Daniel, "Delia," in *Poems and a Defence of Ryme*. All quotations from this sonnet sequence are taken from this edition and are cited by number in the text only.

9. John Harington, trans., *Orlando Fvrioso* (1591), (New York: Da Capo Press, 1970), book 6, stanza 70, p. 46.

10. See for example: Richard Barnfield, *The Poems of Richard Barnfield* (London: Fortune Press, n.d.), 24, 120, 19, 73; Harington, *Orlando Fvrioso*, book 10, stanza 14, p. 66. For discussion of such compounds in Spenser, see Frederick Padelford and William Maxwell, "The Compound Words in Spenser's Poetry," *JEGP* 25 (1926): 498–516.

11. See Spenser in *Concordance*; Gascoigne, *Complete Poems*, 2:335.

12. Angell Day, *A Declaration of al such Tropes, Figures or Schemes, as for excellencie and ornament in writing, are speciallie vsed in this Methode* (1599), edited by Robert Evans (Gainesville: Scholars' Facsimiles and Reprints, 1967), 83, 78.

13. E. A. Abbott, *A Shakespearian Grammar* (London: Macmillan, 1870), 19.

14. See for example: Nicholas Breton, *Poems by Nicholas Breton*, edited by Jean Robertson (Liverpool: Liverpool University Press, 1952), 50, 177, 194; Gascoigne, *Complete Poems*, 1:58, 68; Spenser in *Concordance*. For discussion, see Herbert Sugden, *The Grammar of Spenser's "Faerie Queene"* (Philadelphia: Linguistic Society of America, 1936), 82–87.

15. Peacham, *Garden of Eloquence* (1577), Giiii. For discussions of the adjective, see: R. M. W. Dixon, *Where Have All the Adjectives Gone?* (Berlin: Mouton, 1982); Ian Michael, *English Grammatical Categories* (Cambridge: Cambridge University Press, 1970), 90–107.

16. George Gascoigne, "Certayne Notes of Instruction," in *Elizabethan Critical Essays*, 1:51.

17. Torquato Tasso, *Gervsalemme liberata* (Casalmaggiore, 1581), book 16, stanza 15, p. 151; Fairfax, *Godfrey of Bovlogne*, book 16, stanza 15, p. 283; book 3, stanza 6, p. 40.

18. Southwell, *Complete Poems*, 43.

19. Lily, *Shorte Introdvction of Grammar*, appendix 1, a.iiii; Butler, *English Grammar*, 36.

20. Ivan Poldauf, *On the History of Some Problems of English Grammar Before 1800* (Prague: Prague Studies in English, 1948), 271.

21. Peacham, *Garden of Eloquence*, 146.

22. Puttenham, *Arte of English Poesie*, 176. For discussion of sixteenth-century definitions of this and other figures, see Sister Miriam Joseph, *Shakespeare's Use of the Arts of Language* (New York: Columbia University Press, 1949); Herbert Rix, "Rhetoric in Spenser's Poetry," *Pennsylvania State College Bulletin* 34 (1946); Lee Sonnino, *A Handbook to Sixteenth-Century Rhetoric* (London: Routledge and Kegan Paul, 1968); Tuve, *Elizabethan and Metaphysical Imagery*.

23. Thomas Blundeville, *The Arte of Logicke* (London, 1619), 15.

24. Ibid., 20.

25. Lever, *Arte of Reason*, 161.

26. Ibid., 10.

27. Blundeville, *Arte of Logicke*, 20.

28. For historical discussions of this grammatical distinction, see G. L. Bursill-Hall, *Speculative Grammars of the Middle Ages* (The Hague: Mouton, 1971), 49; Michael Frede, "Principles of Stoic Grammar," in *The Stoics*, edited by John Rist (Berkeley: University of California Press, 1978), 68–69; G. A. Padley, *Grammatical Theory in Western Europe* (Cambridge: Cambridge University Press, 1976), 39; R. H. Robins, *Ancient and Medieval Grammatical Theory in Europe* (London: G. Bell, 1951), 26–27.

29. The scarcity of adjectives in poetry of the 1540s is in the Chaucerian tradition according to Josephine Miles, "The Primary Language of Poetry in the 1640's," in *The Continuity of Poetic Language* (Berkeley: University of California Press, 1951), 15. On Chaucer's use of adjectives, see also Vera Rubel, *Poetic Diction in the English Renaissance* (New York: The Modern Language Association, 1941), 22.

30. John Mendenhall, *Aureate Terms* (Lancaster, Penn.: Wickersham, 1919), 14.

31. Alfred North Whitehead, *Science and the Modern World* (New York: Free Press, 1967), 54. See also, Murray Cohen, *Sensible Words* (Baltimore: Johns Hopkins University Press, 1977), 38–40; Paul de Man, "The Epistemology of Metaphor," in *On Metaphor*, edited by Sheldon Sacks (Chicago: University of Chicago Press, 1981), 14; Otto Jesperson, *The Philosophy of Grammar* (New York: Henry Holt, 1948), 74–75.

32. Roger Ascham, "The Scholemaster" (1570), in *English Works*, edited by William Wright (Cambridge: Cambridge University Press, 1970), 182.

33. Blundeville, *Arte of Logicke*, 27.

34. For discussion of the phrase *inward heart*, see Ferry, *The "Inward" Language*, 59–70. For uses of *constant heart* see for example: Shakespeare, Sonnet 53; *Tottel's Miscellany*, 1:160; Harington, *Orlando Fvrioso*, book 43, stanza 21, p. 360.

35. Some examples are: Gascoigne, *Complete Poems*, 1:358, 403, 407; Googe, *Eglogs, Epytaphes, and Sonettes*, 76, 87; Harington, *Orlando Fvrioso*, book 14, stanza 46, p. 106; book 23, stanza 96, p. 184; Southwell, *Complete Poems*, 93.

36. Edmund Spenser, "Ruines of Rome," *Minor Poems*, 2:152.

37. Wilson, *Rule of Reason*, 26.

38. Blundeville, *Arte of Logicke*, 91.

39. Wilson, *Rule of Reason*, 19–20.

40. Michael, *English Grammatical Categories*, 255.

41. Sidney, *Poems*, 84.

42. On the development of a history of the language, see R. F. Jones, *The*

Triumph of the English Language (Palo Alto: Stanford University Press, 1966); J. L. Moore, *Tudor-Stuart Views on the Growth, Status and Destiny of the English Language* (Halle: Niemeyer, 1910); A. C. Partridge, *Tudor to Augustan English* (London: André Deutsch, 1969). On the development of dictionaries, see James Murray, *The Evolution of English Lexicography* (Oxford: Clarendon Press, 1900); De Witt Starnes, *Renaissance Dictionaries* (Austin: University of Texas Press, 1954).

43. On the teaching of Latin, see Foster Watson, *English Grammar Schools to 1660* (New York: Augustus M. Kelley, 1970), 233.

44. Derek Attridge, *Well-weighed syllables* (Cambridge: Cambridge University Press, 1974), 45; W. Keith Percival, "Grammar and Rhetoric in the Renaissance," in *Renaissance Eloquence*, edited by James Murphy (Berkeley: University of California Press, 1983), 303; Michael, *English Grammatical Categories*, 203.

45. Wilson, *Rule of Reason*, 18, 117.

46. Clerk, *Dictionarie*, 325.

47. Richard Sherry, *A Treatise of Schemes and Tropes* (1550), (Gainesville: Scholars' Facsimiles and Reprints, 1961), 70.

48. Lily, *Shorte Introdvction of Grammar*, Appendix 1, a.iiii; Cooper, *Thesavrvs Lingvae*; Blundeville, *Art of Logicke*, 17.

49. Ramus, *Rvdimentes*, 2.

50. Peacham, *Garden of Eloquence*, 14.

51. Puttenham, *Arte of English Poesie*, 180–82; Peacham, *Garden of Eloquence*, 16.

52. Golding, *Metamorphosis*, book 7, lines 686-87, p. 179.

53. Barnfield, *Poems*, 19.

54. Gascoigne, *Complete Poems*, 1:151.

55. Watson, *Poems*, 54. A source for Shakespeare in Textor's *Epitheta* is suggested by Ong, *Interfaces of the Word*, 183–84. Wilson's *The Arte of Rhetorique* is the source suggested by Douglas Peterson, "A Reliable Source for Shakespeare's Sonnet CXXIX," *Shakespeare Quarterly* 5 (1954): 381–84.

56. *Tottel's Miscellany*, 1:137; John Donne, *The Divine Poems*, edited by Helen Gardner (Oxford: Clarendon Press, 1966), 11.

57. Becon, *Reliques of Rome*, fol. 163.

58. Lily, *Shorte Introdvction of Grammar*, Appendix 1, a.iiii.

59. Wilson, *Rule of Reason*, 15.

60. Ibid., 17.

61. John Rainolds, *The Svmme of the Conference Betwene Iohn Rainoldes and Iohn Hart* (London, 1584), 538.

62. Sherry, *A Treatise of Schemes and Tropes*, 20.

63. Peter Ramus, *The Logike of the Moste Excellent Philosopher P. Ramus Martyr* (1574), trans. by Roland MacIlmaine, edited by Catherine Dunne (Northridge: San Fernando Valley State College, 1969), 29–30. For discussions of the etymology of names, see Curtius, *European Literature*, especially pp. 43–44, 495–500. On the incorrectness of Old Testament etymologies of names, see James Barr, *The Semantics of Biblical Language* (Oxford: Oxford University Press, 1975), 109.

64. Ramus, *Logike*, 31.

65. Sylvester, "Babilon. The second Booke of the second Day, of the second Weeke," in *Bartas*, 425.

66. John Marbeck, *A Booke of Notes and Common places* (London, 1581), 521.

For discussion of Reuchlin's belief in the "wonder-working" name of the Son, see Joseph Blau, *The Christian Interpretation of the Cabala in the Renaissance* (New York: Columbia University Press, 1944), 49.

67. Camden, *Remaines*, 26, 18.

68. Carew, "Excellency of the English Tongue," 2:287.

69. Rainolds, *Svmme of the Conference*, 609.

70. Elyot, *Gouernour*, 2:227.

71. Mulcaster, *Elementarie*, 188.

72. Wolfgang Musculus, *Common places of the Christian Religion*, trans. by John Man (London, 1563), fol. 367.

73. Wilson, *Arte of Rhetorique*, 165–66.

74. Wilson, *Rule of Reason*, 23.

75. Carew, "Excellency of the English Tongue," 2:288.

76. Wilson, *Rule of Reason*, 24.

77. Carew, "Excellency of the English Tongue," 2:287–88; Mulcaster, *Elementarie*, 102; Day, *Declaration*, 87.

78. Lever, *Arte of Reason*, 2.

79. Wilson, *Rule of Reason*, 24.

80. Mulcaster, *Elementarie*, 102.

81. Carew, "Excellency of the English Tongue," 2:287.

82. For further discussion of the etymology of names, see K. K. Ruthven, "The Poet as Etymologist," *Critical Quarterly* 11 (1969): 9–37.

83. Ben Jonson, *Ben Jonson*, edited by C. H. Hereford and Evelyn Simpson (Oxford: Clarendon Press, 1954), 8:52.

84. Peacham, *Garden of Eloquence*, 147. For a historical discussion of epithets, see Bernard Groom, "The Formation and Use of Compound Epithets in English Poetry from 1579," *S. P. E. Tract* 49 (Oxford: Clarendon Press, 1937).

85. Peacham, *Garden of Eloquence*, 146.

86. Puttenham, *Arte of the English Poesie*, 176.

87. Wilson, *Arte of Rhetorique*, 6.

88. For examples of these epithets, see Sidney, *Poems*, 59; Golding, *Metamorphosis*, book 1, line 317, p. 12; *Tottel's Miscellany*, 1:159; Barnfield, *Poems*, 67; Spenser, *Concordance*.

89. Peacham, *Garden of Eloquence*, 147.

90. Puttenham, *Arte of English Poetry*, 182.

91. Ibid., 255–56.

92. Day, *Declaration*, 84, 78, 80; Peacham, *Garden of Eloquence*, 9; Edmund Spenser, "The Teares of the Muses," in *The Minor Poems*, 2:66; Sir Thomas Wyatt, *Tottel's Miscellany*, 1:42. Quotations from Wyatt's poems which appeared in the miscellany are taken from this edition because it was in Tottel's version that they were known to later sixteenth-century poets.

93. Peacham, *Garden of Eloquence*, 12.

94. Ong, *Interfaces of the Word*, 169.

95. Ascham, *Scholemaster*, 247.

96. Sherry, *Treatise of the Schemes and Tropes*, 38.

97. William Cooper and John Ross, "Word Order," *Functionalism* (Chicago: Chicago Linguistic Society, 1975), 63–111.

98. Wilson, *Arte of Rhetorique*, 167–68.

Chapter Three

1. Paul Ricoeur, *The Rule of Metaphor*, trans. by Robert Czerny (Toronto: University of Toronto Press, 1977), 24.

2. Fraunce, *Arcadian Rhetorike*, 15; Wilson, *Arte of Rhetorique*, 176.

3. Sherry, *Treatise of Schemes and Tropes*, 40; Cawdrey, *Table Alphabeticall*, 82–83; Wilson, *Rule of Reason*, 208; Puttenham, *Arte of English Poesie*, 178, 180, 154; Fraunce, *Arcadian Rhetorike*, 18; Peacham, *Garden of Eloquence*, 9; Hoskyns, "Direccions for Speech and Style," 121.

4. Ernesto Grassi, *Rhetoric as Philosophy* (University Park: Pennsylvania State University, 1980), 33.

5. Peacham, *Garden of Eloquence*, 1.

6. Hoskyns, "Direccions for Speech and Style," 121.

7. Puttenham, *Arte of English Poesie*, 178; Fraunce, *Arcadian Rhetorike*, 3. For discussion of Aristotle on this point, see Marcus Hester, *The Meaning of Poetic Metaphor* (The Hague: Mouton, 1967), 14.

8. Carew, "Excellency of the English Tongue," 2:288.

9. George Chapman, "To the Understander," *Achilles Shield* (1598), in *Elizabethan Critical Essays*, 2:305; Mulcaster, *Elementarie*, 173; Cawdrey, "To the Reader," in *Table Alphabeticall*, 5; Puttenham, *Arte of English Poesie*, 154.

10. E. K., "Dedicatory Epistle" to "The Shepheardes Calender," by Edmund Spenser, in *The Minor Poems*, 1:9.

11. More, "Confvtacion," 437.

12. Elyot, *Gouernour*, 1:242–45.

13. Hoskyns, "Direccions for Speech and Style," 121.

14. Peacham, *Garden of Eloquence*, 11–12.

15. Lever, "The Forespeache," *Arte of Reason*.

16. Abraham Fraunce, *The Lawiers Logike* (1588), (Menston: Scolar Press, 1969), 2–3.

17. Tyndale, "Obedience of a Christen man," 166.

18. Ascham, *Scholemaster*, 200.

19. For discussions of the term *literal*, see Owen Barfield, "The Meaning of the Word 'Literal,'" in *Metaphor and Symbol*, edited by L. C. Knights and Basil Cottle (London: Butterworths Scientific Publications, 1960), 48–63; R. M. Grant, *The Letter and the Spirit* (New York: Macmillan, 1957). For historical discussions of biblical interpretation, see Robert Grant, *A Short History of the Interpretation of the Bible* (London: Adam and Charles Black, 1965); Philip Rollinson, *Classical Theories of Allegory and Christian Culture* (Pittsburgh: Duquesne University Press, 1981).

20. Hooker, *Lawes of Ecclesiastical Politie*, 130.

21. The term "lyterall cense" is used for the reader's "construccyon" not distinct from grammatical arrangement by Stephen Hawes, *The Pastime of Pleasure* (1555), (London: Percy Society, 1845), 24.

22. Tyndale, "Obedience of a Christen man," 166.

23. Tyndale, "The Supper of the Lord" (1533), in *The Whole workes*, 469.

24. I. A. Richards, *The Philosophy of Rhetoric* (New York: Oxford University Press, 1950), 71; Ricouer, *Rule of Metaphor*, 78.

25. Peacham, *Garden of Eloquence*, 2.

26. Mulcaster, *Elementarie*, 102.

27. Brinsley, *Lvdvs Literarivs*, 208. For full discussions of the commonplace tradition, see Otto Bird, "The Tradition of Logical Topics: Aristotle to Ockham," *JHI* 23 (1962): 307–23; Harry Caplan, *Of Eloquence* (Ithaca: Cornell University Press, 1970); Elbert Harrington, "Rhetoric and the Scientific Method of Inquiry," *University of Colorado Studies* 1 (1948): 1–64; Sister Joan Marie Lechner, *Renaissance Concepts of the Commonplaces* (New York: Pageant Books, 1962); Walter Ong, *The Presence of the Word* (New Haven: Yale University Press, 1967), *Rhetoric, Romance, and Technology* (Ithaca: Cornell University Press, 1971).

28. Wilson, *Rule of Reason*, 89; Pierre Gerard, *A Preparation to the Most Holie Ministerie*, trans. by N. B. (London, 1598), 176–78.

29. Gerard, *Most Holie Ministerie*, 176. For a full discussion of the places as mnemonic devices, see Frances Yates, *The Art of Memory* (London: Routledge and Kegan Paul, 1966).

30. Wilson, *Arte of Rhetorique*, 214; Sidney, "Apologie for Poetrie," 1:183.

31. Wilson, *Arte of Rhetorique*, 213.

32. See, for example, Robert Cawdrey, *A Treasvrie or Store-Hovse of Similes* (London, 1600); the metaphor is still in use in a mid-seventeenth-century example: John Spencer, *Things New and Old. Or, A Store-House of Similes, Sentences, Allegories, Apophthegms, Adagies, Apologues, Divine, Morall, Political, &c. With their severall Applications* (London, 1658); Andreas Hyperius, *The Practis of Preaching*, trans. by John Ludham (London, 1577), 12, 30.

33. Clerk, *Dictionarie*, 43, 45. The importance of this commonplace book is discussed by Starnes, *Renaissance Dictionaries*, 168–80.

34. Clerk, *Dictionarie*, 91–102.

35. For discussion of *Astrophil and Stella* 1 in relation to Ramist ideas of invention, see Thomas Sloan, "The Crossing of Rhetoric and Poetry in the English Renaissance," in *The Rhetoric of Renaissance Poetry From Wyatt to Milton* (Berkeley: University of California Press, 1974), 234–36. The importance of "the *de inventoribus* trope" to Shakespeare's Sonnet 59 is discussed by Rosalie Colie, *Shakespeare's Living Art* (Princeton: Princeton University Press, 1974), 60.

36. Harington, *Orlando Fvrioso*, book 1, stanza 42, p. 4; book 37, stanza 1, p. 306.

37. Alpers , *Poetry of "The Faerie Queene,"* 156.

38. Desiderius Erasmus, *Flores aliquot sententiarum ex variis collecti scriptoribus. the flowers of sencies* gathered oute of sundry writers by Erasmus in Latine and Englished by Richard Tauerner (London, c. 1555). See Ong, *Interfaces of the Word*, 179: "*Anthologia* is the Greek word for which the Latin *florilegium* is a calque: both mean etymologically 'flower collection,' for which the English equivalent is posies, a term which figures in not a few Elizabethan collections of poems." I have not, however, found a single use of the term *anthology* in this period.

39. Cooper, *Thesavrvs Lingvua*: "*Lego* . . . To gather: to read: to passe by: to choose: to steale"; statutes quoted by Rix, *Rhetoric in Spenser's Poetry*, 12.

40. Clerk, "The Preface to this *last Edition*," in *Dictionarie*.

41. Wyatt, *Tottel's Miscellany*, 1:38; Gascoigne, *Complete Poems*, 1:92–93.

42. Booth, "Commentary," in *Shakespeare's Sonnets*, 172.

43. Clerk, "The Preface," in *Dictionarie*; Thomas Newbury, *A booke in Englysh metre* (London, 1563).

44. Peacham, *Garden of Eloquence*, 25. For differences on this point from some later thinking about metaphor, see W. B. Stanford, *Greek Metaphor* (London: Basil Blackwell, 1936), 9.

45. Puttenham, *Arte of English Poesie*, 178.

46. George Lakoff and Mark Johnson, *Metaphors We Live By* (Chicago: University of Chicago Press, 1980), 36; Paul Ricoeur, "The Metaphorical Process as Cognition, Imagination, and Feeling," in *Philosophical Perspectives on Metaphor*, edited by Mark Johnson (Minneapolis: University of Minnesota Press, 1981), 143.

47. Richards, *Philosophy of Rhetoric*, 96. For discussion of these and alternative terms, see Monroe Beardsley, "Metaphor," in *The Encyclopedia of Philosophy*, edited by Paul Edwards (New York: Macmillan, 1967), 5:285; Paul Henle, "Metaphor," in *Philosophical Perspectives*, 90–91.

48. Peacham, *Garden of Eloquence*, 9.

49. Abraham Fleming, trans., *A Panoplie of Epistles* (London, 1576), 10, 402.

50. Daniel, *Delia* 23; Henry Howard, Earl of Surrey, *Tottel's Miscellany*, 1:3; Wyatt, *Tottel's Miscellany*, 1:71; Spenser, *Amoretti* 18.

51. Wyatt, *Tottel's Miscellany*, 1:42; Spenser, "The Teares of the Muses," *Minor Poems*, 2:66; Day, *Declaration*, 80.

52. Watson, *Poems*, 127.

53. Sir Walter Ralegh, *The Poems of Sir Walter Ralegh*, edited by Agnes Latham (Cambridge, Mass.: Harvard University Press, 1962), 5.

54. Reference to this belief in a "Song" by Donne is noted by Helen Gardner in "Commentary," in *The Elegies and the Songs and Sonnets* (Oxford: Clarendon Press, 1965), 155.

55. Sidney, *Poems*, 70.

56. Puttenham, *Arte of English Poesie*, 183–84. For a history of the term *metalepsis*, see Hollander, *Figure of Echo*, 133–49.

57. Peacham, *Garden of Eloquence*, 23.

58. Puttenham, *Arte of English Poesie*, 183; Wilson, *Arte of Rhetorique*, 175; Day, *Declaration*, 79.

59. Peacham, *Garden of Eloquence*, 23, 24.

60. Wilson, *Arte of Rhetorique*, 175; see also Sherry, *Treatise of Schemes and Tropes*, 41–42.

61. Cawdrey, "The Epistle Dedicatorie," in *Treasvrie*, A2.

62. Spenser, "Epithalamion," 2:246.

63. Wyatt, *Tottel's Miscellany*, 1:32. For arguments about the differences between pun and metaphor, see Donald Davidson, "What Metaphors Mean," in *On Metaphor*, 33.

64. M. M. Mahood, *Shakespeare's Wordplay* (London: Methuen, 1957), 51.

65. Blundeville, *Arte of Logicke*, 16.

66. Lever, *Arte of Reason*, 2–3.

67. Sir Thomas Wyatt, *The Canon of Sir Thomas Wyatt's Poetry*, edited by Richard Harrier (Cambridge: Mass.: Harvard University Press, 1975), 104.

68. Among numerous discussions of Spenser's punning, see Fletcher, *Prophetic Moment*, 101–6; Giamatti, *Play of Double Senses*, especially pp. 82, 93, 107; Quilligan, *Language of Allegory*, especially pp. 33–42.

69. Jonson, *Ben Jonson*, 8:81.

70. Peacham, *Garden of Eloquence*, 56–57.

71. Puttenham, *Arte of English Poesie*, 207.

72. Peacham, *Garden of Eloquence*, 57.

73. Blundeville, *Arte of Logicke*, 16; Wilson, *Rule of Reason*, 162; Fraunce, *Lawiers Logike*, 26.

74. Blundeville, *Arte of Logicke*, 58.

75. Wilson, *Rule of Reason*, 162.

76. Lever, *Arte of Reason*, 3.

77. Fraunce, *Lawiers Logike*, 26–27.

78. Aristotle, *A Briefe Art of Rhetorique*, trans. by Thomas Hobbes (London, 1637), 154–55. For discussion of these two views, see Ricoeur, *Rule of Metaphor*, 19.

79. Wilson, *Rule of Reason*, 24.

80. Ibid., 163.

81. Ibid., 162; Puttenham, *Arte of English Poesie*, 154.

82. For recent discussions of Sonnet 138, see Joel Fineman, *Shakespeare's Perjured Eye* (Berkeley: University of California Press, 1986), especially pp. 165–67 and the reply by Denis Donoghue, "Shakespeare in the Sonnets," *Raritan* 6 (1986): 136–37.

83. William Empson, *The Structure of Complex Words* (Norfolk, Conn.: New Directions, n.d.), 350.

84. Ibid., 368.

85. Ibid., 366.

86. Donne, *Elegies and Songs and Sonnets*, 79.

87. Empson, *Structure of Complex Words*, 352.

88. Blundeville, *Arte of Logicke*, 14.

89. Ibid., 17.

90. Hoskyns, "Direccions for Speech and Style," 121.

91. Tyndale, "Obedience of a Christen man," 183; Peacham, *Garden of Eloquence*, 27.

92. Sidney, *Poems*, 39. For discussion of this poem as an example of Sidney's "emblem technique," see Forrest Robinson, *The Shape of Things Known* (Cambridge: Mass.: Harvard University Press, 1972), 182–84.

93. Sir Philip Sidney, *The Countess of Pembroke's Arcadia* (The Old Arcadia), edited by Jean Robertson (Oxford: Clarendon Press, 1973), 106–7.

94. Christopher Marlowe, *The Complete Works of Christopher Marlowe*, edited by Fredson Bowers (Cambridge: Cambridge University Press, 1973), 2:536.

95. Wilson, *Arte of Rhetorique*, 172.

96. Fairfax, "The Allegorie of the Poem," in *Godfrey of Bovlogne*. See Angus Fletcher, *Allegory* (Ithaca: Cornell University Press, 1964), 2n1.

97. Day, *Declaration*, 79; Musculus, *Common places of the Christian Religion*, fol. 272.

98. Puttenham, *Arte of English Poesie*, 186–87.

99. Spenser, "The Shepheardes Calender," 1:22; E. K., Ibid., 27.

100. Puttenham, *Arte of English Poesie*, 186–87.

101. Fraunce, *Arcadian Rhetorike*, 15.

102. Puttenham, *Arte of English Poesie*, 186–87.

103. Tyndale, "Obedience of a Christen man," 166; Day, *Declaration*, 79–80.

104. Gascoigne, *Complete Poems*, 1:68. See also, Sir Edward Dyer, *The Life and Lyrics of Sir Edward Dyer*, edited by Ralph Sargent (Oxford: Clarendon Press,

1968), 194; Breton, *Poems*, 194; Wyatt, *Tottel's Miscellany*, 1:64; Spenser, *Concordance*.

105. For discussion of this poem, see Alastair Fowler, *Conceitful Thought* (Edinburgh: Edinburgh University Press, 1975), 98–100.

106. "The first Sunday in Advent," in *Book of Common Prayer* (London, 1586). Unless otherwise specified, all quotations from the English liturgy are taken from this edition, which incorporates revisions made in 1552, 1559, and 1561.

107. "On good Friday" in *Book of Common Prayer*.

108. Romans 13:13, *The Holy Bible, Revised Standard Version* (New York: New American Library, 1974), 152.

109. Wilson, *Arte of Rhetorique*, 175.

110. "The fift Sunday after the Epiphanie," "The third Sunday in Lent," "The Communion," "A Catechisme," in *Book of Common Prayer*. William Kempe, "The Education of children in learning" (1588), in *Four Tudor Books on Education*, 217; Sidney, *Poems*, 275.

111. Gascoigne, *Complete Poems*, 1:58; Breton, *Poems*, 50.

Chapter Four

1. For a recent study of Spenser's Protestant affiliations, see Anthea Hume, *Edmund Spenser: Protestant Poet* (Cambridge: Cambridge University Press, 1984).

2. Andrew Maunsell, "The Epistle Dedicatorie," in *The First Part of the Catalogue of English printed Bookes* (London, 1595).

3. Reginald Scot, *The discouerie of witchcraft* (1584), 234. For discussions of magic in relation to Spenser's poetry, see Gross, *Spenserian Poetics*; A Bartlett Giamatti, *Exile and Change in Renaissance Poetry* (New Haven: Yale University Press, 1984), 76–88.

4. Scot, "To the Readers," in *The discouerie of witchcraft*, Bij; 433, 234.

5. Marbeck, *Booke of Notes*, 120; Rainolds, *Svmme of the Conference*, 582, 580. For full studies of Protestant attitudes toward the aspects of Catholicism condemned as magic, see Keith Thomas, *Religion and the Decline of Magic* (New York: Charles Scribner's Sons, 1971); D. P. Walker, *Spiritual and Demonic Magic* (London: Warburg Institute, 1958); D. Douglas Waters, *Duessa as Theological Satire* (Columbia: University of Missouri Press, 1970).

6. This is an instance of what is called "the principle of symbolic parody" by Northrup Frye, "The Structure of Imagery in *The Faerie Queene*," in *Essential Articles for the Study of Edmund Spenser*, edited by A. C. Hamilton (Hamden, Conn.: Archon Books, 1972), 163.

7. Henry Smith, *Gods Arrow Against Atheists* (London, 1604), 42, 83. For uses of the term, see also William Vaughan, "Of the Art Magick," in *The Golden-groue*, 2d ed. (London, 1608), book 3, chapter 45.

8. Scot, *Discouerie of witchcraft*, 217.

9. Andrew Tuer, *History of the Horn-Book* (London: Leadenhall, 1896), 1:55.

10. The term is used twice in "The workes of a young wyt" (1577) by Breton, *Poems*, 29, 31.

11. Tuer, *History of the Horn-Book*, 1:80.

12. For evidence of this belief, see Becon's discussion with the marginal heading "The wonderful vertue of bels," in *The Reliques of Rome*, fol. 81.

13. Scot, *Discouerie of witchcraft*, 236.

14. "The Supper of the Lorde," in *The Booke of the Common Prayer* (1549), in *The First and Second Prayer Books of Edward VI* (London: Dent, 1968), 222.

15. "Of Ceremonies," in *First and Second Prayer Books*, 289.

16. Augustine Baker, "Treatise of the Venerable Father Augustin Baker," in *Memorials of Father Augustine Baker*, edited by Dom Justin McCann and Dom Hugh Connolly (London: Catholic Record Society, 1933), 16.

17. Tuer, *History of the Horn-Book*, 1:53; Charles Butterworth, *The English Primers* (Philadelphia: University of Pennsylvania Press, 1953), 178n14.

18. Johnson, *New Booke of New Conceits*, 212.

19. Quoted by Butterworth, *English Primers*, 178.

20. Ibid., 257, 253. The identification of the A.B.C. with religious texts is further shown by the fact that in 1557 John and Richard Day were granted sole right to print "the psalmes of David in English meeter with notes to singe them, the A.B.C. with the little catechisme . . . the Catechisme in englishe and lattyn" according to H. S. Bennett, *English Books and Readers 1558 to 1603* (Cambridge: Cambridge University Press, 1965), 167.

21. Tuer, *History of the Horn-Book*, 1:81.

22. "To the Christian Reader," in *An Alphabet of the holy Proverbs of King Salomon* (London, 1596). The use of the alphabet in psalms and by Saint Augustine is discussed by Maren-Sofie Røstvig, "Structure as Prophecy: the influence of biblical exegesis upon theories of literary structure," in *Silent Poetry*, edited by Alastair Fowler (London: Routledge and Kegan Paul, 1970), 50–52, 66.

23. For discussions of these occult studies, see John Burke, "Hermetism as a Renaissance World View," in *The Darker Vision of the Renaissance*, edited by Robert Kinsman (Los Angeles: University of Los Angeles Press, 1974), pp. 95–117; Wayne Shumaker, *The Occult Sciences of the Renaissance* (Berkeley: University of California Press, 1972); Lynn Thorndike, *A History of Magic and Experimental Science* (New York: Columbia University Press, 1941), 5: 134–36. On acrostic patterns made out of the Hebrew alphabet, see Alastair Fowler, *Triumphal Forms* (Cambridge: Cambridge University Press, 1970), 7.

24. Charles Nauert, *Agrippa and the Crisis of Renaissance Thought* (Urbana: Illinois Studies in the Social Sciences, 1965), 324–25.

25. Scot, *Discouerie of witchcraft*, 444.

26. William Shakespeare, *The Tragedy of Richard the Third*, 1.1.509.

27. Smith, *Gods Arrow Against Atheists*, 100.

28. William Caxton, *The Mirrour of the World* (c. 1481–90), edited by Oliver Prior (London: Kegan Paul, Trench Trübner, 1913), 34; Hall, "A Commendatory Preface," in *Lvdvs Literarivs*, 1; Sylvester, "Babilon. The second Booke of the second Day, of the second Weeke," in *Bartas*, 425.

29. Sylvester, "Babilon," in *Bartas*, 425.

30. Sidney, "Apologie for Poetrie," 1:157.

31. Ibid., 1:185.

32. Ibid., 1:154.

33. Ibid., 1:195, 154, 206, 172.

34. Ibid., 1:156.

35. Scot, *Discouerie of witchcraft*, 354–55.

36. For discussions of the religious language of Sonnets 105 and 108, see John

Bernard, "'To Constancie Confin'de': The Poetics of Shakespeare's Sonnets," *PMLA* 94 (1979): 85–88; Jane Roessner, "Double Exposure: Shakespeare's Sonnets 100–114," *ELH* 46 (1979): 357–78.

37. The liturgical formulas and repetitions of Sonnet 105 are noted by Murray Krieger, *Poetic Presence and Illusion* (Baltimore: Johns Hopkins University Press, 1979), 27.

38. Sidney, *Poems*, 111–13. For discussion of such forms, see Hollander, *Figure of Echo*, especially pp. 27, 33–34, 83–84.

39. Wyatt, *Tottel's Miscellany*, 1:71. The suggestion that Wyatt's poem is based on a French rondeau itself derived from a sonnet by Petrarch, *Ite, caldi sospiri, al freddo core*, is made by Joost Daalder, "Appendix," in *Sir Thomas Wyatt Collected Poems* (London: Oxford University Press, 1975), 236.

40. "Of Matrimonie," in *Book of Common Prayer*. For discussion of these religious formulas, see Booth, "Commentary," 337. The association of repetition in poetry with "a litany" is also made by Russell Fraser, *The Language of Adam* (New York: Columbia University Press, 1977), 189.

41. Hooker, *Lawes of Ecclesiasticall Politie*, 56.

42. Cawdrey, *Table Alphabeticall*, 92; Puttenham, *Arte of English Poesie*, 226; Day, *Declaration*, 90; Smith, *Gods Arrow Against Atheists*, 73; cited in the *O.E.D.* from John Foxe, *Actes and Monuments*, 2d ed., p. 1299.

43. Johnson, "New Booke of New Conceits," 211.

44. "An Ordre for Euensong," in *The Booke of the Common Prayer*, 29.

45. "An Order for Evening Prayer," in *Book of Common Prayer*.

46. Michael Drayton, *The Works of Michael Drayton*, edited by J. William Hebel (Oxford: Shakespeare Head Press, 1932), 2:337.

47. Giles Fletcher, *The English Works of Giles Fletcher, the Elder*, edited by Lloyd Berry (Madison: University of Wisconsin Press, 1964), 100.

48. "An Order for Morning praier," in *Book of Common Prayer*. Examples of enumeration in praise of the universe are discussed by Kitty Scolar, *Natural Magic* (Oxford: Clarendon Press, 1965), 19.

49. Bartholomew Griffin, *The Poems of Bartholomew Griffin*, edited by Alexander Grosart (Manchester, 1876), 31.

50. Sylvester, "Babilon. The second Booke of the second Day, of the second Weeke," in *Bartas*, 426.

51. "Publyke Baptisme," in *Booke of the Common Prayer*, 240.

52. "Publique Baptisme," in *Boke of Common Prayer* (1552), in *Prayer Books of Edward VI*, 398.

53. "The Letanie," in *Book of Common Prayer*.

54. Scot, *Discouerie of witchcraft*, 233.

55. Quoted by Helen White, *The Tudor Books of Private Devotion* (Madison: University of Wisconsin Press, 1957), 216; the prayer is discussed on pp. 216–29.

56. *A Booke of Christian Prayers* (London, 1590), 62–63.

57. Quoted by Frances Yates, *Giordano Bruno and the Hermetic Tradition* (Chicago: University of Chicago Press, 1964), 201.

58. Peter French, *John Dee* (London: Routledge and Kegan Paul, 1972), 8–9.

59. "The Sunday next before Easter," in *Book of Common Prayer*.

60. *Booke of Christian Prayers*, 62–63.

61. Cooper, *Thesavrvs Lingvae;* Cawdrey, *Table Alphabeticall,* 27.

62. F. E. Brightman, *The English Rite* (London: Rivingtons, 1921), 2:1022–23.

63. Among many discussions of this passage, see Donald Cheney, *Spenser's Image of Nature* (New Haven: Yale University Press, 1966), 25; A. C. Hamilton, "On Annotating Spenser's *Faerie Queene:* A New Approach to the Poem," in *Contemporary Thought on Edmund Spenser,* edited by Richard Frushell and Bernard Vondersmith (Carbondale: Southern Illinois University Press, 1975), 43–44; Patricia Parker, *Inescapable Romance* (Princeton: Princeton University Press, 1979), 71; Maureen Quilligan, *Milton's Spenser* (Ithaca: Cornell University Press, 1983), 101–2; Quilligan, *Language of Allegory,* 256; Mark Rose, *Spenser's Art* (Cambridge: Mass.: Harvard University Press, 1975), 7; Kathleen Williams, *Spenser's World of Glass* (Berkeley: University of California Press, 1966), 2.

64. Sidney, *Poems,* 36.

65. Quilligan, *Language of Allegory,* 256.

66. Watson, *Poems,* 204, discussed by Alpers, *Poetry of "The Faerie Queene,"* 156–57.

67. Patricia Vicari, "Spargamos: Orpheus among the Christians," in *Orpheus,* edited by John Warden (Toronto: University of Toronto Press, 1982), 66.

68. Sidney, *Poems,* 208.

69. Golding, *Metamorphosis,* book 10, lines 93–96, p. 251.

70. Smith, *Gods Arrow Against Atheists,* 34; Edgar Wind, *Pagan Mysteries of the Renaissance* (London: Faber and Faber, 1958), 24–25.

71. Sidney, *Apologie for Poetrie,* 1:158.

72. Graham Castor, *Pléiade Poetics* (Cambridge: Cambridge University Press, 1964), 26–29.

73. Clement, "Petie Schole," 93–94. See also Puttenham, *Arte of English Poesie,* 6; Sidney, "Apologie for Poetrie," 1:151.

74. Sylvester, "The third Day of the first Weeke," in *Bartas,* 93.

75. Castor, *Pléiade Poetics,* 26–27.

76. Dee, "Mathematicall Præface," Aiij. For the association of Moses with Hermeticism, see French, *John Dee,* 84–85.

77. The association of Archimago making the false Una with Pygmalion is made by Millar MacLure, "Nature and Art in *The Faerie Queene,*" in *Essential Articles,* 176.

78. Scot, *Discouerie of witchcraft,* 395. For discussion of such incantations, see Maurice Bouisson, *Magic,* trans. by G. Almayrac (New York: E. P. Dutton, 1961), 93–125.

79. Kurt Seligmann, *The History of Magic* (New York: Pantheon Books, 1948), 346.

80. Sylvester, "The second Day of the first Weeke," in *Bartas,* 31.

81. Guillaume de Salluste Dubartas, "Second Iovr De La Sepmaine," in *La Sepmaine* in *Les Œvvres de Salvste* (Geneva: 1582), 1:31.

82. For historical accounts of the blazon relevant to this discussion, see Robert Pike, "The 'Blasons' in French Literature of the 16th Century," *Romanic Review* 27 (1936): 223–42; P. B. Wilson, *Descriptive Poetry in France* (Manchester: Manchester University Press, 1967), 7–26. For discussions of the blazon of Belphoebe, see Harry Berger, *The Allegorical Temper* (New Haven: Yale University Press, 1957), 120–49;

Louis Montrose, "The Elizabethan Subject and the Spenserian Text," in *Literary Theory / Renaissance Texts*, edited by Patricia Parker and David Quint (Baltimore: Johns Hopkins University Press, 1986), 326–28.

83. Donne, *Elegies and Songs and Sonnets*, 17–19.

84. Puttenham, *Arte of English Poesie*, 244.

85. Gascoigne, "Certayne Notes of Instruction," 1:48.

86. Geoffrey de Vinsauf, "Poetria nova," in *Three Medieval Rhetorical Arts*, edited by James Murphy (Berkeley: University of California Press, 1971), 55.

87. Gascoigne, *Complete Poems*, 1:448.

88. Sidney, *Poems*, 85–90; William Ringler, "Commentary," in Sidney, *Poems*, 410.

89. Sir Arthur Gorges, *The Poems of Sir Arthur Gorges*, edited by Helen Sandison (Oxford: Clarendon Press, 1953), 23. Connections among these three sonnets are discussed by Anne Prescott, *French Poets and the English Renaissance* (New Haven: Yale University Press, 1978), 54–59.

90. Henoch Clapham, *Three Parts of Salomon his Song of Songs* (London, 1603), 6; Dudley Fenner, *The Song of Songs* (Middleburgh, 1594), Biij.

91. A. C. Partridge, *English Biblical Translation* (London: André Deutsch, 1973), 81–82; Fowler, *Conceitful Thought*, 108.

92. Fenner, *Song of Songs*, Di.

93. David Quint, *Origin and Originality in Renaissance England* (New Haven: Yale University Press, 1983), 245n.48. For Spenser's use of the Canticles, see Israel Baroway, "The Imagery of Spenser and the *Song of Songs*," *JEGP* 33 (1934): 23–45.

94. Fenner, *Song of Songs*, Biij.

95. The relation of tenor to vehicle in this passage is discussed by G. K. Hunter, "Spenser's *Amoretti* and the English sonnet tradition," in *Theatre for Spenserians*, 139.

96. Puttenham, *Arte of English Poesie*, 192.

97. Theodore Beza, *Master Bezaes Sermons Vpon the Three First Chapters of the Canticle of Canticles*, trans. by John Harmar (Oxford, 1587), 163.

98. For Spenser's use of the Geneva version of the Canticles in this passage, see Naseeb Shaheen, *Biblical References in "The Faerie Queene"* (Memphis: Memphis State University, 1976), 34.

99. Sidney, *Poems*, 89.

100. Gascoigne, *Complete Poems*, 1:448.

101. Watson, *Poems*, 90.

102. Gascoigne's correlative blazon is inset into his prose narrative, "The aduentures of Master F. I," in *Complete Poems*, 1:448.

103. William Fulwood, *The Enimie of Idlenesse* (London, 1582), 285–86.

104. Sidney, *Poems*, 88.

105. Golding, *Metamorphosis*, book ten, lines 265–311, pp. 256–57.

106. *Tottel's Miscellany*, 1:126. Daniel in *Delia* 13 compares Pygmalion and the poet-lover who must "carue his proper griefe vpon" the lady's "stony harte."

107. Jonson, *Ben Jonson*, 8:52.

108. Andrew Marvell, *The Poems and Letters of Andrew Marvell*, edited by H. M. Margoliouth (Oxford: Clarendon Press, 1927), 1:26–27.

109. For discussion of Archimago as the creator of a counterpoem to Spen-

ser's, see Ernest Gilman, *Iconoclasm and Poetry in the English Reformation* (Chicago: University of Chicago Press, 1986), 75–76.

110. Spenser, "Epithalamion," 2:245.

111. Sternhold and Hopkins, "Psalme Cxliiii," in *Whole Booke of Psalmes*.

112. Sidney, "Apologie for Poetrie," 1:158.

113. Spenser, "Epithalamion," 2:246.

114. John Foxe, *Actes and Monuments* (London, 1610), 25; Tyndale, "Supper of the Lord," 469; Smith, *Gods Arrow Against Atheism*, 73.

Afterword

1. Theodore Beza, "The Epistle Dedicatorie," in *The Psalmes of David*, trans. by Anthonie Gilbie (London, 1580); Sidney, "Apologie for Poetrie," 1:154–55.

2. Sidney, "Apologie for Poetrie," 1:155.

3. J. C. A. Rathmell, "Introduction," in *The Psalms of Sir Philip Sidney and the Countess of Pembroke* (New York: New York University Press, 1963), xxvii.

4. A connection between Milton's translation of the fourth psalm and Sidney's is suggested by Margaret Boddy, "Milton's Translations from the Psalms," in *A Milton Encyclopedia*, edited by William Hunter et al. (Lewisburg: Bucknell University Press, 1979), 7:55.

5. Sidney, *Poems*, 270–71.

6. Ibid., 273.

7. Milton, "The Shorter English Poems," in *Works*, 1:123–24.

8. Sidney, *Poems*, 279.

9. Ibid., 275.

10. Ibid., 271.

11. Ibid., 278.

12. Ibid., 273–74.

13. Rathmell, "Introduction," in *Psalms of Sidney*, xix.

14. Milton, "The Shorter English Poems," in *Works*, 1:126–28.

Index

A.B.C. books, frontispiece, 131, 195n.20. *See also* Alphabet
Agrippa, Cornelius, 132, 147
Alpers, Paul, 11, 46–47, 93
Alphabet, 1–2, 19–21, 128–33, 195n.22
Ariosto, Ludovico, 92
Aristotle, 57, 58, 73, 83, 84, 110, 118
Ascham, Roger, 59, 78, 88–89
Augustine, Saint, 89

Bacon, Sir Francis, 28, 132, 184n.54
Baker, Augustine, 130
Bakhtin, Mikhail, 6
Baret, John, 16, 19, 32–33, 182n.16
Barnfield, Richard, 54, 67, 186n.10, 189n.88
Barthes, Roland, 8
Batman, Stephen, 32, 184n.67
Becon, Thomas, 17, 68–69
Beza, Theodore, 162, 174, 198n.97
Bible, xvi, xviii, 1, 28, 71–72, 75, 122, 123; Apocrypha, 144, 145; Canticles, 152, 159–63, 164, 167; Genesis, 30, 133, 153, 160, 169; Hebrews, 121; Psalms, 131, 152, 167, 169; Revelation, 131; Romans, 120, 121
Blundeville, Thomas, 57, 58, 60, 61, 65, 106–7, 109, 113, 114, 187n.23, 193nn.88, 89
Bodenham, John, 17, 182n.17
Booke of Christian Prayers, 146–48
Boke of Common Prayer (1552), 129, 143, 146
Book of Common Prayer (1586), 122, 140, 143–47, 194n.110
Booke of Common Prayer (1549), 130, 142–43, 145–46
Booth, Stephen, 95
Boys, John, 28, 184n.55
Breton, Nicholas, 55, 119, 124, 129, 186n.14, 194n.104
Brinsley, John, 38–39, 91, 191n.27
Bruno, Giordano, 147

Bullokar, William, 16, 22, 40, 55, 181n.16, 183n.40
Butler, Charles, 22, 55, 57

Calvin, John, 174
Camden, William, 10, 22, 72, 189n.67
Campion, Thomas, 21
Carew, Richard, 33, 35, 72–75, 85, 185n.79, 189nn.68, 75, 77, 81, 189n.81, 190n.9
Catullus, 92
Cawdrey, Robert, 17, 19, 20, 84, 91, 105, 141, 148, 182n.17, 190n.3, 191n.32, 192n.61, 196n.42
Caxton, William, 133, 195n.28
Chapman, George, 85
Chaucer, Geoffrey, 5–6, 10, 58, 67, 109, 149, 151, 152
Cicero, 98
Clapham, Henoch, 160, 198n.90
Cleland, James, 29, 184n.58
Clement, Francis, 16, 153, 181n.16
Clerk, William, 21, 65, 91–93, 95–96, 183n.34, 188n.46, 191nn.33, 34, 40
Cooper, Thomas, 9, 16, 65, 148
Coote, Edmund, 19–22
Cox, Leonard, 17, 182n.17
Curtius, Ernst, 13, 26, 28

Daniel, Samuel, 28, 52–54, 78, 98, 106, 139, 140, 145, 159, 184n.54, 192n.50, 198n.106
Day, Angell, 54–55, 74, 77–78, 98, 103, 117, 118, 141, 184n.54, 186n.12, 189n.77, 193n.97
Dee, John, 28, 147, 154, 184n.56
DeNeef, A. L., 11
Donne, John, xii, 68, 112, 114, 157
Drayton, Michael, 144
Du Bartas, Guillaume de Saluste, 28, 34, 35, 92, 153, 155–56, 160
Du Bellay, Joachim, 159
Dyer, Sir Edward, 119, 193n.104

Elyot, Sir Thomas, 18, 20, 33, 36–37, 73, 86–87
Empson, William, 112, 116, 123
Erasmus, Desiderius, 17, 93

Fairfax, Edward, 4, 6, 7, 8, 56, 116–17, 119
Fenner, Dudley, 160, 161, 198nn.90, 92, 94
Ferry, Anne, xii, xiii
Ficino, Marsilio, 153
Fleming, Abraham, 98
Fletcher, Giles, 144
Florio, John, 16
Foucault, Michel, xvii–xviii, 15–16, 27, 28
Foxe, John, 141, 147, 163–64, 168, 196n.42, 199n.114
Fraunce, Abraham, 6, 17, 84, 85, 87–88, 109, 110, 118, 180n.11, 182n.17, 190nn.2, 3, 193n.73
Fulwood, William, 163–64

Gascoigne, George, 34, 55, 67–68, 94–96, 99, 106, 119, 124, 139, 158, 163, 186n.14, 187n.35, 193n.104
Geoffrey de Vinsauf, 158
Gerard, Pierre, 91, 191nn.28, 29
Golding, Arthur, 21–22, 50, 67, 152, 164, 183n.37, 186n.3, 189n.88
Googe, Barnabe, 50, 186n.4, 187n.35
Gorges, Sir Arthur, 159
Greaves, Paul, 55
Greene, Thomas, xii, 179n.3
Greville, Fulke, Lord Brooke, 27
Griffin, Bartholomew, 145
Gross, Kenneth, xiv–xv, 179n.12
Guarna, Andrea, 38, 185n.84

Hall, Joseph, 18, 133, 182n.21, 195n.28
Harington, Sir John, 53, 54, 60, 92, 132, 186n.10, 187nn.34, 35
Hart, John, 16, 18, 32, 182n.26
Harvey, Gabriel, 132
Hawes, Stephen, 89, 190n.21
Helgerson, Richard, xiv, 179n.11
Heywood, John, 13
Hollander, John, xvii
Homer, 78
Hooker, Richard, 29, 38, 89, 140
Horace, 153
Hoskyns, John, 29, 84–87, 113–14, 190n.3
Howard, Jean, xiii, xiv, 179nn.7, 9
Hyperius, Andreas, 91, 191n.32

Johnson, Thomas, 33, 131, 141, 184n.69, 195n.18, 196n.43
Jonson, Ben, xii, 76, 107, 165–66

Kempe, William, 122, 194n.110

Lacan, Jacques, xiv–xv
Levens, Peter, 20–21
Lever, Ralph, 16, 17, 30, 51, 57, 58, 74, 87, 109, 182n.17, 189n.78, 190n.15
Lily, William, 37–38, 64, 65, 69, 186n.19
Locke, John, 59
Lydgate, John, 58

Marbeck, John, 72, 127, 188n.66, 194n.5
Marlowe, Christopher, 115, 132
Marot, Clement, 169
Maunsell, Andrew, 126, 194n.2
Marvell, Andrew, xii, 166
McCanles, Michael, xiv, 179n.10
Miles, Josephine, xvii
Milton, John, 41, 42, 62, 67, 112, 114, 170–77
Montaigne, Michel de, 16
Montrose, Louis, xiv, 179n.8
More, Sir Thomas, 18, 33, 86
Mulcaster, Richard, 17, 18, 19, 30, 32, 73–76, 85, 184n.65, 189n.77, 190n.9
Musculus, Wolfgang, 74, 117, 189n.72, 190n.97

Nashe, Thomas, 132
Newbery, Thomas, 96

Ong, Walter, 20
Ovid, 67, 149, 151, 152

Peacham, Henry, 17, 23, 35, 36, 37, 55, 57, 66, 69–70, 76, 77, 78, 84, 87, 90–93, 96–100, 102, 103–5, 108, 114, 117, 182n.17, 183n.44, 190n.3, 192n.44
Petrarch, Francis, 94, 139, 196n.39
Plato, 73
Primaudaye, Pierre de la, 16, 182n.16
Puttenham, George, 10, 22–23, 57, 66, 77, 84, 85, 94, 97, 102, 103, 108, 110, 117–18, 141, 158, 162, 181n.4, 189n.86, 190nn.3, 9, 197n.73

Quilligan, Maureen, 11

Rabelais, Francois, 6
Rainolds, John, 70, 73, 127, 188n.61, 194n.5
Ralegh, Sir Walter, 100, 102, 119
Ramus, Peter, 16, 17, 66, 70–71, 182n.17
Richards, I. A., 90, 97
Ricouer, Paul, 90
Robinson, Robert, 16, 182n.16
Romei, Annibale, 183n.44
Ronsard, Pierre de, 164

Scot, Reginald, 126, 128, 129, 132, 136, 142, 146, 147, 155, 195n.35
Shakespeare, William, xii, xiii, 2, 3, 9, 39, 61, 62, 78, 83, 106, 110, 114, 132; *Lvcrece*, 26–27; *Richard the Second*, 25–26; *Richard the Third*, 132; *Second Part of Henry the Fourth*, 26; *Sonnets: 3*, 113, 114; *18*, 2, 22, 61, 62, 83, 134–38, 151; *21*, 62, 83; *24*, 95–96; *33*, 135; *35*, 137; *53*, 187n.34; *59*, 191n.35; *62*, 25; *64*, 54, 100–1; *65*, 136–38, 141; *66*, 144; *76*, 141; *105*, 2–3, 138–42, 144–46; *106*,156; *108*, 137–38, 158; *114*, 135; *126*, 2; *129*, 68; *130*, 83, 156, 161; *135*, 76; *136*, 76; *138*, 110–12; *143*, 76
Sherry, Richard, 65, 70, 78, 84, 190n.3
Sidney, Sir Philip, 8, 9, 50, 76, 132, 139, 147, 154, 158, 167; *Apologie for Poetrie*, xi, 5, 91, 133–36, 152, 153, 167, 169, 170, 191n.30, 197n.73; *Arcadia* poems, 4, 7, 27, 50, 62–63, 66, 101–3, 105, 114–15, 116, 119, 139, 149, 150, 152, 158, 161, 163, 164, 189n.88; *Astrophil and Stella: 1*, 92; *6*, 173; *7*, 141; *9*, 107, 108, 120; *11*, 13–14; *15*, 92; *49*, 116; *71*, 13; *Psalms: 122*, 169–77, 194n.110
Skelton, John, 131–32
Smith, Henry, 132–33, 141, 168, 196n.42, 199n.14
Southwell, Robert, 27, 56, 187n.35
Spencer, John, 191n.32
Spenser, Edmund, 6, 8–15, 17, 18, 23, 24, 25, 27–28, 29, 34, 39, 40–41, 46–48, 50–53, 58, 60, 61, 62, 75–78, 93, 98, 122–24, 132, 139, 148, 153, 155, 156, 158, 167, 172; *Amoretti: 1*, 49, 51; *9*, 83–84; *18*, 98, 192n.50; *30*, 141; *56*, 100, 103; *64*, 158; *67*, 107; *79*, 61; *81*, 158; *Epithalamion*, 46–47, 48, 105, 158, 160, 167–68; *Faerie Queene:*

1.1.7–9, 148–53; *1.1.35–37*, 125–27; *1.1.45*, 154; *1.2.12*, 122–23; *1.2.43*, 75; *1.3.13*, 128; *1.4.36*, 23; *1.10.3*, 127; *1.10.12–14*, 41–48, 116, 117, 119; *1.10.19*, 20, 127–28; *1.10.33*, 66–67; *1.11.28*, 4, 7; *1.11.46*, 23–24; *2.1.34*, 122; *2.3.22–24*, 156–58, 160–61; *2.3.24*, 12; *2.3.28*, 159–61; *2.6.12–13*, 150–51; *2.9.41–43*, 80–82; *2.12.74*, 53–54; *2.12.75*, 56; *3.2.33*, 24–25; *3.8.6–7*, 154–55; *3.8.7*, 166–67; *3.9.2*, 23; *3.10.15*, 34; *4.2.32*, 148; *4.2.41–44*, 141–42; *4.5.45*, 25; *4.11.40*, 67; *4.12.25*, 24; *5.2.47*, 35; *5.9.26*, 31; *5.9.27–28*, 39–40; *6.8.42*, 162; *Ruines of Rome*, 60; *Sheaperdes Calender*, 86, 117; *Teares of the Muses*, 78, 98, 192n.51
Sternhold, Thomas, and John Hopkins, 10, 167, 169, 170
Surrey, Henry Howard, Earl of, xii, 98, 192n.50
Sylvester, Joshua, 28, 34, 35, 72, 92, 133, 145, 153–56, 188n.65, 195nn.28, 29, 196n.50

Tasso, Torquato, 53, 56
Textor, John, 78, 188n.55
Thompson, John, 4
Tottel's miscellany, xii, 4, 7, 8, 51–52, 68, 94, 165, 187n.34, 189nn.88, 92
Tuve, Rosemond, xvi–xvii
Tyndale, William, 17, 18, 88–90, 114, 168, 182n.17, 199n.14

Vaughan, William, 194n.7
Virgil, 78, 102, 103, 151

Watson, Thomas, 33–34, 68, 93, 99–100, 102–3, 106, 119, 150, 163, 164
Whitehead, Alfred North, 59
Wilson, Thomas, ix, 1, 17, 31, 61, 65, 69, 70, 74, 77, 79, 84, 91, 103, 104, 109, 110, 121, 182n.17, 189nn.73, 74, 76, 87, 190nn.2, 3, 191nn.28, 30, 193nn.73, 79
Winters, Ivor, xii
Withal, John, 92, 93, 149
Wyatt, Sir Thomas, xii, 78, 94, 98, 106, 107, 139, 192n.50, 194n.104